THE ITALIAN EXILES
IN LONDON
1816—1848

THE ITALIAN EXILES
IN LONDON
1816–1848

BY

MARGARET C. W. WICKS, M.A., Ph.D.

Essay Index Reprint Series

BOOKS FOR LIBRARIES PRESS, INC.
FREEPORT, NEW YORK

First published 1937
Reprinted 1968

LIBRARY OF CONGRESS CATALOG CARD NUMBER:
68-16987

PRINTED IN THE UNITED STATES OF AMERICA

To KIT
WHO LOVED ITALY

PREFACE

THE collecting of material for any study is pleasurable, and one of the greatest rewards that await the researcher is the friendly contact with many people who are willing to help. I am happy to have this opportunity of expressing my gratitude to all who have helped me. I would thank especially the Authorities of King's College and University College, London, for placing at my disposal letters dealing with the Chairs of Italian and the appointments of Gabriele Rossetti, Valerio Pistrucci, Antonio Panizzi and others ; and Mr. F. C. Nicholson, librarian of the Edinburgh University Library, for the loan of books and for frequent acts of kindness. Professor T. B. Rudmose-Brown of Trinity College, Dublin, Mr. Henry Enfield of Bramcote, Nottingham, Mr. Mazzini Stuart, the Signora Giglioli, the Keeper of ·the Archives du Nord, Lille, and the Faculty of Advocates, Edinburgh, have generously lent me letters and other documents and supplied me with information. Miss Dorothea Douglas read through for me the papers of Charles Nodier in the Library at Besançon and made notes on his relations with Lady Mary Walker. The late Mrs. Janet Ross entrusted to me for the period of six months the infinitely precious letters written to her grandmother, Mrs. Sarah Austin, by Santorre di Santa Rosa. Her gracious act and the permission to publish the letters were the greatest inspiration in the course of my work, and the memory of my visit to her in her lovely Florentine villa one hot sunny spring day when flowers were everywhere in bloom is very precious.

To my friends Dr. Constance Brooks and Miss Ella Stewart I am much indebted for help in compiling the index, and to Miss Margaret K. B. Sommerville for help in the arduous task of proof-reading. Dr. James Watt of Edinburgh was ever ready with advice on legal points, and to his great kindness I owe the photostats of the wills and assistance in many other ways. I am not able adequately to express my gratitude to Mr. John Purves of Edinburgh University, who first suggested to me the subject of this study and then throughout the years of my labours was a never-failing guide and counsellor. Mr.

Purves even allowed me to benefit from his own researches, and gave me a copy of the correspondence between Gabriele Rossetti and Charles Lyell of Kinnordy before the publication of his own work on the subject. The example of his fine scholarship was constantly before me and his interest made me persevere when my courage had almost failed.

To Professor Piero Rèbora, formerly Professor of Italian at the University of Manchester, I owe the interest taken by the Manchester University Press in this book and their offer to publish it. To the Secretary of the Manchester University Press, Mr. H. M. McKechnie, I express my grateful thanks for his endless patience with me in the unforeseen delay which has attended the publication, and for his technical help. The Carnegie Trust have generously undertaken responsibility for a proportion of the loss, should the interest of the general public in the history of the Italian exiles in London a hundred years ago prove less than my own, and I thank them.

And now, after some twelve years of work on the ' Exiles ', at times engrossing and arduous, at times almost laid aside, my task is ended. I can only say that it has enriched my life.

MARGARET C. W. WICKS.

April 19th, 1937.

CONTENTS

INTRODUCTION

THERE was a period in the nineteenth century when a knowledge of the language and literature of Italy could almost be taken for granted among Englishmen of culture. The epic struggle for independence and unity sent many patriots into exile before their great aim was achieved. Their endeavours to earn the wherewithal to provide for their daily needs drove numbers of them into teaching and journalism, and even into the higher ranks of literature. New editions of the Italian classics were issued, magazine articles appeared on all subjects, economic, historical and literary. But behind all this activity there was also the desire to spread Italian culture and to win friends for Italy, and even to give the Italians themselves a living interest in the treasures they possessed in common and thus to draw them together.

The French Revolution had sown its seeds too well for them not to be forced into life by the reactionary policy in Europe that followed the collapse of the Empire in 1815. But the Italian struggle was of a different type from the French, different in origin and different in aim, There was no rising of oppressed classes of workers against a tyrannical aristocracy ; but the birth of a spirit of independence and nationality that sought to drive out the foreign power that stifled its growth. The revolution was led by the enlightened nobility and professional classes, who in spite of many reverses had to set themselves the task of moving the masses, and of infiltrating a wholesome living spirit of revolt and independence into their unreasoning, superstitious obedience. There was no overthrow of religion. A deep, strong faith inspired the leaders, which sought by an enlightened, liberal and reformed Catholicism the uplifting of the people. It was this religious consciousness that won for the patriots the sympathies of the Free Church adherents in England. Quakers, Unitarians and others offered their friendship and hospitality unstintingly to the hundreds of exiles who sought refuge in these islands during the greater part of the nineteenth century. There was undeniably a political motive behind much of it. It was a part of liberal and radical policy to befriend those who were struggling to attain their freedom.   In the earlier days the centres of Whig influence, Holland House and Lansdowne House, by opening their hospitable doors to the exiles gave the lead to Whig society.   Balls, parties and dinners were given in their honour, and no social gathering was complete without the presence of some of the exiled patriots. London society has been criticized for the way in which, after lavishing every attention upon the refugees, it as suddenly neglected them.   Yet this exaggerated reception was only a season's fashion, inspired often by curiosity rather than by real sympathy, and expected to last by no one less than the refugees themselves.   The more stable elements, the real friends of liberal thought, were enduring in their friendship.

In this contribution to the study of the unification of Italy, the aim is to show something of the lives of the exiles who settled in London. An endeavour will be made to trace their struggles to earn an often precarious livelihood, and to follow them in their relations with each other and with the English families with whom they came in contact. The most valuable sources of information are private letters which have been generously placed at the author's disposal.   The secret police reports would have been useful in determining the movements of individuals.   Unfortunately, however, a careful search of the documents in the Records Office, London, only revealed the fact that the Alien Office ceased to exist in 1836 and a recommendation of the Secretary that the papers should be kept.   It seems that it is or was the custom that departments dispensed with should send their files to be re-pulped, that they might be credited with the amount to Stationery. This laudably economical procedure is a possible cause of the paucity of documents available relating to the exiles.

The differences in character, ability and origin of the exiles themselves were cause of the differences in their spheres of influence. Foscolo was not content to accept the hospitality offered him as a tribute to his genius, but tried to take his place as an equal among the wealthy members of the English nobility, and ruined his health and fortune in the attempt.   Panizzi became one of those among whom he had come to live, thought as they did, acted as they, but kept his love for Italy untouched.   He used his power to influence the minds of Britain's statesmen and to win their support for his native land. Others, by the force of their example and their patient endurance of the changes that exile had brought into their lives, inspired respect for the country which could produce such men.   The few who brought discredit on the name of Italy have passed into oblivion.   The prominence given to Foscolo is due to his position as initiator and pioneer in the Italian emigration, and the place he took in London among the refugees who looked upon him as their head. The seeming neglect of Mazzini arises from the impossibility of giving more than a brief outline of his first period of exile in England. His influence permeates the whole of the Italian movement from 1831 onwards, and the magnitude of his work can hardly be estimated, but the retirement and simplicity of his first eleven years in London make the tale of them one that is quickly told. The scope of this study includes the period of preparation, insufficient as it transpired, with the unsuccessful revolutions of Naples in 1820, Piedmont in 1821 and the Central Provinces in 1831 ; and the glorious rising of 1848 which called back the exiles to Italy to take their places in army and state, but which ended so disastrously. Professor Benedetto Croce, describing the attitude of the ancients towards history, speaks of it as pessimistic. " They saw much greatness fall," he says, " but they never discovered the greatness that rises up greater after every fall." [1] This surely was the greatness of his own countrymen in the epoch of their *risorgimento*. The second stage in the movement, after 1848, a period of second exile for many and an initiation for others, showed the lessons to be learned from failure, and led up at last to the realization of the great aim of Unity, Liberty and Independence.

[1] *Theory and History of Historiography*, by Benedetto Croce. Translated by Douglas Ainslie, B.A., M.R.A.S., published by George Harrap & Co., Ltd., London. p. 194.

CHAPTER ONE

UGO FOSCOLO

First Years in London, 1816–21

" Ugo Foscolo diede alla nuova Italia una nuova istituzione, l' esilio," says Cattaneo,[1] alluding to Foscolo's last active expression of his love of country, which made exile, with all its horrors of loneliness and poverty, preferable to acceptance of foreign domination. No further justification is necessary for dating this contribution to the study of the history of the Italian exiles in London from 1816, the year of the poet's arrival in England. Foscolo was the first to show by a voluntary renunciation of his rights of citizenship that these rights can be retained at too dear a price ; and his name and fame caused his action to give a lead which great numbers of others followed, and have not yet ceased to follow.

On September 11th, 1816, with Andrea Calbo, who was to act as his secretary and companion, Ugo Foscolo landed in England. From motives of economy the travellers had sailed down the Rhine from Basle. They had then crossed from Ostend to London, in a storm which lengthened the passage to forty-one hours. The expenses of the journey had made considerable inroads into Foscolo's slender means, but he was well in health and filled with hope for the future. His reception by men of standing was warm and immediate ; and eight days after his arrival he had left the Hôtel Sablonnière in Leicester Square and established himself with Calbo in rooms at 11 Soho Square. At Berne in the first week of August, Foscolo had spent some days with an Englishman, whom he calls Mr. Robert Samuel Cook, and introductions of practical value had been exchanged. Cook, who was bound for Italy, was furnished with letters to Giuseppe Grassi and Quirina Magiotti[2] ; and he in return gave Foscolo a letter to Mr. Sicard, Princess of Wales' Apartments, Kensington Palace, in which

[1] *Ugo Foscolo e l' Italia*, p. 34.   [2] *Epist.*, II., p. 268.

he requested the latter to give such assistance in procuring lodgings as a stranger to London would find most useful.[1] This letter is signed ' Saml. Ed. Cook ', but there can be little doubt that the difference in Christian names was an error on Foscolo's part. Foscolo also had a number of acquaintances from the old days in Italy, and he lost no time in communicating with them. Sigismondo Trechi, who was then in England, announced Foscolo's arrival to Giuseppe Binda, who was staying with Lord Holland. Lord Holland expressed a wish to meet Foscolo ; and we gather from the latter's letter to Binda, dated 17th September, 1816,[2] that a visit from Binda to Foscolo must have been the immediate result of the announcement. In this letter Foscolo enclosed a note to Trechi, which was forwarded and reached him on September 22nd. In his reply to it Trechi expresses his pleasure at Foscolo's arrival in England. He is himself at that moment in Perth. " La tua lettera che dovea giungermi a Hawick, non me è pervenuta che jersera in questa amenissima villa del Sig^r. Ferguson. . . . So che a quest' ora devi aver veduto Lord Holland ; che te ne pare di quest' amabilissimo ed amatissimo personaggio ? Gli è quasi impossibile d' incontrare un migliore cuore del suo. So che ti stima infinitamente." [3] Within three days of his arrival Foscolo had written to Sir Robert Wilson, whom he had known in Milan in 1814 [4] ; and he had received from Charles Parr Burney, later Archdeacon Burney, brother of the authoress, a note with an invitation to visit him in Greenwich, and expressing thanks for a letter brought from Mr. Finch, with whom Foscolo seems to have been on intimate terms in Switzerland.[5]

Two years before in Milan, Foscolo had passed through a period of extreme depression, and the one consolation to him was his friendship with William Stewart Rose, who was travelling in Italy at that time. Foscolo spoke of him as " tutto ingegno e tutto cuore ", and added, " s' io non mi lusingo un po' troppo, credo ch' egli, nel dividersi da me, s' accorga come perdendolo, perdo il mio solo conforto ".[6] It is evident that Rose enjoyed the society of Foscolo's friends from the allusions to him in letters from Camillo Ugoni, Giuseppe Grassi and others. It must have been a particular joy to him to welcome Foscolo in England and to return the kindness he had received in Italy. By September 19th in his letter to the Donna Gentile,[7] Foscolo

---

[1] MSS. Lab. See App. I.A, 1. [2] *Epist.*, II., p. 274.
[3] MSS. Lab., Vol. XLII., Sec. A. Dated Sept. 23rd, 1816.
[4] *Epist.*, II., p. 274. [5] *Epist.*, III., p. 344. [6] *ibid.*, p. 336.
[7] *Epist.*, II., p. 276.

was already able to report that Rose, who was then living at Mudiford, near Lyndhurst, had sent his servant to London to guide him during his first days there, and had given him an introduction to a Secretary of State, who would smooth away the difficulties of the Aliens Act, which hampered the movements of every foreigner who set foot in Britain. A number of letters from Rose to Foscolo among the manuscripts in the Biblioteca Labronica deal with the latter's first weeks in England. Several, though undated, were obviously written in September, before Foscolo's first visit to Mudiford, which took place at the beginning of October. In the earliest of these Rose urges Foscolo to come to him and sends him full instructions for the journey.[1] Doubts seem then to have arisen in Foscolo's mind as to his freedom to travel about the country in view of the Aliens Act. Rose made the necessary enquiries and was able to reassure him.[2] An indisposition of Foscolo's, to which he gives the somewhat vague name of " febbre ", appears to have occasioned a postponement of the visit. Dr. Allen prescribed for him,[3] Foscolo having meanwhile become a frequent visitor at Holland House ; and Rose wrote vaunting the restorative powers of the sea air at Mudiford.[4] In the same letter Rose alluded to Count Matexà, who was known to Foscolo, and suggested their travelling down together. It is interesting to find Foscolo's name also coupled with Matexà's in a letter from Rose to William Frere, who was then Master of Downing College, and who seems to have had a fondness for ' lions ', to judge from Rose's reference to the two ' lyons ' he is sending him from Greece.[5] Rose suggests they should be introduced to Dr. Martin Davy, Master of Caius, to whom he also sends a letter on Foscolo's behalf. He refers amusingly to this proposed visit to Davy in a letter to Foscolo ; and speaks of " *Madame son épouse* alla quale dovrette insegnare qualche canzonetta Veneziana, per far vedere che siete *Leone* addimesticato ".[6]

A ' febbre ' of Andrea Calbo's, for which Foscolo himself treated him, caused a further postponement of the visit to Mudiford ; but a letter to Binda, dated October 2nd, held out hopes of Foscolo's being able to leave town the following day. A subsequent letter from Mudiford, with the post-mark of October 8th, contained a graphic account of the journey, which had not been without adventure.[7] The visit was probably of very short duration, in spite of the pleasure it

[1] MSS. Lab. See App. I.A, 2.   [2] *ibid.* See App. I.A, 3.
[3] *Epist.*, II., p. 282.   [4] MSS. Lab. See App., I.A, 4.
[5] *ibid.* See App., I.A, 5.   [6] *ibid.*, Vol. XLII., Sec. A.
[7] *Epist.*, II., p. 279.

gave to both Rose and Foscolo, who were inspired by their discussions of English and Italian literature. The first letter among the manuscripts in the Biblioteca Labronica that Lord Holland wrote to Foscolo is dated October 1816, and invites him to Holland House on his return from Mudiford, to meet some people who will be of assistance to him in his literary work. Perhaps Foscolo, during his quiet sojourn in the country, missed the brilliant circle at Holland House ; but his speedy return to town is more probably accounted for by the state of his finances. Lord Holland enclosed a letter of introduction to Longman, the publishers,[1] and also a note to Murray, whom, however, he did not know personally. Rose also gave Foscolo a letter for Murray,[2] and it is interesting to see the result of these intro-ductions. Longman treated the Italian coldly and was unwilling to take any risks ; Murray entered into an agreement with him for a series of letters on the " Customs, Literature and Political History of England and Italy ", to be published in three volumes.[3]

The month Foscolo had spent in England had been, from a social point of view, a triumphal success. Invitations poured in on all sides, and people vied with each other in introducing the famous poet to those who would be useful to him in his exile. Foscolo's proud spirit could not accept hospitality without making some return, and from various notes of thanks, dated from the first months of his residence in London, we gather that the return frequently took the form of gifts of his own works. But his life of social engagements could not go on for long. The journey from Zurich had cost some £68, and Foscolo arrived with barely enough to keep Calbo and himself, living with economy and care until the winter. The travelling expenses involved, in the acceptance of invitations alone were by no means light. Already in his letter of September 19th to the Donna Gentile, Foscolo points out the necessity of appearing in easy circumstances, if he is to succeed. This notion, which ultimately became an obsession, never left him— a curious complex in one who had such extraordinary powers of con-centration and the will to perform positively herculean labours. A week sufficed to show Foscolo that his mode of living would require

[1] MSS. Lab. See App. I.A, 9.
[2] *ibid.*, Vol. XLII., Sec. A. " Pero mi dispiace . . . che il librajo, al quale v' indirizzava il Lord Holland, abbia trattato freddo ; chè m' immagino che sarà stato uno di quelli che non vorrebbero nemmeno giuocare une scudo. Ma voi non dite nulla di *Murray* pel quale io vi avea dato una lettera."
[3] Chiarini, *Vita*, p. 343.

a fixed income of about five hundred pounds a year, if he were to keep Andrea Calbo.[1] The fact that he confessed so much showed his uneasiness, and not even the kindly suggestions that by giving public lectures he could earn a thousand pounds in the half year from January to August, seemed quite to still his fears. Meanwhile January was still far off and present needs were great. An appeal to his brother, whose careful savings had already saved Ugo from destitution, does not seem to have brought him the required aid. One has a painful impression of the poverty-stricken family in Italy straining every nerve to help the exiled son, who was lavishly playing the part of a man of fashion in London and striving to appear as an equal in the brilliant and wealthy society which had received the new ' lion ' with open arms.

Foscolo hid his poverty from the eyes of his many new acquaintances, but in Italy the Donna Gentile, with almost maternal love, sensed the state of things without waiting for a confession. Among the Foscolo manuscripts in the Biblioteca Nazionale in Florence there is the draft of a letter to Rose from Quirina Magiotti, written on the back of a letter dated July 27th, 1816.[2] Knowing Foscolo's intention of going to London she doubtless felt that he would be in need of a true friend. Foscolo's improvidence had already brought him into difficulties in Italy, and with exquisite sensitiveness she probably foresaw the dangers ahead. Foscolo's letter to her of October 23rd contains an acknowledgment of thirty zecchini, sent presumably to Calbo, and weakly remonstrates with her for the action she has taken. The Donna Gentile knew well that the lavish hospitality shown to the famous exile would only be accepted in the ' grand manner '. The timely gift was probably a relief in more ways than one, for Foscolo was able to throw down the mask and confide his difficulties to the friend who understood him best. He confessed his powerlessness and his galling dependence on the favours of others. " —pur troppo ! ho bisogno dell' ajuto altrui ; e per ottenerlo, è necessità somma ch' io m' arrenda spesso alle altrui vane carezze, e ch' io sempre spenda più di quello che posso " ; and then the thought which haunted him throughout the eleven years of his exile in England and which, if it be based on truth, is a deep disgrace to the nation which prides itself on its hospitality, its justice and its truly democratic principles, " ma in questo paese è grande smacco l' essere povero, e il parere bisognoso : nessuno ti guarda ; e nessuno si degna, come diceva l' Ortis, di collocare il beneficio frà cenci." [3] The very postage

---

[1] *Epist.*, II., p. 277.   [2] See App. I.A, 6.   [3] *Epist.*, II., p. 283.

on his letters was now an expense too great to be incurred frequently, and the outlook to the future was depressing in the extreme. The lovely weather of the first weeks of October evidently changed towards the end of the month into the fogs which herald the arrival of November. In the letter to the Donna Gentile of October 25th Foscolo speaks of his excellent health, but attributes the melancholy of his spirits to the fog which attacks his eyes and lungs. The same day, writing to Binda, he complains that he does not feel well and that ·his annual attack of asthma seems about to come on.[1] The illness seems to have kept him a prisoner, and the time was spent in writing, with Calbo's aid, a lengthy article in reply to Chateaubriand's *Bonaparte et les Bourbons*, which never seems to have seen print. At last, on November 21st, Foscolo wrote to Binda that the doctor had sanctioned his going out for a little to enjoy the few minutes of sunshine.[2] The depression of spirit which his circumstances, his health and the cold, damp weather helped to increase, seems to have suggested thoughts of suicide which he confided to Rose. Rose, more accustomed to the climate and knowing his friend's mercurial temperament, wrote a comforting letter, affirming his confidence in Foscolo's ultimate success.[3] In the letter to the Donna Gentile of March 25th, 1817, Foscolo refers to his illness, which cost him for drugs and medical attendance far more than his slender purse could afford, and which proved the test which Calbo's friendship and gratitude were unable to stand, for the faithful Achates, having had his fare paid for him from Zurich to London, chose this moment to take his departure.

Looking back with all the information now in our possession, these first weeks of Foscolo's exile in London offer a clue to much that is otherwise inexplicable in the years to come. His pride erected a wall between what one might almost call his two lives : on the one side lay what was known to himself and those of his most intimate friendship, his family and Quirina Magiotti, namely the blankness of the future and the soul-destroying struggle to find money adequate to the expenses of his new life ; on the other side was what Foscolo chose to show to the world. In judging the society which received him with such extravagant warmth, only to desert him later when his circumstances were becoming increasingly difficult, we must keep before us the fact that from the first Foscolo's position had been a false one. His sponsors in society were Lord and Lady Holland.

[1] *Epist.*, II., p. 285.   [2] *ibid.*, p. 288.
[3] MSS. Lab. See App. I.A, 8.

Some letters of introduction he had brought with him and some he had received from Rose, but the overwhelming reception which greeted him was due to the place made for him in the Holland House circle. In 1816 the position occupied by Holland House was unique. It was the stronghold of the Whig party, indeed almost a political party in itself. The liberal policy of extending protection to all sufferers in the cause of liberty found supreme expression in the lavish hospitality dispensed there. Lord Holland himself was a constant champion of true liberty, and his friendship was a thing to have and to hold. Other attractions of Holland House drew men of all shades of opinion. The wide interests of its far-travelled hosts, their intimate knowledge of literature both ancient and modern, English and foreign, their sparkling wit, Lady Holland's beauty and Lord Holland's charm of manner, all combined to bring together the most brilliant intellects of that brilliant age. When Foscolo arrived in London the Hollands had not long returned from a visit to Italy, where they had known of his fame. They could look back with delight to their old friendship with the Countess of Albany, which dated from their long residence in Florence in the early years of their married life. Giuseppe Binda, the Lucchese, who in the capacity of financial secretary and later of librarian lived for many years as a dependant in Holland House, had known Foscolo in Florence, and he eagerly renewed his acquaintance with him and introduced him to the Hollands. From shortly after his arrival until the following May or June, Foscolo was a most frequent visitor at Holland House. His brilliant conversation was another ornament to the famous circle, and Lady Holland's kindness to him made him a ready victim to the charm of her extraordinary personality. Lord Holland expressed later to Roger Wilbraham that he considered him the man of greatest value he had ever met in all his life.[1] He received him with signal attention as a man of letters, but it was as a victim of a despotic government that he was taken up and fêted and lionized by the rest of Whig society.

The society at Holland House must have been a revelation to Foscolo. In the *salons* he had frequented in Venice and Milan and Florence there had certainly met together men of note, both Italian and foreign ; but there was a superficiality, a frivolity and, it must be confessed, a shabbiness born of insufficient means in the gatherings, that was entirely absent from the circle at Kensington. The wealth of the hosts made the setting at Holland House of the most luxurious. The entertaining was on a sumptuous scale, and the brilliance of the

[1] Segrè, p. 403.

conversation and the warmth of the welcome made such men as
Samuel Rogers, the poet, Sydney Smith, Sir James Mackintosh,
Lord John Russell, Brougham, Jeffrey, and Hallam *habitués* of the
house. The rare library of many thousands of volumes, which Lord
Holland had inherited and enriched, was not the least of the attractions. In those days, when books for consultation were very difficult
of access, the courtesy which threw open the library to so many
students of letters, and the generosity which prompted the lending
of many priceless works, showed Lord Holland's sympathy with
learning. The Princess Liechtenstein paints a vivid picture of the
scene in the library at Holland House, where " all the antique gravity
of a college library was so singularly blended with all that female
grace and wit could devise to embellish a drawing-room ".[1] Portraits
of famous men and women hung on the walls wherever spaces were
left between the shelves loaded with the literary treasures of many
countries and of many ages ; and living men and women, not less
famous, discussed in groups the politics of the day, or art or travel
or literature. One can picture the success that Foscolo would meet
with in such a gathering. His vivacity, his prodigious memory and
remarkable eloquence soon won him a position among men well
qualified to appreciate his genius. He could have found, in the whole
of the civilised world, no more fruitful ground for his labours. If
we look at the list of his English correspondents whose letters are
preserved in the Biblioteca Labronica, and there are some six hundred
and thirty-seven letters and notes, we can see how many of his friends
and acquaintances he owed to Holland House. The names of the
Duke of Bedford, Lord Brougham, Thomas Campbell, Samuel Rogers,
Roger Wilbraham, Lady Aberdeen, Lady Westmorland, Lady Dacre,
his faithful friend through all his years of adversity, Lady Romilly,
Lady Lyttelton and numerous others recall Lord Holland's hospitality. The people he met vied with each other in procuring him
further acquaintances who might be of assistance to him ; and many,
and among these not the least assiduous were women, invited him
to parties, to dinners and balls, until it seemed as if no gathering
were complete without him. It is not to be expected that Foscolo
would let his real financial position be apparent. He was taken into
society as an equal, not as a poor man of letters ready to accept
the patronage which men of fashion were able and willing to bestow.
He swept all before him with his charming manners and vivacious
conversation, until even he was astonished at the reception accorded

[1] Liechtenstein, I., p. iii.

him by the most formal and unapproachable of nations. But the cost of this new life of Fashion ! London was not Venice. It was impossible to go any distance without heavy expenses, and there were gifts in return for kindnesses received, and no doubt lavish expenditure as long as the money lasted and the eyes of the fashionable world were upon him. Soon Foscolo was brought up against the hard reality. Literary work seemed his only refuge, but the chief difficulty in the way was his lack of knowledge of English. Italian was only known to a very limited number of the reading public, and with them the classics were more in demand than modern works. The letters for Murray were not likely to bring in an immediate return.

By this time Foscolo had doubtless got into some debt and had most likely borrowed money. About the end of November [1] he received some money which saved him for the time being, probably the £100 of which he speaks in his letter of March 25th to the Donna Gentile [2] as coming from Zante. Another Greek, probably his Ionian friend, Giorgio Foresti, who was then in London, came to his aid with £50, whether in loan or as a gift it is difficult to say. In a note to Andrea Calbo, who was living at 19 Gerrard Street, Soho, and maintaining himself by giving lessons to pupils, partly procured for him by Foscolo, the latter begs him to repay at least a part of the money he had lent him. This note is dated February 4th and is followed by another, ten days later, with a pathetic and desperate appeal for repayment; although at the end of the letter with great magnanimity he sends Calbo news of a new pupil who is desirous of learning modern Greek. [3] In October Foscolo had written to the Donna Gentile of his lack of prospects and had suggested as a last resort that he would have to resign himself to going from house to house, giving lessons in Italian, Greek and Latin, [4] to provide his daily bread. The thought was a bitter one. To Foscolo it meant renouncing all claim to social position and acknowledging openly the shame of his poverty. The loans or gifts he received probably tided him over the immediate needs, but as the money became exhausted he was tortured with anxiety. About the middle of February Foscolo began to suffer excruciating agony from an injury to his leg, which dated back to November when he had knocked his shin violently against a chair, causing an attack of pain like sciatica. The surgeon consulted wanted to amputate the limb, but Rose, who was then in London, insisted on Foscolo's consulting another man, who under-

[1] Antona-Traversi and Ottolini, IV., p. 102. [2] *Epist.*, II., p. 295.
[3] Antona-Traversi and Ottolini, IV., p. 102. [4] *Epist.*, II., p. 282.

stood the case and effected a cure.[1] Not the least part of the illness was the expense incurred, which added to Foscolo's distress of mind and increased his feeling of hopelessness. The kindly interest taken in him by all his new friends, who visited him and wrote to enquire about his progress, must have been a source of satisfaction, but here again the two sides of the picture contrast with startling clearness. To none of these friends, unless to Rose, who financially was not in a position to help, was Foscolo able to speak of his difficulties. He guessed intuitively that discussions of ways and means would be unwelcome to his English acquaintances and would most likely oust him from their society. One's income was a subject not to be mentioned among gentlemen. To add to his worries Foscolo was now called upon to pay the consequences of an unfortunate piece of business he had undertaken for the firm of booksellers, Messrs. Orell, Füssli and Co. of Zurich, before leaving Switzerland. He had received the commission, entrusted merely nominally to Andrea Calbo, to buy a quantity of drawing-paper. Badly advised, Foscolo placed the order with a man Angiolo Bonelli in London, who undertook to procure the paper from the manufacturers and forward it direct to Zurich, on condition of immediate payment. Foscolo paid the money, about £42, to Bonelli's clerk in exchange for the receipt, but the invoice was not sent to him. Some two months later Bonelli called to report that the clerk had absconded with £2000, and that he washed his hands of all responsibility. Foscolo, indignant, took the matter into court ; but the accident to his leg prevented his being present to take up the case and he let the matter drop, acting on the advice of a friend who knew the doubtful advantages accruing from legal settlement of such disputes. Having given his word to Hagenbuch, the manager of the firm in Zurich, to send the paper, Foscolo decided to bear the loss himself. He forthwith entrusted the whole business of purchasing and forwarding a further quantity of drawing-paper to a broker, George Mills, and for lack of ready money, gave him a bill payable in three months' time.[2] The three months elapsed about the time of Foscolo's illness, when the additional expenses of surgeons and doctors had well-nigh driven him to despair. With difficulty he

---

[1] *Epist.*, II., p. 295

[2] For this account we are indebted to Professor Viglione, who recovered the facts from the MSS. Lab., Vol. XXXVIII., containing Foscolo's letter to Hagenbuch of March 28th, 1817, which was only partially quoted in the *Epist.*, II., No. 504. See *Ugo Foscolo in Inghilterra*, Viglione, pp. 6–10.

obtained a month's delay ; and then, still as far from being able to settle the bill as in February, to avoid arrest for debt, he turned to a friend, probably General Sir Robert Wilson, and implored him to lend him the necessary sum, to be repaid on Foscolo's receiving payment of a bill of exchange on his property in Zante. The bill was discounted by a banker friend of Foscolo's, Frederick Grig.[1] The danger was averted for the time being ; but one cannot help wondering at the curious sense of honour which made Foscolo take the loss caused by his bad business upon himself, and then draw on his very slender patrimony which he had set aside for the exclusive use of his mother and sister, in order to get himself out of a difficulty which, with greater care on his part, would never have arisen.

His pen was practically Foscolo's sole means of earning a livelihood in London, and it is interesting to examine the labours of his first six months. He read a good deal, especially English works, to acquaint himself, as he said, with English taste in letters. The article in answer to Chateaubriand's *Bonaparte et les Bourbons* does not seem to have been resumed after Calbo's departure. The death of Francis Horner from tuberculosis on February 8th, 1817, at the early age of thirty-nine, was the occasion for perhaps Foscolo's first publication in England. He had known Horner at Holland House and had given him introductions when he went to Italy in search of health. Foscolo translated Horner's Parliamentary speeches and published them in May 1817 with the title of *Discorsi nel Parlamento in morte di Francesco Horner tradotti dall' Inglese*. The translation was dedicated, in memory of their common friend, to Lord Holland's son, Henry ; it was probably chiefly for private circulation. Foscolo seems to have sent copies to various friends. His beautiful letter to Henry Fox is included, with certain omissions, in the *Epistolario*.[2] The other literary work which engaged Foscolo's attention in the spring of 1817 was a new edition of the *Lettere di Jacopo Ortis*, which had unfortunate consequences involving Rose and Quirina Magiotti, and even a friend of Rose's. This new edition was in a way forced on Foscolo by a bookseller, Romualdo Zotti,[3] bringing out an edition

[1] Viglione, p. 8.

[2] *Epist.*, II., p. 298. A copy of the work is to be found in the British Museum ; and another in the Biblioteca Nazionale, Florence, among the Foscolo MSS. belonging formerly to Martelli, Quirina Magiotti's heir.

[3] *Epist.*, II., p. 308 ; also a note in Quirina Magiotti's handwriting on drafts of questions she sent to London after Foscolo's death. ' Stampatori delle Opere edite del Foscolo. . . . R. Zotti, No. 3 Vauxhall Road.' MSS. Fosc., Vol. X.B. Bib. Naz., Florence.

of *Ortis* without the author's permission. Foscolo was induced to take the matter up and come to terms with him, and consequently to supervise the edition. Chiarini mentions no names in his account of the transaction,[1] but Messrs. Antona-Traversi and Ottolini quote a letter from Calbo, recommending a pupil to read the letters of *Jacopo Ortis*, published by Murray some weeks before.[2] There is unfortunately no date on Calbo's note, but there is little doubt that it refers to the edition of 1817, published by Murray and printed by Schulze & Dean. As often happened with Foscolo, the venture proved the reverse of profitable and involved him in further financial difficulties. The bookseller lent him £40, but when the edition was ready, refused to assume the responsibility of the sale of the books, and consequently the loan had to be repaid. In desperation Foscolo borrowed the money from Rose, who, not having sufficient cash in hand at the time, in turn borrowed from a friend. The conditions of the loan were that in the event of Foscolo's not being able to repay Rose by Christmas of 1817 the latter should apply to the Donna Gentile. To understand Rose's position we must recall that from reasons of health he had been obliged to give up a lucrative post ; and before the settlement of the debt his father died, leaving him penniless and in very delicate health. On March 21st, 1817, Quirina Magiotti, having waited long in vain for news of Foscolo, for from his letter to her of March 25th it seems that many of his letters failed to reach their destination,[3] wrote to Rose, begging for news of their friend and asking Rose to lend him, on her behalf, whatever financial aid he required.[4] Rose's first reply to the Donna Gentile was lost, and, hearing this from Foscolo, he again sent her a note of the loan and the conditions.[5] Meanwhile for economic reasons Rose went to Italy. On December 12th, 1817,[6] he acknowledged the Donna Gentile's offer to repay the £40, but expressed a wish to wait until Christmas to give Foscolo time to acquit himself of his debt without her aid. We have Foscolo's account of the affair in his letter to the Donna Gentile of March 10th, 1818,[7] where he expresses his surprise at Rose's prompt action to recover the money after allowing him until December 1818—a year later, be it noted, than the date mentioned by Rose. Foscolo's tone is one of injured innocence, in view of the business-like way he had arranged for the sale of the edition of *Ortis*

[1] Chiarini, *Vita*, p. 342.
[2] Antona-Traversi and Ottolini, IV., p. 101.   [3] *Epist.*, II., p. 293.
[4] MSS. Fosc. See App. I.A, 10.   [5] See App. I.A, 11.
[6] See App. I.A, 12, 13.   [7] *Epist.*, II., p. 343.

by Murray, on Rose's recommendation. Quirina's faith in Foscolo is boundless. ' Sono rimasta maravigliata dello sbaglio sull' epoca del pagamento ', she writes,[1] ' sbaglio certo di memoria di Rose.' References to similar instances of carelessness in financial matters are not uncommon in Foscolo's correspondence. In February 1818 Rose wrote to the Donna Gentile once more about the £40, which she paid and the receipt for which, dated March 4th, 1818, and signed by Nicolò Collalto, Venice, is among the Foscolo manuscripts in Florence.[2]

There is a brighter side to this London edition of the *Lettere di Jacopo Ortis* however. At Holland House Foscolo had quickly become intimate with the English poet Samuel Rogers, and their friendship withstood all the trials of Foscolo's later years of misery. The dedication to Rogers of the new edition of *Ortis* was a graceful recognition of him as a poet and of the honour of his friendship. The dedicatory letter is included in the *Epistolario*, and in it Foscolo laments that his heart is no longer as it was when it left the hand of Nature, but that it has been moulded, perhaps too much, by the world. ' E appunto per rispetto al mondo non mi attento d' intitolare l' intera edizione al nome di lei, ne porvi il mio ; se non se in alcuni esemplari che soli sono accompagnati da questa lettera ; per dirle, che la lettura de' *Piaceri della Memoria*, e l' amicizia che le piace di dimostrarmi accrescono il numero delle rimembranze ch' io custodisco come il men incerto conforto de' miei giorni avvenire.'[3] The last sentence is almost prophetic. Rogers expressed his delight in the great Italian poet's way of honouring him in a characteristic letter which the Florentine editors give in translation in a footnote to the letter quoted above.[4] Foscolo took the opportunity offered by the new edition of the *Lettere* to present the many friends who had shown him kindness with a copy, in some cases specially bound ; although he seems to have expressed his regret that it should be the thoughts and emotions of his early years that he had to offer. There are numerous letters of thanks among the manuscripts in the Biblioteca Labronica, many of them from women friends, and nearly all dated May, the month of the publication. Lady Lyttelton, Thomas Grenville and Lavinia Spencer write in French. I quote from the last. ' Spencer House, ce 18me Mai 1817. J'en suis on ne peut pas plus touchée, et ce sera avec le plus grand empressement que je vais lire un ouvrage ou [*sic*] je verrai

[1] *ibid.*, p. 345, footnote. [2] MSS. Fosc., Vol. X.B.
[3] *Epist.*, II., p. 298.
[4] See App., I.A, 14, for the original text from the MSS. Lab.

les premiers essais d'un génie qui est encore aujourd'hui si rempli de feu et de chaleur, quoi que la froide expérience d'un monde trompeur aurait pu amortir son éclat.'[1]   There are letters in Italian from M. Sandys Wall, and other correspondents who do not sign their names ; and in English from Lady Charlotte Campbell,[2] from Lord Morpeth, and from Lord Carysfort. There is a note in almost illegible handwriting from H.F.R. which gently chides Foscolo for his neglect : ' intanto ·vedo Jacopo Ortis d' appertutto ma in nessun luogo Ugo Foscolo—e così non va bene.'[3]   It is not difficult to guess the tone of Foscolo's reply from a later letter from the same correspondent : ' che caro, che amabile Ugo Foscolo, è questo ! Amo Jacopo Ortis, morto e vivo, ma amo anche più Ugo Foscolo, che d' ogni altro modo così, [sic] è una *bugia* che *nessuna più l' ama* ! '[4]   Not all the copies at Foscolo's disposal were presented now, and to one, which he gave to Henrietta Russell some years later, with a special dedication, we shall refer in due course.

All these signs of appreciation were encouraging, but the worry continued, even increased, all through the spring of 1817, and probably Foscolo was in a state of extreme nervous irritability which he could not always conceal. In a letter in February, which is intended for a letter of reconciliation, he speaks with regret of having fallen into a passion several times in the preceding months, and of himself as ' un individuo che per propria disavventura fu dalla Natura creato di carattere risentito '.[5]   It is easy to guess the scenes that took place from time to time. We know that he expressed himself with vehemence: the state of his nerves during these months probably made his hearers feel themselves often on the edge of a volcano. Even Lord Holland, writing to Horner, regretted Foscolo's intolerance and uncontrollable impetuosity.[6]   His anger amounted at times almost to madness, and some time later, with a cry from the heart, Jekyll, one of the frequenters of the Kensington circle, after a graphic description of Foscolo's passion, exclaimed, ' At Holland House they are sick to death of him.'[7]   The series of letters on the ' Customs, Literature and Political History of England and Italy ', which Murray had agreed to take up, had to be abandoned after a beginning had been made, owing to many difficulties, chiefly the impossibility of an immediate return.[8]   In February Giulio Foscolo wrote reprovingly, beseeching

[1] MSS. Lab., Vol. XLII., Sec. A.   [2] *ibid.* See App. I.A, 15.
[3] *ibid.*, Vol. XLII., Sec. A.   [4] *ibid.*, Vol. XLII., Sec. A.
[5] *Epist.*, II., p. 289.   [6] Segrè, p. 408.
[7] Sanders, p. 324.   [8] Chiarini, *Vita*, p. 343.

his brother to send some repayment to the generous friends who had done much for their mother. A plan to publish the Italian Classics by subscription, which Rose had thought good, was discouraged by Lord Guilford, and Murray, who best understood the difficulty of finding purchasers.

Blow upon blow seemed to fall upon Foscolo, and London, while offering all the social delights and intellectual advantages that man could desire, showed no signs of providing a means of subsistence. Foscolo reluctantly came to the decision that, in order to provide for his present and future needs, he must leave England. The idea of returning to the Ionian Islands gradually took shape in his mind. ' Le mie entrate non reggono a questo paese ', [1] he wrote to Lord Guilford in a draft of a letter probably never sent, but he expressed his grief at the thought of leaving so many kind friends. There is a note in Italian among the Labronica manuscripts, dated ' domenica 22 7bre, 1816 ', from Frederick North, afterwards Lord Guilford, thanking Foscolo for ' suo gentilissimo regalo ' [2] ; and the continuance of an early friendship, added to Lord Guilford's interest in the Ionian Islands, probably encouraged Foscolo to make a frank statement of his affairs to him. With infinite tact and kindly feeling Lord Guilford prevailed upon him to accept a loan, [3] not the first that Foscolo had accepted to help to tide him over till his affairs should be in better order. When his mind was thus tormented with the thought of leaving surroundings where everything was congenial, the cruellest blow struck him that perhaps he was ever to experience, the death of his dearly loved mother. One cannot help feeling that Diamantina Spathis was the very personification of the tenderness, the selflessness and the inexhaustible wealth of a mother's love. Although her married life had been happy, it had been short, and she had early been called upon to bear the burden of poverty and the responsibility of a family of young children. In spite of their love for each other, it could have been with no easy mind that she watched the development and rise to manhood of her stormy, passionate eldest son. All her life she loved him tenderly, and although in the last years of her life the news that reached her was more of him than from him, she never failed to send him her blessing and affectionate messages in the letters of others. To Foscolo she was a being above this earthly sphere, and her love was a protection to him in his times of deepest dejection. He treasured all the messages she sent him throughout his life, and we can see among

[1] *Epist.*, II., p. 300.   [2] MSS. Lab., Vol. XLII., Sec. A
[3] Chiarini, *Vita*, p. 346.

his letters in the Biblioteca Labronica, Leghorn, little slips of paper with lines of Greek, the language which was in very truth his mother tongue. It is curious that it was not until May 24th, nearly a month later, that Giulio wrote to tell his brother of their mother's death on April 28th. When Foscolo spoke of the help he had received from home, from those least in a position to give it, in his draft of the letter to Lord Guilford, he said, ' ho quindi pietà di mia Madre, e vergogna di me,' and at the time he wrote his mother had already passed away and he had done nothing to make up for all the sacrifices of her life. His grief was overwhelming, something more real and purer than the passionate tempers and exaggerated mannerisms which were tending to estrange some of his English friends ; and they brought him their offerings of friendship and sympathy. Lady Holland's beautiful letter in perfect Italian is too well known to require repetition.[1] In it she gives proof of the real goodness of heart which her imperious manner so often masked, and suggests that Foscolo might come and spend some time with them before their departure for the Continent. Lady Charlotte Campbell, too, suggested that he might care to come and talk over his sorrow with her, and shortly after followed this letter with another in which she hints that it was she who had conveyed to Foscolo the news of his loss. Perhaps Giulio Foscolo's letter was carried by hand or enclosed in another. " When six o'clock arrived & then seven and that you came not, I knew my Dear Sir that you had learnt the full extent of the sad tidings—and I felt deeply for you—I felt too, the pain of having been the Person who first convey'd the blow—but I meant it well—do not dislike me for it." [2] Dr. Henry Holland also wrote and asked permission to call to offer personal sympathy, and Lady Flint sent a letter of condolence written in French.[3] At least Foscolo had not the additional pain of feeling himself alone in his sorrow ; but there seemed little left to live for.

By degrees, as spring turned into summer, many of Foscolo's friends left London for the Continent. Rose was among the first to go, then Charles Fox, Lord Holland's eldest son, and Lord John Russell. The Hollands left in June for the Netherlands. A letter of introduction to the Donna Gentile on Fazakerley's behalf is dated June 30th, 1817,[4] and points to a frequent interchange of courtesies between Foscolo and the latter. In July Lady Campbell went to Italy with her daughters, similarly furnished with a letter of introduction to the Donna Gentile, in which Foscolo spoke of the warm friendship she

[1] *Epist.*, II., p. 426.   [2] MSS. Lab., Vol. XLII., Sec. A.
[3] *ibid.*, Vol. XLII., Sec. A.   [4] *Epist.*, II., p. 313.

had offered him and the consolation she had brought him in his recent great sorrow.[1] One would imagine, from the numbers of letters that Foscolo wrote on behalf of English friends, that an introduction from him was greatly sought after by all travellers bound for Italy. The compensation for the loss of so many of his English hosts was to be found in perhaps greater intimacy with those who remained. Foscolo seems in the summer of 1817 to give Italian lessons to several ladies, among them to Lady Flint and Miss Pigou, the latter a young, rather lively friend of the poet Rogers. The lessons were probably a return on Foscolo's part for favours received, and to judge from the letters published in his correspondence, he spared no pains to give his pupils an elegant style in Italian and to correct their foreign turns of speech. There are seventeen letters from Miss Pigou to Foscolo in the Biblioteca Labronica, and from the tone of them one gathers that the friendship bordered on flirtation. Foscolo must have been able to throw off all care at times and to forget his real struggle for existence in the enjoyment of the good the gods provided by means of his friends.

Meanwhile Foscolo's plans for his return to Zante were maturing, and he wrote to Lord Holland in the beginning of July, announcing his intention of returning to Greece with the Ionian deputies, who had arrived in London on June 27th to present the new constitution of the Ionian Islands to the Prince Regent. Among the deputies was Foscolo's cousin, Dionisio Bulzo, who had helped him in the past out of financial difficulties and was to find many further opportunities of rescuing him from desperate straits. Foscolo asked Lord Holland to use his influence with the Provisional Government to obtain him some academic post, and looked forward to being in Greece at the same time as Lord Guilford who was going there on an educational mission. Charles Fox was already there.[2] Foscolo was now beginning to feel intensely lonely. 'Ho bisogno d' amare e d' essere amato', he confessed to Lord Holland, 'e qui dove non ho parenti ne amici che convivano meco, la povertà mi contende d' avere una moglie'[3]; and then he made a clean breast of his financial difficulties, his shame at being forced to accept loans and his inability to earn a living by his writing. Up till this time, although he had undertaken two articles, one for the *Quarterly Review* and one for the *Edinburgh Review*, they had to be translated and were in fact not published until considerably later. To this letter Lord Holland replied in terms of such warm admiration that it must have been balm to Foscolo's troubled spirit. So sure was the poor exile, however, of the futility of battling on in

[1] *Epist.*, II., p. 312.   [2] *ibid.*, pp. 315–16.   [3] *ibid.*, pp. 315–16.

England that he announced his early arrival in Florence to the Donna Gentile : ' fra non molto ci rivedremo ',[1] and to the Countess of Albany : ' E certamente passerò (e forse in ottobre) per Firenze.'[2] Unfortunately the Fates ordained otherwise. All preparations for his departure were made, when, riding one day with his cousin, Foscolo was forced to dismount to prevent his horse, which had got out of hand, from injuring some children playing on the road. In doing so he dislocated his leg, which had already given him much pain during the winter, and had to give up all idea of returning to Greece with the deputies. Bulzo helped him financially during the treatment,[3] and probably left him a sum of money for present needs. When the leg had recovered, the season was too far advanced for Foscolo to undertake the long journey overland with the prospect of crossing the Alps in late autumn, or by sea during equinoctial gales.[4] So he wrote to Lady Flint, with no memory of the original cause of his departure, that, having entrusted the settlement of his affairs in Zante to his cousin, there was no further obstacle to his remaining in England for the rest of his life.[5] A little ready money in his possession and the prospect of publishing a book in the near future soon removed all cares from his mind.

Foscolo now began to long for country air. The surgeon had kept him in an ' immobilità infernale '[6] during the first part of the treatment for the dislocation, and the effect of inaction on Foscolo's impatient nature made a change imperative. He decided to go to Kensington, where he would have the advantages of proximity to town and access to the library of Holland House. On the 20th of September he dated his letters from 19 Edward Square, Kensington. The *Letters from England* were meanwhile progressing and at the same time Foscolo's knowledge of English literature, as he reported to Dr. Allen.[7] To Miss Pigou he confided fragments of an article on Dante, which he intended working up for the *Edinburgh Review*, and even made a request that she should copy them out for him.[8] This was the article which was later sent after considerable misadventure, by Dr. Allen to Jeffrey and which Sir James Mackintosh translated,[9] although to the author's great distress mutilating the text to some extent. It was not published till the following spring, the manuscript having been lost and only found after Foscolo had re-written the article with an infinity of pains and weariness. It was, however, the first of a series for the *Edinburgh*

[1] *Epist.*, II., p. 313.   [2] *ibid.*, p. 314.   [3] *ibid.*, p. 336.
[4] *ibid.*, p. 321.   [5] *ibid.*, p. 321.   [6] *ibid.*, p. 329.
[7] *ibid.*, p. 330.   [8] *ibid.*, p. 327.   [9] *ibid.*, p. 328.

Review on the Italian Classics, and brought Foscolo high praise from all who read it. In the quiet of the country the Fates seemed to smile on him once more. Chiarini reports the cashing of a bill of exchange about the middle of September, and Lady Westmorland sent him £50 with a tactful note that he was not to return the money except when it was quite convenient for him, and, in all probability, she regarded it as a gift.[1] Foscolo began to forget the anguish of the past months. Work brought with it the satisfaction of achievement, and the first of the *Letters*, which was posthumously published as the preface to the *Gazzettino del bel mondo*, was pronounced by Lord Holland as ' de toute beauté—sévère, serrée et claire '.[2]

Later Foscolo left Kensington for new rooms at 22 Woodstock Street, which had the convenience of a central position combined with a very small rent. He retained these rooms even during the more prosperous months of the sojourn at East Moulsey, and returned to them in the spring of 1819, when the failure of Hobhouse's schemes involved him in further financial uncertainty.

All this time the Donna Gentile was patiently waiting for the fulfilment of the promise to see her some weeks hence in Florence. She must have grown weary as the weeks lengthened into months and still no news came from London. At last she wrote, pouring out all the sorrow of her loneliness and disappointment. Nothing could change her love for him. ' Ricordati che non hai altra MADRE che me : io assumo questo titolo con vereconda suberbia, e ne sento anticipato godimento, sperando che MIO FIGLIO non avrà discari i premurosi e teneri ufficj di sua MADRE.' [3] Two months passed before Foscolo replied to this touching letter, and then it was to enlarge on the cause of delaying his journey, and on the difficulties which beset his path in his literary work, not the least of which was his inability to write in English. The famous *Letters*, which were destined to remain a fragment, were spoken of as a completed volume which only the insuperable difficulty of finding a translator kept from seeing the light of day. But the magazine articles, to which he referred so slightingly, were the beginning of his success in English publications. Foscolo found it necessary to explain the humiliating step he had taken in writing for periodicals. ' I più dotti m' hanno qui per oracolo ; e scrissero in un loro giornale, ch' io sono il *genio più grande ch' essi abbiano conosciuto frà' viventi* ;—e notate che gli articoli de' giornali letterarj sono scritti da ricchi e nobili, e talor da ministri.' [4] To Lady Flint Foscolo had

[1] Chiarini, *Vita.*, p. 351.
[3] *ibid.*, p. 335, footnote

[2] *Epist.*, II., p. 334.
[4] *ibid.*, p. 337.

expressed the hope that he might be permitted to end his days in peace in England ; to the Donna Gentile he prays that Thomas Grenville may be able to procure him the protection of a British passport to allow him to live at rest in Florence. It is interesting to find that Quirina Magiotti laughed at the fancied difficulties in the way of his returning to Florence. Any passport would do, the powers that were would oppose nothing to his return and she herself would bear the cost of the journey.[1] But it was to Lady Flint that Foscolo had revealed his real desires.

As the spring of the year 1818 advanced, Foscolo's article on Dante, which had occupied his pen since the preceding August, reached completion and was delivered into the willing hands of Sir James Mackintosh, who had undertaken to translate it for the *Edinburgh Review*. We have noted above the calamity of the loss of the manuscript, and the hours of unnecessary labour spent in re-writing the article. No sooner was the work finished than the original manuscript was found. If Foscolo misused the good fortune which came his way, one cannot dispute the fact that he received more than his share of bad fortune. The article appeared in the February number of the *Edinburgh Review* ; and in spite of the liberties taken by the translator with the text, to Foscolo's own chagrin, everyone else was more than satisfied, and Jeffrey sent him £32 in payment, double the agreed sum. Encouraged by this reception, Foscolo wrote a second article on Dante, " *Osservazioni intorno alla Questione sopra la Originalità del Poema di Dante. Di F. Cancellieri, Roma, 1814,*" [2] which was published in the September issue and was received with even greater praise than the first. A recovery of his self-esteem with the prospect of sufficient earnings from his writings soon had the usual effect on Foscolo's mind ; and we find him in May writing to Quirina Magiotti, giving full rein to his fancy in computing his future gains. The magazine articles were to bring him in some £400 per annum, and the edition of the Italian Classics, a beloved project which he had once abandoned only to take it up again, would ensure him a capital of £10,000. Foscolo's plan was to publish the works of the great Italian poets with their biographies, the history of their centuries and his own notes. The whole series would be complete in thirty-two volumes.[3] He was so sure of the feasibility of his design that he even commissioned the Donna Gentile to find him a copying-clerk to replace the faithless Andrea Calbo.

Inspired by the early summer sun and buoyed up by his hopes,

---

[1] Antona-Traversi and Ottolini, IV., p. 129, quoted from *Epistolario di U. Foscolo e di Quirina Mocenni-Magiotti.*

[2] Viglione, Appendice, p. 319.   [3] *Epist.*, II., pp. 346–7.

Foscolo wrote to Pamela, one of the three daughters of Lord Edward Fitzgerald, then living at Thames Ditton, to find him a house. He was longing for the country, and leisure and quiet to put the last touches to his beloved *Carme delle Grazie*. The house was found at East Moulsey, and the rent of £84 per annum agreed on. Foscolo repeated his former exploits at Milan and Pavia and purchased linen and silver, furniture and the other requirements for an elegant dwelling, and even bought a carriage.[1] The real source of Foscolo's apparent prosperity was an engagement into which he had entered with John Cam Hobhouse, whose acquaintance he had made at the house of his friend and admirer, the octogenarian Italian scholar, Roger Wilbraham, at Twickenham. Hobhouse was newly back from Venice, where Foscolo's name was a byword in all the *salons*. He came to the meeting full of enthusiasm for the poet's genius. His pity was therefore the greater when he learned Foscolo's struggles for his daily bread. An opportunity of assisting him lay at hand. Hobhouse was about to publish notes to the Fourth Canto of *Childe Harold*, and Byron and he had thought of including in the Appendix ' a very short view of the present state of Italian literature '. They found the task beyond their powers, and the meeting with Foscolo suggested to Hobhouse a means of procuring what they required from the foremost Italian literary critic of the day. In his *Ugo Foscolo in Inghilterra* [2] Professor Viglione gives a very full account of the relations between Foscolo and Hobhouse, and we cannot pretend to do more than resume briefly the result of his invaluable researches. Foscolo was pre-eminently fitted for the task of writing a biographical and critical notice of the six greatest Italian poets of his day, Cesarotti, Alfieri, Parini, Pindemonte, Monti, and, at Hobhouse's special request, himself ; although the laudatory remarks in the last were inserted later by Hobhouse, to the dismay of the poet. The essay was published separately, owing to its length, with the title of *Historical Illustrations of the Fourth Canto of Childe Harold*.[3] In fulfilment of Foscolo's condition to acceptance of the task, his share in the work was not mentioned. The Italians, however, recognized immediately the hand of a master and compatriot, and the voices of the slighted and neglected were raised in protest. Ludovico di Breme, in particular, the most ardent of the exponents of the Romantic school, took offence at the designation of the struggle between Classics and Romantics, which to the poets of the day was the centre round which the universe revolved, as an *idle question*. It is

[1] Chiarini, *Vita*, p. 358.   [2] pp. 14–38.
[3] Published by J. Murray, London, 1818.

unnecessary here to enter into the details of the violent controversy aroused ; but Hobhouse took up the cudgels on Foscolo's behalf, repudiated the insinuations that the poet had sold his pen to the Austrians in 1814, and so roused opinion against Di Breme that the latter's health was impaired and he died in August 1820, his end unquestionably hastened by the attack he had himself provoked.

Hobhouse also enlisted Foscolo's help in the writing of an account of the revolutions in Italy. No one was more fitted to tell the tale of the last days of the Regno Italico than the ex-soldier of the Viceroy, who had taken part in the events he described. According to Foscolo,[1] Hobhouse had come to an agreement with a publisher and was to receive £2500. Foscolo, for his share in the work, was to have £50 per month and £400 when it was finished, and he anticipated that it would occupy him for a year. He thus felt justified in his expenditure for his house in East Moulsey. But he was tired and the work seemed to hang fire for a time. The feeling of loneliness deepened, and by November Foscolo felt he could no longer bear his solitary life, for the real emptiness of the social round which had taken up his first year in London was borne in upon him. To Quirina's suggestion that they might meet in Calais for a time, he replied :

Quirina mia, vieni a Calais ; ma col patto ch' io venga a pigliarti, e scortarti in Inghilterra, e condurti in questo mio romitorio dove ho tutto, fuorchè una persona che m' ami,—e però non ho nulla, se non se tristezza sempre, e spesso disperazione mortale. Ma se tu starai alcun tempo, quand' anche non fosse che per due settimane, con me, mi parrebbe di riacquistar tutto, e ringiovenirmi, e rinvigorire ; e lavorerei in un giorno, più che non ora in un mese. Vieni, e quanto più presto puoi ; e troverai preparata ogni cosa a riceverti,—ed il mio cuore che aspetta te sola per aprirtisi e versarsi tutto nel tuo.[2]

But she was not free to come, or she might have prevented Foscolo from many extravagances, and the tragedy of Digamma Cottage might never have been. Work, however, soon helped Foscolo to overcome his depression ; but on December 4th Hobhouse wrote him that he was unable to continue under the same conditions that he had originally proposed, and that he would have to extend the time.[3] An unsuccessful political contest for the constituency of Westminster, which Foscolo called a ' certo misero villaggio ',[4] had cost him £50,000, and the following year Hobhouse, according to Foscolo, found it necessary to go to France for a time to practice his new enforced economy. It is

[1] Epist., II., p. 383.   [2] ibid., p. 381.   [3] Viglione, p. 28.
[4] Epist., II., p. 384.

interesting to note, however, that Hobhouse makes no mention in his diary of his financial loss. The quarrel that followed the announcement of his misfortune has been very fully discussed by Professor Viglione, with, it must be admitted, great fairness to Hobhouse. Foscolo's nerves were in a state of extreme irritability at the time, and the dashing of his hopes of financial security, which had led him into issuing further bills of exchange shortly due, took from him what little self-control he had. Hobhouse did all he could to calm his fury. As the date for the payment of the bills arrived and also of the rent for the house in Woodstock Street, Foscolo launched further bills of exchange and sold at a great loss some of his books and the silver from the house at East Moulsey to save himself from the debtor's prison. A Miss Murray paid the rent of the house, amounting to £14.[1] There is in the Broughton Correspondence in the British Museum [2] a letter, very carefully and legibly written for Foscolo, dealing with one of the bills of exchange. The grateful tone in which he wrote to Hobhouse points to their reconciliation, which did in fact take place.

Foscolo had spent weeks of pleasant enjoyment at East Moulsey in spite of the depression of the beginning. The Fitzgeralds were not far away, and he was able to visit the Wilbrahams, as well as to keep in touch with many of his London acquaintances. The summer of 1818 had also brought him the friendship of Federico Confalonieri, who was in England presumably commissioned to buy some of the recent inventions which were to revolutionize the world. He reported to Foscolo the following year from Milan the success of his various purchases, the steamship, constructed in Genoa, for which he had most likely bought the engines, a gas-engine which supplied a whole house, and spinning machines. He was untiring in his efforts for his unhappy country, up to the moment when the Austrians condemned him to the Spielberg. During his visit to England he cast care aside at times, and enjoyed with Foscolo the unusually warm summer weather. The letters in the *Epistolario* from Confalonieri to Foscolo all testify to the sympathy between the two Italian patriots. Confalonieri suggested as a last meeting a rendezvous at the Hôtel Sablonnière, where probably he had been staying. It was the resort of many of the Italians who visited these islands, whether as exiles or visitors. Foscolo seems to have missed the appointment, and the exchange of letters and papers which was to have taken place.

Foscolo did not remain long at Woodstock Street in the two furnished

[1] Viglione, pp. 28–9, footnote.　　　[2] See App. I.A, 18.

rooms, where he could not ' ricevere anima nata, tanto sono meschine '.[1] He worked there, however, at his articles for reviews, and at the first opportunity, having hidden his poverty from the eyes of his English friends, he removed to No. 154 New Bond Street, where he put into practice his theory of the necessity of appearing a man of independent means, if one wished to succeed in literature in London. Reports of his mode of living and apparent wealth were carried to Italy, and his friends there were under an impression that the articles which he wrote procured him the means to maintain himself in the luxury, which rumour did not understate. Philarète Charles, professor of the *Collège de France*, who made Foscolo's acquaintance in 1819, has left a description of his house, which was as indicative of his love of classic arts as Digamma Cottage itself. ' Tout était payen chez lui. Il y avait des Apollon dans son boudoir, et des Jupiter dans son anti-chambre. Un petit autel portatif lui servait de cheminée, et il regret-tait, j'en suis sûr, de porter le costume moderne.'[2] Charles gives as vivid an account as Cyrus Redding and Sir Walter Scott and others, of the poet's vehement manners and exaggerated speech. Foscolo's own story of his misfortunes was at such variance with the accounts brought to Italy by his London friends, that the Donna Gentile decided to set enquiries on foot to give her a more accurate knowledge of the real state of things. Leopoldo Cicognara, who visited London in 1819, reported on the country house at East Moulsey, and the carriage and coachman, and the rooms in town for occasional visits. He did not omit to add a description of the attractive housekeeper that Foscolo had thought necessary to his well-being.[3] Still, Foscolo was working with ' solida forza d' ingegno ', and was looking forward to amassing a fortune by means of his articles and the cherished edition of the Classics. Silvio Pellico, who knew his friend better than he knew himself and who had repeatedly issued reminders and warnings of the necessity of providing for the proverbial ' rainy day ', once more thought it prudent to bring Foscolo's thoughts to earth. ' Non essere così dimentico, come sei sempre stato, della tua pace avvenire ; aduna un tesoretto per la vecchiaia, affinchè tu possa negli ultimi anni, se sentirai bisogno di rivedere la patria, venirvi indipendente, senza necessità di nulla chiedere.'[4] One disquieting sentence in Cicognara's report spoke of the wanderings of Foscolo's mind, of his wild fancies,

[1] *Epist.*, II., p. 384.
[2] Antona-Traversi and Ottolini, IV., p. 132.
[3] Chiarini, *Vita*, p. 370.
[4] Antona-Traversi and Ottolini, IV., p. 164.

of his melancholy and fears, ' e talora le idee di grandezza lo esaltano. ' The Donna Gentile diagnosed Foscolo's state, and she wrote beseeching him not to let his new love, if such there were, alienate him from his old friends. We shall soon see how rightly her instinct had guided her.

From the age of sixteen, when his Temira had first initiated him into the mysteries of Love, Foscolo had passed through waves of passionate adoration for many women ; but the idea of marriage had only entered into a very few of his loves. In the two years following his arrival in London the intoxication of his remarkable reception and the whirl of gaiety into which he was plunged, left his heart little time for more than flirtations, although of these there were undoubtedly 'many. Among his papers there are indications of a number of attachments, more or less serious. But towards the end of the year 1818 Foscolo became acquainted with the family of Sir Henry Russell of Swallowfield, a retired Chief Justice of Bengal, who was then living in Wimpole Street. He soon was made to feel thoroughly at home in their midst. There were five or six sons [1] and five daughters, the most of whom were still living in the father's house. The mother had died four years before. One imagines that the father had many endearing qualities, and there seems to have been an encouraging absence of ceremony in the household. Foscolo was particularly attracted to Catherine, who was married but spent much of her time with her sisters, and to Caroline, with whom he fell so deeply in love that his life for the next two years was torn between moments of ecstatic joy and agonies of uncertainty. In the letters in the Labronica belonging to the first months after Foscolo's introduction to the family there is no trace of anything but ordinary, friendly intercourse. Invitations to lunch, notes accompanying books returned, notes of sympathetic concern for the poet's health and requesting details of his prescribed diet, that they might offer him what suited him at their table, are the chief communications, which were mainly from Caroline. although Rose Aylmer and Henrietta also had their share in them, Foscolo accompanied the sisters to social functions and took part in those held at Wimpole Street. Before long he found himself on terms of such intimacy there that he was able to undertake the reading of Petrarch with Caroline and her sister, Mrs. Jones. During the spring of 1819 he must have been a constant visitor to the Russells' house, for the explanatory notes on Petrarch, which were a labour of

---

[1] D.N.B. says six on authority of grandson, but does not name them ; Debrett gives five names but no number.

love that absorbed his interest and time for months, produced the famous *Essays on Petrarch* to which most of Foscolo's fame in England is due. It could not have been expected that the poet of the *Grazie* should read the sonnets to Laura with a young, lively, highly intelligent and dangerously fascinating woman, with the dispassionate, academic mind of a language master. Nor did he. He could plead no ignorance of the dangers ahead ; for Sir Henry Russell, who knew well the train of admirers that followed his charming daughter and probably recognized the inflammable nature of his half-Greek, half-Italian guest, issued a timely warning : ' Badate che Carolina vi farà un giorno o l' altro girare la testa.'[1] With open eyes Foscolo walked into the fire. In justice to him we must remember that he cherished some vague, half-formed hopes of Caroline as mistress of his home and mother of his children. Sure of himself and of the invincible power of his love, he set himself to win her, although until her departure for Lausanne in the latter part of the summer of 1819 the relations between them were merely of friendly intimacy. Foscolo's veiled declarations of his love seem to have met with no encouragement, but also with no rebuff. His age (he must have been nearly twice as old as Caroline Russell) and the fact of his being of southern race and a poet probably gave her a romantic interest in him which allowed the dangerous intercourse to continue, and may have blinded her to the almost inevitable results with a man of Foscolo's temperament.

Several of the Russells with some friends set out for Switzerland in the summer, with the intention of remaining some months abroad. Mrs. Jones was then at Lausanne in convalescence after an illness, and Caroline remained with her. Foscolo received permission to write to her ; and from the drafts of some of these letters which have been preserved, we can reconstruct the whole story of his passion for Caroline Russell who had imagined a correspondence of quite different tenour. Jacopo Ortis was no tyro in the writing of love letters, and the opportunity seemed a gift of the gods. In the absence of Caroline herself, Foscolo recalled her image, her every word and the tones of her voice, seeking and finding in her expressions hidden meanings which encouraged him in his suit. He must have given up his thoughts almost entirely to finding suitable form for the outpourings of his heart, for two and three and even five drafts of the same letters are to be found among his papers. As we read his words we can see how his passion, based on an imaginary foundation, created for itself a Caroline far different from the real one. Incapable of believing the

[1] Chiarini, *Vita*, p. 373.

powerlessness of his love, Foscolo continued blindly in the attack, and not until many months later, when Caroline had returned to London and, seeing the futility of attempting to deal kindly with the infatuated poet, had stated her feelings in no equivocal terms, was he made to realize that for once his all-conquering passion had met with a check.

Chiarini has published the results of his laborious researches into Foscolo's relations with Caroline Russell in *Gli Amori di Ugo Foscolo nelle sue lettere*, and he arrives at what one feels is a very just estimate of her character and of her share of responsibility for the poet's hopeless passion. One regrets Professor Viglione's imputations of her refusal to return Foscolo's love to motives of worldly foresight. Commenting on Chiarini's summing up of the relations between them, ' Alle romanze di lui che chiedevano *amore*, ella rispose sempre con una nota molto semplice e molto chiara, no ',[1] he adds, ' Invece il 2 novembre 1824 rispose sì al blasone di Enrico Fortescue, che vantava antenati, baroni, conti e lords : titoli ben più cari al cuore di Carolina che quelli del povero e ramingo cantore dei *Sepolcri*.'[2] He calls her the *orgogliosa signorina*, because she returned to Foscolo the copy of *Adolphe* with marked passages, which he had been tactless enough to send her ; and continues, ' Carolina Russell, cresciuta nell' orgoglio di una casa patrizia, aveva bevuto alla fonte dell' odio contro il poeta di umili natali, non iscritto nel libro d' oro della nobiltà.'[3] In the first place, Caroline Russell herself could hardly be said to belong to the nobility, although her father had been created a baronet in 1812 as a reward for his services in India, and her mother's brother an earl, likewise for public services.[4] Secondly, it is most improbable that Foscolo would give the impression of being of ' umili natali '. Understating the importance of his ancestors was not one of his faults. The attraction that the English girl felt to the famous poet, who explained and commented on the love of Petrarch with such unusual fire and beauty, and who was himself so delightful a companion in the pleasures

---

[1] Chiarini, *Gli Amori*, I., p. 503, quoted by Viglione, p. 183.
[2] Viglione, p. 183. [3] *ibid.*, p. 197.
[4] Messrs. Antona-Traversi and Ottolini rightly give Caroline Russell's mother as Anna Barbara Whitworth on p. 166 of their life of Foscolo, and in footnote 2, p. 168, state that she was reputed a Frenchwoman, thus accounting for Caroline Russell's frequent visits to the Continent. In the latter case they have probably confused Sir Henry Russell with his son Henry, the second baronet, whose second wife was Marie Clotilde (d. 1872), daughter of Benoit Mottet de la Fontaine.

of society, was natural. That the name of Foscolo should be frequently on her lips during her stay in Lausanne, and that her married sister should tease her about his letters is again not to be wondered at. But the moment that she saw that Foscolo refused in all seriousness to believe in her assertions that she did not love him, and persisted in his endeavours to bring her to a declaration of the contrary, she took refuge in a dignified reserve, which increased as the poet's protestations gained in fervour.

The letters from which we reconstruct the story of Foscolo's love for Caroline Russell are only a small proportion of those written by Foscolo, and Caroline Russell's replies are not in our possession. They were returned to her by Foscolo on the tragic day which marked the end of his hopes, and were either destroyed by her or have not been made available for publication. With the intention of utilizing his love story for a novel, which would be a memorial of his maturer years, as *Jacopo Ortis* was of his early youth, Foscolo preserved with care copies of his letters and even drafts of many not sent. They are all written in French, which language Foscolo seemed to prefer for his intercourse with his friends ; for he never mastered the idiom of English completely enough to be *himself* in it. The first letter which Chiarini discusses is dated September 24th, 1819, and from internal evidence seems to be the fourth from Foscolo since Caroline Russell's departure for Lausanne. The others seem to have been an expression of his love for her, which she pretended not to understand. She did not wish to end their friendship, and probably thought she could keep his feelings within bounds by adopting an attitude of friendly reserve. But her absence only caused Foscolo's passion to increase, and his imagination probably led him to place a false interpretation on her words. He had little liking for her philosophic arguments, which were meant to help him to a saner outlook.[1] Writing had always been an outlet for his pent-up emotions, and now letter after letter, pages long, poured out his love for her in a way that would have been impossible if she had been before his eyes. Naturally she felt some annoyance, and wrote to Foscolo that she would consider his third letter as not written. Other letters then passed between them in much the same strain ; but some explanation must have been made, for the letter, dated November 22nd, 1819, which is published in the *Epistolario*,[2] points to their having decided on the relations to be observed in the future, after days of affliction. Caroline, now freed from the fear of embittering the poet's life, and knowing him as he

[1] Chiarini, *Gli Amori*, II., p. 483.   [2] *Epist.*, II., p. 387.

was, could offer him the consolation of her kindness without danger
of his misconstruing it into a manifestation of love. ' La nostra
amicizia sarà d' ora innanzi più aperta.' The letter ends with a beautiful
picture of the poet cherishing her memory when she was no longer
near him, and when he was dead, of her being the one person in
England by whom his tomb would never be forgotten.

The correspondence was resumed with ardour on Foscolo's part,
but we have no record of the letters until March 1820. Caroline
Russell seems not to have written for some time, and then to have
postponed her return home. Foscolo, angry at the delay, wrote to
her and received a reply some time in February, expressing her regret
at the postponement of her return and her desire to keep his friendship. Mad with joy, Foscolo replied immediately, evidently imputing
to Caroline such power over his happiness as to cause her grave displeasure. " I have generosity enough to wish to return in full all
the regard and affection that is felt for me. But you really give me a
power that is too serious and too important when you tell me that I
only have the power of making you very unhappy or happy. As far
as sincere admiration and friendship and gratitude for your kindness
towards me, go, I fear not that you ever have to accuse me of any
change or falling off. . . ."[1] These words seem clear and not unfair,
but there are some scattered rough drafts of Foscolo's reply which
begin with a tirade against the coquetry of women. The reply in
possibly its final form, dated March 17th, 1820, was published by
Chiarini in 1888.[2] It contains some rather curious statements refuting
Caroline's assumption that he considered her the arbiter of his
happiness.

J'ose même penser que la Nature dans sa toute puissance ne saurait
former un individu capable d'usurper pour longtemps un tel arbitre
sur moi. Le premier mérite d'une femme à mes yeux est *d'être digne
de mon amour* ; le second est *de m'aimer* . . . vous n'êtes peut-être
devenue un grand objet pour moi que parce que toutes les choses
étaient depuis longtemps très-petites et indifférentes à mon âme ; si je
me suis fait une illusion, ce ne sera jamais de vous que j'aurais droit
de me plaindre ; le bonheur dont j'ai joui en me créant l'illusion sera
escompté par le malheur de la déchirer de mes mains, ce que [*sic*], à

---

[1] Quoted by Chiarini in *Gli Amori*, I., p. 499. From a letter of
Caroline Russell, dated March 6th, quoted by Foscolo in his reply to
her of May 9th.

[2] *Due Lettere Inedite*. (' Nelle Nozze della Signorina Adele Cerboni
col professore Valentino Cerruti.')

mon opinion, n'arrivera pas ; car mon amour est clair-voyant précisément parce que il [sic] raisonne trop.

We should have attributed other characteristics to Foscolo's love than
too much reasoning. And again—

. . . j'aurais été lâche et cruel en vous inspirant une passion à laquelle
la fortune s'oppose, ou en la satisfaisant avec la plus tolérée, mais selon
moi la moins pardonnable des séductions, celle d'associer perpetuelle-
ment devant la société une femme à la pauvreté et à l'exil d'un homme
qui n'a pas de patrie.

He continues by stating his renunciation of all hope of being able to
live and die at her side, and his prayer that she might marry happily,
though that meant separation from her for ever. He promises not
to speak of the matter again in this world, ' car j'espère d'en causer
de nouveau dans le monde *où l'on ne se marie pas* et où nous connaitrons
mieux l'un l'autre, et n'aurons aucune nécessité de menager nos
phrases, vous pour ne pas m'affliger, et moi pour ne pas vous offenser '.
The reply to this letter seems to have persuaded Foscolo to continue
writing, and, encouraged, he resumed his very long letters, going over
again in detail ' tout ce qui s'est passé dans mon âme depuis Février
jusque à ces jours '. There are two drafts of letters extant, one of
May 9th and the other of the 16th. The former, some eleven pages
long, was published by Chiarini with the letter of March 17th.[1] It
would be tedious to discuss this lengthy epistle in detail, but it contains
a strange passage of several pages in condemnation of coquetry which
merits passing notice, when one considers its context.

Malgré que l'observation de plusieurs années, et surtout en Angleterre,
m'ait convaincu [sic] qu'il y a des femmes qui se font un jeu de leur
coeur et de celui des autres, il m'a toujours été impossible de vous
confondre dans leur nombre. Le monde pense que les malheureuses
qui par nécessité de pain font commerce de leur beauté, et que les liber-
tines et les adultères sont les seules qui se contaminent. . . . Mais
moi, et je ne suis pas le seul, je pense qu'il y a un commerce et une
contamination plus sale et plus abominable que celle du corps : les
jeunes filles qui prêtent leur coeur,—et ne le donnent pas . . . elles sont
ensuite épouses fidèles, et bonnes mères par crainte de lois, par principes
de religion, et par habitude ;—mais le feu divin qui nourrit et illumine
d'une clarté inextinguible les amants et les époux jusqu'à la dernière
vieillesse, s'est déjà évaporé . . . mais que le ciel me preserve d'une
épouse ou d'une amie semblable ! Elle pourrait me tromper pendant
quelque temps mais je m'apercevrais [sic] enfin d'une mauvaise odeur

---

qui tôt ou tard s'exhale de tout coeur où la plus nécessaire et la plus noble des passions a été contaminée de bonne heure. Jamais, Madame, je ne vous ai pas même soupçonnée d'avoir ressemblé à de telles personnes, et de vous être jouée de l'amour.[1]

But confessing himself a year later to Lady Dacre, he alludes to Caroline Russell in a way which suggests that the last statement was not true.

The letter of May 12th, 1820, refers to Foscolo's literary work, and speaks of the Marquis Capponi's expected visit to the sisters at Lausanne after some months in London. The letter of May 16th was Foscolo's thirty-second to Lausanne in reply to Caroline Russell's twelfth. The time was now approaching for the travellers' return home, and Caroline Russell felt the need for making quite clear to Foscolo the hopelessness of his claims. He, on the other hand, suggested lessening his visits to Wimpole Street, gradually at first, so that on her return his absence would not be marked. He dreaded meeting her lest their embarrassment should betray what had passed between them, and, convinced at last that his love was hopeless, he decided to resign himself to his fate.[2]   Like many of his resolutions, however, little came of it, and on Caroline's return home in October he hastened to visit her. From that moment matters quickly came to a crisis. The reserve of her manner at their first meeting, due to her uncertainty as to how Foscolo would behave, was interpreted by the infatuated poet as an indication that she cherished feelings for him which she was endeavouring to hide.   Instead, therefore, of continuing in uncertainty, as he had told her in a letter he wished to do, he visited her on November 17th, determined to force her to a declaration of her feelings. There must have been a stormy scene between them, for Caroline Russell, driven by the poet to express herself in terms that admitted of no misapprehension, succeeded at last in making him understand that there was not, and would never be, any hope. After this farewell scene one would think that Foscolo would have had the tact to avoid the Russell family for some time, but no. A few days later he sought out Henrietta and begged her to do him a favour, which probably was to return to her sister her letters to him. An account of the interview is to be found in one of the fragments of a letter to Caroline, presumably never finished.[3]   Henrietta seems to have confirmed the statement that her sister had never loved Foscolo ; and the latter, hoping doubtless that the conversation would be repeated

[1] Chiarini, *Due Lettere Inedite.*
[2] Chiarini, *Gli Amori,* I., pp. 503–6.
[3] *ibid.,* I., p. 512.

to Caroline, left with the words, ' Je la perdrai en lui laissant le remord
[*sic*] de ma destruction.' According to himself he returned to Wimpole
Street at an unconventional hour of the following Tuesday morning,
to reassure Caroline, who, he feared, might be tortured by the thought
that he had taken his own life.[1] It is also very likely that he took the
opportunity to return her letters which Henrietta had apparently not
accepted. This unexpected visit after what had happened four days
before, and the motive for it, insulted the girl, who treated him with
disdain and cut short the interview. Foscolo left in a fury and for
two days was beside himself with rage. After some weeks in which
to cool down and adopt a more reasonable frame of mind, Foscolo
evidently decided to offer an apology, and after five drafts decided
on the final form of his letter of January 1st, 1821, which accompanied
a New Year gift of a copy of the *Aminta* in Bodoni's edition. One
draft only is dated, presumably the final one, and on it is written in
Foscolo's writing that Miss Russell replied to him the same day.
The changed, resigned tone of Foscolo's letter induced Caroline
Russell to make some amends for the pain she had involuntarily
caused him, by suggesting, after justifying her behaviour, that he
should call to see them from time to time. Foscolo answered this
invitation to Henrietta, regretting his inability to accept it ; and
refused to receive her brother when he called.[2]

At last, on January 11th, Foscolo wrote to the lady herself a letter
of considerable length, which he intended should round off the story
of his love for her. Once more one marvels at Caroline Russell's
patience. He tried to tell her everything, the present state of his
feelings and his dreams that she should lose her fortune and turn
to him.

J'esperais que tandis que les années passaient, mes trois cent livres
par an, le seul [bien] qui me reste, [one wonders if this settled income
is the result of his articles to the periodicals] se seraient augmentées
par mes longs travaux ; et que avec ce que vous pouyiez avoir, nous
aurions pu passer une partie de notre vie à Florence, où avec mille
livres par ans [*sic*] vous n'auriez pas été la dernière Dame à l'égard de
l'aisance—Vous auriez été une des premières pour le rang en portant
un nom connu depuis quelques siècles—[where are the *umili natali* of
which Professor Viglione speaks ?] et vous auriez peut-être [été] la
première non à cause de l'admiration du monde pour le génie de votre
mari, mais à cause de l'estime pour son charactère [*sic*]. . . .

Some time would necessarily elapse before he could carry out his plan,

---

[1] Chiarini, *Gli Amori*, II., VII., letter, d. ' 1 Janvier 1821 '.
[2] *ibid.*, p. 527, VIII., letter, d. 11th Jan.

and their children would therefore be few. Caroline would go to England that they might be born there, even though that meant travelling in mid-winter. He added the doubtful compliment that age would spoil her beauty but not for him. He spoke of the new ideas she had brought back from Lausanne of the ' toute puissance des femmes ', and continued in many pages of the same tone.[1] Then, after this outpouring of the spirit, Foscolo resumed a more or less normal social intercourse with the Russell family, and the only other letter we have from him to Caroline is the famous one accompanying the copy of the *Essays on Petrarch*, which he had had printed in an edition of only sixteen copies, with a special dedication to *Callirhoe* in the one destined for her and in his own. This dedication in English verse is Foscolo's only attempt to express himself in the poetry of the language which he tried to learn for Callirhoe's sake.

This last of Foscolo's *grandes passions* marked the end of another stage in his life's journey, and was perhaps the greatest influence during his exile in London, although the duration of it was comparatively short. It is perhaps hardly fitting that we should pass on to the consideration of his literary labours during the period 1818–21 without some slight reference to his relations with the other members of the Russell family. Professor Viglione, on the authority of Burke (*Peerage and Baronetage*, p. 984), names five daughters, Anne, Caroline, Catherine, Henrietta and Rose Aylmer. The readings of Petrarch took place with Catherine and Caroline. Of Anne there is no mention unless the ' Lady Anne ' spoken of in a letter to Caroline was she, in which case she was probably married. Of the five sons, Charles, who translated part of the *Essays* for Foscolo, seems to have been most intimate with him ; and there is a letter from Whitworth, the fourth son, among the manuscripts in the Biblioteca Labronica. The other sons were possibly in India, except George, the youngest, who was most likely still at school. A most interesting proof of Foscolo's friendship with Henrietta was discovered during the Christmas vacation of 1924 in a second-hand bookshop in Edinburgh. A copy of the *Ultime Lettere di Jacopo Ortis* in the edition to which we have already referred, published by John Murray in 1817, the two volumes specially bound in one in crushed morocco, was picked up for a few coppers.[2] The special bookplate is worded ALLA GENTILE DONZELLE | ENRICHETTA

---

[1] *ibid.*, p. 533.

[2] By Miss Katherine Gower, now Mrs. Romilly John, to whom and to Mr. Purves I am indebted for this information and photographs of the bookplate and inscription.

RUSSELL| UGO FOSCOLO| CANDIDAMENTE D., and the inscription, written with Foscolo's own hand, *A Miss Henr. Russell| Ugo Foscolo| Wimpole St.—17 Marzo* 1819.

> *Come andrà l' alma mia giojosa e paga,*
> *Se impunemente esser potrai sì vaga!*
> > Ippolito Pindemonte.

It is exceedingly interesting to compare this with the inscription in a rare copy of the *Vestigi della storia del sonetto italiano dell' anno* MCC AL MDCCC by Foscolo. Also in Foscolo's handwriting is the dedication *Alla| Gentile Donzella| Luzetta Füsli| Dal Tabernacolo d'Hottingen| La Mattina del dì I gennaio* 1816| *Ugo Foscolo,* and on the opposite page the whole stanza of eight lines by Pindemonte, of which the two lines quoted above are the last.[1] Foscolo's circumstances were not of the best when he made this costly present to Henrietta Russell, for he had written to the Donna Gentile only the day before, telling her of the shattering of his hopes of collaborating with Hobhouse. There is considerable evidence that Foscolo continued to frequent the house in Wimpole Street during the absence of some of the family in Lausanne.

After his final meeting with Callirhoe, for she had now ceased to be that to him, Foscolo was afflicted with insomnia and melancholy. He still mixed a little in society, but one has only to recall the date, 1821, to realize that to a patriot the times seemed heavy with disappointment and failure. Before discussing the Revolution of '21 with reference to Foscolo, we must cast a glance backwards at the work which occupied him after he left East Moulsey. From the readings of Petrarch with the Russells rose up, by a gradual development, the magnificent series of essays on the *Love, the Poetry and the Character of Petrarch,* which was not published in its final form until 1823, but which passed through several intermediate stages. Professor Viglione's very full account of Foscolo's study of Petrarch makes unnecessary more than a rapid survey of the forms it took. The first concrete evidence of the study was an article for the *Edinburgh Review,* which had been promised to Jeffrey for some time. Jeffrey wrote to Foscolo in June and again in August, 1819, to remind him of the anticipated article on the poetry and the age of Petrarch, before it was sent to him translated and ready for the press. Meanwhile Foscolo had sent him an article on Pius VI, which Jeffrey had translated himself from Foscolo's *francioso,* and which was published in the *Edinburgh Review* in the March issue of 1819, and an article on Parga, to which we shall refer later, published

[1] Chiarini, *Vita,* p. 462.

in October 1819, and for which Jeffrey sent him the sum of £50.[1] The Petrarch essay reached Jeffrey's hands on December 13th, but its publication was delayed for some months. Impatient for Caroline Russell's sake to see the article in print, Foscolo had seven or possibly eight copies printed secretly, an expense that he could ill afford, and sent one to Caroline. Until May, 1820, Foscolo curbed his impatience to see his article in the *Edinburgh Review*, but Jeffrey held it up even then to make room for others ' which could not so well bear delay ',[2] and only notified the author in August. Foscolo was so incensed that he withdrew the article and sent it to Murray, who had already intimated his desire to have it for the *Quarterly* ; and he sent Foscolo a hundred guineas for it. The article appeared in April 1821, by which time Foscolo had passed through the fire of his unhappy love, and was not in a state to receive with equanimity the mutilated, almost unrecognizable version which greeted the public. As was to be expected, it aroused no enthusiasm and even provoked criticism. Foscolo found solace in the preparation of a new private edition, the one to which we have already alluded, which he limited to sixteen copies, of the three essays on the *Love, the Poetry and the Character of Petrarch*. The appendices contained translations by Lady Dacre and others of his friends from Petrarch and also from some Greek poets. This edition was an æsthetic delight to Foscolo, and proved to be so to at least one of the recipients of it, for Thomas Grenville, in acknowledging his copy, expressed his appreciation ' as a book-collector ', of the beauty of the volume and the ' rarity attached to it by the very limited number of copies '.[3] To make less obvious his real intention in having the *Essays* thus printed, Foscolo presented no fewer than six copies to various members of the Russell family, but only in Caroline's copy and his own did he print the dedication to Callirhoe. This edition was passed from hand to hand, and at last, when its reputation was firmly established, Foscolo announced to Murray that he was ready to attend to seeing the public edition of the *Essays* through the press. The work was now eagerly anticipated, but for various reasons the printing was only completed at the end of 1822, when Foscolo consulted Lady Dacre about the wording of the dedication to her,[4] who had helped him so materially with her translations.

In 1818, armed with a beautiful letter of introduction in Latin from Cesare Montalti, there arrived in London Francesco Mami, driven into voluntary exile at the age of sixty-four by the deplorable state of

---

[1] *Epist.*, III., pp. 431–2.   [2] Viglione, p. 187.
[3] *ibid.*, p. 198.   [4] *Epist.*, III., pp. 86–7.

his own country. Foscolo lost no time in finding him pupils, and with exceeding care Mami was able to provide for his own modest wants and at the last to help his younger friend, who failed throughout his life to limit his desires by his means. The tangible result of Mami's gratitude to Foscolo was the essay on Pius VI., which appeared in the *Edinburgh Review* of March 1819, translated to Foscolo's great satisfaction by Jeffrey himself. The source of Foscolo's information for this essay was for long unknown, but from papers in the Biblioteca Labronica which Professor Viglione has, with infinite care, ordered and resumed in his discussion of Foscolo's political writings,[1] it has been made abundantly clear that a long series of letters from Mami to Foscolo supplied the facts, which the latter handled with almost too great discretion in the article which brought him a considerable measure of praise. Mami was a native of Cesena, like Pius VI. himself, and had lived some years in Rome with access to the Vatican.

The year 1819 also brought forth the essay on Parga, which was the fruit of Dionisio Bulzo's visit to London with the Ionian deputies in 1817, and of succeeding deputations from the Islands. In October 1818 Maurojanni, an envoy of the Pargiotes to London, tried to persuade Foscolo to be their deputy to the British Parliament and to voice their sufferings [2] ; Foscolo, however, with more knowledge of the British constitution, refused the office, but accepted the papers he sent. ' Ma non essendo io suddito inglese, non posso farne altro uso che di scrivere un giorno la storia della vostra infelice Patria.' [3] This is the first mention of the writings on Parga which occupied Foscolo for two years. The treaty of Paris, though it placed the Ionian Islands under British protection, could not influence the way in which the protection was to be exercised ; and the Lord High Commissioner, Sir Thomas Maitland, though probably less ill-intentioned than was commonly believed, soon made British rule there synonymous with tyranny and oppression. Foscolo frequently helped his Greek compatriots, when they came to London to protest against particularly hard and unjust measures on the part of the Commissioner. Parga was ceded to the Turks in May 1819, and one of the deputies in London obtained Foscolo's help in requesting an audience of Lord Bathurst to ask him to lay their petition before the king. Foscolo's help was again forthcoming in the wording of the petition. Meanwhile Foscolo, provided with documentary evidence by Capodistria and Confalonieri, wrote the article on the Cession of Parga, which was published by Jeffrey, with expurgations, in the October issue of the *Edinburgh Review*, 1819. A

[1] Viglione, pp. 273-88.   [2] *ibid.*, p. 294.   [3] *Epist.*, II., p. 373.

fund had been raised in Devonshire for the benefit of the Pargiotes, with the Duke of Bedford as chairman of committee, and Foscolo seems to have been nominated to receive subscriptions. Delay in the transaction of their business, which the death of George III. and consequent dissolution of Parliament increased, caused much suffering to the Ionian deputies. Foscolo seems to have helped them personally as far as he could, and Lord John Russell sent a sum of money for their use. In acknowledging the latter's generous gift, Foscolo explains that the deputies were only willing to accept money for his sake, in order that they might refund to him what he had advanced them.[1] At the same time he refers to Lord John's promise to take up their case in the House of Commons, which he did in June of that year, but with no very decided result at the time. In his letter to Hobhouse of the preceding August Foscolo had intimated his intention of publishing a history of Parga, under his own name, in the event of Jeffrey mutilating his article,[2] and he wrote the book with infinite labour. The mass of documents and notes in the Biblioteca Labronica testify to the care Foscolo took that all his statements should be based on fact. The history was translated by several people apparently,[3] and a considerable part of it by the author's friend and admirer, J. H. Merivale. It became known from the readings which Foscolo gave of the manuscript while he was occupied with it, and he received encouraging letters urging him to publish the work. But it was destined not to see the light ; for a sudden fear, whether of being sent out of the country under certain terms of the Alien Act for too bold a criticism of the British rule in the Ionian Islands, which is most probable ; or of compromising certain of his friends, not the least those who had supplied him with much valuable secret information, and who were already sufficiently compromised by the Revolution of 1821, caused Foscolo to delay the publication and finally, although Murray had already announced it, to suspend it altogether.

As a relief from the toil of writing for the periodicals, Foscolo returned to his translation of Homer, a poetical task which gave him such joy that his health improved and his depression almost vanished. Capponi took with him on his return to the Continent the finished translation of the third book of the *Iliad* for insertion in the *Antologia*, although Foscolo amended it two years later until its original form was

[1] Correspondence of Lord John Russell, 1819–60, B.M. See App. I.A, 19.
[2] Broughton Correspondence, Vol. IV., B.M. See App. I.A, 20.
[3] Viglione, p. 301.

almost lost.[1] The delight at finding his poetic gift unspoiled by years
of magazine writing inspired Foscolo with a longing to write tragedies,
but the needs of life were inexorable and he had to satisfy himself with
re-publishing his *Ricciarda*, which brought him warm praise from
Merivale, Mrs. Maria Graham [2] and others of his friends, but left
him with a debt to the printer.

Many causes combined to make life hard for Foscolo in the years
1818 to 1821. His health was not good. He was afflicted with
insomnia, and overwork affected his eyes. The course of his love
for Caroline Russell was too uncertain to bring him more than very
short flashes of joy, and the turn of events after her return to London
plunged him into melancholy. The years of preparation for literary
work in England had passed, and he forced himself to the exhausting
labour of writing magazine articles which had to be copied and translated before they could be set before the eyes of the editors. He seems
constantly to have been in debt. His long-suffering cousin, Dionisio
Bulzo, met his bills of exchange for a time, but refused at last to advance
him money to repay others. Baron Trechi came to his aid at least
once,[3] and we shall never know how much was given him and lent
him without written record. To all these distresses one more was
added before the year 1821 was well on its way. The woes of Parga
roused the Greek blood in him to defend his native land, and now news
of the failure of the revolution in Piedmont with its widespread influence in all Italy filled him with grief for the land of his adoption.
Forty-six of his friends were imprisoned in various cities by the
Austrians, and his deeply loved friend Silvio Pellico, whose letters had
always been full of the tenderest affection and kindly brotherly advice,
was among them.[4] Foscolo himself had passed away before many of
them saw the free light of day again. Luigi Pellico wrote from Turin
in June 1821, of Silvio's sufferings in Venice (he was not sent to the
Spielberg until February, 1822), and of the refugees from Piedmont
seeking safety in foreign countries.[5] The Donna Gentile, writing on
May 9th, 1821, reported the mysterious disappearance of Silvio
Pellico's protector, Count Porro of Milan, of whom we shall hear more
later. The authorities in Milan were panic stricken, education was
at a standstill, ' le cose di Napoli hanno dato l' ultima rovina alle
speranze italiane.' [6] From this time forth, however, life was stirring
in the people of Italy, and, although much blood was yet to be spilt

[1] *Epist.*, III., p. 71. [2] See Viglione, pp. 301–2, footnote.
[3] *ibid.*, p. 289, footnote. [4] *Epist.*, III., p. 27.
[5] *ibid.*, p. 446. [6] Antona-Traversi and Ottolini, pp. 171–2.

and many lives dragged out in exile, yet the active struggle leading to the unification of Italy had really begun.

This terrible year of 1821 marks the close of the long first chapter in Foscolo's life in London. The second was to begin joyfully and hopefully, to open up a vista of life as he had dreamed it might be in his declining years, peaceful and harmonious and dedicated to the Muses ; but it was to end only in disaster and flight. The whirl of gaiety of the early months of his exile, followed by the calmer and more intellectual pleasures of Holland House, had filled his life for a time. Certain characteristics, however, which would tend to make him unpopular in a society which could not be entirely composed of wits, have been recorded. ' He had the greatest dislike to be asked a question which he did not consider important, and used to say, " I have three miseries—smoke, flies, and to be asked a foolish question." ' [1] Yet he must have been lovable. His enduring friendships with so many great and good men and women testify to it. With women he seemed to show his best nature in friendship. Love was a selfish passion in him which left him depressed and vengeful when the madness passed. He was a curious mixture of extremes. His mercurial temperament kept him in a state of change between melancholy and boundless hope. He had an innate love of luxury, allied to extreme moderation, almost frugality, in the pleasures of the table. The most scrupulous neatness and cleanliness in his own dress and that of any of his servants was an essential with him, and any departure from it seemed to give him real agony.[2] Restriction irked him. ' Io ho bisogno di poter andare dove voglio, quando e come voglio,' [3] he said once, and yet he could force himself to the most exacting slavery in trying to earn a living by his pen. In the midst of his wide circle of friends and acquaintances he complained of constant loneliness, which was simply another name for home-sickness. He almost acknowledges it in his letter of March 1820, to Capponi, bidding him good-bye. ' E mi dorrebbe che tu non ricevessi da me un altro addio . . . innanzi che tu rivegga l' Italia : tanto più ch' io bramo assai di rivederla, non però n' ho lusinga :

E il desir vive e la speranza è morta.

Pur vo alle volte tentando ; e se potrò armarmi d' un passaporto che

[1] The Mirror of Literature, Oct. 6th, 1827, p. 229.
[2] ibid., p. 229.
[3] Giornale Storico, 1885, Vol. V., p. 221. Letter of Dec. 28th, 1807, to the Contessa Marzia Martinengo Cesaresco.

mi copra delle greche ali inglesi, trapianterò, appena appena avrò il modo, i miei tabernacoli presso Firenze . . . parlerei non foss' altro italiano.' [1]   Two months later he wrote to Caroline Russell '. . . il me parait [sic] que . . . la conscience d'aimer et d'avoir l'âme pleine de quelque chose qui l'échauffe, est un instant et une nécessité que les mortels doivent d'une manière ou d'une autre satisfaire ; . . . moi, ne pouvant—n'ayant plus comment ni qui aimer tranquillement et sagement, je suis obligé d'aimer souvent en fou et d'user toutes mes forces à faire la guerre contre moi-même pour devenir plus calme '.[2] For nearly a year longer he was to ' aimer en fou ', and then, when that was past, he had but a short time to wait before he found someone whom he could love *tranquillement*, and with whom there was a hope of the domestic calm he longed for, though not in the way he had pictured it.   He was to find his daughter.

[1] *Epist.*, III., p. 15.   [2] Chiarini, *Gli Amori*, II., p. 507.

CHAPTER TWO

UGO FOSCOLO—*contd.*

Digamma Cottage and After, 1821–7

IN 1804, having asked to be sent once more on active service with the army, Foscolo had been posted to the Italian Division on the coast of France, which was awaiting Napoleon's orders to help in the invasion of England. With his old rank of Captain, he was sent to Valenciennes in charge of the depot, to his great disgust. Among the English civilian prisoners there was a family with which Foscolo seems quickly to have become intimate. He learnt English from the daughter, as a relaxation from his dull round of duty, and taught her Italian in return. It is improbable that he fell deeply in love with her, or she with him, as far as one can judge from subsequent events ; but she bore him a daughter whom he cannot have seen, as he was ordered away in the early spring of 1805. What we know of this child is gleaned from Foscolo's own account of her birth in three letters which he wrote in 1826, to his sister, to Capponi, and to Dionisio Bulzo ; by inference from the draft of a letter to ' Fanny ' among his papers ; and from scattered mention of her, greetings and so forth, in letters from Mami and others. From the fact that Foscolo spoke of her sometimes as Miss Emerytt and assumed this name himself when he went into hiding, it has been supposed that that was her mother's name. On the other hand, an indiscreet reference by Pickering in a letter to Foscolo in November 1824, and a similar reference elsewhere,[1] to ' Miss Hamilton ' point to Foscolo's daughter, and make it seem possible that Fanny's name was Hamilton and not Emerytt, and that the child, when adopted by her grandmother, took the latter's name.[2] Although

[1] MSS. Lab., Vol. XLVI. Letter from George Robinson, dated Oct. 29th, 1825.
[2] Considerable additional research has been done since this was written, and the question is dealt with in Appendix VI.

in the eleven years that had intervened since his child's birth Foscolo
does not seem to have given her a thought, yet he must have made
some enquiries when he reached England, for he elicited the information
that the mother had married, leaving her child to the care of her own
mother, who brought her up in the country.[1] We shall never know
what communication Foscolo had with the grandmother ; but events
proved that he must have had some.

Whether Foscolo was in slightly better circumstances in the latter
half of 1821, it is difficult to prove ; but he found it possible to send
his sister a sum of money by the Ionian deputies, who passed through
Venice on their way home.[2] The reports of his prosperity were a
comfort to his sister, although, knowing her brother, she added in her
letter of thanks, ' Pur troppo il mondo giudica dall' apparenze.' In
any case, he probably felt that the fruit of his labours for the magazines
was beginning to suffice for his wants. His studies of Homer led to
two lengthy articles, one on the *Homer* of Payne Knight, and the other
the *History of the Æolic Digamma* which was published in the *Quarterly*
in April 1822, and which to his astonishment added more to his reputation as a scholar than any of his previous studies. In the spring of
1820 he had described to Caroline Russell the ' cottage ' of his dreams,
where he would live and work in peace, surrounded by his dearest
friends. The idea was probably constantly in his mind, even after
the catastrophe of his love, and no detail of the house unplanned. It
thus happened, when his daughter's grandmother died at the beginning
of 1822, leaving her £3000 and entrusting her to her father's care,
Fate played into his hand. Exhaustive search for the grandmother's
will in the records in London has yielded nothing whatsoever, contrary
to Professor Viglione's expressed hopes.[3] It must have been lodged
elsewhere. A knowledge of the terms of the will and the powers of
the somewhat credulous trustees would have thrown considerable light
on Foscolo's later proceedings. His own accounts leave too many
legal loopholes to be truthful. Whether the trustees thought that
they were acting for the best, or whether Foscolo persuaded them
against their better judgment, it is impossible to say, but Foscolo's
later accounts of the matter in his letters of 1826, referred to above,
state that they invested the £3000 in land on a ninety-nine years' lease,
and in three villas in the new district of Regent's Park, of which two
were already built and the other was to be built in accordance with
his own design. Professor Viglione quotes the title of the contract

---

[1] *Epist.*, III., p. 226.   [2] *ibid.*, p. 447.
[3] Viglione, p. 64, footnote 3. See App. VI.

entered into on February 12th, 1822, between Charles Davis of 102 Gt. Titchfield Street in the County of Middlesex, bricklayer, and Ugo Foscolo of 16 Wigmore Street (he had left 154 New Bond Street a short while before, for what reason we do not know), for the construction of a villa to be ready by the following Michaelmas. The villa was to be let to Foscolo on a twenty-one years' lease at the annual rent of £87.[1] If the death of the grandmother really took place in 1822, Foscolo had lost no time in disposing of his daughter's legacy, for the land must have been already purchased by February 12th. If any extenuation is possible of this extraordinary breach of trust, it can only be found in the fact that 1822 and 1823 were years of phenomenal prosperity in the British Isles, when such a wave of activity in building and road-making and canalization swept over the country as it had never experienced before. The face of our cities was changed in incredibly short time. House property and land may have seemed a safe investment.

Whatever the ultimate purpose of the newly acquired property in Regent's Park, the real owner was kept out of sight, probably at school in the country, and Foscolo went alone to South Bank to occupy one of the villas already built, of which he sent Lady Dacre a minute description.[2] At the beginning of March he was already there. The situation of the ' cottage ' suited him, one mile from town and yet with the advantages of the country. Regent's Park was not taken into London until 1825. The disadvantage of the house which seemed all doors and windows, admirably constructed to let in draughts, was that it had been constructed as a *cottage fashionable* instead of a *cottage confortabile*, to suit the prevailing taste for outward show. Foscolo went on to tell Lady Dacre that he was having a house built to his own design, and, unable to confess the source of his means to her, and the existence of the poor child who reasonably hoped to make her home with him, he added : ' Essendo ormai rassegnato a vivere e a morir solo, la mia casa non sarà più spaziosa di quel che abbisogni ad *un solo padrone*.' [3] In this abode of rest and peace he would write his books, ' alcuni per *vivere*, ed altri—non oso più dir per la patria, ni per la gloria—ma per la segreta gioja che emerge dall' esercizio delle nostre facoltà '.[4] The change in Foscolo's ambition is interesting. Comfort, not appearances, was now his object, the modest home of a bachelor whose whole interest was in his books. He had, of course, to emphasize the modesty of his desires, for he knew that the many friends who had

[1] Viglione, p. 65.　　　　　　　　　[2] *Epist.*, III., pp. 57, 58.
[3] *ibid.*, p. 58.　　　　　　　　　　　[4] *ibid.*, p. 59.

helped him with gifts, and loans that would probably never be repaid, would wonder at his sudden increase of fortune. The presence of his daughter, too, would require very careful handling. It was impossible that he could take her into his house without her becoming known.

The intensive study and writing of the past months had fatigued Foscolo to such a degree that his health was affected and his eyesight seriously impaired. With furious energy he had written, early in 1822, a series of articles on Italian literature for the *New Monthly Magazine*, of which five were published, while others probably served for future issues. Certainly the articles were short and in no way comparable with the famous articles for the *Edinburgh Review* and the *Quarterly*, but they followed closely on the study for the Homer essay, and the fatigue must have been very great. It is interesting to note that these essays are signed with a digamma, which Foscolo henceforth adopted as a personal mark and which he even chose for the name of his famous villa. Acting on advice, he decided to try the waters at Chatsworth as a cure for his eyes ; and from his letter to Lady Dacre, written on June 12th, 1822, from Sale, where presumably he was staying with Jonathan Hatfield while on the way from Manchester to Liverpool, we have a detailed description of his travels. It was the first time he had had an opportunity of exploring England north of London. He visited Cambridge, with the friend who accompanied him on his journey, and was welcomed at the University. Cambridgeshire pleased him with its flatness, but not Leicestershire. Derbyshire enchanted him as having the beauty of Switzerland without its ' unpleasant inhabitants '. A memory of the first unhappy months of his exile ! A week at Chatsworth proved beneficial, but he did not dare to stay longer away from his beloved Digamma Cottage. He took the opportunity of visiting Manchester, which failed to exercise over him its real fascination, and only oppressed him with a sense of the sufferings of the workpeople and the slave-driving of the employers. He made an interesting forecast of the labour troubles of a later day. '. . . i vostri figli, o più tardi i vostri nipoti, si accorgeranno che la vera rivoluzione sarà qui prodotta, da un lato, dalla miseria della moltitudine, e dall' altro, dalla dovizia de' nuovi ricchi '.[1] Liverpool impressed him more favourably, and he had the pleasure of meeting with Roscoe. Before June 20th he was again in London. The poor Donna Gentile had been neglected for more than three years, and in July Foscolo, writing to Capponi about his literary work, lamented the fact that his correspondence brought his friends in Italy more annoy-

[1] *Epist.*, III., p. 67.

ance than pleasure, on account of police supervision ; and his English friends travelling on the Continent proved very uncertain messengers.[1] Meanwhile it was obvious that Digamma Cottage could not be finished by Michaelmas, and Foscolo found himself obliged to renew his lease of the smaller house for a year at a rent of £40.[2] About the beginning of October Digamma Cottage was ready for occupation, and Foscolo handed over his small house, which he now called Cappa Cottage, to Samuel Carter Hall, the author and editor, who had only recently arrived in London, aged twenty-two. Foscolo had met Hall and John Banim at a dinner-party given by Eyre Evans Crowe, the historian, probably just before Crowe set out on his visit to Italy [3] ; and soon after he engaged Hall, who was beginning to make a name for himself in journalism, as a kind of literary secretary.[4] It seems that the secretary's duties were light, as Foscolo had very little work on hand, except such as concerned the furnishing of his beloved villa. The editor of the *New Monthly Magazine* had suggested in October that Foscolo had sent him too many articles on Italian literature. The poet consequently broke off all dealings with him. Jeffrey had hurt him by delaying the insertion of the essay on Parga in the *Edinburgh Review*, and Foscolo sent him nothing more for some years. His pen being his sole means of support, however, and submission to others galling to his proud spirit, he decided to found a review himself, of no political colour and of European interest. He expressed his intention to Thomas Campbell, the poet, to J. H. Wiffen and to Lord John Russell, and he sent an outline of his design to Henry Hallam.[5] Fortunately perhaps for his finances, the plan was never put into execution.

One of Foscolo's greatest delights was flowers and he spared neither pains nor money to embellish his garden at South Bank. From the arid source of accounts Professor Viglione learns the names of the plants that found a place there, magnolias, camelias, jasmines and other beautiful and rare trees. On the garden Foscolo spent £200. His friends delighted in sending him gifts of plants, and he acknowledged a present of a pineapple plant from Miss Caroline Fox,[6] who had not forgotten him, although he had ceased to be a regular visitor at Holland House. He received several plants from the famous gardens at Woburn Abbey, where he had visited the Duke of Bedford and made the acquaintance of the Quaker, Jeremiah Holmes Wiffen, who helped

---

[1] *ibid.*, p. 69. [2] Viglione, p. 66.
[3] *Epist.*, III., p. 68, letter of introduction to Grassi, and p. 380, Grassi's acknowledgment, dated Feb. 14th, 1823.
[4] Viglione, p. 75. [5] *Epist.*, III., pp. 76–80. [6] Viglione, pp. 70–2.

the Duke in his literary work. Foscolo also presented flowers to some
of his hostesses. Lady Aberdeen thanked him for a jasmine he had
sent her,[1] and as late as 1824 a note signed Isabella Stansfeld (?) asks
him to send for his ' Cape Jessamine ' which he had lent them and
which ' smelt so sweet while it was here '.[2]

At the same time Foscolo was hard at work preparing his *Saggi sul
Petrarca* for the press, and his letters to Lady Dacre of September to
January are chiefly concerned with the translations from Petrarch
which were to form one of the main sections of the book. He was
particularly delighted with her translation of the ' chiare, fresche e
dolci acque ', and never tired of hearing it recited.[3] For some months
Foscolo lived in a ' Fool's Paradise '. The temple for study and the
shelter for his old age was before his eyes, and nothing for the moment
troubled the serenity of his existence. But Foscolo's work on the
Petrarch *Essays* was soon completed. During the last months of 1822,
therefore, he found himself with a secretary and little for either of
them to do. To while away the hours in the evenings he used to play
chess with Hall, who has left an account of their games in his *Retrospect
of a Long Life*.[4] Foscolo was a bad loser and would tear out his hair
in anger and throw the chessmen about if he had the misfortune to be
beaten. Hall's connection with Foscolo as his secretary was of short
duration. Dislike of Foscolo's temperament and real dread of having
his strict religious principles contaminated by the poet's free thinking
were probably the true reasons for the rupture. His approaching
marriage provided Hall with an excuse for ending his secretaryship
amicably.

,Hall's departure left Cappa Cottage once more without a tenant, and
John Banim seems to have wanted it for his own use. Although only
twenty-four, Banim was already known as the author of *Damon and
Pythias* which had been produced at Covent Garden Theatre the preceding year with Macready and Kemble in the principal parts. In a
letter dated January 8th, 1823, he offered Foscolo his services as
translator in lieu of part rent, but his offer was apparently not accepted,
for on February 12th a contract was entered into between them, whereby
Banim was to rent the cottage for a period of five years, at an annual
rent of £65. But like so many of Foscolo's business arrangements, this

---

[1] Viglione, p. 71. Prof. Viglione dates this letter of thanks 1822 (it
bears the date June 27th), but this year is impossible, as Foscolo was
not in Digamma Cottage until Oct. 1822.

[2] MSS. Lab., Vol. XLVI.   [3] *Epist.*, III., pp. 73, 82–3.

[4] Viglione, pp. 77–8.

one too was doomed to failure, owing to the refusal of certain trustees to accept his lease of Cappa Cottage as part of the security for a loan. Banim had to go and was naturally annoyed with Foscolo, with whom he had already had a difference over money.[1]

The few short months of bliss that followed Foscolo's entering into possession of Digamma Cottage had passed all too quickly, and by January he was beginning to tumble from the clouds. His conscience became uneasy as the time approached for the payment of his bills. He dared not even pause to estimate his expenditure for the temple of his dreams. Most probably creditors were already knocking at the door, and the old familiar method of robbing Peter to pay Paul was proving less successful than at the beginning of his exile in London. 'He no longer appeared as a martyr to his country's cause, but as a literary man of repute, who owned a splendid villa, with all the elegances that a wealthy gentleman of culture could desire. The friends who used to come to his help with small loans and gifts would not imagine his distress ; and he could not approach them in the face of his recent expenditure and with his former debts unpaid. Many of his friends who deserted him in the course of the years which followed probably had good reason for so doing. It was said by one who knew him well in the Digamma Cottage days, " It is but justice to his friends to add that there were circumstances which justified them in falling away from him." [2] For the present he decided to give lessons in Italian, and confided his plans to Lady Dacre in his letter of January 14th. He himself was resigned to his fate, but to spare his sister's feelings he would refer to himself publicly as the ' author of the Essays on Petrarch '. One might have thought that Rubina, who had struggled all her life against adverse fortune, and who had known the uttermost depths of privation, would have been able to bear with fortitude the shame of her brother's earning an honest living by teaching his native tongue. And his sorrow was great for all those who had shown him hospitality in the certitude of his continuing to live as a gentleman. One might almost take this for the bitterest satire of English society. He would become a visiting teacher to pay his debts and save for his old age, and would write for himself and the Muses.[3] Lady Dacre recognized the urgency of his case, and wrote on the day that she received his letter, to reassure him of their friendship and to offer all the assistance that her sympathy and Lord Dacre's wide experience

[1] Viglione, pp. 91–6.
[2] The Mirror of Literature, Oct. 6th, 1827, p. 229.
[3] Epist., III., p. 89.

could afford him. Foscolo had given Lord Dacre a full account of his failure as an alien to mortgage his property, and of the crushing expenses he had incurred for contracts which were now null and void, and for legal advice. Thoughts of suicide had occupied his mind for a time, but he felt he had not the right to die while his debts remained unpaid. Foscolo's sense of honour, subject though it was at times to serious lapses, did not acknowledge suicide as a way out of worldly difficulties, although it might put an end to the sorrows of unrequited love. Foscolo turned to his friend the barrister, John Herman Merivale, who practised in chancery and bankruptcy, and was in a position to give him the soundest advice. Merivale advised him to sell his houses as the best means of raising money upon them, and unpleasant as the advice was, Foscolo made some effort to follow it. But the offers he received were discouraging, and the attempts to let the two smaller cottages not very successful. Lady Dacre, who was a woman of profound common sense, after her reasonable reply to Foscolo's nonsensical ideas of being a gentleman, came to the rescue with plans for a series of lectures to be delivered by him on Italian literature. The plans were already far advanced by the end of February, for Foscolo in his letter to her of the 25th refers to the prospectus which he is about to send her. He looks forward to realizing some £1000 from the lectures, which will free him from financial anxiety for all time to come. The programme of the lectures was sent to Lord Dacre at the beginning of March,[1] and arrangements were then concluded with Murray for the subscriptions to be sent to him, and the money as received to be used in the settlement of Foscolo's most urgent debts. One hundred and forty people subscribed to the course of lectures, for which the fee was five guineas. The receipts seem to have been £771, which points to a larger sum having been subscribed by some, or to a mistake in the number reported by the Florentine editors in the *Epistolario*.[2] In any case the amount remaining to Foscolo was small. On the conclusion of the lectures Foscolo, forgetting his financial obligations, gave a splendid dinner to the members of the committee, although in justice to him the *strada carrozzabile*, specially constructed for the convenience of his guests, which arouses the astonishment of his biographers, may possibly have been a drive within his own gates which had been left unfinished, or his obligation for a section of South Bank, which was a new road.

It is a curious fact that Foscolo, who could not be in society without

[1] Quoted in the *Epist.*, III., p. 100.
[2] *ibid.*, p. 101, footnote.

becoming at once the centre of interest, and who indeed resented anyone else's usurping his position, had such aversion to appearing before a crowd as to amount almost to a disease. The first mention of this is in the letter to Lord Dacre referred to above, when he speaks of Murray having assumed control of the business part of the lectures, while he reserved to himself the preparation of the material and the steeling of his nerves ' per presentarmi a leggere in italiano a chi mi starà di faccia meno cogli orecchi che cogli occhi. Questo secondo sforzo mi par quasi impossibile.' And yet the cultured audience that gathered to hear him were to a great extent friends of his own, to whose interest in Italian literature he owed their friendship. The names of Lord John Russell, the Duke of Bedford, Lord and Lady Dacre 'Lord Brougham, Thomas Grenville, Hudson Gurney, Hobhouse, Rogers, and the Wilbrahams appear in the list. Foscolo's report of the lectures to Bulzo three years later was unjust to his hearers, to say the least of it. ' Credo che morrei di dolore e di bisogno, innanzi di assaggiare un' altra volta quell' amarissimo calice, d' esporre la mia faccia ad insegnare pubblicamente a gente che non intende, e che accorre chi per curiosità di vedere un animale famoso, e chi per desiderio di fargli la carità.' [1] After giving the lectures he wrote to his sister Rubina of his shame. ' . . . quest' anno mi sono esposto, con la vergogna sul viso e col cuore afflittissimo, a dare lezioni in pubblico, non in un' università, che sarebbe un onore, bensì in una specie di teatro.'[2] Lord John Russell's assurance, in a letter dated evidently in error by another hand ' 1824 ' and placed among the November letters, that the giving of public lectures ' is not in this country any way degrading ',[3] is probably intended to dissipate his dread.

Foscolo's situation became desperate towards the end of 1823. The momentary ease that followed the famous lectures soon gave place to renewed insistence on the part of his creditors. The plan of giving lessons was not put into execution. The rent of the two small cottages was quite insufficient to maintain the large one, and Foscolo still had a staff of three young maidservants, the famous ' Three Graces ', whose ambiguous position in the household seems to have been a subject of common talk. The obvious solution of all problems seemed to be the sale of Digamma Cottage, but its owner dallied with this plan as with others, and kept putting off the evil day. He confided to Lady Dacre his reluctance to part with what he had grown to care for so deeply. It may be that his conscience was pricking him, too,

[1] *Epist.*, III., p. 227.   [2] *ibid.*, p. 123.
[3] MSS. Lab. See App. I.A, 21.

regarding his daughter. Two years had now elapsed since she had been entrusted to his care, and so far he had only thought of her as a justification for the erection of Digamma Cottage. His hesitation in taking her to live with him was more probably due to his inability to explain her presence otherwise than by telling the truth, than to the feeling of delicacy with which Chiarini credits him in not wishing to bring his daughter into the house while the ' Three Graces ' were in occupation. Far from revealing a sense of parental responsibility, it appears to be strongly indicative of where his inclinations lay. The solution in the dismissal of the three maidservants was too simple. Charles Rossi came to Foscolo's rescue in October 1823, when his freedom was seriously menaced by some of his creditors ; and disaster was once more averted for the time being by a promise to settle the debts in the following April. But as the time for the expiry of the grace drew near, Foscolo saw himself as incapable as before of finding the money, and the best solution seemed to be to give up his house and return to the land of his birth. A copy of the memorandum addressed to Lord Bathurst appears in the *Epistolario*, and one in the original English in the handwriting of Andrea Schorno and dated February 17th, 1824, is preserved among the manuscripts in the Biblioteca Labronica.[1] At the end of April, when his affairs were in a particularly unhappy state, he wrote in Greek to a member of the Greek Government, stating his wish for a post in his native land.[2] Ill health and fear of the bailiffs kept Foscolo confined to his house, but at the beginning of March he still hoped to succeed in his efforts to obtain a passport. He wrote to Santa Rosa to say good-bye and to make arrangements about returning books to him.[3] However, as things turned out, he did not succeed in obtaining the passport, and had to set about finding other means of providing for himself and his daughter, and of satisfying the most clamant demands of his creditors. By this time, too, Peel had brought in an amendment to the Alien Bill, to exclude from the provisions of the act ' any Alien who shall have been continually residing in this Kingdom for a Period of Seven years ',[4] which exempted Foscolo from supervision henceforth.

From this time on, Foscolo's life was one of desperate struggle to obtain money, aggravated by ill health, threatened blindness, and real

---

[1] MSS. Lab., Vol. XLV. See Viglione, p. 108, footnote.
[2] *Epist.*, III., pp. 152–3.   [3] *ibid.*, p. 133.
[4] 5° Geor. IV., c. XXXVII. This Act was repealed in May 1836, and the new Act which replaced it limited the time of residence in this country to three years for purposes of exemption.

physical inability to cope with his difficulties. One can imagine the life of the poor girl, Floriana, thus unexpectedly called upon to act the comforter, and possibly to bear the brunt of the short-sightedness of the father who until the early months of 1824 had been practically unknown to her. Her life had hitherto lain in pleasant places, and she was ill-fitted for the anxieties and privations of the years that were in front of her. Having abandoned hope of going to Greece, Foscolo once more resorted to thoughts of teaching, but they were not realized. The labour of writing articles for periodicals, with the expenses of copying clerks and translators, was quite unprofitable. The only hope that yet remained was the long-cherished edition of the Italian Classics.

From a letter from William Stewart Rose we gather that Foscolo had outlined to him his plans of giving lessons in order to earn a more certain income. Rose suggested that teaching might be regarded as a means of earning one's daily bread, but that some other means should be resorted to in order to provide a capital sum for future needs. He referred to his earlier suggestion of a new edition of Dante by subscription, and offered to help.[1] The letters of the previous year had in a way formulated the ideas which Foscolo now decided to elaborate in bringing out an edition of the great Italian Classics. Rose's encouragement decided him to draw up a prospectus, outlining the nineteen volumes in which the works of Dante, Petrarch, Bojardo, Ariosto and Tasso were to be published. Foscolo's first intention seems to have been to publish *in quarto* at his own expense, and to entrust the work to the printer Nichols[2]; but the subscriptions probably being insufficient to guarantee the continuance of the enterprise, he turned for help to Murray. A new prospectus was issued with the changes in plan, and a promise to publish the edition when three hundred subscribers had announced themselves. At the beginning of April Murray abandoned the scheme, and after some further efforts on Foscolo's part, William Pickering was induced to take it up. A third prospectus announced some modifications of the original plan. In May, William Roscoe wrote offering to become a subscriber, but by that time the original plan had already been abandoned.[3]

Meanwhile Foscolo was in town, ' in un quartiere ammobiliato come Dio vuole ', as he announced to Lord Dacre in his letter of April 17th.[4] This ' quartiere ' was No. 1 Well Street, Jermyn Street, as appears from a letter of May 7th from Andrea Schorno, Foscolo's copying

[1] MSS. Lab. See App. I.A, 22. [2] See Viglione, p. 223.
[3] MSS. Lab. See App. I.A, 23. [4] *Epist.*, III., p. 149.

clerk, who was still at Digamma Cottage. Foscolo was still at Well Street on June 21st, when Pickering sent him a cheque for £22 10s— for his work in connection with an edition of Boccaccio.[1] A meeting of his creditors had been held in April, at which six weeks had been granted to him to fulfil his obligations. Meanwhile, not believing Foscolo's statements that he would not shelter behind the Insolvent Act, the creditors met again and demanded immediate settlement. Gregson reported this meeting on April 26th, and advised immediate sale of the property.[2] Foscolo was unwilling to sell his villas without a reserve price, as his debts only amounted to £800, and pled for the full period of six weeks' grace. He was confined to the house at this time for fear of imprisonment for debt, and had difficulty in obtaining papers from Digamma Cottage. The edition of the Classics seemed to hold out some hope of success, and Foscolo longed to raise a loan on the security of the furniture of Digamma Cottage, wherewith to pay off his most pressing bills. Writing to his legal friend Robert Roscoe, not Thomas, as is stated by Professor Viglione, the poet urged the delay of the sale until the plants in the garden should have grown and the property have increased in value.[3] By some means, probably the intervention of friends, delay was obtained until the end of June. The contract with Pickering was now concluded, and when it seemed that nothing could save Digamma, the publisher advanced the necessary sum of £250 to pay the chief creditor, and thus averted disaster. The most pressing debts were paid, but the others still remained.

Foscolo was now free to return to Digamma Cottage. The events of the past months had been a severe strain on him and he was tired and ill. He found solace in the continued kindness of his friends. In June, Rose sent him a gift of twenty pounds of coffee, with a warm invitation to visit him [4]; and a month later Lady Compton tried to persuade him to spend some time in the Island of Mull, where he would have peace to work and opportunity to economize. Before leaving London at the beginning of July, Lady Compton seems to have taken Foscolo's distress to heart and to have begged him to commission her to find a suitable family in the hills, with whom he could board.[5] On July 18th she wrote him from Torloisk, Isle of Mull, not from the ' campagne di Edinburgo ' as Professor Viglione states, to tell him that a family of Macleans would be delighted to have him,

---

[1] MSS. Lab., Vol. XLVI.   [2] Viglione, p. 105, footnote 3.
[3] *Epist.*, III., p. 155.   [4] MSS. Lab., Vol. XLVI.
[5] Viglione, pp. 108-9.

' avrà due camere che non fumano ',[1] and giving most interesting details of the journey, which we venture to repeat.

Arriverà qui (da mia madre) per dieci lire—si riposerà, e vedrà un poco del paese ; poi passerà a Pennycross, che sarà un' affare di sette ore—ed io sono incaricata di farle un' invito dalla parte di Mr. Maclean e la di lei moglie, per venire a farli una visita di un mese. . . . Le spese sono a ragioni di dieci lire, e cosi si fa il conto.

Then follows a minute estimate of the cost of the journey, the passage to Edinburgh, the cost of the hotel, meals, etc. : té 2s., bed 2 days 14s., lunch 2s. 6d., dinner 4s. 6d., coach to Glasgow 10s. 6d., boat from Glasgow to Aros and horses from Aros to Torloisk.

Mia madre dice che le manderà cavalli da qui e che la consiglierebbe di approdare non ad Aross [sic], ma ad Tobermorry [sic], perchè la strada (se strada deve nominarsi) è molto migliore. . . . Noi abbiamo fatto questo viaggio tale quale come l' ho accenuto per lei, e ci abbiamo trovato un gran commodo ed un gran risparmio : e questo bellissimo piacere di risparmiare credo che sia il destino di tutti i figli di Adamo. . . .

There are, however, also among the 1824 letters some notes less welcome than Lady Compton's, reproaches from ladies he had neglected to visit, a request for an autograph, gushing invitations and the like— the ' nonsensical biglietti delle perpetuamente scriventi signore inglesi, le quali scrivendo di nulla, ti astringono a perdere tempo e parole a rispondere nulla '.[2]

Although the summer of 1824 saw Foscolo once more in residence in his beloved villa, the relief from financial pressure was only momentary. There was no immediate prospect of return from the edition of the Classics, and still a large number of debts were outstanding, apart from sums of money owing to friends. There is an echo of the uncomfortable feelings which must have been shared by many of Foscolo's friends, in a letter from Hatfield, written in June 1824, while Foscolo was still living in town. Finding himself unable to repay the money he had borrowed from Hatfield, he had passed over the date of payment in silence.[3] Probably many other similar loans were allowed to drop, and the lenders gradually permitted their intercourse with Foscolo to lapse. Tired though he was, Foscolo dared not leave London and had to work for his daily bread. A timely subsidy from abroad, through his brother, roused in him hopes that the villa would soon be free of claims.[4] Meanwhile he entered into

[1] MSS. Lab., Vol. XLVI.   [2] Epist., III., p. 164.
[3] MSS. Lab. See App. I.A, 24.   [4] Viglione, p. 110.

an agreement with Walker of the *European Review* for a series of
articles, which occupied him for the last nine months of 1824. Unfortunately Walker's demands for articles were beyond his ability to
utilize them, and payment was only sent when they appeared in print.
Foscolo, who was under an obligation to pay his creditors at the
beginning of November, would therefore be compelled to seek work
elsewhere, unless the editor of the *European Review* were willing to
pay him a definite sum weekly, adjusting their accounts quarterly,
and he wrote to him to this effect. But Walker was unmoved, and
was as a matter of fact himself in an unsound position financially. At
last, in November, he sent Foscolo a bill for £54 which Pickering
agreed to cash and divide among certain creditors. Hearing, however,
of Walker's financial instability, Pickering refused to pay when the
creditors appeared, and one of them, a tailor, furious at the treatment he had received, had Foscolo arrested on November 19th. The
arrest could not have lasted long, but it was followed by weeks of con-
cealment, during which, however, his daughter visited him.[1] If the
facts stated in a document written by Foscolo, dealing with his contracts
with Pickering, are true, he took a half-furnished cottage in Hampstead
for three months, but owing to the dampness of the house, left after a
short time.[2]

On December 5th John Finlayson, Foscolo's house agent, announced
the sale of the furniture of Digamma and Cappa Cottage, which
realized £400,[3] £200 of which was given to Pickering in part payment
of the debt due to him. It would seem that the houses were sold the
following month for £1400 to Eliza Wartridge, who had rented Green
Cottage for September and October of 1824. According to Foscolo's
friend and legal adviser, Hoggins, this entire sum was divided among
the creditors in complete settlement of the debts.[4] Hoggins' statement points to the debts having been far greater than Foscolo himself
had reckoned. It is also difficult to understand what actually had
been sold, for Foscolo's letters of 1826 to Dionisio Bulzo and Rubina
contain accounts which are difficult to reconcile with each other.
Probably the furniture of the cottages was sold, and a mortgage taken
out on the rest of the property, of which Eliza Wartridge was the
holder. Foscolo, after the settlement of his debts, took a cottage at

[1] MSS. Lab. See App. I.A, 26.
[2] " A circumstantial statement of the facts in the matter at issue
between Mr. Foscolo and Mr. Wm. Pickering." MSS. Lab., Vol.
XLVIII., Sec. N. II. See Viglione, p. 113.
[3] *ibid.*, p. 114.   [4] *ibid.*, p. 115.

Hendon to which his books and the furniture of Green Cottage were
sent. At last he was free of the incubus that had tormented his days,
but he was faced with the need to provide for himself and his daughter
solely by the work of his pen. Half measures were never his policy,
and refusing to be pitied by those whose admiration he had courted,
he changed his name and retired into seclusion. Digamma Cottage
itself, which had been the realization of his dreams and the cause of
his misfortunes, was taken down later to make way for the new railway
and Marylebone station, and South Bank and recently even North
Bank have been swallowed up in a gigantic power station. Pickering's
letter announcing the despatch of Foscolo's possessions, is addressed
to *Mr. Marriatt, Parson St., Hendon*,[1] and subsequent letters to *Ivy
Cottage*, Hendon, which may be the same place. One of these conveyed an invitation from Jonathan Hatfield to Foscolo to use his
country-house for as long as he liked. All Pickering's notes at this
period are extremely friendly in tone, and he wrote much about the
edition of Dante, and forwarded such necessities as paper and pens.

In May 1825, not June or July as Professor Viglione suggests,[2]
Foscolo left Hendon for Totteridge, to judge by a letter from Hoggins
of May 30th, addressed to him there. Unharassed by debts, Foscolo
could now look forward to uninterrupted work, and he chose for his
retreat, in the beautiful, bracing country north of London, the little
village of Totteridge in Hertfordshire. The Florentine editors,
unacquainted with the district, misread the abbreviation *Herts.* of
the county and the curiously un-English ' Totteridge Hertz ' has
found a place in all the Foscolo biographies since. The new house
consisted of no less than ten rooms. There seems to have been a
stable attached and a well-stocked garden. The inventory of the
furniture, which has come down to us,[3] suggests a comfortable, tasteful
house, without any of the exotic luxury of the ill-fated Digamma
Cottage. Unfortunately Foscolo's relations with Walker and Pickering
were far from being the solution of his financial difficulties that he
had hoped. His dealings with them have been examined by Professor
Viglione [4] with such scrupulous care that a mere indication of the
main points is all that is necessary here. The trouble began while
Foscolo was still at Digamma. The first four volumes of the edition
of the Italian poets were under a bond to pay the debts for his house,
and the articles for the *European Review* were to pay for the daily
needs of the household. Unfortunately, Walker was unable to meet

[1] MSS. Lab., Vol. XLVI.   [2] Viglione, p. 132.
[3] *ibid*., pp. 132-3.   [4] *ibid*., Chapter IV.

his obligations to Foscolo and the poet was able to extract £50 from him only with difficulty. We have seen the unfortunate results of the bill for £54 sent to him in November 1824. Pickering naturally became impatient at the delay in the progress of the Dante edition, due to the work undertaken for Walker ; and Foscolo warned the editor of the periodical of his inability to contribute further. It was November of 1825 before Foscolo succeeded in forcing a promise from Walker to settle his debt to him for articles already published.[1] As we noted, the greater part of Foscolo's debt to Pickering was repaid after the sale of the furniture in December 1824 ; but Pickering made Foscolo sign a bill for the remainder, although he recognized the justice of the poet's claims that the manuscripts sent to the publisher were in fact a part redemption of the debt. In consequence of a firm stand by Foscolo, who stated the absolute necessity of his receiving a regular supply of money if the work were to proceed, Pickering consented in July 1825 to a weekly payment of £4. Meanwhile the publisher took fright at the word of another edition of Dante to be published by Murray, and determined to bring pressure to bear on Foscolo that he might be first in the field. This other edition was announced to Foscolo by his friend Christopher Hoggins in his letter of May 30th. He reported that an intimate friend of Coleridge had spoken to him of a commentary on Dante, about to be brought out by " an Italian—Rosetti [sic] a friend of Mr. Coleridge ".[2] Gabriele Rossetti had just come to London in the preceding year, and Hoggins' comment on his own letter reads delightfully. " So you must have laughed heartily at my writing you about Mr. Rosetti, or some such man—when Mrs. Hoggins had previously mentioned it to you."[3] Pickering did his utmost to hasten on the work, but without result, for Foscolo would never sacrifice the quality of his work to speed or any other consideration. The publisher even suspended the weekly payments for a while in protest. The last of the manuscript of the *Discourse on the text of Dante*, which was to form the first of the Dante volumes, was sent in in November. This unfortunate month, how-ever, marked the rise of the panic fear which swept over the country, causing a run on the banks which brought about the ruin of many old, well-established houses. Pickering began to demand receipts from Foscolo for the money disbursed, under threat of again suspending payment. The *Discourse* was published in November, it seems, but

[1] Viglione, p. 122.
[2] MSS. Lab., Vol. XLVI. Probably S. T. Coleridge is meant.
[3] *ibid,*

so full of misprints that Foscolo was in despair. It is interesting to note that Rossetti, writing to Charles Lyell of Kinnordy on March 15th, 1828, says, ' E cosa nota al pubblico che io pubblicai il mio primo volume nel 1825 con la post-data del 26 : e ch' egli [i.e. Foscolo] pubblicò il suo nel 1826 con l' anti-data del 25.' [1]

Since the middle of November Foscolo had had no income, and only in January was he able to pay his copying clerks by means of a timely gift of £50 from Hudson Gurney, who seems to have been a very good friend to him and to have lent or given him from first to last, according to Mrs. Sarah Austin, not less than £2000.[2] It did not suffice, however, to pay the tradesmen's bills. " Ecco il magnano Buckland, il macellaio White, il panettiere Coldwile, il candelaio Bagget, il lattaio, il cocchiere, il servo, e altri creditori, Harding, Lindurst [sic], Hammond, tutta gente minuta, plebea, insolente."[3] The daily struggles and continual worry decided Foscolo to take Floriana, who seems to have been ill, to stay for a few days with Hoggins at No. 1 King's Bench Walk, Temple, and this he did on January 10th. His absence after some nine days gave rise to the belief that he had run away, and one of his creditors called in fury on Foscolo's host in town ; ' but this together with other previous disagreable [sic] things in that place obliges me to repent indeed having taken my abode amongst them ', wrote Foscolo to his landlord, to whom he owed arrears of rent.[4] The other side of the question does not seem equally clear to Foscolo's biographers. The tradesmen of Totteridge were possibly less conscious of the honour done them by the unknown Mr. Merriatt [5] who took up his abode among them, than of the fact that he allowed his accounts with them to run on without any definite promise of payment. There being no hope of saving the situation otherwise, the only thing left was to sell the furniture of the house at Totteridge. On January 31st, 1826, Foscolo communicated this decision to the surveyor and auctioneer, William Roberts, and put the matter into his hands. The sale was fixed for March 3rd.[6] When it took place it realized only £102, which was not sufficient to meet Foscolo's liabilities.

---

[1] Letters of Gabriele Rossetti to Charles Lyell, from the originals at Kinnordy. Notes on these letters have been made available by the kindness of Mr. Purves.

[2] Ross, *Three Generations of Englishwomen*, II., pp. 24–6.

[3] Viglione, p. 134. [4] *ibid.*, p. 135.

[5] The name is spelt in various ways.

[6] Viglione, p. 135.

The money from the sale at Totteridge was divided among the tradesmen of the district, and none given to Pickering, who still claimed payment in cash of the debt due to him, regardless of Foscolo's suggestion to extinguish it gradually by his literary work. Pickering allowed Foscolo to be arrested on an old warrant, but the detention was of short duration. It is unnecessary here to enter into the weary and soul-destroying negotiations, in which every suggestion put forth by Foscolo was pulled to pieces by Pickering ; while Pickering's conditions were so outrageous as to be beyond Foscolo's consideration, At long last, after Hoggins and Stephen Garrard had done their utmost. Taylor succeeded in obtaining Pickering's signature to the contract. It was then January 3rd, 1827, and Foscolo, worn out with struggling against poverty and adverse circumstances, and weary in mind and sick in body, was only to have a few short months in which to enjoy the comparative peace. Six contracts in all had been drawn up and refused by Pickering before he finally signed the seventh. Towards the end of 1826 Foscolo had again entertained the idea of publishing the *Dante* on his own account, possibly in collaboration with Panizzi ; but Foscolo's determination to vindicate himself in the *Lettera Apologetica*, to be prefixed to the *Dante* edition, was displeasing to Panizzi. The latter expressed his opinion in a letter dated January 4th, 1827,[1] but Foscolo took umbrage at once and the result was a breach of the friendship. In the middle of March of 1827 Foscolo gave in the text and commentary of the *Inferno*, but in spite of the infinite trouble it had cost both publisher and author, it lay in a drawer in Pickering's desk until Mazzini in 1842 induced the bookseller Rolandi to purchase the manuscript for £400. When at last published with Mazzini's anonymous commentaries on the last two books, it did not meet with the reception of which Foscolo had dreamed.

The year 1826, after the sale at Totteridge, was one of great misery and privation, while the struggle with Pickering dragged on wearily. We can trace numerous changes of abode. At the end of February Foscolo wrote to Francesco Mami from No. 6 Devereux Street, Temple, where he lived as the *German gentleman*, under the assumed name of Emerytt,[2] which he adopted now for the first time. Three weeks later, whether for greater security or for greater comfort we do not know, Foscolo was living at No. 2 Duke Street, Adelphi, Strand. None of the houses in which he had lived so far merited the name of *tugurio*, which has been applied to them [3] ; although Foscolo was at this time so reduced in means as to be obliged to sell his books one

---

[1] Viglione, p. 248.   [2] Chiarini, *Vita*, p. 425.   [3] Viglione, p. 115.

by one to provide his daughter and himself with their daily bread.
Foscolo's books and desk and chair had been saved from the sale at
Totteridge. Towards the end of April he removed again, this time
to the country, some twelve miles from London, and from there he
wrote to his copying clerk Giovanni Berra, dismissing him for lack
of means to pay him.[1] He resumed the writing of articles for reviews,
pending the settlement with Pickering. The problem of disposing
of these was solved by another exile, Fortunato Prandi, who had been
five years in England and had made a large circle of influential acquaintances, whose good offices he enlisted on behalf of Foscolo. Without
his intervention the poet and his daughter would have been in sore
straits indeed. Two articles, one on " Boccaccio " and one on " The
Women of Italy ", appeared in the *London Magazine* in the latter half
of 1826, and one in the *Retrospective Review* of 1826, volume XIV.,
entitled " On the Antiquarians and Critics of Italian History ", an
eloquent appreciation of the value of such works of reference as the
histories by Muratori and Tiraboschi. One is appalled at the amount
of work that Foscolo accomplished in the last years of his life ; and a
glance at his closely written manuscript is sufficient corroboration of
all his own accounts of his labours. The full tale of his sufferings is
told in the letter to Hudson Gurney of August 12th, acknowledging a
timely gift of £50. In July, when this saving cheque arrived, Foscolo
was living in a district which can only be called a slum. Poverty and
dirt, noise of shouting and squabbling, drunken men and idle women,
children and cats and dogs without number, created an environment
that wore out the nerves of the supersensitive exile who had always
delighted in cleanliness and beauty and peace. The hot July sun
streamed in through the windows of the little house where he lived,
and to make life still less bearable there was no water in the district.
Chiarini says, ' nel luglio era tornato a Londra, ed abitava nel quartiere
di S. Giles ',[2] but the reference to the necessity for fetching water
from a pump in Euston Square makes one hesitate to accept this
statement. Although the description of his surroundings might well
be applied to the quarter of St. Giles, ' assai lontana ' is a mild epithet
to apply to the distance from there to Euston Square, and it is hardly
credible that water was not to be had nearer his house. Foscolo
himself does not mention St. Giles in his letter. There is in all this
no word of poor Floriana, who was more likely to have been the drawer
of water, and whose sufferings would not be less than her father's.
The first use made of Gurney's cheque was to seek out new quarters ;

[1] *Epist.*, III., p. 184.   [2] Chiarini, *Vita*, p. 428.

and already on August 12th Foscolo was in full enjoyment of an airy flat at No. 19 Henrietta Street, Brunswick Square, which gave him the quiet and cleanliness and fresh water that he longed for. The heat had increased the malady of the liver from which he suffered, and the drowsiness which was a symptom of the disease interfered with his work. There is something indescribably tragic in the thought of the sick man struggling on, and rejoicing in his nearness to the British Museum where he could find books for his work. Plans of future articles, of his cherished novel, of the completed *Dante*, filled his mind ; meanwhile the dispute with Pickering was still unsettled. In August 1826, Foscolo wrote to Gurney that his novel was almost finished and in the hands of a translator. His plan was a series of three novels, *Il mio secondo viaggio in Inghilterra*, *Il mio primo viaggio in Inghilterra* and *Il mio terzo viaggio in Inghilterra*, which should describe the middle, upper and lower classes of society. The one almost finished was the second in the trilogy, and from what we already know from his letters to Lady Dacre, told the story of his love for Callirhoe. From the sale of his novels Foscolo hoped to realize sufficient capital to ensure him a settled income.[1] But the translator died and Foscolo fell ill, and the novel remained in manuscript—a fragment.

Foscolo's own estimate of Pickering's character is probably very much nearer the truth than the scoundrel that later biographers have made him out to be.

Io sono persuasissimo ch' egli è uomo dotato di ottime disposizioni naturali, e desideroso di render servigio altrui ; ma al tempo stesso egli sembra saper del pari simulare e dissimulare, e aver a cuore non tanto i principj assoluti dell' onore, quanto quelli della onestà convenzionale nell' esercizio della sua professione. Egli di più mostra avere una idea incompleta della giustizia, e fidare non tanto nella equità quanto nella legalità.[2]

In this distressful year Foscolo also formed plans of publishing the first volume of his translation of the *Iliad*, with a similar commentary to the one on Dante, and containing a letter to the Greeks with his opinion of their present state and his hopes for their future. He must have spoken of this earlier in the year, because Sinclair Cullen alludes to it in a letter in July.[3] The work on Greece occupied Foscolo's mind seriously at the time, and he wrote to Niccola Piccolo, a Greek man of letters and former professor, to obtain information regarding the state of modern literature in Greece.[4] Another idea regained its

[1] Antona-Traversi and Ottolini, p. 317.   [2] *Epist.*, III., p. 212.
[3] MSS. Lab. See App. I.A, 27.   [4] *Epist.*, III., p. 219.

old place in his thoughts, too. He decided once more to make an effort to return to his native islands. In 1817 and 1824 he had tried to obtain permission to go to Greece and had been unsuccessful, not altogether to his sorrow. Now it seemed to him that Zante would give him a modest livelihood and leisure to compose the works which his fertile brain continued to plan.

A curious impulse, whether actuated by a desire to make amends to his daughter or some half-defined feeling that his life was drawing to a close, made Foscolo seize the opportunity of a messenger to Greece to write a full account of his life in the last years in London, and the confession of his daughter's existence, to three people, his cousin Dionisio Bulzo, his friend the Marquis Gino Capponi, and his sister Rubina. All three letters, with a covering note to Reinaud who had returned to Greece, were written in the last week of September. This time Foscolo was determined to return to Greece, and this time his perseverance would probably have removed any obstacles, but his life was almost ended, and Death turned him from his design. He commissioned Reinaud to find him a house in the country, with a garden of fruit trees and pergolas grown over with vines. To Bulzio he expressed his desires for the future. Public office did not attract him in his country under foreign rule, but he assigned to himself the right ' di guidare alla filosofia ed alle lettere i miei cittadini, amici e congiunti '.[1] Lectures such as he would give in Zante would exalt his heart and not humiliate him as did the course he gave in 1823 to ' gente che non intende, e che accorre chi per curiosità di vedere un animale famoso, e chi per desiderio di fargli la carità '. In proof of his Ionian citizenship, Foscolo repeated to Bulzo his determination to quote his genealogy, supported by documents in the archives of Venice,[2] and it is interesting to note in this connection a letter from Giulio Foscolo from Groß Blasnitz in Moravia, which he had written on April 1st, 1826, and had sent by a friend, Monticelli, to London. The letter was in time to support Foscolo's claim. After a complaint that he had not heard from his brother for many years, Giulio gave news of the family, and proof of their nobility, with a sketch of their coat of arms.[3]

Two magazine articles were among the work of the winter of 1826, the one on the " History of the Democratic Constitution of Venice ", and the other on the " History of the Aristocratical Constitution of Venice ", suggested to Foscolo by the *Memoirs* of Casanova, and by

---

[1] *Epist.*, III., p. 224.   [2] *ibid.*, p. 224.

[3] MSS. Lab., Vol. XLVI.

the *Venetian Memoirs* of Giovanni Gallicioli, published in 1826. Prandi introduced the author to Mrs. Sarah Austin who undertook to translate both articles. She was young then, but her house was already a meeting-place for men of letters and scholars. Some delay in the translation, for which Mrs. Austin apologized, irritated Foscolo who was not satisfied with the work in every particular. The letters that passed between them are extremely formal,[1] and one feels that a certain antipathy to Foscolo, which Mrs. Austin expressed nearly thirty years later to Sainte-Hilaire, existed already. Whatever the reason, Foscolo withdrew the article on the " Aristocratical Constitution of Venice ", and Thomas Roscoe undertook to translate it. After being refused by Murray for the *Quarterly*, it was finally published by Bowring in the *Westminster Review*. Foscolo received £40 for it on January 23rd.[2] The article translated by Mrs. Austin, either by her mediation or Dr. Allen's,[3] was accepted by Jeffrey and appeared in the June number of the *Edinburgh Review*. Mrs. Austin's antipathy to the poet has been ascribed, with some lack of understanding of her character, to disappointed coquetry.[4] As a personality he did not appeal to her, and his mode of living at Digamma Cottage and even before, well known to her or guessed from her intercourse with other exiles and her cousin, Edgar Taylor, became increasingly abhorrent to her as the vivacious, sprightly young woman passed into serious middle life.

Towards the end of the year Foscolo's health made life very hard for him. He decided to write no more for periodicals and to eke out a modest living by giving lessons. He made arrangements to remove once more to a country district, keeping a room in town in which to meet his pupils. This time he settled in Turnham Green, not far from the scenes of his early social successes. By the terms of the contract with Pickering, which was signed in January 1827, Foscolo received the balance of £167 10s. due to him, and one hundred copies of the first volume of *Dante*, containing the *Discourse on the Text*. The money received from Pickering and from the editors of reviews amounted to a substantial sum, but from the fact that help was required from friends in the last months of Foscolo's life, and that he was unable to help Francesco Mami when the latter was in difficulties,[5] we can only suppose that it was used up at once in payments to copying clerks and tradesmen.

[1] MSS. Lab. See App. I.A, 28.   [2] *Epist.*, III., p. 256.
[3] Segrè, p. 412.   [4] Viglione, p. 312.
[5] Chiarini, *Vita*, p. 446.

By the end of April 1827, Foscolo was at Bohemia House, Turnham Green, where he had the much desired change of air. His residence was known to few of his friends, but those who did visit him were faithful to the end, and after his death took over the responsibility of caring for his daughter. Prandi for some time had undertaken the disposal of his manuscripts ; Dr. Negri of Parma, a fellow exile, gave him medical attention during the whole of his long illness ; Francesco Mami visited and comforted him ; Canon Riego, the Spanish exile, sent him small gifts of dainties for a sick man, and cheered him with his society ; Giulio Bossi rendered many a service and was rewarded by Foscolo's collaboration in his *Anthology of Italian Poets*. The English friends were not less assiduous. The lawyers who had helped him to order his affairs, Sinclair Cullen, Edgar Taylor and Robert Roscoe ; Hudson Gurney, whose most generous aid saved Foscolo many times from direst distress ; Charles Fox, Lord Holland's illegitimate son ; and even Lord Holland himself, who sent a gift of choicest wines to him during his last illness, all prove that, whatever his faults, Foscolo had not alienated all his former friends. Some sweetness in his nature, a curious elemental simplicity that made him find contentment in the love for the child he found so late, drew men to him and kept them true, in spite of their judgment and his own excesses. His *antiche nozze* imposed upon him the obligation of living in order to care for his natural daughter, and he himself looked upon the years of toil and poverty that he spent in London after the sale of Digamma Cottage as ' una sorta di espiazione per molte mie passate imprudenze '.[1] This idea of expiation was fixed in his mind, for writing to Hatfield in December 1826, he spoke of being ' costretto a vivere come un profugo messo in bando della società ' : and adds ' ma ho pure la soddisfazione di avere con questi tre anni di fatiche, di privazione e di costanza d' animo, espiato i miei errori '.[2]

Until June Foscolo was able to go to town and attend to his pupils. Although suffering from continuous bilious fever, he had hopes of improvement in health ; and in April he even yielded to the persuasion of friends, Colonel Jones, who had lived at Green Cottage, Hudson Gurney and Francis Palgrave, and sent in an application for the Chair of Italian Literature in the newly founded University of London. He heard later from Thomas Campbell that the professor of Italian would be little more than a language master, as Panizzi found later to his cost, and he withdrew his application. As it happened it was just at

[1] *Epist.*, III., p. 218.　　　　　[2] *ibid.*, p. 251.

this time that the dropsy from which he suffered, and which caused his death, began to grow rapidly worse. He had an operation at the beginning of August, but received no permanent benefit. The dropsy returned as before, and Foscolo announced to his friends his approaching death. It was a rallying call to his old friends, who gathered round him and vied with each other in their efforts to show him kindness. Hudson Gurney visited him towards the end of August and found him at first unable to speak, but his tremendous will asserted itself, and he burst into a flood of eloquence, which recalled his former powers.[1] On the 4th of September a second operation was performed, but the patient was left in such a state of exhaustion as to be unable to regain strength. With a last effort he wrote in large clear letters the touching message to his daughter, which is a recognition of his paternity and at the same time his last will and testament.[2] From the 7th of September he was unconscious, and when Capodistria arrived two days later, it was already too late to say good-bye to his friend. Foscolo passed away on the evening of September 10th, and was buried eight days later in the churchyard of Chiswick Parish Church, where he had told his daughter he wished to lie.[3] Five of his intimate friends, Canon Riego, General De Meistre, Dr. Negri, Manii and Edward Roscoe, saw him laid to rest, and later by the kind offices of Gurney a simple stone, replaced after some years by a small tomb, was set to mark the spot. In after years, while the struggle for freedom in the land he loved was still sending its champions into exile, others came to seek inspiration and consolation at the grave of the patriot, whose example had shown them the way of exile. When their goal had been achieved and Italy was united, the ashes of the poet were removed to her Panthèon, Santa Croce in Florence, the city that had seen much of his triumph and the most enduring and faithful of his loves.

We cannot close this chapter without some reference to the daughter who had lived only four short years with Foscolo before she was called upon to nurse him in his last illness. We know little of their life together, and can only guess that it was happy, perhaps the only solace in Foscolo's life of struggle and care. Messages in letters from his friends to ' Miss Floriana ' and the ' damigella ' show the part she took in the poet's life. To Reinaud Foscolo wrote : ' Or addio anche da parte della Floriana, che sta benissimo, e ingrassa, e strimpella il suo pianoforte, e mi fa ridere anche quando sono malato.'[4] In a letter

---

[1] Antona-Traversi and Ottolini, pp. 334–5. [2] *Epist.*, III., p. 268.
[3] Chiarini, *Vita*, p. 453. [4] *Epist.*, III., p. 255.

to Edgar Taylor at the end of 1826, congratulating him on the birth of a daughter, his love for Floriana and the comfort that her devotion brought him are reflected in the praise he bestows on daughters.[1] When he felt his end near, he gave instructions that his funeral should be very simple so as to leave as much money as possible for Floriana. Strangely enough, Hoggins and Taylor, two of Foscolo's most intimate friends, were of opinion that she was not really his daughter but merely adopted.[2]

After Foscolo's death the little money there was, and his papers passed into Floriana's hands. Her first thought was to repay Hoggins, who had guaranteed the rent of the house at Turnham Green during his illness. She was worn out after the privations and anxieties of the last years, and the strain of months of nursing. Canon Riego acted as her guide and counsellor, and Bossi and others comforted and helped her. A plan of publishing Foscolo's literary remains for her benefit occurred to some, and William Stewart Rose took the matter up, but it came to nothing.[3] Rooms were found for her in Bernard Street, Brunswick Square, after her father's death ; but before another month was over, Frances Dorothy Cartwright, the poetess, who was then only forty-seven years of age, not about sixty as Taylor suggested to Gurney, moved to pity by the lonely girl's plight, wrote to Taylor offering help if Floriana were deserving. Canon Riego thought she should be sent to a school as assistant, where she might also complete her education. Miss Cartwright meanwhile saw Floriana, liked her and wrote to Gurney regarding plans for her future. She mentioned the extreme delicacy of her appearance and the traces she bore of her terrible past sufferings. Gurney continued his generous help to her. For nearly a year Floriana lived at Hadley, either in a post or to recover her strength ; and while there became engaged to a young tradesman of Barnet. Although the match was not what Miss Cartwright would have hoped for her, it was a relief to Floriana to feel herself no longer a charge on the generosity of her father's friends. In July 1829 an effort was made to raise a fund to set up the young man in business for himself.[4] In September Floriana was back in town, living near Canon Riego, but he expressed to Mami in a letter his doubt that she would see the fulfilment of her desires. Probably she was then too ill to hold out hope of recovery. We do

[1] *ibid.*, p. 253.
[2] *Giornale Storico*, Vol. XCII., Anno XLVI., Fasc. 276, pp. 306–7.
[3] Chiarini, *Vita*, p. 457.
[4] *Giornale Storico*, Vol. XCII., pp. 306–8.

F

not know exactly when she died, but she left her father's manuscripts to her faithful old friend, Riego.[1]

Evidently after her father's death Floriana handed over his papers to Sinclair Cullen for safe custody. Bossi had warned her not to dispose of them without consulting Panizzi as to their value. In April of 1829 Cullen wrote to Hobhouse in a postscript, ' I wish too you would apply to me for Foscolo's MSS.'[2] A year later he notified him that he had sent the Foscolo papers,[3] and in May of 1830 he pressed the sale of them on Hobhouse.[4] Possibly Floriana had not yet died, since Cullen had the disposal of the manuscripts, but her death and bequest to Canon Riego would take the matter out of his hands. We know that they were sold by Riego in 1835 to the Marquis Gino Capponi, Enrico Mayer and Pietro Bastogi, and in 1844 they were placed in the Biblioteca Labronica in Leghorn, whose chief treasure they are.

[1] Chiarini, *Vita*, p. 458.
[2] B.M. MSS. Broughton Correspondence, Vol. X., f. 106.
[3] *ibid.*, Vol. XI.   [4] *ibid.* See App. I.A, 29.

CHAPTER THREE

FOSCOLO'S FRIENDS AND FELLOW EXILES

FOR more than four years Foscolo reigned supreme in London society as the great Italian patriot who had chosen the way of exile in preference to submission to foreign domination. The revolutions of 1820 and 1821, ending in disaster, sent hundreds of the best of Italy's sons into exile ; and the next few years saw the arrival of many of them in London, driven in turn out of Switzerland, France and Spain, where they had sought hospitality in countries freer than their own but which nevertheless felt their presence as an embarrassment. England was to them the home of liberty, and the joyous sense of freedom compensated for many of the sorrows of living in a strange land, although eventually the climate drove great numbers of the refugees back to the Continent, to Paris, Brussels, and wherever else the government of the day encouraged their presence or at least overlooked it. One of the first to arrive in England was General Guglielmo Pepe,[1] who set foot on these shores in the middle of August 1821, accompanied by Colonel Pisa and a servant. His name was already famous. The affairs of Naples had for years been of vital interest in this country, especially since Nelson's connection with the Neapolitan Kingdom ; and the struggles which had just taken place between the Constitutionalists and the King, who relied on the Austrians for support in his autocratic policy, had been watched with keen attention in Britain. Pepe had had a military career of conspicuous brilliance, in spite of the changes of ruler from Bourbon to Joseph Bonaparte, from Joseph to Joachim Murat, then back again to Ferdinand IV. His absolute fearlessness and outstanding ability and integrity brought him to the front after certain vicissitudes in his earliest days, including imprisonment in irons at the age of sixteen and his first taste of exile. Pepe first became acquainted with the doctrine of the Carbonari in 1813

[1] He spells his name Pépé in the English translation of his autobiography.

67

and looked upon the sect as " a useful agent for the civilization of the popular classes ".[1] Seven years later he decided to assume direction of the Carbonari in the two provinces under his command, and to organize them into military order. He enrolled personally five thousand militia who were all members of the sect.[2] He was already a lieutenant-general, when at the age of thirty-seven, in July 1820, during the momentary constitutional rule after the revolution, he was appointed General-in-Chief of all the forces in the United Kingdom of the Two Sicilies. But Ferdinand repented of his liberal gesture, and the Austrians helped him to return to the absolutism of his fathers. A timely warning sent Pepe for the second time into exile, but a sentence of death was passed on him, with the confiscation of all his property.

Pepe presents a curious contrast to the other refugees, which is rather difficult to define. Perhaps the effect is produced to a considerable extent by his own memoirs, in which the *sum pius Æneas* attitude carries one back into an earlier age. His directness and simplicity emphasize the soldier, the man of action, rather than the thinker, but from the first he was filled with an intense love of country, which reverses only strengthened. His exile in 1799 was caused by his having signed the " solemn oath of freedom or death ", when General Championnet took Naples with French troops and established freedom in the name of the French Republic.[3] Speaking of this first great grief he said, while in his second exile,

I did not quit the country of my birth without feelings of bitter anguish. Nature has imprinted upon the human heart such deep and indelible feelings of love for our fatherland, that I sorrowfully quitted a country, which, twenty years later, I was obliged again to forsake and perhaps for ever, a country to which I have devoted the most intense and persevering, though vain, attachment during the whole course of my existence, and for whose sake my heart has been so often and in many ways torn with anguish.[4]

After the Revolution of 1820 Pepe fled to Spain, and in Madrid met many of the Piedmontese officers who were expiating there the failure of their rising in February 1821. There were some two hundred of them, bearing each other company in misfortune. Pepe could not long remain inactive, and he determined to take steps to prevent in future such disasters as they had just experienced. The revolutionaries of Naples and Piedmont had made their preparations inde-

[1] *Memoirs of General Pépé written by himself*, I., p. 317.
[2] *ibid.*, II., pp. 162–3   [3] *ibid.*, I.   [4] *ibid.*, I., p. 116.

pendently of each other, and in ignorance of each other's plans. The strength in united action that might have led to success was thrown away, and this was the lesson that Pepe drew from their failure. To prevent a repetition of their mistakes in the future he founded a society which he called the " Constitutional Brothers of Europe ", with the object of enabling the members to correspond and of precluding any possibility of want of union.[1] Colonel Pisa, a Piedmontese officer, was one of his chief helpers, and Pepe himself undertook the responsibilities of much of the propaganda. He decided therefore to go to London, and sailed from Lisbon for Falmouth.

Pepe was not without English connections, and Queen Caroline had expressed a wish that he should come to London, although he arrived too late to see her again before she died. The Marquis Antaldi of Pesaro met him on his arrival,[2] and, his reputation having preceded him, he rapidly made friends. Naturally he turned to men of liberal opinions, although he was placed in the difficult position of having to explain the recent failures. " I did not like to associate with those whose political opinions were at variance with my own," he wrote, " and even the society of the radicals was often irksome to me from the perpetual necessity I found of justifying my unfortunate countrymen for having lost their freedom." [3] Among others he met Sir Robert Wilson, the famous Radical general, Foscolo's friend, whose career was not altogether unlike his own, and who in 1821 was dismissed from the army for taking action against the mob at Queen Caroline's funeral.[4] Wilson introduced him to the Duke of Sussex, to Lord Holland, Earl Grey and others. At Holland House his acquaintances increased. Another of his friends was Lieut.-Colonel Napier, who could share his interest in Spain, and Sir Francis Burdett, a friend of a number of the refugees in London. He met Major Cartwright, then an old man, and was a frequent visitor at his house, when Fanny, the host's niece, whom we know already as the lady who came to the help of Floriana Foscolo, had to play the part of interpreter. At his house he became acquainted with John Gilchrist, the orientalist, who joined with Cartwright in befriending the exiles of any country, and there were many in London at that time. Through Foscolo, Pepe met Thomas Campbell, and the friendship proved a lasting one. Having arrived in England with little or no knowledge of the language, Pepe first took some lessons, for which he paid 7s. each, as he points out. His friends Campbell and Gilchrist then helped

---

[1] *ibid.*, II., p. 208. [2] *ibid.*, II., p. 226.
[3] *ibid.*, II., p. 228. [4] *D.N.B.*

him to attain proficiency, in exchange, in Campbell's case, for Italian and in Gilchrist's for French. The pamphlet which he wrote in 1824, however, on the causes of the downfall of liberty in Naples, Spain and Portugal, was written in French and translated into English by Cartwright's niece. The subject bade fair to be a popular one, and a bookseller offered him £300 for it, £100 of which he accepted in money and the remainder in copies for distribution among friends in England and in Italy.[1]

Pepe's financial position in London gave him an advantage over many of his compatriots, who were obliged to keep the wolf from the door by laborious teaching and journalism of a wearisome kind. His brother Florestano seems to have kept him supplied with sufficient means for his necessities. He was therefore free to devote himself to the furtherance of his schemes. The society of " Constitutional Brothers " met with no success in England, where secret societies were quite foreign to the nature of the people, and in point of fact unnecessary. A certain dread of the clause in the Alien Bill, which reserved to the Secretary of State the right to deport aliens, kept Pepe's activities within bounds. Had he but known it, his every movement was watched and duly reported in secret to the Alien Office ; and the Home Office Records, which give such clear evidence of the destruction of much that would have been invaluable to us, have carefully preserved the secret file headed : *General Pepe 1822. Reports of G.P.'s movements.*[2] After submitting a most interesting water-colour copy of a charter with designs round the border of a sun with a face, three nails, a cross and battle-axes, a crown of thorns, a red cap of Liberty and other devices,[3] sent from Naples for distribution to certain persons in London including six members of Parliament, the reports deal with an expedition to Spain which Pepe planned in the first six months of 1822, with Macerone's help and the knowledge of the Spanish Ambassador who provided them with funds. Joachim Murat's widow also seems to have sent them money, and an order was placed with two firms for small arms. The active help of a certain Captain Johnston, a smuggler, was enlisted, who seems to have been public-spirited enough to offer his pension as security to the principal of a foreign gambling-house for a loan of £2000 to pay for Macerone's purchases of arms and accoutrements. Colonel Pisa's return to Spain was reported and the movements of a Major Baldwin, who was to raise men in Ireland, while a Mr. McDermott was to do the same in Scotland.

[1] Pepe, II., pp. 228-30.   [2] Records Office, H.O. 5.
[3] See App. I.B, 1 (1) to (7).

A landing in Calabria was the ultimate aim of the expedition. An earlier report, evidently from a different source (dare we say spy ?) notes the existence of a society calling itself " The Confederation of European Constitutionalists ", which was probably the society founded by Pepe in Spain, and to which belonged Sir Robert Wilson, Wood—probably Alderman Wood—and Waithman, who was Lord Mayor of London the following year. Little knowing the interest the British Government had been taking in his movements, Pepe was rather surprised when Customs officers proceeded to read his papers, at Lord Castlereagh's instigation, as he was about to leave Falmouth for Spain to join his expedition.[1] The plot came to naught, as the Constitutional Government in Spain refused to help the conspiracy of the French liberals, who were thus unable to create the necessary diversion, and the Greeks likewise withheld their aid. The news of the punishments meted out to his former Neapolitan friends, condemned to thirty-two years' imprisonment in chains, completed Pepe's distress and made his persevering patriotism appear to him almost a crime, as he said himself.[2] He returned to London, leaving Pisa in Spain. In April 1823 the Spanish deputies authorized the French and Italian exiles to serve under the tricolour, but it was too late. They lost their own liberty and constitution, and with them perished the hopes of the invasion of Calabria. Pisa spent two years in prison before he returned to London.

In the meantime Pepe's compatriot and former friend, General Carascosa, had come to London from Malta, with the express purpose of challenging Pepe to a duel. The latter was surprised, for although he had broken with Carascosa on account of his deserting the constitutionalists for the king, he had not seen in that any cause for fighting. For once Pepe's propensity for duelling was not at fault. The meeting took place, and, after wounding his adversary, Pepe became reconciled to him and friendly intercourse was resumed, until Carascosa's criticism of the Neapolitans in his memoirs on the Revolution of Naples made Pepe refuse to meet him again.

Something positive for the good of the refugees Pepe did achieve in London. He induced Joseph Hume, Alderman Wood, Cartwright and Gilchrist, all intimate friends of his, to form a committee of their political friends for the assistance of the Italian exiles, some of whom were in great distress. The women were not less active than the men, and a series of efforts were made to raise money by means of bazaars and balls and concerts for the relief of the poorer patriots.[3] As we

[1] Pepe, II., p. 238.   [2] ibid., p. 238.   [3] ibid., p. 234.

shall find later, the channel for distribution of the funds raised was a corresponding committee of the exiles themselves.

On the accession of Francis, Duke of Calabria, to the throne of the Two Sicilies in January 1825, Pepe wrote a letter to him urging him to do some good in his country as he had given proof of liberal ideas, but the result was what one might have expected from a Bourbon. The letter was, nevertheless, a sign that the old spirit had not been quenched in Pepe in spite of his exile. During the years that followed Pepe spent the greater part of the summers in Belgium, where he made friends with exiled French liberals. France as an asylum was still closed to him, in spite of anything that Lafayette could do, with whom he had carried on for years a vigorous correspondence. In December 1826 Thomas Campbell wrote inviting him to accompany his wife and himself to Scotland, where he was going to pay a visit to Glasgow as Lord Rector of the University. Pepe had remained in Brussels and could not accept. In 1830, at the first murmurs of the July Revolution, he hastened to Paris, entering France disguised as a servant. He met Lafayette and at once tried to extract a promise of help for his great plan. Two thousand men and ten thousand muskets, and a couple of frigates to transport them, were what he wished to start his revolution in Calabria ; but once more he found that a liberal government is not necessarily anxious to help every other, and delay ended in refusal. He met Lord John Russell in Paris, and the hopes of the Whigs running high, he returned to London, trusting to find capitalists there willing to finance an expedition to Italy, and a government ready to help. He visited Brougham, Nugent, Hume and Grey, but when the Whig party came into power he found that the ministry were pledged to reform and to a reduction of expenditure, and also not to meddle with the internal affairs of any other country.[1] England's help to Italy was limited to *wishing her well*. Pepe's activity did not diminish in France ; but henceforth, as London ceased to shelter him, the details of it belong to other records than ours.

Pepe had remarkable insight into the weakness of the conditions obtaining in Italy for the realization of the great purpose of unity and independence, which he had so much at heart. He was fully conscious of the enormous difficulty of rousing the common people, belonging to provinces differing so widely in culture and institutions that only the language seemed common to all. All the revolutions in Italy which marked the progress of the *risorgimento* movement were organized by the upper classes, and a great work had to be undertaken to

[1] Pepe, II., pp. 310–13.

foster the growth of a desire for independence and then for unity among the masses of the population. Pepe was one of the first to see that the successive risings in different parts of the peninsula and their subsequent failure, were the best lessons the country could have, that, if the will to put down absolute government and to drive out the foreigner was to achieve anything, the desire for unity must be fostered in every heart. The measure of success that greeted the efforts of each revolutionary province for never so short a time showed what could be done. " The experience of their own strength, bought however dearly during the last few years," wrote Pepe, " will effectually tend to the eventual freedom and union of the people of the great divisions of the Peninsula." [1] Mazzini was to accomplish the task of rousing the masses ; meanwhile the true patriots neglected no opportunity, however small the chance of success, of striking a blow in the cause of liberty. Pepe's *Memoirs* were published in English in 1846, and two years later he followed the call of his country and returned to fight for her. In 1823, when he wrote to Foscolo before leaving for his ill-fated expedition from Spain, he recalled the Athenian in Marathon who attempted to stay the flight of an enemy ship. " Gli venne troncato il braccio dritto, ed egli impiegò il sinistro ; e perduto anche questo, si ajutò co' denti, finchè troncata ebbe la testa." [2]

Three days after Pepe's defeat at Rieti on March 7th, 1821, which led to his exile, revolution broke out in Piedmont. In the South, Carbonarism was widespread in the army and had the republican aims of its founders, republican refugees who had fled to the Abruzzi and Calabria from Joseph Bonaparte's rule. It was first directed against the French, later against the Austrians, as represented in the successive Neapolitan rulers, and thus aimed at driving out the foreigner and at the independence of Italy, with occasional thoughts of a united country. In the North the movement had a different complexion. The Piedmontese Carbonari, recruited from the younger nobility and officers of the army, were in the main Royalists, but strove for a constitution. Their king himself was anti-Austrian; and the wider view of Italian independence only gained extent as Carlo Alberto, Prince of Carignano and heir to the throne, foresaw the increased power of the House of Savoy, if the Lombards succeeded in freeing themselves from Austrian rule. Unity was conceived, except by very few, as a union of the northern provinces. In Lombardy the movement was literary, expressing itself in a spreading of liberalism in romantic dress, as opposed to the old hide-bound classicism : a literary revolt with a strong political bias.

[1] Pepe, III., p. 341. [2] *Epist.*, III., p. 451.

The organ of the party was the magazine edited by Silvio Pellico, the *Conciliatore*, which proposed to conciliate *tutti i sinceri amatori del vero* and counted among its contributors Di Breme, Borsieri, Giovanni Berchet, Giuseppe Pecchio and his brother, and Sismondi of Geneva. After not quite a year of life the magazine was suppressed in 1819 by the Austrian Government, and gave place in secret to more definitely political aims. Ideals of social reform inspired the Lombard patriots, and " schools of mutual instruction " were opened by Arrivabene in Mantua, Confalonieri and Porro in Milan, and Filippo Ugoni in Ponteviso,[1] and carried on with enthusiasm until, arousing the hostility of the Government as being symbolical of liberalism, they were suppressed. In 1820 Porro, Confalonieri and Arconati Visconti imported a steamboat, and everything possible was done to further the progress and well-being of the people. As the plans for the Piedmontese rising matured, the possibility of revolution spreading into Lombardy induced the Lombard liberals to take steps to deal with the situation. A company of five, Benigno Bossi, Pecchio, Borsieri, Castiglia and Arrivabene, met one snowy day in February 1821 at Pecchio's villa on the outskirts of Milan and discussed suitable names for the Committee of Government and plans for the formation of a National Guard. Pecchio acted unofficially as *liaison* officer between Lombards and Piedmontese, and induced Arrivabene to give him 1000 francs to help to equip the revolutionaries of Piedmont,[2] although Arrivabene considered the greater plan of extending the rising beyond Piedmont to embrace Lombardy and clear the country of the usurper, as a task beyond their strength.

The Piedmontese Revolution, fired perhaps by the example of Naples, broke out in Alessandria, when the garrison proclaimed the Spanish Constitution and greeted Victor Emmanuel as King of Italy. Turin followed, and on March 14th the list of the provisional *junta* was signed by Carlo Alberto, appointed regent by the King who had abdicated in his fear, and by Ferdinando Dal Pozzo.[3] So far all was well and perfect order was maintained, but Carlo Alberto, to the surprise of the Constitutionalists, deserted the cause and left Turin on the night of the 21st, either intimidated by the Austrians or regretting the step he had taken. Santa Rosa, the Minister for War, at once issued an order of the day, which *The Times* in a leader says, " if not the act of an admitted madman, is perhaps the boldest political production that ever issued from a ministerial pen ".[4] He threw down the

---

[1] *Memoirs of Count John Arrivabene*, translated from the original by C. Arrivabene.   [2] *ibid.*.
[3] *The Times*, 1821, March 23rd.   [4] *The Times*, 1821, April 2nd.

gauntlet to Austria and called eloquently on the commandants of corps, officers, subalterns and soldiers to unite round their standards and run to plant them on the banks of the Ticino and the Po. The land of Lombardy was expecting them, and would rise to devour its enemies when the van-guard of the Piedmontese appeared.[1] Lack of careful preparation in drawing the masses of the people into the cause, neglect of opportunities, delay and easy discouragement brought about the inevitable result ; and the war against Austria ended in the easy rout of the Constitutionalists at the disastrous battle of Novara. Exile was henceforth the only way to escape imprisonment or death open to those who had taken a part, however small, in the effort to win for their country free institutions and the right of self-government. Crowds of refugees passed through Genoa, many destitute of the barest necessities of food ; and the city waited until their retreat was safe before surrendering to the united army of loyalist Piedmontese and Austrians. Numbers of the exiles made their way straight to England ; others, and among them the leaders, lingered nearer home, until circumstances drove them to a country where Austrian influence was powerless to force the government to refuse them shelter.

There is very little evidence available of the earliest days in London of the majority of the refugees. Certainly the English public had had their interest aroused by the events of the past eighteen months, and they were prepared to receive the victims of despotism with open arms. Foscolo had established himself in London society. Many of the men of note had travelled extensively on the Continent and had been welcome guests in the *salons* of the aristocracy of Venice, Milan and Turin. We can safely assume, therefore, that there were few Italians among the leaders who did not find some English friend to guide and help in the first bleak days. The financial position of the refugees varied as much as their home circumstances and the unpreparedness of their departure would lead one to imagine. Some men of wealth had been able to realize at little more than a moment's notice a sum sufficient to supply their needs for some time. One of these was Arrivabene, who after a term of imprisonment in one of the Venetian prisons pending his trial was acquitted, but fled with his lifelong friend, Giovita Scalvini, shortly after the news of the arrest of Confalonieri, Pallavicino and others in January of 1822. Arrivabene borrowed 18,000 francs on the security of some of his property, although he left half of it to be returned to the lender when he considered the distress he would cause to the peasants who occupied his farms, if they were suddenly ejected.

[1] *The Times*, 1821, March 24th.

Others of the exiles were able after a while to have remittances sent to them secretly from home, and Florestano Pepe kept his brother supplied with funds during the whole of his exile.   Later the sequestrations of property removed from even the wealthy any hope of supplying their daily needs, except by their own efforts ; and of course large numbers of refugees were young men of no personal estate, and these were brought to the brink of starvation, until public subscriptions afforded them a modicum of relief.   In the absence of the Alien Office records, the only means of knowing the date of arrival in London of any of the exiles is from memoirs or chance references in correspondence.   The Neapolitans and Piedmontese were the first to arrive ; and the Lombards followed, when it was seen that arrests were being made on the merest suspicion that a man was a member of the Carboneria, or even that he knew of members and failed to denounce them.   The panic fear of Carbonarism spread to Modena and the Duke caused numbers of men to be arrested there.   Among those who escaped were Antonio Panizzi, of whom we shall have more to say later, and his friend Ambrogio Berchet.   The forging of passports must have been brought to a fine art during the period of emigration, for very few of the emigrants were provided with valid papers.

The most interesting of the groups of refugees in London was the one which centred round Foscolo.   It was a fortunate chance that the poet was in possession about the years 1822 to 1824 of a small house which he could place at the disposal of his fellow countrymen.   The first Italian residents of Green Cottage seem to have been Santa Rosa and Luigi Porro, who lived there from April to September of 1822. One is tempted to take Pecchio's advice and omit the title of Count to which nearly all had claim.   Porro belonged to one of the wealthiest families in Milan, and had kept open house for all men of distinction who visited that city.   He had formed friendships with many noted Englishmen before leaving Italy ; and Silvio Pellico spoke of meeting Byron, Hobhouse and Brougham in his house.[1]   He must have been a man of extraordinarily bright temperament, for references to " il lieto Porro ", " il loquentissimo Porro " are frequent in the letters of his friends.   Referring to a visit which Porro paid to him at his villa at Zaita, with his three sons and their tutor, Silvio Pellico, Arrivabene spoke of the " youthful vivacity of Porro ", and another time said, " His amiable character and distinguished manners rendered him popular everywhere."[2]   One feels that he must have put courage into a good many of his friends who felt it difficult to bear up against

[1] *Le mie Prigioni*, p. 93.   [2] Arrivabene, p. 11.

the melancholy which threatened to take hold of them. There is an interesting note addressed to Hobhouse, dealing with Porro's arrival, one of the very few of the Alien Office records extant. It is apparently an extract from the Alien Entry Book and is filed in a letter-book marked ' secret '.[1] It shows at any rate that Porro had nothing to fear in London from lack of protection.

MR. HOBHOUSE—
Count Luigi Porro of Milan has arrived from Geneva via Paris und. the assumed name of Monr. Millenet—he left Milan in March last & has since resided in Switzerland. He is now brought to the Alien Office for permission to assume his real name, by a Mr. Yeates Brown No. 4 Cumberland St. Portman Sq. who says he is well known as the son of Timothy Brown & that he is himself recently arrived from Milan & that Lord Gwydir & Lord W[m]. Bentinck will be responsible for Count Porro—4th Feby. 1822.

It is interesting to remember that Foscolo provided Yates Brown —he spells the name thus—with a letter of introduction to Velo de' Sette Comuni, when he was about to visit Vicenza in 1821.[2] Over a year elapsed before Porro joined forces with Santa Rosa at Green Cottage, but wherever he lived he cultivated his old friendships, both English and Italian, and made new friends among the more recent arrivals from Italy and the London families who welcomed them. He visited Mrs. Sarah Austin with Santa Rosa, and later the latter's other friends at Nottingham. In 1825 he was one of those sent to take money to the Greeks to help them in their struggle for independence, but he returned after a short sojourn. We know that he was obliged to give lessons in Italian and literature when he found himself deprived of means, and he adapted himself quietly and contentedly to his new mode of living, like others of his compatriots more resigned than Foscolo. Arrivabene tells us that his patriotism and love of liberty never left him, and he seems to have been a welcome guest wherever he went. Pecchio referred to a visit from him in a letter to Panizzi of April 1831.[3] Visits to the Continent also helped to pass the time of exile, and he seems to have spent most of the year 1828 abroad and to have met his daughter, who had been three years married, in Marseilles.[4] In 1838, after the amnesty, he returned to Italy. We have a letter from him to Panizzi, written in 1847, introducing a young sculptor who was going to England, but in it he only mentions one English

[1] Records Office, H.O. 5, 35. [2] Epist., III., p. 33.
[3] Lettere ad A. P., p. 99. [4] ibid., p 72.

family, the Duckworths, and writes as if he were a little out of touch
with the city where he had lived for so long.[1]

In August 1823 there arrived in London another Milanese friend
of Foscolo's, Giuseppe Pecchio, and he too rented one of the rooms
of Green Cottage for two months, after which he preferred to remain
in town.[2]   As one of the most active liberals and Confalonieri's right
hand, Pecchio had been accused of high treason and cited to appear
before the Special Commission at Milan.   Realizing only too well the
futility of defence, he had escaped into Switzerland before his accusation was published on October 19th, 1822.   The document is interesting and imputes the crime of high treason to ' Don Giuseppe
Pecchio ' under four headings : (a) of having made himself the propa-
gator in Lombardy of a secret society, called the *Federati Italiani*, in
consequence of the revolutions made in concert with some of the
principal Piedmontese conspirators towards the first days of February
1822, with the design of overturning the legitimate Austrian government in Italy ; (b) of having formed with several Austrian subjects the
plan of a National Guard, organized in Lombardy ; (c) of having with
several Austrian subjects formed the plan of a provisional government,
which should at the moment of the Piedmontese invasion usurp the
sovereign power, and (d) of having falsely guaranteed powerful co-operation in Lombardy and solicited the chiefs of the revolutionary government in Piedmont to invade the country.   The bird having flown,
the sentence of death on the gibbet was passed on October 9th, 1823.
Pecchio was by then safely in London.   Shortly after his arrival he
published *Anecdotes of the Spanish and Portuguese Revolutions*, giving
an account of the events in the Peninsula in which he had taken part
on leaving Switzerland.   He told of the disregard of General Pepe's
scheme to form a cosmopolitan corps there, and of the limiting of the
services of the Piedmontese to allowing a few hundred of them to form
themselves in Catalonia under General Mina.   The book is in the
form of letters to an English lady and is most graphically written.
Pecchio mentions the conduct of the Genoese and their help to the
refugees, of whom six hundred set sail from Genoa.   He estimated
the number of Piedmontese in Spain at about five hundred, who
received a monthly allowance from the Spanish Government.   Radice
was one of his companions, and like himself had been condemned to
death, but nearly two years earlier by Carlo Felice.   In November 1821
Pecchio went to Portugal and met some of the Piedmontese, who were

[1] Panizzi Correspondence, B.M., Add. MSS. 36715, Vol. II.
[2] Viglione, p. 100.

about to join the Greeks. His letters were full of the sorrowful tale of proscriptions, which increased daily in his unhappy country, but he sent a message to the Italians who frequented the correspondent's hospitable house in London, that he was glad to be able to share the honour of exile. His letter of March 12th, 1822, announces his departure that night on his first visit to England. He had become greatly attached to John Bowring, then in business in Madrid, a man of most varied accomplishments, a great linguist and of similar interests to his own. Bowring was a friend of Jeremy Bentham's. It is easy to picture the reception that Pecchio found awaiting him. His intention was to stay only a month in London, and his letter of May 10th from Lisbon is full of interesting observations on his visit. He thought John Bull worked too hard, merely for his daily bread and clothing, and the habit seemed to have taken hold of his old friend Foscolo, whom he met again after a separation of six years. " Of all the living writers of Italy," he wrote, " Foscolo is he whom I most admire." [1] He described Foscolo's cottage in South Bank, the forerunner of Digamma, and commented on his excessive labour for the London periodicals. Even at that time, when Pecchio was only a passing visitor, he felt the Alien Bill like a sword of Damocles over the heads of his exiled countrymen and had no great hopes of help for Italian liberty even from the English Radicals. In 1824 he published a *Journal of Military and Political Events in Spain*, and in spite of not very robust health seems to have led a by no means idle life, studying, writing and teaching ; and the same year, while living at West Cottage, South Bank, to which he had removed from Green Cottage, he planned an Italian periodical which would include on the editorial committee Scalvini, Dal Pozzo, Giovanni Berchet, Santa Rosa, Mossotti, himself and some others.[2] The plans did not materialize, probably on account of Santa Rosa's departure for Greece. He spent a short time in Nottingham in the spring of 1825, carrying on the teaching which Santa Rosa and then Porro had relinquished, but at the beginning of March he too left for Greece, one of the bearers of the sum raised to help the Greeks. He left for England again on June 11th,[3] saddened by the loss of a very dear friend, and disappointed in the achievements of the people he had hoped to see triumph over their enemies. On his return he published " A Picture of Greece in 1825 ", first in the *New*

[1] *Anecdotes of the Spanish and Portuguese Revolutions*, by Count Pecchio, 1823, p. 150.   [2] *Lettere ad A. P.*, p. 52.
[3] *Relazione degli Avvenimenti della Grecia*, by Giuseppe Pecchio, 1826. Preface.

Monthly Magazine, then along with two similar narratives by others in two volumes. The original Italian version was published by Vanelli in Lugano in 1826, with the title *Relazione degli Avvenimenti della Grecia nella primavera del 1825*. This book increased his reputation in London, where he was already well known.

Professor Viglione quotes from Cyrus Redding's *Memoirs*[1] an account of a luncheon party at Digamma Cottage at which Santa Rosa, Porro, Pecchio, Filippo Ugoni, Campbell and Redding were present ; and there were most probably many such reunions, and even more quiet evening gatherings for conversation or chess. Count Filippo Ugoni, the youngest brother of the more famous Camillo, was a provincial, from Brescia, and had been an active propagandist of the forbidden doctrines in his native city and the surrounding district. With a slight difference in the wording he shared the accusation and condemnation of Pecchio. Giovita Scalvini, another Brescian, Arrivabene's intimate friend, after completing a term of imprisonment, had fled with him and Camillo Ugoni in the early summer of 1822, knowing the most probable fate in store for him otherwise. He arrived in London in the autumn. Arrivabene most probably accompanied him and shared rooms with him in London. Apart from casual mention of them, we know nothing more until in October of 1823 Scalvini and Ugoni rented Green Cottage for three months. Hardly a week had passed, when for some reason Foscolo and Ugoni quarrelled ; and Foscolo, considering himself the offended, challenged his former friend to a duel. Probably hot temper on both sides had a great deal to do with it, and certainly Santa Rosa considered himself unable to second Foscolo, although his friend Collegno undertook the office for Ugoni. Fortunately the matter was amicably settled by a written apology on both sides.[2] Ugoni continued to live in Green Cottage until April 16th, 1824, three months after Scalvini had left ; but the fact of Foscolo's preferring to write to Scalvini rather than direct to his own tenant, to ask him to warn Ugoni three weeks before his lease came to an end, that a board with ' *To let* ' was about to be put up under one of the windows,[3] would imply that the relations between them were not very cordial. Something happened three years later which so reduced Ugoni's income that he was obliged to turn language master to keep himself ; and he bent his steps towards Cheltenham, where he taught for a while, before betaking himself to Paris to join his brother Camillo and others of his friends, that the expense of London life and the climate had driven from England. He must have been a lively

---

[1] Viglione, p. 8.   [2] *ibid.*, pp. 100–1.   [3] *Epist.*, III., p. 142.

young man, judging from his letters to Panizzi; and Pecchio referred to his energy.

Count Giovanni Arrivabene was of a different type, ' sweet Arrivabene ', as Santa Rosa called him, and one can see from his *Memoirs* that exile only made him more patient, more understanding of others' faults, and as he says himself he learned to content himself with little and to " accept with toleration the sincere opinions of others ".[1] He looked upon his sufferings in the same spirit as Silvio Pellico, and was grateful for the circumstances which chastened his faults, although his vision was directed outwards and his energy for the good of his fellow men. The habit formed in Mantua of interesting himself in the conditions of the masses led him to study social conditions in England. Speaking of the large numbers of institutions in England, hospitals, asylums, schools and the like, Pecchio refused to describe them, because he said, " Uno stimabile amico mio, il conte Arrivabene di Mantova già da due anni con ardore si occupa in questa impresa. Non che sorpassare io non potrei mai neppure eguagliare la diligenza e il fervore ch' egli ha posto in un lavoro in cui il suo cuore seconda la sua mente." [2] In 1828 Arrivabene was in Paris,[3] where he lived for some years before transferring himself to Brussels. He visited London from time to time and corresponded at intervals with Antonio Panizzi, whom he called years after, when introducing a Roman exile of 1849, *il padre di tutti gli emigrati italiani che si propongono di caminare sulle vostre traccie.*[4] Panizzi was able to execute small commissions for him and evidently to show kindness to young exiles whom he introduced.[5] Fagan includes in his *Lettere ad Antonio Panizzi* a most interesting letter from Arrivabene written on March 30th, 1845, announcing a visit to Mantua which he was about to make, and showing his continued interest in England and in the progress of Belgium. " Molti odiano l' Inghilterra ", he wrote, " ma nessuno non può non ammirare la sua fortezza, la sua costanza, lo spirito nazionale suo." [6] In Belgium, which he loved almost as much as his native Italy, Arrivabene was one of those who partook of the lavish hospitality which the wealthy Marquis Arconati-Visconti, himself an exile of '21, dispensed to his fellow countrymen in one of the *châteaux* which he owned there. Arrivabene was born

[1] Arrivabene, p. 110.
[2] *Osservazioni semi-serie di un Esule sull' Inghilterra*, by Giuseppe Pecchio, p. 332.   [3] *Lettere ad A. P.*, p. 72.
[4] Panizzi Correspondence, B.M., Vol. III., 1849–53, fol. a 510.
[5] Panizzi Correspondence *cit.*, Add. MSS. 36714, fol. 448, and 36715, fol. 14. See Appendix I.B, 2.
[6] *Lettere ad A. P.*, p. 153.

in 1787 and was still alive when Panizzi's Letters were published in 1880.[1] His dear companion in his youth and in exile, Scalvini, left him to return to Italy in 1839. Scalvini's interests were literary and artistic rather than economic, and his work partly translations from German, including Goethe's *Faust*.

Another of the group of Lombards who were sentenced to death *in contumaciam* in 1823 was Giacomo Filippo de Meester-Haydel of Milan, better known as General de Meester, or as some of his friends wrote ' de Meistre '. He was likewise accused of plotting to cause an insurrection to break out in Milan, and to proclaim the Spanish Constitution, of having approved of the plan of the National Guard and of having co-operated in Piedmont for the revolutionary army to enter Lombardy.[2] He too is one of the patriots who flit through the background of our story, and his name occurs only now and then in connection with Santa Rosa, and then for a time with the administration of the Refugees Fund, of which he was treasurer and secretary in 1824. He evidently was in difficult circumstances some years later, for in 1832 Dal Pozzo helped to raise among other exiles a sum of money to assist him. Dal Pozzo entered in his letter-book a note of 30th April to San Marzano and to Baldissero on the subject, and a recommendation to San Marzano to speak of the matter to Della Cisterna. On May 14th he wrote to Count Flahaut for a subscription and the following day sent the total of 265 francs to a Signor Mirri. The subscribers are interesting and were as follows : S. Marsan 40 frs., Cisterna 25, Orsini 40, Baldissero 20, Flahaut 40 and himself apparently 50 francs. Of Di Prie we know still less. Santa Rosa mentioned him and wrote to him from Nauplia a letter which Pecchio published in his *Picture of Greece in 1825*. We quote from the English edition. " Thou hast, my dear Demetrius, the gift of prophecy ; and I fancy I see thee on the sofa when, with the air of a man certain of his assertion, thou didst predict to me the issue of my journey to Greece." Then after news of Porro and Collegno, he continued, " As to the fair sex—of whom thou hast ever been an elegant adorer—I must tell thee that in Athens I saw some very handsome faces . . . but in truth, their beauty was materially assisted by a paste, made with consummate art. It is chiefly in our sex that the elegant and shapely forms, for which Greece was so famed, are beheld." [3] His name also appears along with those of Dal Pozzo, Baron Ugoni and Berchet in a letter which Pecchio wrote in March

[1] *Lettere ad A. P.*, footnote to p. 154.   [2] Arrivabene, p. 126.
[3] Pecchio, *A Picture of Greece in 1825*, p. 186.

1824 to Lady Morgan, and which was published by *Freeman's Journal* in Dublin during the stupid controversy which raged about a letter of criticism, alleged to have been written by Foscolo, of Lady Morgan's work, *The Life and Times of Salvator Rosa*.

Giovanni Berchet, one of the most ardent of the Romanticists, had been one of the chief contributors to the *Conciliatore*, and when the political tenets of the new romantic school brought them into conflict with the Austrian Government, he too was obliged to go into exile to evade the fate that befell some of his unhappy collaborators. In some ways he was better prepared than most of his fellows for making his way in a foreign country, for he had had a commercial training under his father's guidance, and was a proficient linguist. In London he found a post in the business of a compatriot, which enabled him to live without anxiety as to the providing for his daily needs. He devoted much of his spare time to literature, and the years of his exile were productive of a considerable number of poems from his facile and patriotic pen. Santa Rosa spoke of evenings spent together, when the poet recited his works and he acted as a friendly critic. In 1824 Berchet published his *Profughi di Parga*, which dealt with a subject of burning interest to the friends of liberty, that Foscolo had also treated in one of his most important works written in England, but which he had suppressed in its final form for fear of the consequences. The same year saw the publication of two romances, *Clarice* and *Il Romito del Cenisio*, of national inspiration, followed in 1827 by *Il Rimorso*, *Matilde*, *Giulia* and *Il Trovatore*. One can well understand the effect such poems as Berchet's would have on his compatriots in exile, even if they were not of the immortal. In 1829 he left London for the Continent and we hear of him as one of Arconati's daily guests in Belgium. He returned to Italy in 1847, and was in Florence when in the following year the Provisional Government of Lombardy, after the Cinque Giornate, called him to Milan to take over the portfolio of Public Instruction. His friendship with Antonio Panizzi probably dated back for many years, and his correspondence with him from Milan in 1848 gives a graphic account of the political situation. Panizzi was his medium of unofficial communication with the British Government, and a supporter of his policy of fusion with Piedmont. It is curious to find this poet, who stigmatized Carlo Alberto after 1821 as the *Carignano esecrato*, telling Panizzi to make clear to the English that " Carlo Alberto noi lo vogliamo, noi lo avremo ".[1] He forbade the inclusion of his poem

[1] *Lettere ad A. P.*, p. 160.

against him in all future editions of his works, and was big enough to acknowledge his change of opinion. It was his conviction that the opposition to Carlo Alberto in England was due to republican propaganda ; and he confessed to Panizzi, " Non tocca a me di fare il panegirico al Re ; ma come galantuomo che adora sopra tutto il vero, ti dico che, lasciato stare il passato, del quale siamo rei tutti, e veduto con occhio scrutatore il solo presente dal principiare dell' opposizione sua all' Austria fino adesso, Carlo Alberto si conduce davvero in modo schietto, onesto, lodevolissimo." And then he added, " Avresti mai creduto che io dovessi dire di queste parole ? " [1] His ardent advocacy of fusion with Piedmont did not leave out of account the larger issues. " L' unità assoluta dell' Italia verrà col tempo ", he wrote, " chè in politica come in natura nulla si fa di un tratto, d' un solo sbalzo." [2] He distrusted France, whom he accused of continuing the old pre-republican policy of opposing the formation of large states on her borders. " Non s' accorgono che un' Europa nuova si prepara, la quale vuole vedute nuove di diplomazia, di politica, di relazioni internazionali." He even thought of the possible necessity of ceding Savoy to France to silence her opposition. [3]

After his return from Greece, Giuseppe Pecchio went to Manchester College, York, as professor of Italian, and there met Sydney Smith, who was vicar of the parish of Foston, not far from York. They seem to have been intimate friends, and Camillo Ugoni was of the opinion that no other of Pecchio's English acquaintances had so just an appreciation of his gifts as the famous wit. [4] He must already have been one of the *habitués* of Holland House, and Sydney Smith alluded in a letter to Lord Holland in July 1828 [5] to Pecchio's forthcoming marriage to Philippa Brooksbank, whose parents he had reassured as to the suitability of the bridegroom. After their marriage Pecchio and his wife settled in Brighton, where the climate probably suited the exile's health better than that of the north. In 1831 Pecchio published his *Osservazioni semi-serie di un Esule nell' Inghilterra*, and, although he is inclined to look at England through rose-coloured spectacles, the book is most entertaining and affords one some insight into another's views of our institutions and customs. " Il più bel sole

---

[1] *Lettere ad A. P.*, p. 162.   [2] *ibid.*, p. 154.   [3] *ibid.*, pp. 167–8.
[4] Ugoni, *Vita e Scritti di Giuseppe Pecchio*, pp. 48–9. Quoted by Carlo Segrè, *op cit.*, p. 365.
[5] *A Memoir of the Reverend Sydney Smith by his Daughter Lady Holland*, II., p. 286.

dell' Inghilterra è la libertà ", " L' aura vitale d' un inglese è l' indipendenza ", are expressions which show the chief charm of England
in Italian eyes. He speaks of her hospitality to all oppressed peoples
and draws a graphic picture of London in 1823. " Nel 1823 Londra
era popolata d' esuli d' ogni specie e d' ogni paese ; costituzionali
volenti una sola camera, costituzionali volenti due camere, costituzionali alla francese, altri alla spagnuola, altri all' americana.
Generali presidenti dismessi di repubbliche, presidenti di parlamenti
sciolti a bajonetta in canna . . . e uno sciame di giornalisti, poeti,
e uomini di lettere. Londra era l' Eliso (un satirico direbbe il Botany
Bay) d' uomini illustri e di eroi *manqués*." [1] He criticizes the effusive
welcome accorded to the exiles on their arrival and the subsequent
neglect of them. " Non v' è tomba tanto vasta come Londra che
ingoi i nomi più illustri per sempre. È un onnivero oceano. La
celebrità d' un uomo in Londra splende e sparisce come un fuoco
d' artifizio. Gran chiasso, grandi inviti, grandi elogi, grandi esagera-
zioni per pochi giorni, poi un silenzio perpetuo." [2] In the crowd of
exiles of every rank and shade of opinion it was not astonishing that
there should be at times dissension, and Pecchio does not hide it.
He admires the system of party government. " Il vantaggio del-
l' opposizione non consiste tanto nel bene reale che fa, quanto nel
male che risparmia." [3] What strikes him perhaps most is the silence
of the London streets, the quietness of the home life, the equable
docile minds of the English women, and the quiet studies and amuse-
ments, which foster the peacefulness that is apparent everywhere.
Like most of his compatriots, he singles out for admiration the women
he meets, their gentleness and sympathy, their frankness and lack
of coquetry. He has a word of criticism for the evil effects of industry
on the population, which are not yet properly apprehended. And
he devotes a whole chapter to sailors, sailors who sing *Hearts of Oak*
and *Haul away, yeo ho, boys*, and *Rule, Britannia* in their taverns,
and are invincible in storms at sea. In 1827 he published *L' Anno
Mille ottocento ventisei dell' Inghilterra*, an account of the disastrous
year of bank failures and widespread distress, and in 1830 his much-
discussed life of his former friend, Ugo Foscolo. William Stewart
Rose announced Pecchio's intention to write Foscolo's life, in a letter
to the Donna Gentile of May 20th, 1830 ; but by that time the work
must have been almost completed, for Pecchio, exactly one month
later, told her that it had been sent to the Continent to be printed.
He admitted the slightness of his biography, but blamed the poet's

[1] Pecchio, pp. 104–5.   [2] *ibid.*, p. 106.   [3] *ibid.*, p. 94.

many friends who had failed to fulfil their promises to supply him with letters, and excused himself by saying that he had written not for the English but for a nation to whom *il far niente* was so sweet. The letter, and still more the book on its appearance, roused the indignation of the Donna Gentile, who was deeply wounded by the tone of levity and the criticism which Pecchio did not mask.[1] One must admit that Pecchio did not let absence of documentary evidence stand in his way, and his works, though eminently readable, do not always carry weight. The years in Brighton were apparently happy, and enlivened by the society of William Stewart Rose, Madame Zorzi, and Panizzi's old friend, with whom he made his escape, Ambrogio Berchet. Berchet taught Italian in Brighton but had difficulty in finding pupils. We hear little of him except that he sends greetings to Panizzi ; and then in 1848, on October 5th, Casati mentioned to Panizzi in a letter that he had not seen him. A postscript to Giovanni Berchet's letter of May 25th, which was omitted by Fagan, said simply, " Ambrogio Berchet è a Parma comand^te· la Guardia Nazionale." [2] A lively interest in the affairs of Italy, and an assiduous correspondence with his compatriots in France and Brussels and with Panizzi in London, kept Pecchio in touch with every movement for freedom ; but he refused to be drawn in by Ugoni's enthusiasm to take part in any of the plotting, which was doomed to failure from the first. He died in 1835 in Brighton, regretted by all his numerous friends.

One of the oldest and most distinguished among the refugees was Ferdinando Dal Pozzo, whose name is met with frequently in correspondence and narrative dealing with the exiles, and who seems to have been an extensive traveller, even after the disasters which banished him from home. He was born in 1768 near Moncalvo, and after studying law served the House of Savoy until the arrival of the French. He held many offices under the Napoleonic régime, and was deputy for the department of Marengo to the French legislative body and senior president of the Court of Appeal of Genoa. The Emperor bestowed on him the Légion d'Honneur and made him a baron of the Empire. He resigned office at the Restoration and retired to Turin, where he devoted himself to his profession and criticized the Government in a series of *Opuscoli politico-legali*, which appeared anonymously in 1817–19 in Milan. The Revolution of 1821 found him identified with his profession, no conspirator nor

---

[1] MSS. Fosc., Vol. X.B. Bib. Naz., Florence.
[2] Panizzi Correspondence, B.M., Add. MSS. 36715, fol. 462.

member of a secret society, but a liberal. Carlo Alberto held him in high esteem and owed him gratitude for certain personal services in connection with his patrimony. It was not surprising therefore that Dal Pozzo was made Minister of the Interior on March 14th, the outbreak of the revolution, and held office until Carlo Alberto deserted the cause seven days later. Dal Pozzo remained true to his liberal opinions and had to flee after the defeat. Geneva sheltered him first, until in 1823 Austria brought pressure to bear on the Government, and he had to leave for London with others in the same position.[1] He found a circle of friends in England, and settled, probably in lodgings, at 31 Alpha Road, Regent's Park,[2] a house in which Santa Rosa also lived for a while before he went to Nottingham. That there is little to tell of his life in London is not strange, if one considers his own words in a letter to the Avvocato Pollano in Paris on May 17th, 1832, regretting his inability to provide a certain Signor Licheri with introductions for England. " Otto anni e più io ho dimorato nelle isole britanniche ; ho fatto così poche relazioni, che quasi non me ne so render ragione io stesso. Si è lungi colà dal commercio sociale e facile che esiste in Francia e in Italia." [3] But he did express a desire to be appointed Sardinian Minister in London.[4] We know that he lived in other cities as well as London and that he was in Edinburgh for a time, when he would have the delight of his friend De Marchi's companionship. His wife died in 1830, and the following year he married a young Englishwoman, Mary Richardson, who seems to have made him very happy, in spite of the hostility which he drew down upon himself from his compatriots, by the publication in 1833 of a brochure, *Della felicità che gl' Italiani possono e debbono dal Governo austriaco procacciarsi*. In 1831 he removed to Paris, where he found conditions much more congenial. The *copialettere* of his correspondence from August 24th, 1831, to June 2nd, 1832, which is in the Biblioteca Nazionale, Florence, and which has been published, but with omissions, for the Biblioteca della Società Storica Subalpina, is written in an ordinary exercise book of some two hundred and twenty-eight pages, either in Dal Pozzo's handwriting or in that of

---

[1] *Dieci mesi di carteggio di Ferdinando Dal Pozzo*, Pavia, 1916. Introduction by J. C. Bollea. The MS. *copialettere* is in the Biblioteca Nazionale in Florence and has not been fully published.

[2] Bib. Lab., MSS. Fosc., Vol. XLVI. See App. I.B, 3 (a).

[3] *Dieci mesi*, p. 97.

[4] *Copialettere*, MS., p. 11. Letter to the Countess Caccia di Romentino in Turin ; d. Sept. 2nd, 1831.

his secretary, Giovanni Battista Ronna, who was also an exile. It was bought by the Biblioteca Nazionale in 1915 from a bookseller, but its origin was not revealed. The whereabouts of the rest of Dal Pozzo's papers seem to be unknown, but the present heirs say that they may be in the Archivio di Stato of Turin. The letters are extremely interesting to us, for they show the arrangements Dal Pozzo made for the winding up of his estate. Rolandi had many commissions to fulfil: to forward correspondence; to attend to the letting of his house at 87 Regent Quadrant, which he retained until in 1832 he applied for naturalization as a Frenchman ; to distribute some of his pamphlets to certain friends ; to dispose of certain articles of furniture, and countless other matters. Care had to be taken not to sell certain things belonging to his wife, " nemmeno un certo *silver mug* che le apparteneva, essendo ancora ragazza ". He contemplated visiting London soon and bringing his horses over. He kept up his membership of the Literary Union Club, and we know returned frequently to London. The letters to his banker, Filica, agent of Gandolfi & Co., are interesting in the attention to detail that they show. What strikes one most on reading the letter-book is the real kindness of heart and readiness to help others that is evident from several communications. No trouble is too great for him to take in making arrangements for some children, the family of Baron Viarigi, who seem to have lived in various parts of England and in Edinburgh, and in whom Lady A. M. Elliot is interested. He fits the boy out suitably before he goes to take up a bursary at the École Polytechnique, and tries to have the girl Sophie entered for Saint Denis.[1] His dislike of Turin is such that he never wants to go back, and therefore he sells his property there and succeeds in realizing sufficient capital to ensure him an annual income of twenty thousand francs in Paris.[2] His friends warn him of the danger of sequestration of his possessions in Piedmont and he decides to sell everything to his wife to avoid the loss.[3] It is sad to think that the next years of his life were embittered by the hostility of his former friends. Filippo Ugoni even went so far as to credit him with having accepted money from the Austrian Government.[4] Pecchio, although he is furiously eloquent, is not unfair, and Panizzi and he both refuse to consider him a traitor. As a matter of fact, Dal Pozzo remained to the end a

---

[1] *Copialettere*, MS. See App. I.B, 3.

[2] *Dieci mesi*, etc. Letter to De Marchi, Edinburgh of March 15th, 1882, p. 94.

[3] *ibid.*, p. 59.   [4] *Lettere ad A. P.*, p. 119.

Piedmontese, without the wider feeling of belonging to a united Italy. " Io non sono dell' avviso dell' unione di tutta l' Italia, la riguardo come un romanzo. Questa è un' opinione come un' altra, al quale non esclude per niente il mio attacamento, anzi il mio vivo amore per l' Italia," he wrote to Pecchio in the letter of March 13th, 1832, thanking him for his Life of Foscolo, which he promised to read " con meno di distrazione, che voi non avete fatto rispetto la mia ' brochure ' intitolata *Motifs de la publicité*, etc., mentre scriveste all' amico Ugoni che io dava per consiglio l' introdurre l' uso della lingua francese in Piedmonte, quando non vi è neppure una parola di questo ".[1]

Many of the other refugees are nothing but names to us to-day. 'Santa Rosa wrote to Panizzi of the arrival of Ravina and again of the Conte Palma, and we know that Gabriele Rossetti called the former a " celebre morditore de' pacifici galantuomini " and accused him of writing an article in the *Foreign Review*, holding up his *Dant.* to scorn.[2] Dal Pozzo let his London house to a Signor Puzzi. Foscolo's copying clerks alone are a goodly number who have left little or no history. Bossi went to Mexico after Foscolo's death. The Home Office Records contain a list of " natives of Piedmont ", among them Giovanni Berra, who had tried to embark for Greece in 1823 but had been sent back to Dover from Calais.[3] In 1824 *The Times* made an appeal for subscriptions on behalf of " not less than 83 Italian gentlemen, expelled from their country for endeavouring to ameliorate its institutions—utterly destitute—actually starving ".[4] The allowance from the Refugee Fund was, we know, as low as 7s. per week.[5] Even Baron Raffaele Poerio has left little trace of his exile in London. He signed a protest against the first Italian Committee in 1824, and we find Pecchio in 1832 or 1833 giving him an introduction to Panizzi,[6] because, he says, " Mi sono immaginato che ti piacerebbe di conoscerlo. D' altronde gl' Italiani che cooperano per *la chimère qui se réalisera*, è bene che si conoscano fra loro. Non v' è altro modo di rimpastar l' Italia, che stritolando insieme tutti i suoi frammenti."

There is one more exile, however, whom we must not pass by

[1] *Dieci mesi*, etc., p. 83.
[2] Letters of Gabriele Rossetti to Charles Lyell of Kinnordy, for notes on which I am indebted to Mr. Purves.
[3] Records Office, H.O. 5. See App. I.b, 4.
[4] *The Times*, 1824, August 28th.
[5] *Lettere ad A. P.*, p. 42.
[6] *ibid.*, p. 110.

without notice and that is Fortunato Prandi, without whose aid in disposing of his manuscripts Ugo Foscolo would have been in still greater distress than he suffered. He earned a modest livelihood, like many others of his fellows, by teaching Italian. Crabb Robinson spoke of his " once fanatical liberal Italian friend " acknowledging the truth of Wordsworth's Sonnets,[1] and called him a " high-minded virtuous patriot, but on his own national politics rather wildish ". " I made him confess ", he added, " the duty of striving at least to keep the vanquished Soul beneath the stern control of *awful prudence*— not an Italian virtue in this age." [2]   Prandi must have given Crabb Robinson Italian lessons, for he speaks of their reading Filicaja and comparing him with Wordsworth, and Mary Wordsworth talked of his plodding at Italian and of her bearing " that Italian Man " a grudge if he kept Crabb Robinson from visiting them.[3]   Prandi was also Lucy Austin's Italian master, and her daughter, the late Mrs. Janet Ross, remembered him when he returned with his English housekeeper to Florence in his last years.   At one time he must have been in great financial straits and Mrs. Sarah Austin took up his case and tried to help him out of his difficulty.[4]   In 1840, when Andryane visited London after years of imprisonment in the Spielberg for his adopted country, Prandi showed him hospitality, and we are glad to be able to read his grateful thanks and his pleasure in meeting some of the exiles for the cause.[5]

[1] *Correspondence of Henry Crabb Robinson with the Wordsworth Circle*, by Edith J. Morley, I., p. 383.
[2] *ibid.*, p. 263.   [3] *ibid.*, p. 322.
[4] Letters to F. Place, Vol. I.   B.M. Add. MSS. 37949, fols. 217–19. See App. I.B, 5.
[5] Letters to Fortunato Prandi lent to me by Mrs. Ross.   See App. I.B, 5.

CHAPTER FOUR

SANTA ROSA, 1822–4

" QUEL est donc cet homme avec lequel on préfère l'exil aux douceurs de la patrie et de la famille ? Il est impossible d'exprimer le charme de son commerce. . . . Son coeur était un foyer inépuisable de sentimens affectueux. Il était bon jusqu'à la tendresse pour tout le monde. . . . Aussi était-il impossible de le connaître sans l'aimer. Je doute que jamais créature humaine, même une femme, ait été autant aimée." Thus wrote Victor Cousin,[1] and we shall find that Santa Rosa's greatest consolation in the period of exile, the last of his life, which he spent in England, was the love and unfailing loyalty of his friends. It was the sweetness and sincerity of his own nature which won for him the affection of the noblest of those among whom his lot was cast, and caused them to shed tears as they wished him good-bye on what proved to be the last long journey of his life. The record of the months of his exile in England is a record of his friendships, as will be seen from the letters which we have been privileged to reproduce.

After the disastrous battle of the Bicocca di Novara in April 1821, which put an end to the hopes of the Constitutionalists, Santa Rosa was taken prisoner by the soldiers of the King of Sardinia ; and as one of the leaders of the revolution, the one indeed who, to the last, had striven to rally the Piedmontese Constitutionalists and infuse new life into them, that they might present a united front to the Austrian advance, he would have paid the penalty with his life, had it not been for his miraculous rescue by the Polish colonel, Subula. Four years later, when Collegno was making enquiries in the Turkish camp for his missing friend after the attack on Sphacteria, a man standing near started at the name of Santa Rosa and explained that he was a Polish officer and had been the means of saving the life of the leader of the '21 by rescuing him from the *carabinieri*. Now this soldier of fortune

[1] *Revue des Deux Mondes*, 4me Série, 1840, tome XXI., p. 646.

had been one of the leaders of the Turkish soldiers who had caused his death.

After the failure of the Piedmontese rising Santa Rosa escaped with his companions to Genoa, whence the majority set sail for Spain to aid the liberal cause there. A few months in Switzerland followed, which Santa Rosa, who was not among the Spanish volunteers, devoted to the writing of the account *De la Révolution Piémontaise*,[1] partly, as he says, a reply to the histories already published, which give a biased view of the revolution. One of these in particular, *La Révolution du Piémont*, by M. de Beauchamp, published in Paris in 1821, adopts a tone of moral reproof towards the revolutionaries, that must have been galling to those whose failure to achieve their object cannot, at any rate, be held due to lack of loftiness of purpose and purity of motives. " J'écris dans une langue étrangère ", writes Santa Rosa at the beginning of his history,[2] " parce qu'il importe au bien de mon pays que les étrangers me lisent."

In November 1821 the Swiss Government, yielding to pressure from Turin and Vienna, intimated to Santa Rosa their inability to shelter him any longer, and he left Lausanne for Paris towards the end of the month. There he spent some months living in the greatest retirement under an assumed name, studying and writing during the day and finding great consolation in his friendship with Victor Cousin, which he owed to the unconscious revelation of his own character in his account of the Piedmontese Revolution. The introduction of Santa Rosa to the philosopher was brought about by a mutual acquaintance and they soon became intimate friends. They spent the evenings together, and many times Santa Rosa remained all night by Cousin's bedside, watching over his invalid friend with exquisite tenderness. The secret report on General Pepe, dated ' 29 April 1822 ', gives an account of his purchase in England of arms and ammunition for the cause, and of the efforts to raise men ; and ends with this interesting sentence, " Santa Rosa is now the Corresponding Agent in Paris." [3] Suspected by the police of corresponding with the Carbonari in Piedmont and accused of conspiring against the French Government, Santa Rosa left Paris with Victor Cousin for Auteuil, where they spent the first months of 1822 together in the utmost seclusion. A sudden aggravation of Cousin's illness one day took him back to Paris in search of medical advice, and Santa Rosa was tempted in his anxiety to follow his friend. He was arrested on his way to his lodging,

---

[1] Published in 1822, without the author's name.
[2] *De la Révolution Piémontaise*, p. 2.   [3] Records Office, H.O. 5.

and kept two months in prison. He was tried and pronounced " Not Guilty ", but was forced to remove to Alençon with the other Italians arrested with him, and there he had to report daily to the authorities. Irked by this curtailing of his freedom, he wrote an open letter of protest to the minister Corbière and was transferred in consequence to Bourges, and his freedom still more restricted. After some delay he was presented at his request with a passport for England, but a last indignity was offered him of being escorted to Calais by a gendarme, although he was granted permission while passing through Paris to say good-bye to Victor Cousin.[1]

On a dull, misty October day Santa Rosa arrived in London. He knew no one except Ugo Foscolo, who seems to have offered him hospitality, which he refused in a letter dated October 30th, 1822,[2] and had a very imperfect knowledge of English. It is therefore not strange that the exile's bright hopes of a happier life in England, full of freedom and rich in opportunity for literary work, were turned to despair, as he realized his own loneliness and the distance that separated him from those he loved best on earth. A letter from Sismondi, whose friendship with Santa Rosa dates from the time that the exile passed in Geneva, seems to be a reply to one announcing the latter's intention of going to England if the authorities would grant him a passport. It holds out promise of a warm welcome there, although it contains a warning note. The letter [3] is dated *Genève, 26 juin 1822*, and ends thus : " Si l'on vous laisse passer en Angleterre, je puis vous promettre que vous y serez bien reçu, que vous y avez déjà excité un vif intérêt, que votre livre y a eu un grand succès. Mais cet accueil et la sûreté personnelle suffiront-ils pour vous dédommager de la tristesse que cause une langue étrangère ? et la presque impossibilité de communiquer toute votre âme ? " That Santa Rosa did find in England a friend in whom he was able to confide his whole heart, we shall see later when we consider the letters written to Mrs. Sarah Austin, whose acquaintance he made in the month following his arrival.

There is an unconscious echo of Sismondi's words in the last letter which Mrs. Taylor wrote to her daughter in February 1823. She had just commented on the hard winter and consequent aggravation of the sufferings of the exiles ; and had expressed her satisfaction that

[1] " Santa Rosa," by Victor Cousin. *Revue des Deux Mondes*, Vol. XXI., 1840.
[2] Viglione, p. 97.
[3] *Memorie e Lettere Inedite di Santorre Santa Rosa*, 1877, p. 116.

her daughter had learnt to speak foreign languages so well, that she could talk with these men in their own tongue. She had evidently just read some letters from Santa Rosa, which Mrs. Austin had forwarded for her perusal, and adds, " The mortification of being with such people and having no access to their minds is very great. It would now exclude you from some of your greatest enjoyments."[1]

Immediately on his arrival in London Santa Rosa must have written to his friend Sismondi, because the latter's answer from Geneva is dated October 11th, 1822. Sismondi's letter is particularly interesting on account of the introductions it contains, of which, from references in letters to Mrs. Austin, we know Santa Rosa took advantage. With an apology for suggesting introducing anyone so well known as he, in a country where men are free, Sismondi recommends him to call on Mr. William Smith, M.P., of Park Street, Westminster, who has already shown much eagerness in receiving all the Italian refugees. At the same time Sismondi's sister-in-law, Miss Fanny Allen, is writing to her friend Miss Smith to tell her to bring about a meeting between Santa Rosa and Sismondi's brother-in-law, Sir James Mackintosh ; and by his means or her father's to procure him introductions to everyone he wishes to know among the leaders of the Opposition, or among men of letters. Sir James Mackintosh is to take him to see Jeremy Bentham. There is an amusing entreaty at the end of the letter to send his address, " car dans un pays comme Londres où la police ne prend pas vos noms et vos demeures, et où la distance extrême du bureau des postes fait qu'on connaît à peine l'usage de la poste restante, un étranger perdu au milieu d'un million d'hommes n'est pas facile à trouver ".[2]

The acquaintance of the Smiths could not but be of value to Santa Rosa, for William Smith was a friend of Rogers the poet, of Wilberforce and Sir James Stephen. Possibly he was introduced to the Austins by Miss Smith, who was a friend of Mrs. Austin. Certain it is that the charm of the home at 18 Queen Square and the beauty, vivacity, intelligence and, above all, the sympathy of its mistress exercised from the first a fascination over the lonely exile. Mrs. Austin spoke Italian fluently, and it is evident that the friendship between them made rapid strides from the first letter from Santa Rosa

[1] *Three Generations of Englishwomen*, Memories and Correspondence of Mrs. John Taylor, Mrs. Sarah Austin, and Lady Duff Gordon, by Janet Ross, I., p. 44.

[2] *Memorie e Lettere Inedite* . . . . pp. 116–18.

to her, which has the postmark ' 26 Dec.' [1]. Curiously enough there is no mention of Christmas time nor any expression of good wishes ; but a description of the " dinner I was present to yesterday " probably refers to a Christmas festivity. Love of a quiet home life and thoughts of his wife and children are the chief notes in the letter, which suggests by its tone that Mrs. Austin is a sympathetic listener. Writing to Victor Cousin on November 26th, Santa Rosa commented on the new acquaintances he had made in London. Among others " M. Austin et sa famille, jeune avocat encore obscur, mais tête très pensante, disciple de M. Bentham, que lui et sa femme connaissent particulière-ment. Celle-ci est une personne d'un excellent caractère, prodigieuse-ment instruite pour une femme, mais n'en étant pas moins aimable. Elle veut bien me donner quelques leçons d'anglais, dont je profite peu, malgré l'attrait que pourraient offrir les leçons d'une femme de vingt-sept à vingt-huit ans, d'une figure très agréable. C'est une connaissance intéressante que je cultiverai avec soin, et voilà tout." [2]

At the time when Santa Rosa made Mrs. Austin's acquaintance, the latter had been married for some two and a half years, and was the mother of a small daughter. The baby girl must have been a warm friend of Santa Rosa whose thoughts were constantly turned to his own children at home, for he frequently sends her messages in her mother's letters, and is obviously delighted that Lucy still remembers him, even after some absence.

This then was the circle into which Santa Rosa was introduced, and as for himself, we cannot do better than quote Victor Cousin's descrip-tion of him, written some fifteen years later for the Prince della Cisterna :

Santa Rosa avait à peu près quarante ans; il était d'une taille moyenne, environ cinq pieds deux pouces. Sa tête était forte, le front chauve,

---

[1] This letter and all those which follow from Santa Rosa to Mrs. Austin, most of which are unpublished, with the exception of isolated sentences which are noted, were lent to me for six months by Mrs. Janet Ross. I include them in chronological order in Appendix II.A. The constant references to other refugees and to the English friends who helped them, and the intimate revelations of Santa Rosa's own character make them invaluable to us. This letter is quoted in full by Mrs. Ross in *Three Generations of Englishwomen*, and excerpts from it in Italian by Professor Guido Ferrando, in *Un' Amica inglese di Santa Rosa*, p. 6, extract from *La Vita Britannica*, review published by the British Insti-tute, Florence, II. Yr., No. 6, Nov.–Dec., 1919.

[2] " Santa Rosa," by Victor Cousin, p. 670.

la lèvre et le nez un peu trop gros, et il portait ordinairement des lunettes. Rien d'élégant dans les manières ; un ton mâle et viril sous des formes d'ailleurs infiniment polies. Il était loin d'être beau, mais sa figure, quand il s'animait, et il était toujours animé, avait quelque chose de si passionné, qu'elle en devenait intéressante. Ce qu'il y avait de plus remarquable en lui était une force de corps extraordinaire. Ni grand ni petit, ni gros ni maigre, c'était un véritable lion pour la vigueur et pour l'agilité. Pour peu qu'il cessât de s'observer, il ne marchait pas, il bondissait. Il avait des muscles d'acier, et sa main était un étau où il enchaînait les plus robustes. Je l'ai vu lever, presque sans effort, les tables les plus pesantes. Il était capable de supporter les plus longues fatigues, et il semblait né pour les travaux de la guerre. Il aimait passionnément ce métier. Il avait été capitaine de grenadiers, et personne n'avait plus reçu que lui de la nature, au physique comme au moral, ce qui fait le vrai soldat. Son geste était animé, mais sérieux ; toute sa personne et son seul aspect donnaient l'idée de la force. Je n'ai jamais vu de plus touchant spectacle que celui de cet homme si fort . . . se métamorphosant en une véritable soeur de charité, tantôt silencieux, tantôt gai, retenant sa parole et presque son souffle pour ne pas ébranler la frêle créature à laquelle il s'intéressait. . . . Il n'avait aucune ambition ni de fortune ni de rang, et le bien-être matériel lui était indifférent ; mais il avait l'ambition de la gloire. De même en morale il chérissait sincèrement la vertu, il avait le culte du devoir, mais aussi le besoin d'aimer et d'être aimé, et l'amour ou une amitié tendre était nécessaire à son coeur.[1]

Mrs. Austin's house was the rendezvous of many well-known men of the time, who had pleasure in the society of its beautiful and clever mistress and in the conversation of her brilliant husband. Jeremy Bentham was a neighbour in Queen Square and regarded Mrs. Austin with fatherly tenderness. The literary men who frequented the house were often called upon to help the political exiles, who always found a warm welcome there ; and Jeffrey, in particular, was appealed to to consider articles written by some of the refugees. Foscolo, San Marzano, Porro, Dal Pozzo, Pepe, Panizzi, Arrivabene, Ugoni, Cucchi, Radice, Floresi, Prandi, Vecelli, Pecchio were only some of the Italians who found their way to Mrs. Austin's house. Her ability to speak their language was a first attraction, but the charm of the woman herself soon made them look upon her as " la santa protettrice di tutti gli esuli, una santa bella come quelle che Raffaello ha dipinto ".[2]
Sarah Austin was not long in appreciating the sweet nature and

---

[1] " Santa Rosa," by Victor Cousin, pp. 647–8.
[2] Pecchio in a letter to Mrs. Austin, *La Lettura*, Anno XXIV., No. 7, p. 483.

nobility of character of Santa Rosa, and he was singled out from among the others for an intimacy of friendship, which was infinitely precious to both, and which after Santa Rosa's death was the bond that united Victor Cousin and Mrs. Austin in warm friendship as long as they lived. Shortly after they met, as we have seen, Mrs. Austin offered to teach Santa Rosa English, and the first two letters, as well as from one friend to another, are from pupil to mistress. At this time Santa Rosa was full of hope that he would soon be able to master the difficulties of the language. That the first effort to which we have just referred, had called forth Mrs. Austin's approbation, is evident from another dated ' Sunday morning '—an unfortunate habit of dating which adds to the difficulty of arranging Santa Rosa's letters chronologically—and bearing the postmark ' 30. Dec. 1822 '. In this letter we have the first of a series of delightful character sketches, " un portrait à la mode de Mad^e. de la Fayette ", as Santa Rosa says,[1] which appear from time to time in the letters. Apparently the previous evening Santa Rosa had had a social evening in his rooms, at which San Marzano, " a Savoie fellow, and a big Piedmontese outlaw, the Logician, and a Napolitan Lawyer " were present. The Neapolitan lawyer, Paladini, is the subject of this first character sketch.[2] Santa Rosa announces the arrival of the Marquis di Priè in London, " courties as to manners ; patriot as to principles ". In this letter Santa Rosa expresses his political belief, that the only hope of the Bourbons' retaining the crown of France, illegally acquired in 1814 and 1815, was in their adopting a constitutional government in home affairs, but he does not hesitate to state his dislike of Bourbons and Bonapartists alike. This letter and the four which follow allude to an illness which Santa Rosa appears to have had at this time. He suffered from frequent depression, which was increased by anxiety about his family of whom he had no news. Reading and the company of his Italian friends served to pass the time, but he longed to see Mrs. Austin again and to be able to speak of his children to her understanding heart. She sought to lighten the tedium of illness by sending the patient books. The newspapers, too, interested him deeply. The reports of meetings held about this time throughout the country, where the government was freely criticized, served but to emphasize the difference between England and his own unhappy country. His great love for his own country kept him loyal to her in her misfortunes, and made it impossible for him to renounce his nationality, although he longed to see his own people enjoy the freedom of the English.

[1] Letter to Mrs. Austin. App, II.A, 13.   [2] App. II.A, 2.

H

Persecution in whatsoever form was abhorrent to him, and his indignation broke out at the thought of an intolerant archbishop.

After the first two letters Santa Rosa renounced writing in English. Possibly the difficulty of expressing his thoughts was greater than he imagined in the first joy of finding ' a better way out for improving '. His French letters, however, seem to have called forth a reply in French from Mrs. Austin, and that brought down upon her a reproof, and was at the same time a reminder to himself to express himself in Italian. In this letter there was a remarkable description of a journey undertaken by Radice to Ireland, presumably on holiday or to prospect, for he returned to this country not very long after. The letter is undated but inscribed in another hand ' 1823. About Feby.' That it preceded the letter marked ' 1823 Lent '.[1] seems evident from the reference to Radice, where Santa Rosa thanks Mrs. Austin for her " kindly attentions with regard to our friend Radice ", probably introductions he had requested for him to friends in Ireland. It is also addressed to Queen Square and therefore must have been written before the 23rd of February, by which time Mrs. Austin was in Norwich.

Santa Rosa dated his next letter, which was unsigned, ' Thursday evening ', which seems to be a mistake for ' Tuesday evening ', as he alluded to its being ' the last of the merriments ' before Lent and to the following day being ' Ashes Day '. The postmark is unfortunately incomplete owing to the seal of the letter and gives no help. He reported to Mrs. Austin a visit from General Guglielmo Pepe, which is particularly interesting as a friendly continuation of the relations between them, referred to in the Secret Report in the Home Office Records. Pepe had been in this country since the Neapolitan Revolution of 1821. Before the month was out Santa Rosa was to find himself called upon to second his compatriot in the duel between the latter and Carascosa, brought about by their mutual recriminations regarding their procedure in the war of 1821 against the Austrians. There seemed some justification for Foscolo's complaint to Capponi, that Italians, whoever and wherever they be, are possessed of a spirit of ' Discordia calunniatrice '.[2] Santa Rosa himself made the first note in his diary since his arrival in England, under the date February 28th, 1823, and it is as follows : " Eccomi a Combwood aspettando l' ora dį sangue. Due Italiani me presente, verranno al ferro ; tristo effetto delle memorie nostre. Non ho potuto negare di assistere Guglielmo Pepe. Men duole."[3]

[1] App. II.A, 7.   [2] *Epist.*, III., p. 238.
[3] *Memorie e Lettere Inedite*, . . . p. 92.

About the third week in February Mrs. Austin was summoned to Norwich to her mother's sick-bed. Mrs. Taylor's last letter to her daughter, to which reference has already been made, was written shortly before that, and shows the intimacy that existed between them, and the interest Mrs. Taylor took in her daughter's activities on behalf of the refugees. After reading Santa Rosa's letters, as we saw, her ready sympathy at once seized upon the same cause of sadness and home-sickness that Sismondi had spoken of, the difficulty of expressing one's ideas in a strange tongue. With fine intuition Mrs. Austin had discriminated between the refugees in her endeavours to give them practical help. For some she strove to find publishers and encouraged them in literary work, for others she advised the teaching of their native language. She sent Cucchi and Radice to Norwich and enlisted the help of her own family and friends, among the latter Mrs. Opie, in finding them pupils. In Mrs. Taylor's letter there is mention of both. " You inquire about Cucchi ; the only intelligence I have had is from Mrs. Opie. She likes him and will endeavour to procure him pupils ; she thinks him more fit for the world than poor Radice, who is too sensitive and delicate." [1] In a very short time ' poor Radice ' was to suffer shipwreck off the coast of Ireland and have a struggle to save his life.

Porro seems about this time to have gone to live with Santa Rosa, who found pleasure and renewed strength in his company. Santa Rosa refers to him in his letter to Mrs. Austin of February 23rd, and also to General Pepe, hinting that he has something to tell her about the latter, probably the duel, when he once more occupies his favourite seat in the chimney corner at Queen Square. Mrs. Austin's continued absence was a source of anxiety to him and he longed to see her again. Meanwhile news had come from Italy to cheer the exile in his loneliness. His wife cherished the thought of sending their eldest son to him and of joining him herself, but he would have none of it. To him the sacrifice appeared too great. If they had come to England, who knows but that the sacrifice of his own life at Sphacteria might never have been made !

Mrs. Taylor's illness kept her daughter longer in Norwich than had been at first intended, and from Santa Rosa's letter of March 19th it is not difficult to gather that Mr. Austin had written to his wife, begging her to return home. Mrs. Austin, torn between conflicting duties, had written to Santa Rosa to ask his advice. The friendship between them was now so intimate that Mrs. Austin had allowed

[1] *Three Generations of Englishwomen*, I., p. 44.

herself, without fear of being misunderstood, to speak of her learned husband's love of solitude, to the exclusion even of herself. During the five years of her engagement Sarah Taylor from being " flirtatious, dazzling, attractive, imposing ", had become " the most demure, reserved and decorous creature in existence "[1]; and no doubt from time to time flashes of the old spirit leaped forth and called in question the even tenour of her married life. Santa Rosa, although he was not at ease with Mr. Austin, even to the extent of fearing to invite him to spend an evening with him lest he should receive a " gelata risposta ",[2] yet appreciated the brilliant qualities of his mind, and had understood what great depths of feeling lay hidden under his undemonstrativeness. In this same letter Santa Rosa made a spirited defence of his friend Porro, in answer, it seems, to some remark in Mrs. Austin's letter which may have referred to the enlivening effect of Porro's company. The hospitality of Mrs. Austin's friends was extended to Santa Rosa and some of the other refugees, and they had opportunities of meeting with some of the leading Whigs. In this letter he referred to his many social engagements, and to a visit Porro and he paid to the house of Mr. Fry, the Quaker. Evidently Cucchi was meeting with success in his work in Norwich and had thirty-two pupils ! He had written to Santa Rosa in praise of Mrs. Austin, and Santa Rosa pretended to a spark of jealousy.

Santa Rosa wrote to Victor Cousin of his English connections in September 1823, " Je t'ai écrit que je ne plaisais guère aux Anglais, et en général c'est assez vrai ; mais il y a cependant quelques personnes sur l'amitié desquelles je crois pouvoir compter. Je connais, entre autres, une famille de quakers, la famille Fry." [3] In his *Ricordi* he describes this family so vividly that the passage is worth quoting in full. Whether the visit referred to is the first or the second he paid to the Frys, is not mentioned, but from the introductory tone of the description it is probably the former. He writes :

Questi Inglesi sono della religione degli *Amici*, conosciuti al mondo sotto il nome di Quackers [*sic*], salvo una delle figliuole che si sposò ad uno della Chiesa anglicana e prese quella fede. Il padre è un ricco banchiere e provveditore di thè a mezza Inghilterra, piccolo, rotondetto, viso colorito e fresco, buono, affettuoso nei modi, e lieto e sereno. La moglie ha molto nome per la cura ch' ella prende delle

---

[1] Mr. Fox, the Unitarian clergyman, quoted by Mrs. Ross in *Three Generations of Englishwomen*, I., p. 36.

[2] See App. II.A, 13.

[3] " Santa Rosa," by Victor Cousin, p. 673.

donne prigioniere. Ella ammaestra, conforta quelle infelici, e provvede che abbiano da lavorare e si giovino del prodotto. La sua carità diligente, e la sua eloquenza del dire, hanno dato autorità al suo nome. Questo è noto in tutta la Gran Bretagna e in Francia. La Marchesa Giulietta [1] le scrisse per avere consigli, e per partecipare i suoi pensieri a pro delle donne prigioniere di Torino. Con grande piacere vidi una sua lettera, colla quale ella raccomanda alla Signora Fry Cesare Balbo. Ma essa allora non potè vederlo, perchè stava fra afflizioni e solitudini domestiche. La prima figliuola, che ha nome Caterina, ritrae una nostra divota, una nostra monaca restituita al secolo, ma è giovane, di viso modesto e delicato, i modi suoi sono schietti, si muove agevolmente a tranquillo e dolce ridere. L' altra, disertrice dei quaqueri, disse a Porro : " Mai non mi piacquero le discipline degli Amici. La mia natura non vi si accorda." Mi piacquero molto le tre altre fanciulle, l' una di 14, l' altre fra 9 e 12 anni : semplice vestire, aria lieta. Benedette creature ! siete felici, e si legge nei vostri occhi. Una di esse, sentendo che io era padre e lontano dei miei cinque figliuoli, mostrava di non voler credere. La riunione del mattino mi rasserenò l' animo. Il padre lesse un capitolo del Vangelo e un salmo con semplicità e raccoglimento. Poi tutti seduti a una lunga tavola, ed un aspetto di letizia e di pace dolcissima. Vennero due convitati in fasce, zio e nipote. Bimbi di cinque mesi, l' uno figlio, l' altro nipote del signor Fry, nati lo stesso giorno. Presi il primo in braccio, e lo accarezzai. Ma ho detto che erano in fasce ; no, essi avevano bracchia libere ed una vestina agiata. Tornerà, spero, alla villa degli amici. Ne ho bisogno per tornare in me.[2]

In June of the same year, writing from Green Cottage, Southbank, to his friend Luigi Provana, Santa Rosa ends his letter with a reference to the Frys : " Se vedi la marchesa G.B., dille che ho avuto il piacere di sentire a parlare di lei dalla Signora Elisabetta Fry, che io fui due volte a visitare nella sua casa di campagna, e vidi nelle prigioni di Newgate. Donna di alto sentire e di cristiana virtù sublime, e riverita come madre amorosa dalle cattivelle prigioniere." [3]

The next letter from Santa Rosa to Mrs. Austin is undated, but has been inscribed ' February 1823 ', altered to ' April 1823 '. As it announces Santa Rosa's removal on the following day to Foscolo's cottage at South Bank, which Porro and he rented for six months, the latter date is probably correct. The endless round of calls in which Santa Rosa soon found himself involved, the dinner parties where precious hours were wasted over the wine which he always allowed to pass him by, and the dissipation of his energy in a social round which depleted his purse and kept him from his beloved studies, had

---

[1] La Marchesa Giulietta Barolo.
Memorie e Lettere Inedite, pp. 95-6.   [3] *ibid.*, p. 100.

decided him to remove to the comparative quiet of the outskirts of London. The change of residence seemed to suggest to Santa Rosa a possible change in his friendship, the beginning of a new life, and he appealed to Mrs. Austin to continue to hold him in affection. Curiously enough San Marzano, who seemed such a general favourite, had evidently frightened Miss Smith, and Santa Rosa referred to this. The two exiles had just been once more to see *Othello* with Kean in the title rôle. Santa Rosa found particular pleasure in going to Shakespearian plays and refers to them several times in his letters.

The Austins too had now removed, to Henrietta Street. There is no mention of the change in any of the letters, but the lapse of time between those of March and April may account for this, and we know for certain that Santa Rosa had seen Mrs. Austin at least once since her return from Norwich.

Thoughts of Italy were always in Santa Rosa's mind. The ' meetings ' held throughout the country to discuss Parliamentary Reform struck him more forcibly by the contrast they presented with his own unhappy country. The 23rd of March recalled to his mind the events of 1821. We find this entry among his *Ricordi* : "Ventitrè marzo ! non è questo il giorno in cui pubblicai la proclamazione che restituì alla patria la vita e le speranze ? vita che fu breve, pur troppo ! speranze che si dileguarono ! Ma mi rimase l' onore di non aver disperato della libertà italiana." [1] Santa Rosa had been suffering from depression about this time and had given expression to his discontent in a letter to Mrs. Austin which has not been preserved. Perhaps she destroyed the written record of a passing mood which her friend soon after regretted. In his next letter of June 2nd he referred to " la lettre que je vous ai écrite dernièrement " in a tone which indicated that the mood had passed, and that he was a little ashamed of having revealed himself to her. At South Bank, where he then was, Santa Rosa made friends with Berchet, who had a post in the business of one of his compatriots in London, and who also frequented the Austin's house ; and he mentioned him in this letter for the first time. He spoke of him in several letters to Cousin and always in terms of the highest praise.

It is interesting that in all the letters to Sarah Austin from Green Cottage there is no mention of Foscolo, although Santa Rosa with the other exiles living in Foscolo's house often spent the evening with him. Even when he announced his change of address to South Bank, he omitted to mention the owner of his new home to her, although

[1] *Memorie e Lettere Inedite*, pp. 94–5.

he spoke of him to Victor Cousin. Without doubt he was fully aware
of Mrs. Austin's dislike of the poet, and this fact made him avoid a
subject which would in any way disturb the harmony of their friendship.

While struggling to maintain himself by journalism, work which
fatigued and discouraged him, Santa Rosa gave Berchet every
encouragement to write the poetry which he dedicated to the cause
of liberty. The book referred to in the letter inscribed ' June 1823 '
is probably *I Profughi di Parga*, which was published in London in
1824 and in which Berchet fearlessly condemns the English policy
with regard to that unfortunate city.

In the second week in June Mrs. Austin had received news of a
relapse in her mother's condition and had set off at once for Norwich,
only just in time to see her before she passed away. The letter dated
June 12th is an expression of Santa Rosa's sympathy with her on the
death of Mrs. Taylor. He alludes, too, to San Marzano's journey to
the Continent, where he remained nearly three months. But when
one friend departs, another arrives to take his place ; and Santa Rosa
is able to announce Dal Pozzo's arrival from Switzerland. The
necessity of providing for the moment was exhausting all his energy,
and he was dissatisfied with himself, that so far he had been unable
to begin his self-imposed task, the work he had planned on the ' Con-
gresso di Verona ', which he intended to publish with his name.[1]

During these summer months of 1823 Santa Rosa lived very much
in the company of his fellow-exiles. There are references now and
then in his letters which indicate evening reunions of friends. Mrs.
Austin seems to have been present at one at least of these, and perhaps
some young French exiles who inspired the Italians afresh with
thoughts of freedom.[2] Since April Santa Rosa had shared with
Count Luigi Porro the tenancy of Green Cottage, South Bank, where
they had a study and a bedroom each and shared a dining-room. The
rooms were furnished as Foscolo knew how to furnish, and nothing
was lacking in their surroundings, at least, to make the exiles forget
the discomforts of enforced residence in a foreign land. In August
they were joined by Giuseppe Pecchio on his arrival in England for
the second time, after being expelled from Spain. Green Cottage
was a home to many refugees, as we have already seen, and it was
after Santa Rosa's departure at the beginning of October that Giovita
Scalvini and Filippo Ugoni went there to live. The inhabitants of
Digamma and Green Cottage exchanged frequent visits and spent

[1] See Prof. Ferrando, *Un' Amica Inglese*, p. 8.   [2] App. II.A, 13.

many hours talking of the future of Italy. Foscolo in particular loved to dwell on the history of the land of his fathers. Santa Rosa had a very real affection for Foscolo, and seemed to be able to appreciate the good in him and bear with patience the explosions of mad fury, which from time to time shook the poet and destroyed for a while his powers of reasoning, even when they were directed against himself.[1] A letter from Santa Rosa to Luigi Provana from Green Cottage, dated in error ' 14th June, 1824 ' (Santa Rosa was in Nottingham in June 1824), gives a glimpse into the life of the exiles who were Foscolo's neighbours and tenants in the summer of 1823. This letter, first published by Nicomède Bianchi in the *Memorie e Lettere Inedite di Santorre Santa Rosa* in 1877, contains much that is of present interest and we venture to quote from it again. The criticism of English institutions and character shows that Santa Rosa's eyes were wide open to what was around him. He finds much to admire but is conscious of his own social shortcomings. The business of social pleasure has no charm for him. His joy is in quiet intercourse with a few chosen friends. His picture of Foscolo is a kind one and is sent to one who also knew him.

Credo . . . di conoscere abbastanza la costituzione della società inglese per poterti dire senza taccia di temerità che essa ha una saldezza incredibile, e che assicura all' uomo una porzione di libertà e uno sviluppamento delle sue facoltà, maggiori che negli altri Stati di Europa. L' America inglese è superiore alla madre patria per la maggiore uguaglianza introdotta nelle istituzioni ; ma nell' Inghilterra c' è più vita, c' è più nobiltà d' animo. Stolta cosa il blaterare contro l' aristocrazia inglese, benchè qui si faccia da uno sterminato numero di persone. Un' aristocrazia che è sottomessa alle leggi, e alla quale può sorgere agevolmente chiunque per l' industria propria o dei suoi si fa ricco, è un elemento necessario in una nazione grande e ricchissima, nè può mai dirsi trista a ragione.

Se tu vedessi crescere le proprietà, sorgere le case, nascere i giardini, le vie come per incanto, tu benediresti l' incognita divinità autrice dei prodigi.

Here Santa Rosa is painting a true picture of the development of the Regent's Park district in 1823, and recalls the building fever that swept the country like an epidemic. He continues :

Ma non è incognita : la *Libertà*, ma vera, non di parole ; non iscambio di aristocrazie oppressive, non un anelare verso l' uguaglianza perfetta, che la natura delle cose respinge, non un governo che

---

[1] See Redding, *Fifty Years' Recollections*. Quoted extensively by Prof. Viglione in *Ugo Foscolo in Inghilterra*.

parlando di libertà si fa arbitro delle vostre azioni tutte, o indiscreto guidatore della vostra foggia di vivere.   Grandi difetti ha tuttavia la società inglese ; leggi penali atroci, leggi civili intricatissime, e in Irlanda esercizio abbominevole d' intolleranza religiosa. Ma questi difetti, questi mali, si vanno menomando e risanando. Le difficoltà da superare sono grandi, e lo debbono essere, come argomento della solidità dell' edifizio : ma gli sforzi dei buoni sono incessanti e misurati, onde la vittoria è certa.   .

Della natura degli Inglesi ho osservato due cose principali, la sincerità e la benevolenza. La prima di queste virtù è quasi universale. Sarebbe espulso dalla società chi fosse riconosciuto macchiato dell' opposto vizio. Ma gli Inglesi sono piuttosto buoni che amabili. L' amabilità è una certa combinazione d' ordine e di varietà. Ora questi Britanni hanno molto del primo, e quasi niente del secondo. Nella vita di ogni Inglese havvi una certa serie necessaria di fatti, è come una rotaja d'onde non mai escono di leggieri. Noi Italiani siamo generalmente graditi dagli Inglesi ; io meno di quasi tutti i miei compatriotti, perchè non ho l' abilità di sapermi accomodare ai loro tempi, e alcuni dei modi inglesi del vivere mi riescono insopportabili. I pranzi inglesi sono diventati per me *una paurosa cosa*, e mal sapevo dissimularlo.

Of Foscolo he says :

Sei o sette anni di soggiorno qui, hanno innestato alquanto il *gentle-man* inglese sull' italiano e sul greco. Ma se scavi più addentro, trovi Ugo. È vero che Ugo non conosce e non calcola i progetti degli Italiani dal 1814 in qua, d' onde nascono alcune sue idee meno giuste. Egli è volonteroso di parlare, ma si fa udire volentieri massime da chi prende diletto dei casi anche minuti d' Italia.[1]

In August of 1823 the Austins spent some time at Dorking with or near the family of James Mill, the utilitarian philosopher. The time seemed long to Santa Rosa, whose Italian friends had all left South Bank except Pecchio, lately arrived in England. A consolation in his loneliness was the meeting with Collegno who had striven with him in 1821 to give firmness to the Piedmontese rising and fixity of purpose to its unhappy Royal leader. Full of hope, Collegno had gone to Portugal and then to Spain to strike a blow for freedom, but disillusioned he returned to England in 1823 after the engagement of Bidassoa. Mrs. Austin had sent Santa Rosa a gift for his little daughter, and the kindly thought had lifted his depression. In his letter of thanks, dated August 19th, he mentioned Radice's return from Ireland and his intention not to return to Norwich. News had come from San Marzano too. Di Priè and Colonel Jones had been at South Bank and both left about the time of the letter. Santa Rosa was

[1] *Memorie e Lettere Inedite*, pp. 98–9.

anticipating with misgiving the middle of September, which probably marked the expiry of his lease of Green Cottage. Meanwhile
he was persevering in his reading of English. Shakespeare was
possibly too difficult, hence his lack of assiduity, but he delighted in
Pope. His love of English was then such that he hoped within the
next four years to read, write and appreciate it better than any other
foreigner. This hope was not fated to last long, for little more than a
year later he wrote despairingly from Nottingham of his inability to
sustain an ordinary conversation without mortal anguish.

The reason for Radice's not returning to Norwich is hinted at in
the next letter, dated August 30th, with a postscript of September 1st.
He had brought some disgrace upon himself which necessitated his
finding another centre, and from the tone of Santa Rosa's references
to him, one is tempted to consider him as a rejected suitor for the hand
of some fair lady. Three letters were enclosed from San Marzano
to Mrs. Austin, but they are not among the letters which have come
down to us in the correspondence that was in the possession of the
late Mrs. Janet Ross. As the days pass, Santa Rosa's resolution to
begin his independent work became more fixed, and, as an additional
incentive to a task in the way of which there appears to be every
obstacle, he settled a date for beginning. For some unexplained reason
he decided not to send this long letter, and the next day wrote a short
letter giving in brief the same news. It is difficult to know how the
letter of August 30th—September 1st came into Mrs. Austin's possession, and hence found a place among the letters which are the historical
basis for this narrative. Either another ' caprice ' induced him to
send the long letter after all (he had apparently intended leaving it
himself when he called at Henrietta Street on the 2nd of September),
or Mrs. Austin persuaded him later to let her have it, as it was ' con-
damnée ' but obviously not destroyed.

In September Santa Rosa's lease of Green Cottage elapsed, and in
the next letter to Mrs. Austin, dated October 3rd, we find him in
new quarters. Presumably ' 91 Alpha Road ' and ' 31 Alpha Cottages '
are one and the same house. The latter address appears on all the
letters following this one. From a map of the period the name Alpha
Road is given to the main road almost parallel with South Bank to the
south, and also to the three short roads which branch from it. The
district of Regent's Park, between St. John's Wood and Marylebone,
was a favourite one with the refugees. Santa Rosa seemed to enjoy
the solitude which his new abode had brought him, but looked forward
to Mrs. Austin's continuing to visit him on her return. She was

expected home from Dorking on the 11th and Santa Rosa hoped to be able to introduce to her his two friends, Dal Pozzo and Collegno. Muschietti was going to Manchester to establish himself. He had also been a visitor at Henrietta Street and is mentioned in several letters. It is most interesting to see how the exiles looked upon London as their headquarters, from which they spread to different parts of England and Scotland, where there seemed most opportunity for them to earn an honest livelihood. Porro had gone to York, possibly on holiday, and had enjoyed the music there, no doubt in the Minster. " Sa lettre est presque un hymne ", says Santa Rosa, " mais elle paraît griffonnée par le diable ", a description, incidentally, which might well be applied to his own, of all his letters perhaps the most difficult to decipher. His writing, like Foscolo's, varies very much according to his moods.

Two and a half months elapsed before Santa Rosa wrote again to Mrs. Austin, unless some letters have been lost. The London winter had demanded its toll again and Santa Rosa had been ill. Everything conspired to increase his depression. Even news from his wife was for once incapable of rousing him. He was anxious about his children's future. The thoughts of being unable to bring up his own children became a torment, and he dreaded their being handed over to the Jesuits by the king, in the event of his restoring to them their father's possessions. Bowring had then an article in his hands for publication, which Mrs. Austin had apparently translated ; but he seemed to have had some doubt about it as it stood, and submitted it, without the author's permission, to John Stuart Mill, " S.A. le Prince Héréditaire John Mill ", as Santa Rosa calls him, who was then only seventeen years old, and probably a fit product of his remarkable education. Santa Rosa found it difficult to hide his annoyance, and only controlled himself when he recalled Bowring's goodness to the refugees. The work of writing for periodicals was exceedingly distasteful to him at any time, and he had little patience for episodes of that kind. Mrs. Austin lost no time in defending John Mill from any imputation that he might have influenced Bowring against the article. She was touched, however, by the dejected tone of Santa Rosa's letter and offered him introductions to new acquaintances, which he gently but firmly refused in a note in reply, as he was unwilling to assume any new responsibilities, even social. San Marzano had returned from the Continent ; letters had arrived from Italy for Santa Rosa, and his spirits were again in the ascendant.

There are two letters dated merely with the day of the week and there is some difficulty in ascribing them with anything like certainty. On the one dated ' mardi ' is written, in another hand, ' June 1823 ', which has been altered to ' 1824 '. That both of these are wrong is evident, since Santa Rosa was at Green Cottage, South Bank, in June 1823 and in Nottingham the following year. As the letter is addressed from 31 Alpha Cottages, it must have been written between October 1823 and April 1824. The reference to an absence from London might allude to the visit to Brighton, of which Santa Rosa speaks in the next letter dated ' lundi '. It might equally possibly refer to his transfer to Nottingham. The second letter, dated ' lundi ', can be assigned fairly conclusively to January, from its reference to Confalonieri's sentence, which we know to have been pronounced towards the beginning of 1824, " nel principio del 1824 ", says Silvio Pellico.[1] Santa Rosa had just returned from his holiday in Brighton and was filled with sadness at the news.

Doubtless letters are missing which would have filled in the gap of some months before the next one in our possession, dated May 9th. We may picture long weeks of hard work writing articles for the newspapers, and depression accompanying the weary struggle for existence in the huge city where living was so costly. Santa Rosa had a horror of debt and, whatever else he might be unable to do, on one thing he was determined, to provide for his own needs by his labour ; and so, tired of writing articles and of translating, he resolved to try teaching, although he confessed later that he was totally unfitted for the post of pedagogue. Writing to Foscolo from Nottingham in June 1824, speaking of the latter's edition of the Italian Poets, he said :

L' impresa non è di quelle cui vi bramerei in qualche modo consecrato ; ma io credo che sia miglior cosa che il fare articoli. Tra quello che ne ho provato io e ciò che ne ho sentito da voi, ho preso gli articoli in una tale avversione, che preferisco logorarmi qui il petto insegnando la nostra lingua (talvolta a chi non la imparerà mai, mai), anzichè spendere le mie facoltà nello studio altrui con poco guadagno e senza riputazione. Dacchè lasciai Londra, ebbi alcune aperture relativamente a Giornali ; ma non esitai nel rifiuto neppur un momento.[2]

Mrs. Austin, anxious to do all in her power to help, wrote to her friends, the Needhams, who lived at Lenton, to ask whether there was an opening for one of the refugees as a teacher of languages in Nottingham. The reply was evidently satisfactory, because shortly after, about the beginning of March, Santa Rosa took up residence there ;

---

[1] *Le mie Prigioni*, p. 144.   [2] *Epist.*, III., p. 455.

and before long, with the aid of introductions from Mrs. Austin, he had made a circle of friends whose goodness to him was one of the greatest comforts in his exile.

During the early spring months of 1824 Santa Rosa was filled with anxiety not about his own future but Foscolo's. Worried by creditors, distracted by the constant thought that he had given his word that they would be paid in April, or might then have recourse to legal means of recovering the money due to them, and seeing no prospect of being able to clear himself, Foscolo resolved to leave the country which had, with some happiness, brought him so much misfortune. His letter to Lord Bathurst, Minister for the Colonies, asking for a passport for Greece, was written on February 17th,[1] and no answer had been received when Foscolo wrote the letter to Santa Rosa on March 1st, bidding him good-bye. Foscolo was living in hiding at that time on account of a warrant for his arrest, that some of his creditors had taken out. "Oggi mi trovo più infermo che mai", he wrote, "e pur troppo non potrò dirvi addio : bensì s' io dovrò partire vi scriverò ; e vi scriverò anche se non potrò partire. Se credete, date l' indirizzo vostro al signor Andrea,[2] sì che le mie lettere possano arrivarvi ;—se no, mene informeranno gli amici nostri." Then, after information about some of Santa Rosa's books which had been lent to Sir Francis Burdett, "Intanto addio da tutta l' anima, L'amico vostro."[3] Immediately on receipt of this Santa Rosa hastened to Digámma Cottage, but not finding Foscolo there, only ' la fanciulla ' Floriana, he wrote him the touching letter, full of affectionate concern, which is published at the end of the *Epistolario*. With two or three, even four months provided for, Santa Rosa implored Foscolo to come to him if circumstances made him wish for a few days of obscure peace. "Io ho creduto alcuna volta di potervi disamare quando mi avete afflitto ;—ma ho fatto sperienza di non poterlo," he added with Christian charity. Knowing Foscolo's passionate devotion to his mother, he appealed to him in her name to do what she would have approved. Some thought of offering himself in the cause of the Greeks was even then in Santa Rosa's mind, for he ended his letter with the words, "Dio ci possa riunire sotto il cielo delle due sole contrade del mondo che io amo, Italia e Grecia, nutrici degl' ingrati popoli d' Europa !"[4]

[1] *Epist.*, III., pp. 143–4.
[2] Andrea Schorno, Foscolo's copying clerk.   [3] *Epist.*, III., p. 133.
[4] *ibid.*, *Lettere a Ugo Foscolo*, p. 454. Quoted in full by Nicomède Bianchi in *Memorie e Lettere Inedite*, p. 102.

By the date of his next letter to Sarah Austin, May 9th, 1824, Santa Rosa was already established in Nottingham and on terms of friendship with the Enfield family. The children brightened his life and made him forget, for a time at least, the drudgery of his daily round of lessons. The optimistic days were past when he hoped in four years time to have mastered the English language better than any of his compatriots. A period of discouragement had set in. He was thinking back over the events of his life and the cause of his exile, and realized now, when it was too late, where he had acted wrongly "Le souvenir de mes fautes politiques m'accable," he wrote to his friends in London.[1] He begged for a long letter full of news of all his friends, and his request met with a speedy fulfilment, because a fortnight later he acknowledged not only the letter, but also receipt of the portraits of his children which Mrs. Austin had forwarded. These portraits had been painted by Santa Rosa's order, hence perhaps his displeasure at the artist's failure to catch the likeness of his little daughter. The lonely exile loved to talk of his children, and not only Mrs. Austin but the new friends in Nottingham were willing listeners. He used to lay the miniatures on his table in turns, as his companions during breakfast,[2] and we know that they went with him to Greece. Collegno tells the story of the accident to the miniature of Teodoro in his *Diario dell' Assedio di Navarino*, and also in his résumé of the events leading up to the last scenes of Santa Rosa's life. It is from the latter that we quote. "Portava sempre sul petto i ritratti de' suoi figliuoli, e il 20 [aprile] essendosi accorto d' aver mezzo cancellata l' immagine di Teodoro, volendola rasciugare, ne provò una tristezza profonda, anzi mi confessò che non poteva tenersi dal vedere in quest' accidente un augurio sinistro, e il domani scrisse a un suo amico a Londra : Tu ne riderai, ma dopo ciò sento ch' io non debbo più rivedere i miei figli ! "[3]

Radice kept up a correspondence with Mrs. Austin and she sent his letters on to Santa Rosa, sure that they would be read with a

[1] App. II.A, 23.

[2] *Memories of Lenton*, by M. C. M. (Constance Martineau), p. 13, published in 1910 by the Arden Press, Letchworth, for private circulation, and made available to me by Henry H. Enfield, Esq., of Bramcote, Nottingham, and his sister, whose father was the "little Dick" of Santa Rosa's letters. See App. II.B.

[3] *Diario dell' Assedio di Navarino, Memorie di Giacinto Collegno, precedute da un Ricordo Biografico dell' Autore scritto da Massimo D' Azeglio*, Torino, 1857. (The diary was written by Collegno in French and translated into Italian by Achille Mauri.)

sympathetic eye. He did not appear to find teaching any more
entrancing than Santa Rosa, but his friend in exile could find words
of encouragement for him. He spoke affectionately of him as ' le
cher enfant '. Radice was young and liked to be petted, and at times
exile weighed heavily on him. Mrs. Austin had also reported bad
news of San Marzano's health, which caused Santa Rosa some anxiety.

During this last summer of his life Santa Rosa was surrounded
by affectionate friends who did all in their power to mitigate his
many hardships. He was frequently at Lenton, Mrs. Needham's
house some three miles from Nottingham, and at the Enfields' ; and,
although he thought himself a dull companion, he won the admiration
and affection of all. " Maria Enfield and I especially worshipped
·him," said Anne Needham.[1] The daughters of Mr. Needham used
to call at Santa Rosa's lodgings in Parliament Street on their way
from school and leave gifts of flowers, eggs or books ; and felt
honoured if they chanced to see him, and still more if he spoke to
them. Happy summer evenings were spent sitting on the verandah,
or gathered round the drawing-room window at Lenton, when Santa
Rosa and Mr. Needham's daughters and Henry and Maria Enfield
sang favourite Italian songs. The invalid daughter sat at an open
window upstairs and listened, and the mother was sometimes with
her and sometimes with the merry party below.

The revolutionaries of 1821 were characterized by deep religious
conviction, conviction which in their exile brought them into immediate and sympathetic touch with the members of the English Free
Churches. There is no doubt that the mainspring of Santa Rosa's
life was an enlightened faith, and his belief in a hereafter was unswerving. Many were the discussions between Santa Rosa and
Victor Cousin, during the year of their friendship in Paris, on the
question of the immortality of the soul, and to Santa Rosa all was
crystal clear. His strong tendency to theological discussion would
naturally attract the interest of the Frys, the Needhams, the Enfields
and others with whom the spiritual side of man's life was a constant
subject for thought. Anne Needham reported Porro's first visit to
Lenton in a letter to her friend, with a comment on his faith. " He
is a Unitarian, Santa a reforming Catholic, and the first time they
were here together they had a most spirited conversation on the
subject of Catholicism."[2] The news of Santa Rosa's death was

[1] See footnote 2, p. 110.
[2] Letter, undated, from Miss Anne Needham (afterwards Mrs. William
Enfield) to Miss Mitchell.

such a blow to her that his own certainty of a life beyond the grave was the only solace. " The determination to meet him hereafter was a sort of crisis in my religious life."

Although Santa Rosa had left London, he had not cut himself off from his friends there, and his fellow-exiles often visited him, as we have seen from his letters to Mrs. Austin. The Enfields and the Needhams received them all with kindness. Radice, Arrivabene, San Marzano, Porro, Pecchio and Muschietti were all welcome guests at Lenton.

Not a day passes just now without some peculiar interest [wrote Anne Needham to her friend, Miss Mitchell]. I allude principally to the frequent visitations we have lately had from Santa's illustrious compatriots. On Monday evening the garden contained a singular and interesting assemblage. There were Santa Rosa, the Marquis Charles de San Marsan, and Count Porro and Castiglione, wandering about the garden and distributing amongst us the favour of their rare conversation. . . . Whoever else we see, Santa must always stand at the head of our affections and admirations. We always love him with a peculiar love, when we see him with his friends.[1]

News of Foscolo, who was hard at work on his edition of the Italian Poets, was brought to Santa Rosa by Porro and also by Ciani, another exile who passed through Nottingham ; but the desire to hear from Foscolo himself induced Santa Rosa to write him the letter of June 21st, from which we have already quoted, with a pathetic appeal to Foscolo to order his life so as to free himself from the overwhelming incubus of debt which was draining his strength and paralysing his mind.

Spero di risapere da voi [he wrote], che l' edizione di cui mi sì disse vi assicurerà un capitale, e due o tre anni d' ozio. Mio caro Ugo, io ve ne scongiuro a mani giunte ; se vi riesce di uscire da quell' insoffribile stato di angoscia dell' aver debiti e non mezzi da pagarli, dell' essere obbligato di lavorare collo spasimo, di dovere interrompere talora il vostro lavoro per trovare un bel ragionamento da ispirare la pazienza o la confidenza ad un creditore, . . . se ciò vi riesce (lasciatevene pregare e ripregare da chi vi ama, e vi desidera sinceramente pace e gloria), ordinate le vostre cose in modo da non incominciare una nuova serie di piccole ma pur amare calamità. Forse le grandi calamità esaltono l' uomo ; ma le piccole lo contristano e lo abbassano.[2]

Schiller expresses this same thought through the lips of Mary Stuart,

In großes Unglück lehrt ein edles Herz
Sich endlich finden, aber wehe tut's
Des Lebens kleine Zierden zu entbehren.[3]

---

[1] See note 2, p. 111. [2] *Epist.*, III., p. 455.
[3] *Maria Stuart*, Act I., Sc. 1.

It is curious to note that Santa Rosa, commenting on Foscolo's earlier intention of going to help the Greeks, expressed the opinion, which he himself had later only too unfortunately an opportunity of proving true, that it was imprudent to go to Greece without a good number of pounds sterling in one's possession. Referring to his own present situation, he remarked that few people are interested in Italian and hence he had few pupils. " Mi trovo precisamente sul campo che il povero Tedaldo coltivava. Ei ci moriva di fame ; e così farei io se non fossi stato raccomandato efficacemente." [1] Touched though he was by his friend's love for him, Foscolo yet delayed three months before replying, and then a letter was only dragged from him by Porro, who was to bear it to Nottingham. The answer was long and sad. Foscolo was oppressed with work, and tired.[2]

We have no letter to Mrs. Austin between May 24th and July 28th. Santa Rosa complained of her long silence too, but it is still possible that a letter is missing. In the July letter Santa Rosa speaks of the visits of his fellow-exiles, which dates fairly conclusively the letter from Anne Needham to her friend.

About this time efforts were being renewed to help the Italian refugees in London, whose plight was in many cases pitiable. Mrs. Austin was one of those who were active on behalf of the unfortunate exiles ; and the Editor of *The Times*, in his appeal on August 28th, 1824, for subscriptions to save the eighty-three Italian gentlemen from starvation, added, " Many most respectable names of all parties of Englishmen are to be found on the list of voluntary managers of whatever little fund may be raised for this pious object." [3] An English and an Italian committee were already in existence, but in spite of the singleness of their aim, some friction had arisen in the administering of the funds, and of this we shall find echoes in the letters from Santa Rosa to Mrs. Austin written at the end of July and beginning of August. In the letter of July 28th, however, Santa Rosa spoke only of a ' statement ' which seems to be a statement of the case of the exiles that would appeal to British sympathies, and make clear the exact purpose for which the fund was required.

The following day Santa Rosa, having received a further communication from Mrs. Austin enclosing letters from Radice, wrote an acknowledgment, in which he spoke freely also of San Marzano. The dissensions among the refugees seemed to have embittered the latter, and Santa Rosa was afraid that his contempt for certain men

---

[1] *Epist.*, III., p. 456.   [2] *ibid.*, p. 162.
[3] *The Times*, August 28th, 1824, p. 2e.

I

might lead him to condemn the cause for which he had already suffered so much. That Mrs. Austin, in her desire to dissipate these fears, gave some indication of them to San Marzano is evident from San Marzano's letters to Mrs. Austin which we shall consider later. Santa Rosa on his removal to Nottingham, had resigned membership of the committee, where probably his moderation and patient tolerance might now have settled the differences which threatened to divide the exiles into opposing factions, and alienate the sympathies of the English public. In *The Times* of July 20th,[1] appeared a letter from the English Committee which was active on behalf of the Italian refugees, dated July 18th, 1824, and signed John Smith, chairman. The letter was addressed to " General de Meester, as member, treasurer, and secretary of the Italian Committee ", and expressed the fullest satisfaction, after careful examination of the accounts, of the manner in which the ' Monies ' entrusted to the Italian Committee had been expended. In the issues of the following date an apology was made for the omission of the signature of Colonel Jones, the honorary secretary, which should have appeared in addition to that of the chairman. On the 28th July a very long letter was published in *The Times*, headed *The Italian Committee*, and addressed to the Editor, in which were voiced the grievances of a section of the Italian refugees against the Italian Committee of which General de Meistre was secretary. The letter, after expressions of gratitude to the English . Committee, states in no measured terms the case against what it refers to as " the dismissed Italian Committee ". The latter appears to have refused, " arrogantly " their assailants write, to exhibit their accounts at the request of the refugees. There then follows under six headings with two sub-sections, the explanation of the situation. According to the writer of the letter, Colonel Raffaele Poerio, chairman of what was presumably the committee of investigation, the

ate Italian Committee, composed of Marchese San Marzano, Conte Porro, and Messrs. Demestre, Cornari and Angeloni, was appointed by the Italians with limited powers, and for the sole object of receiving the monies granted by several Philanthropic Societies, the English meeting, or private English and Italian beneficence, for the relief of the wants of the Italians, and distributing them equally, after having faithfully stated the different sums to the parties concerned. [The second ' explication ' goes on to state] that the said committee having exceeded all the powers given them, and abused the confidence of their countrymen, these, after having exhausted all conciliatory means to

---

[1] *The Times*, July 20th, 1824, p. 2e.

make them return to reason, observing the uselessness of their attempts to obtain justice, were obliged to dismiss them from a charge which they exercised in an inhuman, partial, and arbitrary manner, and in which they exerted themselves to continue by means far from honourable.[1]

The writer then criticizes the examination of accounts referred to by the chairman of the English Committee, as being of only a part of the committee's administration ; states that the committee had received considerable sums of money for the relief of the Italian refugees, the receipt or use of which they had taken particular care to keep a secret, and challenges the equity and correctness of the distribution of the money. One instance of the committee's want of equity is cited, where they had not given " any relief for the space of nearly two months to ten individuals, who had perhaps a particular claim to consideration, depriving them thus of all means of subsistence, and leaving them exposed to hunger and wretchedness ".[2] The exclusive right of examining the Italian Committee's accounts of the money granted to the Italian exiles who had fought for the cause of Liberty in Spain, apart from those dealing with the funds received from the English Committee, is claimed for the exiles themselves and their ' new managers '. " We finally add ", writes Poerio,[3] " that Marchese San Marzano and Conte Porro against all expectation, instead of giving the asked for account of their administration, have removed from London, and that the ex-Treasurer, Signor Demestre, has not been able to make any answer to the Official demands made him both by the Italian Committee, and Mr. Chippendale, attorney, for the rendition of the said accounts." The last paragraph is an appeal in the name of justice to the English public, to observe that the Italian refugees had been provoked to come to such extremities by those who till now wanted to oppress them. If the English public should now withdraw its support " the Italians will endeavour to console themselves in their undeserved disgrace [4] by the consciousness of their having preferred hunger and all the attendants of misery to the humiliation and degradation their oppressors had condemned them to, and to whom in their turn they leave the barbarous and disgraceful satisfaction of so base a vengeance." It is hardly astonishing that San Marzano was affected by attacks such as this.

[1] *The Times*, July 28th, 1824, p. 2e.
[2] *ibid.*, July 20th, 1824, p. 2e.
[3] *ibid.*, July 20th, 1824, p. 2e.
[4] disgrazia, i.e. misfortune.

Santa Rosa communicated to Mrs. Austin the gist of Porro's reply to General de Meistre, in which he admitted the justice of the claim that all accounts should be submitted to every legally constituted committee ; but he contested the legality of any committee elected in a meeting of a section of the exiles. Santa Rosa is an amazing example of patience and tolerance, and even the attacks on his friends, which involved himself to a certain extent, as a former member of committee, cannot rouse a spirit of bitterness. He imputes to the bad influence of a few unruly members, perhaps agents of the enemy, the dissension in their ranks. Bowring took a very prominent part in the work of the committee, and was a fit person to look into the accounts if the work had been allotted to him, for finance occupied most of his attention in after years.

On August 5th, San Marzano wrote to Mrs. Austin about the fears regarding his political opinions which Santa Rosa had conceived and had, wisely or unwisely, communicated to her.

Ce qu'il vous a dit à mon égard [he said referring to Santa Rosa], est un des plus parfaits nonsenses qu'il ait jamais dit dans cette matière. Je le plains. S'il peut seulement lui venir dans l'esprit que quelques individus dont ni le nombre, ni les talens, ni les actions ni les richesses, ni la position sociale ne rendent d'aucune importance pour leur pays soient capables par leur bassesse d'altérer les principes qui ont dirigé ma conduite politique. Je dis que je le plains si cela est, pour cette raison que lors même qu'il n'aurait pas une haute idée de mon caractère il devrait en avoir assez de mon sens commun pour savoir que ce n'est pas la conduite d'un petit nombre de brigands qui pourrait changer mes opinions à l'égard de l'humanité toute entière.[1]

He went on to defend the fundamental simplicity of his principles as tending to greater stability than metaphysical abstractions, and authorized Mrs. Austin to communicate this part of his letter to Santa Rosa, which, however, as we see from the letter from Santa Rosa to Mrs. Austin, dated August 28th, she decided not to do. From the thanks expressed by San Marzano, it is evident that Mr. Austin had helped General de Meistre with his advice on the legality of the latter's refusal to submit the accounts of the Italian Committee to the refugees who had decided that it was their business to examine·them.

A certain success was now meeting Santa Rosa's labours in Nottingham, and he was able to set aside a number of guineas in excess of his expenditure ; but a life of teaching in a small country town could

[1] Unpublished letters from San Marzano to Mrs. Austin. See App. II.c.

not satisfy him long, and he hinted to Mrs. Austin that he was seriously contemplating a change to an active life. The scene that appealed to him was Greece, a land he loved like his own, " nutrice degl'ingrati popoli d'Europa ". It was not mere discontent that made him give up his quiet life in Nottingham, for it had brought him warm friendships and a reasonable freedom from the practical cares of existence ; but inaction galled him, and the love of liberty that burned like a flame within him, could only find expression in deeds. Collegno wrote of him, " Il motivo principale, che indusse il Santa Rosa a partire da Nottingham, fu, a quanto pare, quella forzata nullità a cui si vedeva ridotto. Fare il maestro di lingua, quando si ha il pensiero e la capacità di grandi cose, è un martirio da non sapersi comprendere se non da chi l' ha provato ! Intorno a questo tempo egli scriveva ad uno de' suoi amici : *Quando si ha un' anima forte, conviene operare, scrivere e morire.*" [1] Santa Rosa offered himself to the Greek deputies in London, and asked for command of a battalion. The time of waiting for a reply and for orders was long, and probably Santa Rosa considered it wise to say nothing of his plans to his friends, until they had sufficiently materialized to enable him to give them definite details. In his letter of August 24th, 1824, to Luigi Provana, four days before the letter to Mrs. Austin, there was no mention of any change in his life, but only of what he calls later ' un certo stato di scoraggiamento e di languidezza che mi avevano preso purtroppo a Nottingham '.[2]

Nulla, nulla qui mi consola [he wrote on August 24th], nulla mi diletta. Lavoro per vivere ora e forse questo mi rende più stupido che non sarei quando io fossi in altre circostanze. Tuttavia è una consolazione il campare del proprio lavoro. La mia mente non è decaduta ; anzi, io credo di vedere le cose morali e sociali molto da alto. Ma il cuore è misero, la memoria scemata, l' immaginazione soventi[sic] sorda alle chiamate del cuore.
Continuo a leggere l' istoria, e massimamente d' I alia. Sono, più che mai non fossi, italiano in tutta la mia esistenza, salvochè non scrivo più la mia lingua patria con quell' eleganza acquistata con tanta fatica, se pure acquistata mai. . . . Pensiero terribile ! Io non la vedrò più mai quella terra dove ho i più cari amici, dove amai, dove crebbi, dove soffrii, dove sperai. . . . Quel pensiero, come un fantasma che persegue il reo, seguita il tuo povero amico.
Sono stato accolto assai bene in questa città dove campo lavorando. Ma non ho facoltà di corrispondere col cuore alle gentilezze d' ogni

---

[1] *Diario dell' Assedio di Navarino*, p. 24.
[2] *Memorie e Lettere Inedite*, p. 107.

maniera che ricevo. [Then, speaking of his affection for Porro, he added] ma Luigi mio, le affezioni degli amici vecchi sono le sole che penetrino le parti più intime della misteriosa esistenza del cuore. Scrivimi, Luigi, se mi ami ancora. Scusa il dubbio. Ma io penso troppo soventi [sic] che niuno più si cura di me in questo mondo. È un pensiero ingiusto, ingiustissimo, ma che mi opprime, ma che mi percuote.[1]

The longing for his native tongue was perhaps one of the causes of his dissatisfaction with his English. Always to be obliged to speak in a foreign language imperfectly understood has, after a time, the effect of vitiating one's style of expression. "Mi son cacciato in capo d' imparare l' inglese. Qui mi tocca di parlarlo sempre ; ma che volete ? Mi trovo mancar le parole e le frasi, un dì più che l' altro, e non ci fo altro guadagno che di dimenticare il mio francese, e di scrivere l' italiano viepiù stentato e scorretto," he wrote to Foscolo.[2]

Having decided to see the Greek deputies personally, Santa Rosa planned to go to London, and he announced to Mrs. Austin on October 19th [3] his intention of spending a week there, but did not divulge the purpose of his visit, although he said his own doubts were almost dissipated. He looked forward to talking over his future with her.

The Chair of Spanish and Italian in Dublin University was vacant about this time and Radice a candidate for it. Lady Charlotte Bury had made his acquaintance a short time before (Clifton is not far from Bath), and in support of his candidature, wrote renewing her old friendship with Foscolo, and begging him to send a letter in his favour.[4] Pecchio was a rival candidate for the chair and had Santa Rosa's support. For some reason Radice was hurt at Santa Rosa's preference and ascribed it to Pecchio's noble birth. Santa Rosa criticized with scorn his young friend's lack of judgment of himself for he had always shown him affection and had taken the greatest interest in his welfare ; but he knew the man's super-sensitiveness, and forgave him. Even in his note to Mrs. Austin announcing the postponed hour of departure for Greece, he had a thought for Radice, and a feeling of thankfulness that the misunderstanding between them had been cleared up. We know that Radice was appointed, and was professor of Spanish and Italian in Trinity College, Dublin, from 1824 till 1849. The honorary degree of LL.D. was conferred upon him by the College on April 13th, 1833.

While Santa Rosa's thoughts were busy with the great change he

---

[1] *Memorie e Lettere Inedite*, pp. 104–5.   [2] *Epist.*, III., p. 456.
[3] See App. II.A, 29.   [4] See App. I.A, 25.

contemplated in his life, his kind friends in Nottingham had remembered his birthday with gifts of books. His acknowledgment, written the same day as the letter to Mrs. Austin announcing his intention to go to London, has a message for each one ; and, besides offering a glimpse into Santa Rosa's friendly relations with the Enfield family, is a proof against his despairing assertion that his English is so bad, as to have destroyed all his hopes of mastering it. The letter which is addressed to " Maria, Henry, Anna, Richard, Harriet ",[1] makes no mention of the impending change.

Two days later came unexpected news that the ship in which he was to sail was on the point of departing, and Santa Rosa was obliged to take hasty leave of all his dear friends in Nottingham. Anne Needham's account of his last days there, and of the sorrow that his departure occasioned them, is sufficient evidence of the place he had taken in their lives.[2] Porro and Muschietti, the latter from Manchester, went to him immediately, and Porro accompanied him to London. Having had no time to hear from Mrs. Austin in answer to his letter of October 19th, he was unaware of her absence from London, until he arrived at Dal Pozzo's house in Air Street, Piccadilly, on October 25th. He wrote at once to her, giving her the date of sailing, Thursday, October 28th, and expressing a wish to see her again, if it were possible. Immediately on receipt of this letter, Mrs. Austin announced her return to London ; and the fortunate chance of the postponing of the ship's sailing made it possible for the friends to meet once more. On November 1st Santa Rosa wrote her a last word of good-bye, before leaving the shores of the country that had been his home in exile.[3]

At least one other farewell letter, full of kind messages to friends, and written two days before sailing, has been preserved to us. It is abundantly evident that the most poignant grief is the lack of news from Piedmont ; but, as we see some lines further on, a letter from Madame de Santa Rosa arrived in Nottingham on the Tuesday after her husband had left for London, and was forwarded by hand so that it might reach him in time. In a letter to Luigi Provana from Nauplia, Santa Rosa, speaking of his last days in England, said, " a Nottingham ho imparato a conoscere il cuore degli ottimi Inglesi. Vidi lagrime, vere lagrime sparse nell' ultimo dir loro addio.

---

[1] It is interesting to note that Maria Enfield was 18 years of age at this time, Anna 10, Dick 7, and Harriet 5. See App. II.B, 1.

[2] See App. II.B, 4, letter to Miss Mitchell dated ' November 1824 '.

[3] See App. II.A, 32.

Quivi io v' era pure onorato con ogni delicatezza di modi." [1]   And
the reality of the grief which his departure occasioned is read in every
line of the letter written by Anne Needham to her friend Miss Mitchell,[2]
in which she described Santa Rosa's last days in England.

The story of the voyage to Greece on the *Little Sally* is told in
detail by Collegno, who had striven with Santa Rosa to steady and
guide the ill-prepared Piedmontese rising of '21, had shared his exile
in England, and finally had set out with him for Greece, deluded
by the Greek deputies in London into believing that their services
would be valued in the cause of freedom.   Santa Rosa's modest
request for command of a battalion, was met with hints of far more
important posts waiting for him in Greece, of the administration of
the war and the setting of the finances in order.   He was provided
with open letters of introduction in flattering terms, and with sealed
ones, which he later discovered contained warnings against employing
him, lest his name should embarrass the Greek Government with
the Holy Alliance.   For four days the *Little Sally* was held up by
adverse winds at the mouth of the Thames, and the beginning of the
voyage was symbolic of the volunteers' reception by the Executive
body in Greece.   The bright hopes of rendering service to the Greeks
which had encouraged the six men who sailed together on the *Little
Sally*, soon faded, as the dilatoriness of the Greek command made
it increasingly evident that they were less concerned with winning
the war than with keeping themselves in favour with certain powerful
allies.   The little company of volunteers landed at Nauplia on
December 10th, and Santa Rosa remained nearly a month there,
endeavouring to extract a promise from the Greeks to employ him
adequately.   As no success greeted his efforts, Santa Rosa decided
to see something of Greece and set out on an extended tour to Athens
Marathon, Cape Sunium and other hallowed places of antiquity.
An attack of fever delayed his return, but he eventually rejoined
his friends in Nauplia about the beginning of March.   Preparations were now being made for the siege of Patras, and Santa Rosa
renewed his efforts to obtain a command, with the same result as
before.   By this time he realized that his fame was against him, and
his friends tried to persuade him that he had fulfilled all his obligations
to the Greek Government, and could safely and honourably return
to England.   However, with greater determination than ever to
accomplish at least some part of what he had set out to do, Santa

---

[1] *Memorie e Lettere Inedite*, p. 106.

[2] See App. II.B, 4.   Letter dated ' November 1824 '

Rosa enlisted as a private under his middle name of Derossi. He took part in the relief of Navarino and entered the city on April 21st, with Prince Maurocordato's troops. The next two weeks he spent reading Shakespeare, Davanzati, and his friend Provana's works, as the weakness of the garrison of Navarino made it impossible to follow up with a new offensive. Meanwhile Pecchio and Gamba had arrived in Greece, and had brought letters for the earlier volunteers. Collegno left Navarino for some days but returned in time to spend a few days with Santa Rosa, before the latter left for Sphacteria on what proved to be the last journey of his life. On the 8th of May Collegno received a note from his friend, requesting him to forward a supply of biscuit; but that same day Santa Rosa fell in the ranks of the Greeks, who had failed conspicuously to justify the faith placed in their courage by so fine a band of the friends of liberty. Enquiries in the Turkish camp produced no certain information about him, and his name was not even pronounced in the funeral oration for the fallen at Sphacteria, which formed part of a requiem held on June 5th at Nauplia. It was with very heavy hearts that Santa Rosa's friends returned to England, some of them on the same boat, the *Little Sally*, that had brought them out six months before. The personal loss of so sweet a friend was only enhanced by the sense of the uselessness of the sacrifice, and the disillusionment that had destroyed their enthusiasm and killed their hope. Pecchio returned with Collegno to England, Gamba proceeded to Zante and Porro remained for some time longer in the land of the Greeks they had set out to help to free.

Santa Rosa's friends in exile were soon scattered over the British Isles and their history lost to London. Muschietti settled in Manchester, as we have already seen, whence he came to bid good-bye to Santa Rosa on the latter's departure for Greece. Cucchi was in Norwich where Mrs. Austin's influence and Mrs. Opie's friendship continued to help him to earn a livelihood. Radice, after a short sojourn in Bath, seems to have been attracted to Ireland; and in spite of his alarming experiences of shipwreck on the occasion of his first visit, did not hesitate to apply for the Chair of Italian and Spanish at Trinity College, to which he was appointed on November 11th, 1824, in succession to Alfonso Pelegrini. It is interesting to find that, in the Records of the Home Office, the secret letter book which we have already mentioned in connection with Porro and his application to resume his own name, contains also a reference to Radice's arrival in England.

Evasio Radici,[1] late Captn. of Artillery in the Piedmontese service is also arrived having quitted Turin in April last, from the same Political cause. He retired to Spain & has a Spanish Passport under the name of Jean Solo Major. He also now applies to resume his proper name, he is the bearer of many Italian letters to different persons in London, particularly Cam Hobhouse, Col. Sorreno, Mr. Beckenteth Lawyer of Lincoln's Inn & others. Both these persons [2] have been reported to me as having visited Genl. Pepe some days since and are connected with the Report lately made respecting Italy. 4 Feb. 1822.[3]

The letter, which is unsigned, is addressed to " Mr. Hobhouse."

San Marzano seems to have been more fortunately placed than some of his compatriots, in that he was apparently independent of lessons or journalistic work for his livelihood. He was able to return to the Continent for three months in 1823 and he made a prolonged tour in Scotland in 1824, when his journey took him to Edinburgh and from there as far as Inverness, then by the Caledonian Canal to the West Coast and to Glasgow and back to Edinburgh. Anne Needham, in a letter to a friend, gives a description of his personal appearance which brings him vividly before our eyes. She speaks of his grace and nobleness of deportment, " of his height and slenderness, his brown waving hair and restless eyes ", and mentions the wound in his hand which he received in Russia, where he was aide-de-camp to Napoleon. He was thirty years of age when he visited Santa Rosa in Norwich in 1824, but had already had experiences which might almost have filled a longer life. We have already referred to his work on the Italian Committee in London and to the unfortunate criticisms of his administration of the funds. From his references to Santa Rosa's fears lest his allegiance to the cause of liberty in Italy had suffered under the unjust attacks of his fellow exiles, the character of the man is not hard to judge. He had himself a singleness of purpose, which gave him a distaste of principles founded on metaphysical abstractions. In some ways he had an almost youthful impatience of another's different point of view, and, one feels, a certain hardness of judgment which a sense of humour would probably have mitigated. His letters to Mrs. Austin [4] are curiously abstract in expression and in the highest degree impersonal, compared with those of Santa Rosa. It is, by the way, diverting

---

[1] The name is often found spelt *Radici*, even in the Trinity College records.

[2] i.e. Porro and Radice.

[3] Records Office, H.O. 5, 35. Letter Book—Secret. H.O. Alien Entry Book, B, 10/5.

[4] See App. II.c.

to read, in a more than usually illegible letter, written transversely across the front page, this sentence : " Comme je n'aime guere à perdre le sens d'une partie de vos lettres je vous prie, surtout quand vous écrivez de travers de soigner un peu plus votre écriture." [1] After some years in England San Marzano transferred the home of his exile to Paris, following the example of a goodly number of his com-patriots, who found France probably a less costly and more congenial country than England, and also in closer touch with affairs in Italy. In April of 1832 [2] Dal Pozzo noted in his letter book the appeal he had sent to San Marzano in favour of General Demestre. A fortnight later he noted, among other subscriptions received, the sum of forty francs from San Marzano. On the same day, May 15th, he wrote to San Marzano in Paris, remarking on the brightening of the horizon for the political exiles, as shown in certain mitigation of sentences and permission to return to Italy ; and strangest of all in San Marzano him-self dining that very day on Sardinian soil as the guest of the Sardinian Ambassador in Paris, the Count Sales. And so, little by little, the martyrs of the Piedmontese rising of '21 found the way reopening for their return home.

[1] See App. II.c, 1.
[2] *Dieci mesi di carteggio di Ferdinando dal Pozzo.*   MS. in Bib. Naz., Florence, p. 207.

CHAPTER FIVE

ANTONIO PANIZZI

In the spring of 1823, while Santa Rosa was enjoying the peace and comfort of Green Cottage which Porro and he had leased from Ugo Foscolo, there arrived in London after many vicissitudes the young Modenese patriot, Antonio Panizzi, who from that time forth was to adopt England for his home, and in spite of his ever-living and active interest in the affairs of his native land, to give her unstintingly the fruits of his remarkable intelligence and indefatigable energy. After the crushing of the Neapolitan and Piedmontese revolutions of 1820 and 1821, the governments of the petty Italian states were seized with panic fear and took every measure in their power to repress the growing liberal movement. Many arrests were made of persons suspected of being members of secret societies. After a semblance of a trial they were sentenced to death or to imprisonment on evidence extracted often by means of torture.[1] In 1820 Francis, Duke of Modena, published a decree stating that all who continued to be members of the Carboneria, a secret society having for its aim the independence of Italy under a constitutional government, and the destruction of all governments whose power was not vested in the nation ; or all who, knowing of members of the society, failed to denounce them, were guilty of high treason, a crime punishable by death, or in the latter case of imprisonment for life.[2] After numerous arrests some of the Carbonari of Modena were about to be brought to trial, when Besini, chief of police, who had been appointed by the Duke also to judge the cases, was murdered. The trials took place the following month at Rubiera, and Antonio Panizzi, a young lawyer of Bresciello, who had more than professional interest in the proceedings, was present as an observer. Forty-seven sentences were passed, one of

[1] *The Life of Sir Anthony Panizzi, K.C.B.*, by Louis Fagan, I., p. 30.
[2] *Antonio Panizzi, Scholar and Patriot*, by Constance Brooks, Ph.D , pp. 6–7.

death.[1] Panizzi himself seems not to have been a member of the Carboneria and to have stated so in after years, but there are some grounds for believing that he was a member of an affiliated society, the *Sublimi Maestri Perfetti*.[2] Shortly after the trials at Rubiera, Panizzi was arrested, but by the help of friends succeeded in escaping.[3] Another version of the story is, that he was warned in time and able to elude the grasp of the authorities. However it may be, Panizzi, provided with a passport which he had had the forethought to obtain some time before, crossed the frontier into Switzerland. His cousin Zatti and two friends, Minzi and Montani, had accompanied him as far as Cremona, where unfortunately he had been obliged to leave his luggage and take to flight, while the suspicious Austrian official was making enquiries as to the genuineness of his papers.[4] Panizzi decided to settle at Lugano, but he made this impossible by writing there an account of the trials at Rubiera, which he published under the title *Dei Processi e delle Sentenze contra gli imputati di Lesa-Maestà e di aderenza alle Sette proscritte negli Stati di Modena*, and with the date .*Madrid, 1823*.[5] The authorities requested him to leave the town, and he made his way to Geneva, where he met other exiles ; but his stay there too was of short duration, for the representatives of Austria, France and Sardinia were sufficiently powerful to interfere in the Swiss right of asylum and to procure his expulsion. After some hesitation and prospecting, a small company of refugees set forth down the Rhine for England and arrived in London on May, 1823.[6]

Panizzi soon found himself a welcome visitor in the little circle of exiles that surrounded Santa Rosa, and was presented to their doyen, Foscolo, who had then been in occupation of Digamma Cottage for some months. Foscolo often joined the company at Green Cottage, and it is not difficult to picture the delightful evenings spent there, when the youthful enthusiasm of the latest of their number to arrive from their beloved native land would stimulate the poet to the highest flights of his astounding eloquence. But Panizzi had arrived in London with a very small sum of money between himself and starvation, and in spite of his extreme care, living in an attic and limiting his daily expenditure on food to fourteen pence,[7] means had to be found to provide

---

[1] *ibid.*, p. 30. [2] *ibid.*, p. 32. [3] Fagan, I., p. 41
[4] Brooks, p. 14. [5] Fagan, I., p. 25.
[6] *ibid.*, pp. 42–3. The writer of the article on the life of Sir Anthony Panizzi in the *Quarterly Review* of April 1881, says July, but there are so many obvious inaccuracies that we hesitate to accept it as authoritative.
[7] Fagan, I., p. 43

for the ordinary needs of life. There seemed little opportunity in London for new-comers. The number of refugees already trying to earn a livelihood was greater than could be supported, and the provinces offered a better chance of success. Armed with letters of introduction from Foscolo to William Roscoe and Dr. William Shepherd, whose interest in Italy and liberal sympathies made them particularly warm friends to the victims of despotism, Panizzi made his way to Liverpool, where his own industry and force of character helped him to overcome the initial difficulties and to earn a living. Roscoe's influence gave Panizzi the *entrée* into the intellectual society of Liverpool, and he soon made acquaintances who most probably helped him to find pupils. An allusion in one of the letters to him from Santa Rosa shows that there were already two Italian teachers in Liverpool, and evidently Panizzi's first weeks there were not less difficult than the time he had spent in London. He was young however, only twenty-six, of great strength of body as well as mind, and Santa Rosa's kind encouragement and advice was seed on good ground.[1] Dogged perseverance brought him through the difficulties of learning a foreign language, which we judge he set about with characteristic thoroughness ; and of teaching his own to pupils who lived in widely scattered districts, involving miles of walking in depressing wintry weather.[2] He met with considerable success as a teacher ; his type of brain with its orderliness and meticulous attention to detail marked his peculiar fitness for the work that had been thrust upon him by circumstances. But he would have little patience with triflers, and his ideas on the teaching of modern languages, which he set out in detail in a letter to the Warden of London University some years later,[3] make it abundantly clear that his method was no " Italian without tears ". Hence perhaps came his dislike of teaching beginners, whose enthusiasm often outran their diligence and ability, but with whom he dared not quarrel, providers as they were of his daily bread. In 1825 [4] Panizzi was so far advanced as to be able to give in English, in the Royal Institution of Liverpool, two courses of lectures on the results of his study of the Italian language, leading up to Tasso and Ariosto, and these seem to have met with very great success if one may judge from the appreciatory reports in the *Liverpool*

---

[1] *Lettere ad A. P.*, p. 12.   [2] Fagan, I., p. 53.

[3] Correspondence in the possession of University College, London, and made accessible to me by the Librarian. Panizzi's letters, No. 1179. Quoted by Brooks, p. 203.

[4] Fagan gives 1824 and 1825 as the dates of the lecture (p. 60), but Dr. Brooks (p. 25) proves that both series were delivered in 1825.

Mercury of the day.[1] In 1826 Panizzi's improved circumstances made it possible for him to change his abode to 93 Mount Pleasant, where he remained until his removal to London. By this time his place in Liverpool society was assured and he had many friends, not the least of whom was Francis Haywood, who was just a year older and therefore a companion on more equal footing than Roscoe, whose age made his attitude to Panizzi rather that of a father than a contemporary. The round of dinners, a species of social function which called forth many and various criticisms from the refugees who were obliged to submit to this particularly English institution, had already become a part of Panizzi's life and in August of 1826 Foscolo warned him of the dangers of too much roast beef and beer and even of the wine the English drink, " da che quant è più pregno di acquavite, tant' è (più) prelibato per essi ".[2]

During the years in Liverpool Panizzi took advantage from time to time of opportunities to visit other parts of the country. He spent some holidays in London, where he renewed his old friendship with fellow-exiles. Santa Rosa had passed from them, but Filippo Ugoni, Scalvini, and Dal Pozzo, until ill health compelled him to seek the less rigorous climate of Paris,[3] were still there, and Pecchio not far away. Foscolo, although always more of a patron than an intimate, received Panizzi with great pleasure and reproved him, in a letter of July 1826, for leaving him for three weeks without news after they had parted.[4] Panizzi had devoted much of his time since his exile to the study of Italian literature, and in January of 1826 went to Oxford to consult and compare thirteen manuscripts of the *Divina Commedia* in the Bodleian Library. From his notes he prepared a letter which he destined for the editor of the *Antologia* in Florence and was about to send it, when a copy of Foscolo's *Discorso sul Testo di Dante* came into his hands. It was his enthusiasm for Foscolo's scholarship that led him to write at once and submit his own notes for the poet's perusal. He offered to consult other Dante manuscripts available not far away, in the possession of Sir Thomas Mostyn, if Foscolo so desired, and also the manuscript belonging to " Signor Colke di Olkam ",[5] an unconscious revelation incidentally of Panizzi's difficulty at that period

---

[1] Quoted by Brooks, pp. 195–7, from the *Liverpool Mercury* of Friday, March 18th, 1825, and of Nov. 11th, 1825.

[2] *Lettere ad A. P.*, p. 40.

[3] *Epist.*, III., p. 469.   [4] *Lettere ad A. P.*, p. 36.

[5] *Epist.*, III., pp. 460–1. The reference is to Thomas William Coke of Holkham, first Earl of Leicester (1752–1842).

in pronouncing the English aspirate *h*. Foscolo answered the letter almost by return and expressed his appreciation of the value of Panizzi's researches, which he intended to make use of.[1] The correspondence marked the renewal of the relations between Panizzi and Foscolo, which Foscolo's tragic circumstances had prevented during Panizzi's visit to London the previous summer ; and they must have met frequently during his next visit in 1826, to which we have already referred. Foscolo had evidently found such sympathetic response in Panizzi's company that he was inspired to write him a long account of his lessons, which had necessitated a change of dwelling to Henrietta Street, a more suitable part of the town ; and of his many troubles with Pickering. His letters to Panizzi are incredibly long and deal with his health, his struggles and his reluctance to write for the periodicals, and add nothing to what we have already discussed in connection with the last years of his life. Panizzi had the same kindly thought as Lady Dacre three years earlier, and suggested that a series of lectures in Liverpool, combined perhaps with one in Manchester, would yield Foscolo a sum of £120 in the space of three weeks, but of course his name would have to be published in order to attract an audience. The plan was good, but Foscolo's morbid dislike of facing a company of people and of seeing his name in advertisements made him refuse to consider it. Some correspondence passed between Foscolo and Panizzi on the subject of a translator for the novels dealing with the former's life, as we have seen, and Dr. Shepherd was to undertake the work. The question, too, of the publishing of the *Lettera Apologetica* roused Panizzi to a spirited and courageous defence of his native land, and caused a very long heated discussion with Foscolo.[2] Panizzi's tone was strengthened. It was no longer from disciple to master, but the voice of one who knew the Italy of his day and the brave struggles her children were making to set her free. This difference of opinion may have contributed largely to the reluctance which Panizzi always displayed, to speak of his great countryman. Still the breach was not irreparable if breach there was, for Foscolo seems to have invited Panizzi to stay with him at Turnham Green in June, 1827,[3] not three months before he died. A more probable cause of the lack of deeper feeling for Foscolo than gratitude dictated, was the reputation which the prodigal poet had made for himself in London society, a reputation which brought discredit on all Italian exiles, and prevented many

---

[1] *Lettere ad A. P.*, p. 34.
[2] *Epist.*, III., pp. 463–4, and *Lettere ad. A. P.*, p. 50.
[3] *Medusa, Anno I.*, 1902, N. 4, quoted by Brooks, p. 41.

Englishmen from discriminating between the truly noble and the less worthy among the refugees. In after years Panizzi must have heard criticisms of Foscolo from some of the leading men of the period, who had known him well, and the criticism of the *man* would wound the feelings of the *compatriot*. Santa Rosa's maxim, which he sent to his young friend in the early days in Liverpool, became also Panizzi's rule of life. " Possiamo onorare il nome italiano nella Gran Bretagna coll' intierezza della vita, coll' utilità dei lavori, colla dignità dei discorsi e dei costumi, e col sopportare anzi vincere la povertà colla costanza e col lavoro." [1]

On March 23rd, 1827,[2] the trial was held at Lancaster of the two brothers, Edward Gibbon and William Hayward Wakefield, accused of the abduction of an heiress, Ellen Turner who had been a pupil of Panizzi's. It was only natural that Panizzi should take an interest in the proceedings, and he seems to have journeyed to Lancaster with Henry Brougham, who was the counsel for the prosecution. It is not certain when the young exiled Italian lawyer first met the famous advocate. They both knew Francis Haywood and may have met at his house. In any case their intimacy deepened after the Lancaster trial, when they most probably had ample opportunity to discuss the case, and there seem grounds for believing that Panizzi was able to give some help owing to his knowledge of continental marriage law. It will be remembered that both brothers were sentenced to three years' imprisonment, and that Edward's marriage to Ellen Turner which was performed at Gretna on March 7th, 1826, by the blacksmith, David Laing, was cancelled by a special Act of Parliament.

The outcome of the friendship between Brougham and Panizzi was the preference of the latter in the candidature for the Chair of Italian in the newly founded University of London. The plan was mooted in 1826 of creating a university in London, where a general system of education should be established, independent of all religious teaching. As was to be expected, the promoters of the scheme were chiefly of Whig sympathies and Dissenters. Brougham was one of the most influential members of the Council, and his support of Panizzi resulted in his appointment. However, the coveted chair was as yet a treasure

---

[1] *Lettere ad A. P.*, p. 14.
[2] *The Annual Register for the Year 1827*, Law Cases, etc. The King *v.* Edward Gibbon Wakefield, William Wakefield, Edward Thevenot, and Frances Wakefield, pp. 316–26 ; but the *D.N.B.* dates the sentences of the brothers from 1826, although the sentences were pronounced May 14th, 1827.

of unknown value, and Panizzi seems to have hesitated in accepting it, as his position in Liverpool was assured and he had many friends there. The University of London was still untried. A visit to London early in February 1828, brought Panizzi into contact with Leonard Horner, the warden of the new University, who evidently showed him much kindness. One of the subjects discussed by them in connection with Panizzi's appointment was the defining of the duties of the new professor. Panizzi apparently expressed then to the Warden his great objection to teaching beginners, and his desire for an assistant to take this burden from him. It is rather interesting to find this young professor of thirty-one, although becomingly grateful for the honour done him in appointing him to the chair, quite clear in his own mind as to the conditions under which he was willing to work, and quite firm in his statement of them.

In Panizzi's letter of thanks to Horner for the kindness shown him during his visit to London, he broached the subject of the assistant and suggested as a suitable man for the post a Roman, Pistrucci, whom we have no reason for disbelieving to be related to Valerio Pistrucci, who succeeded Gabriele Rossetti in the chair of Italian at King's College in 1849. Dal Pozzo seemed to agree with Panizzi in his estimate of Pistrucci, who was of " good character, and of agreable [sic] and gentlemanly manners ". The only disadvantage was that he knew English " but indifferently ", and he would have to learn it thoroughly before he could be considered competent.[1] Panizzi ended his letter with a statement of the method of teaching Italian which he had found most successful. After eight or ten lessons on pronunciation and elementary grammar points, with exercises from English into Italian, he introduced the pupil to historical books for translation into the foreign tongue. Syntax was taught as required for correction of the errors made. Italian prose was then read by the teacher, repeated by the pupil and translated literally into English. Impromptu translation from English into Italian followed, and last of all, when the pupil was familiar with the verbs, dialogues and phrases were learnt and conversation in the foreign tongue attempted. Panizzi followed up this outline of his own method by a condemnation of the " so-called Hamiltonian system, which is a great humbug ".[2] The next letter to the Warden, dated March 6th, 1828, was an acknowledgment of the formal letter of appointment, and a statement of his opinion regarding the respective duties of the professor and his assistant. The same

[1] University College MSS., No. 932. See App. III.A, 1.
[2] *ibid.* This passage on method is quoted in full by Brooks, p. 203.

directness which was afterwards so characteristic of him is noticeable here. He had no hesitation in suggesting to the Council, and it must be remembered that he was only thirty-one years of age and a stranger in a strange land, that, after consulting with the other professors, they should adopt a uniform plan for the study of all modern languages and literatures. In the same letter Panizzi stated his intention of publishing a selection of extracts from the best Italian prose writers for the use of his students.[1] There was enclosed in this letter a private note for Horner begging that no financial arrangements be entered into with the assistant without reference to himself, and preferably only through him—an evidence of his strong sense of discipline which was so essential to him later at the British Museum. The scheme of work for Italian was submitted towards the end of March, and suggested Roscoe's *Leo X* as the text for translation into Italian.[2]

In the covering note to the syllabus there is evidence that the Council did not approve of the choice of Pistrucci as assistant, and Panizzi, acknowledging his own responsibility for the elementary teaching, stated his determination to undertake the work himself for the first year if necessary. He proposed, however, an intimate friend of his upon whom he could rely.[3] In a later letter Panizzi pointed out that in wishing to exclude the beginners from his lectures in Italian, he was looking more to their profit and to his own credit than to fees, an indifference to gain as such, that characterized him throughout his career.[4] His interest in the budding University was shown in his request for copies of the University Report for circulation in the news-rooms in Liverpool, and indeed he was successful in disposing of some shares in it to some of his friends in the north. He spared no pains to induce the Corporation of Liverpool to become " proprietors ", and although most of the shareholders were Dissenters he conceived plans for interesting " C. of E. Gentlemen ".[5] With a sigh of resignation Panizzi offered to renounce his claim to an assistant if the Council so desired, but was quite indifferent to the loss to himself financially that an assistant would incur. The beginners in Liverpool must have been a great trial to their Italian master to cause the " repugnance " [6] which he expressed again and again in his letters. " This is a point on which I particularly insisted at the time of my appointment," [7] he wrote. As the opening day of the new University drew near, the question of the introductory lecture was touched on, but to judge from

[1] University College MSS., No. 933.
[2] *ibid.*, No. 1179.   [3] *ibid.*, No. 938.   [4] *ibid.*, No. 934.
[5] *ibid.*, No. 943.   [6] *ibid.*, No. 936   [7] *ibid.*, No. 937.

a letter to the Warden, dated Nov. 22nd, no students had presented themselves. Robert Browning, then just over sixteen, had been entered in 1828 ' among the students of Italian at London University, Gower Street ', as one of his biographers expresses it, although we shrewdly suspect his name was the only one. It was withdrawn in favour of German before the classes began, as a good Italian master, Angelo Cerutti, was available for private lessons near his home [1] ; and thus Panizzi lost the honour of being the great poet's guide to the *dolce favella*. The Council apparently had decided to guarantee certain professors the sum of £200 for one year, provided the fees of their pupils did not amount to that sum. Panizzi stated his willingness to give instruction at any time he might be required, and added, " to receive a remuneration which I shall have in some manner deserved, will not diminish my gratitude, but will be more pleasing to my feelings".[2] He then outlined a course of lectures on the Romantic Narrative poets which might attract an audience. The disappointment must have been keen, after the bright hopes which induced him to leave his work and friends in Liverpool. This course was delivered, and at the end of March Panizzi submitted subjects for a further course, which was attended only by two people, " Mr. Booth and Mr. Romilly, who would not have attended if they had not been my private friends ".[3] One solution of the difficulty was found in giving a course of lectures which ladies might attend, but this had to be outside the sacred precincts of the University,[4] and Willis's Rooms were chosen. About fifty people enrolled, all of them Panizzi's own friends, as he said in his letter of May 1st, 1835, appealing against the decision of the Council that he should prepare and deliver a course of lectures, notwithstanding the failure of all previous courses. The Chair of Italian at London University does certainly seem to have merited the name of " barren honour ", which an opponent of Panizzi's bestowed on it.[5] The question of an assistant came up once more for discussion in October, 1833, and Panizzi proposed Rosteri, of whom he said, " He looks like a gentleman, and that is a good thing." [6] But the correspondence continued regarding the wisdom of announcing further lectures which

[1] *The Life of Robert Browning*, by W. Hall Griffin and H. C. Minchin, p. 90.
[2] University College MSS., Box XXXI., No. 20
[3] *ibid.*, No. 3379. See App. III.A, 5 and 7.
[4] *ibid.*, Box XXXI., No. 1. See App. III.A, 6
[5] *Foreign Quarterly Review*, XV., p. 49.
[6] University College MSS., No. 3173.

attracted no audience. The Senate seems to have decided they should be announced, but history is dumb regarding the effect on attendance.

Some letters passed between Panizzi and the Warden on the subject of the promise made by the Council to lend the former £250 per year for the first two years, on which condition alone he had agreed to leave Liverpool. The decision of the Council which guaranteed certain professors £200 per annum was made later ; and Panizzi felt that the first agreement with him was still binding, entitling him " as a matter of *right* and not of favour £50 more ".[1] He bowed, however, to the will of the Council and did not press his claim. His loyalty to the University remained unbroken, and he was ready in 1830 to write to the Council in defence of the Warden, who had apparently been attacked by some malicious persons in the Sunday press.[2] In April 1831 the question of remuneration was again raised, and Panizzi appealed for the payment of the whole of his fees, without the stipulated deduction of one-third by the Council, in view of his having only nine students. " It is evident that if the almost total failure of my class had been foreseen, neither would the Council have appointed a Professor of Italian, nor would I have accepted the appointment," [3] he wrote. The following year the Committee of Management evidently decided to put on a settled footing the question of remuneration of professors situated as Panizzi was, although an extract from the account book shows that of £40, the sum received from eight students in fees, £26 13*s*. 4*d*. was Panizzi's share.[4] By this time Brougham had once more come to the rescue, possibly feeling that he had been instrumental in bringing Panizzi to London, and that he must compensate him for the unexpectedly inauspicious beginnings of the Chair of Italian. 1830 saw the rise of the Whig party to power and Brougham was raised to the peerage and made Lord Chancellor. As an ex-officio Trustee of the British Museum he was able to use his influence to secure the appointment of Antonio Panizzi as Extra-Assistant Librarian. Two of Panizzi's old friends, Francis Haywood, and William Ewart [5] whose interest in public libraries may first have been aroused by the great librarian, stood security of £500 each for him, as was required by the rules of the British Museum. The duties of the University being little more than nominal, Panizzi held the two posts concurrently.

In 1832 a chance meeting at dinner with Dr. Roget, the secretary of the Royal Society, led to Panizzi's being asked to revise the proofs of

[1] *ibid.*, No. 1530.   [2] *ibid.*, Box XXXI., No. 5.   See App. III.A, 8.
[3] *ibid.*, No. 2444.   [4] *ibid.*, No. 2725.
[5] Carried a Bill establishing free public libraries, 1850. *D.N.B.*

the new catalogue of the library. After examining the proof sheets he refused to undertake the correction of so inaccurate a production. The committee acknowledged the justice of his criticism, scrapped the work already done and invited him to compile a new catalogue, which was begun in October 1833. Payment was promised on a basis of the number of titles written, but Panizzi was mortified by the refusal of the committee to accept his computation, and in two successive years he had to force his claim, before it was finally recognized. Further difficulties were placed in his way during the revision of the proofs, and the interference of the catalogue committee hampered his work. Although the opinion of bibliographs was in favour of Panizzi, the committee resolved that he be no longer employed. Panizzi's determination brought him full settlement of his claim in spite of opposition, but he stated his case in fullest detail to the Duke of Sussex, who was then president of the Royal Society.[1]

Panizzi's work at the British Museum was in the preparation of a general catalogue of the printed books ; and the enthusiasm which he always brought to whatever task he undertook resulted in his being specially commended, and recommended for additional remuneration by the Sub-Committee of Finance in June of 1835. The General Meeting in the following month refused to ratify the recommendation, although concurring in the opinion expressed as to Panizzi's zeal and ability.[2] In the same year a Parliamentary enquiry was held into the condition, management and affairs of the Museum, and Panizzi gave valuable evidence based on his experience of famous continental libraries, to the examination of which he devoted much of his holiday time. He suggested improvements in the conditions at the British Museum,[3] and the value of his services was recognized two years later, when the resignation of Baber, the Keeper of the Printed Books, took place. It is unnecessary here to go into the details of the opposition raised when Panizzi was called upon, over the head of his senior, Cary, the well-known translator of Dante, to succeed to the office of Keeper. Cowtan and Fagan both state that Panizzi only applied for the post, when he was assured that Cary's nomination would be set aside on the grounds of his ill-health. In spite of meetings of protest against the " foreigner " and the out-cry in the Tory press, he was appointed on July 15th, 1837.[4]

As this appointment precluded the holding of any other, Panizzi

[1] Fagan, I., pp. 121–30.   [2] ibid., p. 132.
[3] A Biographical Sketch of Sir A. Panizzi, by Robert Cowtan, p. 17
[4] Fagan, I., p. 134.

was obliged to resign the professorship of Italian at London University, although the duties were far from onerous. We have devoted considerable attention to the correspondence dealing with this period of his life, chiefly because, in the biographies of Antonio Panizzi, the great honour of the position is vaunted, without sufficient regard for the small beginnings of what is now so important a part of the work of University College, London. The letter intimating his resignation shows a remarkable advance in power and correctness of expression, and a complete mastery of contemporary English epistolary style.[1]

In 1831, probably because he was unwilling to accept the privileges of hospitality without fulfilling the obligations of a citizen, Panizzi decided to apply for naturalization. At that time still a special Act of Parliament was required in each case, after the petition for naturalization with the necessary sponsors was presented. Panizzi's petition is most interesting in its simplicity. No mention is made of the cause of his leaving his native land ; the years of his exile until his appointment to the Chair of Italian are dismissed with the bare and rather vague expression of " literary pursuits ", and his whereabouts during that time are ignored. The tenure of such important offices as the professorship of Italian in London University and an assistant-librarianship at the British Museum are deemed sufficient grounds for the conferring of the privilege of naturalization. Panizzi's sponsors were Lord Auckland, whom he knew as a member of the Senate of the University, and Lord Sandon.[2] The bill was read in the House of Lords for the first time on January 20th, 1832,[3] and passed without hindrance. The final act is dated March 24th, 1832, and from that day Panizzi could style himself an Englishman.[4]

When Panizzi had made the decision to leave Liverpool for London, the friends he had in Lancashire saw to it that he was provided with the necessary introductions to give him a place in London society. Roscoe gave him a letter to Samuel Rogers, who, as we know, was one of the Holland House Circle, and a man of great influence among the eminent men of his day. He was a valuable protector for the young exile, whose restless spirit and boundless energy needed wide scope for their expression. Brougham continued his good offices by making

---

[1] University College MSS., No. 4193. See App. III.A, 9.
[2] Records Office, H.O. 1, 15, 1835. Naturalization Bills. See App. III.B, 1, 2, 3.
[3] *ibid.* Letter from E. G. Walmisley, Clerk of the Journals, H. of L., to the Hon. George Lamb, Under-Sec. of State in the Home Office.
[4] Fagan, I., p. 117.

him known to Lady Dacre, whose love for Italian literature had already made her a good friend to Foscolo. Lady Dacre must have been a woman of singular charm. She was certainly gifted far beyond the average, and seems to have had a very merry wit. William Brougham had spoken to her of Panizzi, and some six months after the latter had settled in London, Henry Brougham introduced him to her by letter in most flattering terms. The friendship was not only literary, and was extended to the whole family, who seemed to regard Panizzi as an intimate of their circle. When they first met, Panizzi was busy with his study of the Romantic Narrative Poets of Italy, including his edition of Bojardo, of which we shall speak later, and the Ariosto which he published in 1834 and in which he was permitted to incorporate some of Lady Dacre's translations. Their correspondence is most assiduous for the first ten years or so of their acquaintance, although their friendship lasted until the death of Lady Dacre in 1854. In the early days Panizzi was a welcome guest at 2 Chesterfield Street and visited the Dacres also at Welwyn, their country home. Lord Dacre's ill health and, after his death, Lady Dacre's age and infirmities made their intercourse less frequent after a while, but it continued to be animated by warm friendliness to the end. The first of the many letters from Lady Dacre in the British Museum deal chiefly with their literary interests, with translations from the Italian poets, that Panizzi seems to have suggested as fit subjects for her pen, and with the edition of Lady Dacre's translations from Petrarch which was published in 1836, and which certainly was helped and encouraged by Panizzi, if the idea of the collection did not originate with him. He presented Lady Dacre with a beautifully printed and bound book in 1833, which was a suggested model for the volume of Petrarch, but it seemed too splendid, too pretentious to the authoress, who was passing through a stage of depression and dissatisfaction with her efforts.[1] Other matters claimed her attention for the next few years, although she persevered with her work ; but it was not until 1835 that she definitely decided on the publication, in which Panizzi undertook to be her unofficial collaborator, and to provide her when required, with explanatory renderings of the Sonnets. Her own poetic translations were subject to the criticism of other friends also. Her letters were henceforth full of references to the work in hand, and she stated her difficulties in finding suitable renderings. So much that was lovely in the original Italian would not bear translating into English. One passage in particular, in which the beauty lay in the language rather

[1] Panizzi Correspondence. Vol. I., fol. 298. B.M., Add. MSS. 36714.

than in the thought, gave her such trouble that she had to cut out the greater part of it. She wrote a delightfully witty letter to Panizzi, relating all her woes, and another passing on " Mr. Smith's " [1] criticism of one of her renderings.[2] Panizzi seems to have approved of her translation of the difficult passage however, and his encouragement inspired her to sit down and translate another sonnet, in spite of the disturbances attendant on a house full of guests.[3] A further difficulty arose when the sonnets were ready for the press. A preface had to be written. As the Dacres had by then gone to Ireland, all kinds of distractions made the writing of it an arduous and dissatisfying task. Several attempts were sent to Panizzi with the authoress's comments on their inadequacy, and finally a preface was dispensed with and the translations left to speak for themselves. The proof correcting was probably done by Panizzi. It certainly took up little of Lady Dacre's attention, and her remarks show that she limited herself almost to the insertion of a few commas. She left the choice of setting and type to Panizzi's good taste and superior knowledge [4] ; and the result of his labours filled her with delight. " The book is really perfection ! ! " [5] she wrote in her enthusiasm, although she was a little ashamed later that her " poor attempts " should have cost so much money, " when anybody had rather read the worst novel that ever was written ".[6]

There are of course, as well, many personal allusions in the letters from Lady Dacre, which show the affection in which Panizzi was held by the family ; many chance remarks, which offer a peep into Panizzi's own life. One of the earliest letters suggests that the professor of Italian at London University had some ambition to become Italian tutor to the Princess Victoria, but even the Archbishop of Canterbury, whose aid Lady Dacre tried to enlist, was powerless to help.[7] A note of much later date, 1845, leads one to suspect that the idea was not finally given up for some time.[8] Invitations are frequent, and news of Lady Dacre's grandchildren, whose mother was the Miss Wilmot of Foscolo's lengthy epistle from East Moulsey.[9] Panizzi is asked for his

---

[1] ' Bobus ' Smith, Sydney Smith's brother.
[2] Cf. Panizzi Correspondence. Vol. I., fols. 410, 412–13. B.M., Add. MSS. 36714. See App. III.c, 1 and 2.
[3] ibid., fol. 414.
[4] ibid., fols. 456 and 458. See App. III.c, 3 and 4.
[5] ibid., fol. 460.   [6] ibid., fol. 469.
[7] ibid., Vol. XIII., fols. 49 and 50. B.M., Add. MSS. 36726. See App. III.c, 5.
[8] ibid., Vol. II., fol. 22. B.M., Add. MSS. 36715. See App. III.c, 6.
[9] Epist., II., p. 355.

advice on the choice of suitable books, French, Italian or German for Mrs. Sullivan's daughter. Lady Dacre is " particular about morality and delicacy ",[1] and in another letter asks not for *new* books but *good* books, " approved works and books of information of any age ".[2] Panizzi gave the child Italian lessons, too, and she made excellent progress, although the grandmother says in one letter of the younger child, " The little Gertrude finds what you told her to do very difficult." [3]   He was asked to recommend an Italian teacher, preferably " some very safe tidy comfortable little old *compatriot* ",[4] a woman, for Lady Becker's daughter ; and to give his opinion on a poor exile, whom Lady Dacre had allowed to teach her granddaughter to save him from starvation.   Lord Dacre was apparently the means of introducing Panizzi to Thomas Coke of Holkham, Norfolk,[5] of whose magnificent library Roscoe, who had catalogued it, had spoken years before.[6]   With eager anticipation the Dacres awaited Panizzi's verdict, and invited him to visit them at once on their return from a five weeks holiday in Ireland.   " This morning brings your welcome proposal for next Wednesday.   We shall be delighted to see you and to hear all about Holkham, and tell you all about Ireland." [7]   In after years, when afflicted with ill-health, complete deafness and other infirmities, Lady Dacre acknowledged Panizzi's friendly calls of enquiry by making him one of the first of her visitors, when her medical advisers permitted her once more " to enjoy the society of those who contributed by their kindness and their talents to the pleasantness of my better days ".[8]

But we have wandered on into the future.   There were many other friendships formed in those early years in London.   Panizzi was a sociable man and an asset to all functions.   He was in the plenitude of his powers and a compelling personality.   He soon became a frequent visitor at Holland House and remained a friend of the third Lord Holland and his famous wife to the end, and continued in touch with their successors, although he quarrelled with Lady Holland in Naples,

---

[1] Panizzi Correspondence, Vol. II., fol. 115.   B.M., Add. MSS. 36715.
[2] *ibid.*, Vol. XIII., fol. 48.   B.M., Add. MSS. 36726.
[3] *ibid.*, Vol. II., fol. 16.   B.M., Add. MSS. 36715.
[4] *ibid.*, fols. 53–4.
[5] *ibid.*, Vol. I., fol. 442.   B.M., Add. MSS. 36714.   See App. III.c, 7.
[6] Fagan, I., p. 66.
[7] Panizzi Correspondence, Vol. XIII., fol. 39.   B.M., Add. MSS 36726.
[8] *ibid.*, fols. 53–4.

owing to her contributing to a fund for Austrian soldiers. The whole of Whig society was open to him in those days of struggle for the supremacy of ideas of freedom and liberalism ; although he made friends even among the Tories, and indeed in Liverpool had preferred them to the Whigs, and both to the Radicals.[1] Brougham's interest in him gave him a start, and the names of the committee of the new university are sufficient to show how wide the circle was into which he was received. We find the names of the Rt. Hon. James Abercrombie, Lord Auckland, Alexander Baring, George Birkbeck, Thomas Campbell, Viscount Dudley, Isaac Goldsmid, Olinthus Gregory, George Grote, Joseph Hume, the Marquis of Lansdowne, Zachary Macaulay, Sir James Mackintosh, James Mill, the Duke of Norfolk, Lord John Russell, Benjamin Shaw, John Smith, William Tooke, Henry Warburton, Henry Waymouth, John Whishaw and Thomas Wilson as well as that of Henry Brougham himself.[2] A number of these became firm friends of Panizzi's, and the gatherings at Lansdowne House added to his acquaintances. The famous dinners given by the Rt. Hon. Thomas Grenville, dignified and exquisite, most probably formed the habit of dining out for which Antonio Panizzi was noted throughout almost the whole of his long life in London. There is one other friendship to which we must refer at this period of Panizzi's life, and that is with a man whose connection with Foscolo was closer and longer than that of any other Englishman, William Stewart Rose. Rose was living in Brighton when Panizzi came to London, and in constant touch with the Italian exiles there, of whom Pecchio and Berchet were old friends of Panizzi's ; and his letters in the British Museum cover the years from 1828 to 1836. The letters are written in Italian until 1830, when Panizzi's English is so good as to cause Rose to renounce the foreign tongue ; and they address Panizzi as 'Professore' until Berchet tells him to omit the title. The very frequent greetings from Madame Zorzi show that Panizzi must have been a fairly regular visitor to Brighton, although we have no definite knowledge of his accepting Rose's many invitations to stay with him. As one would expect, the early letters deal chiefly with literary matters, requests for books and discussions on the *Orlando Furioso*, which study engrossed both correspondents. Apparently the idea of publishing his lectures had occurred to Panizzi, as a means of making himself known ; and Rose encouraged him, although a little doubtful of the value of his advice from lack of know-

[1] *Epist.*, III., p. 465.
[2] From a letter from Gabriele Rossetti to Charles Lyell of Kinnordy of Dec. 11th, 1827.

ledge of conditions.[1] Rose helped him with suggestions as to his Early English reading, advising particularly metrical romances and of the prose only the *Morte d'Arthur*,[2] with a warning to distinguish between the stories of the Round Table and those of Charlemagne.[3] Panizzi was commissioned by Rose to seek him a suitable house in London, as the air of Brighton did not suit him, but the prices were too high for Rose's diminished resources.[4] A letter of August 1829 refers to Panizzi's visit in the summer and expresses thanks for a gift of two hams.[5] Rose had advised Panizzi to give the course of external lectures, and recommended Willis's Rooms, King Street, St. James's Square, where we know they were held, and in the following February he suggested repeating the same course in Brighton, where there was a sufficiently cultured society for it to be appreciated.[6] Panizzi was in Liverpool in the autumn of 1830, and Rose commented on his announcement of Huskisson's tragic death at the opening of the Manchester to Liverpool railway.[7] Most of the other letters deal with the edition of Ariosto, to which Rose contributed translations. He was warmly appreciative of its value, although he tactfully pointed out one or two misuses of words in the English text.

So far it would seem that Panizzi's interests were now entirely in his adopted country and that he had ceased to have anything to do with the affairs of his native Italy, but nothing could be further from the truth. Of all Italians who were exiled during the great *risorgimento* movement, few played a more important part than Antonio Panizzi. But his was rather a method of propaganda in the great country of free men that he had chosen for his home ; and by keeping in close touch with events in Italy, he was able to present the true state of things to the statesmen of Great Britain in a way that no one else could. He first consolidated his own position, and when his opinions had gained weight with them, he could influence them to support the great cause of the Independence of Italy. In the first years in London, while he was yet making his way, and it must always be kept in mind that Antonio Panizzi saw clearly the goal before him and had a breadth of outlook and strength of purpose which helped him finally to reach it, he kept himself free from the plotting and scheming of some of his companions in exile, but received their confidences and helped them with his sane sound reasoning. Rose wrote to him once in a way that showed appreciation of Panizzi's practical good sense. " Quantunque

---

[1] Panizzi Correspondence, Vol. I., fol. 125. B.M., Add. MSS. 36714.
[2] *ibid.*, fol. 128.   [3] *ibid.*, fol. 132.   [4] *ibid.*, fols. 136, 138.
[5] *ibid.*, fol. 143.   [6] *ibid.* fol. 160.   [7] *ibid.*, fol. 177.

io mi astenga dal parlar di rivoluzioni italiane co' vostri compatriotti, amerei assai di parlarne con voi quando ci trovassimo insieme." [1]

The departure of Santa Rosa for Greece in 1824 had, in a way, broken up the little group which had welcomed Panizzi on his arrival. Pecchio after his return to England, as we have seen, betook himself to York, and after his marriage, settled in Brighton. His letters to Panizzi bulk by far the most largely in the published correspondence and there are others among the manuscripts in the British Museum. The first reached Panizzi shortly after he had gone to Liverpool, and was a continuation of a discussion they had had together in London when several of the exiles had determined to join in founding a political and literary magazine, which by the date of Pecchio's letter, October 6th, 1824,[2] seemed to offer a chance of success that Santa Rosa's departure dissipated. There was a gap of some years in their correspondence after that, but Pecchio's admiration for his younger compatriot was sufficient to bridge the gulf. So many of their friends had returned to the more genial climate of the Continent, to France and Belgium if not to Italy, that there was the more reason for those who were left to keep together. Knowing Panizzi's friendship with Brougham, Pecchio saw the possibility of using it to inspire Brougham to a new philippic against the Austrian influence over the governments of the Italian states.[3] Not all Pecchio's letters dealt with politics. He was warm in his congratulations to Panizzi on the publication of his work on the Romantic Narrative Poets.[4] It is easy to comprehend the sympathy between the two exiles. They both saw the futility of small insurrections, and realized that a war was the only power to galvanize the different provinces of Italy into action. The central committee in Paris could do little at that unsettled time of French affairs, when the new government after the July Revolution was still not firmly established. The only possibility, then, was to wait in patience until their time came, and meanwhile to consolidate the forces of the refugees so that they would be of real help. Pecchio was perfectly clear about the powerlessness of individuals to change the lot of their country. The people must rise as a whole, and we know that years had to pass before defeat taught them the necessity of co-operation, and Mazzini's great work inspired them with a sense of nationality and of one-ness. Pecchio kept Panizzi well informed as regards the operations of the Paris committee, and acted towards him in the capacity which Panizzi afterwards filled between his native land and the British statesmen ;

[1] *ibid.*, Vol. XIV., fol. 340. B.M., Add. MSS. 36727.
[2] *Lettere ad A. P.*, pp. 51–3.   [3] *ibid.*, p. 75.   [4] *ibid.*, p. 76.

and both followed British politics with the keenest interest. The course of events in the rising in Central Italy of 1831 proved the sanity of Pecchio's arguments ; and who knows how great an influence he had over the young Modenese, whose hot blood might have led him into paths that would have meant destruction for him, and would have prevented the great work that he achieved in after years ! The two patriots remained in close touch until Pecchio's death in 1835. Panizzi must have felt deeply the passing one by one of the men he had looked up to as the leaders of the liberal movement in Italy, men who had initiated the struggle for life which was to last so long before it ended in victory. With Ferdinando Dal Pozzo Panizzi evidently kept in touch, although the references to him are few. We know he helped the young professor in his search for a suitable assistant, and that they met from time to time as long as Dal Pozzo remained in London. Nothing is more interesting in Panizzi's relations with his fellow exiles than the mode of their address. Ugoni, Berchet and the other friends of his youth maintain the intimate *tu* ; the older men, the leaders of the Revolution of 1821 whose position compelled respect, though mingled with the utmost friendliness, and whom Panizzi had only known personally in their exile, use *voi* ; and with very few is the stately, distant *Lei* the form adopted, but of these the Cavaliere Dal Pozzo is one. It is a significant fact in Panizzi's case, for his sympathies were quick and whole-hearted.

The years that elapsed until his appointment to the Keepership of the Printed Books in 1836, marked Panizzi's greatest activity as a man of letters. Creative literature was not his bent, and the works that came from his pen arose nearly all out of his other interests. He arrived in England with his reputation to make, and with a strong determination to make it. His first production was an article on the Holy Alliance for the *Edinburgh Review* in July 1824, written in Italian and translated. The same year saw the mocking reply to the document sent to him by the *Ispettore ed Esattore di Finanze* at Reggio, demanding payment for the expenses of his accusation, sentence and execution *in contumaciam*. Panizzi's admiration for Foscolo's *Commedia di Dante Alighieri*, and his longing to help the great poet in his distress, inspired him to write an article on the book for the *Westminster Review*. As a matter of fact there is little of criticism of Foscolo's work in it, but a great deal about Italy in general and the unifying influence of Dante. One feels that the young reviewer is overawed by the greatness of his author. This was his first work in English for publication,[1] and it

[1] Fagan, I., p. 67.

appeared in the January number of 1827. The following year saw the reviews of three books in the *Foreign Review and Continental Miscellany*, one of which was Gabriele Rossetti's *Dante*. Panizzi's criticism of Rossetti's theory fanned the author's animosity, already roused by his loss of the professorship of Italian ; and the full result of this was apparent in the attack on Panizzi by Keightley in 1835 in a so-called review of Panizzi's *Italian Romantic Poetry*, where the reviewer embraced Rossetti's cause for personal revenge. The year 1828 saw the publication of two books for use in the teaching of Italian to his students, an *Elementary Grammar* and a book of *Extracts from Italian Prose Writers*. Four years later an article on the " Political Condition of the Italian State " appeared in the *Edinburgh Review* ; and then 1834 marked the completion of the edition of the Romantic Narrative Poets, in nine volumes, which was the great literary achievement of his life. The full title of the work is the *Orlando Innamorato di Bojardo : Orlando Furioso di Ariosto : with an Essay on the Romantic Narrative Poetry of the Italians : Memoirs and Notes by Antonio Panizzi*, and it represents the fruit of the study begun in 1824, which first expressed itself in the lectures in Liverpool, and continued to engross the author for the next ten years. The first volume was dedicated to Roscoe, to whom Panizzi was so deeply indebted for his start in Liverpool ; and numerous letters of thanks prove that the author repaid many of the kindnesses shown him in England by presenting copies to his friends. In 1835 Panizzi published one edition of Bojardo's sonnets which he dedicated to the Rt. Hon. Thomas Grenville, and to this we shall refer later.

The result of Panizzi's thoroughness in his method of learning English was soon apparent in his style. His first letters to the Warden of London University are laboured in expression, and contain un-English turns of expression and even mistakes in spelling. The style becomes easier after a while and the last letters are free from all foreign idiom. At first his writing showed a tendency to verbosity and heaviness which it lost as he advanced in years and experience. He lacked the sense of *le mot juste* which Foscolo possessed to a remarkable degree, and this quite apart from any consideration of Italian or English. Panizzi's real love of English life and institutions, combined with his great natural adaptability, soon brought about an English trend of thought which expressed itself naturally in a purely English dress. The later correspondence shows complete mastery of his medium, or rather complete unconsciousness that it is not native to him. Only at very rare intervals a word betrays hesitation, but generally it is not more than one finds in the case of those whose reading is chiefly in a foreign tongue, or who have lived much out of England. Perhaps it is the same hesitation which prompted his inordinate love of colons in his writings. At this distance of time it is not possible to judge of the fluency of his speech, but it must have been such as to make his hearers forget the foreigner in their contact with his mind. Certain peculiarities, however, he seems to have retained and one was an inability to pronounce that bugbear of foreigners, the English *th*.[1]

The appointment to the Keepership involved residence at the Museum, and Panizzi had to remove from the rooms at 2 Gower Street which he had occupied since he first arrived in London to take up the professorship at the University. From the moment of the great change in his position, he set out to justify the choice of the Trustees by giving his whole tremendous energy and industry to the furtherance of the work of the Museum. Quick decision, an iron will, impatience of stupidity and a lightning directness of attack made Panizzi's task no easier in dealing with his fellow workers. His physical strength was given to few men and what he exacted from himself, he expected also of others. Unfortunately there was a complete lack of sympathy between him and the Principal Librarian, Sir Henry Ellis, who was then only sixty years of age, but unprogressive, even undecided in character, although control on both sides enabled them to work together for nineteen years. While Panizzi was still an assistant librarian, he was called upon to give evidence before the Select Committee on the British Museum of 1835–6,[2] and had an opportunity to express his views as to the purpose and utility of the institution, which after years of determined struggle on his part were at last accepted as the principle for which the Museum stood in the life of the community. The subject of Panizzi's work at the British Museum has been dealt with so fully by his two biographers, Fagan and Cowtan, who as colleagues had an inside knowledge of affairs and a vital interest in that part of his life, that it would be superfluous to do more than refer to it here. One of the first tasks he had to perform was the superintending of the removal of the library of printed books from Montague House to the new building prepared for them, and he did this in person, watching over the treasures with an eagle eye, and scolding in no measured terms any of his subordinates who handled them carelessly or allowed a book to fall.[3] The stupendous task was performed without any interruption to the readers. The other great matter to which Panizzi's attention was called, was the preparation of a catalogue.

[1] Brooks, p. 161.   [2] Fagan, I., p. 146.   [3] Cowtan, p. 25.

His views on the subject were strong and his condemnation of Sir Henry Ellis's system equally so. In 1839 the rules drawn up by Panizzi and his colleagues in the library for the preparation of the new general catalogue were sanctioned by Parliament, and published two years later. The question of the catalogue being settled satisfactorily, Panizzi gave his mind to determining the deficiencies in the library, and embodied the result of his investigations in a report issued in 1845. The Trustees forwarded it to the Treasury, with the statement of their opinion of Panizzi's qualifications for assuming the responsibility of a large increase in expenditure in the purchase of printed books. The reply of the Treasury was a preliminary grant of £10,000, which was followed by an annual grant of the same amount.[1] It is not difficult to imagine the enormous increase in work that the purchase of many new books entailed, and Panizzi spared no ounce of his great strength in developing the library as a National Collection worthy of the name. The library was his life, although even in these years he had some moments to spare for the cultivation of his ever-increasing circle of friends and for the interests of his beloved Italy. Panizzi's name is also associated with two other libraries in London. As a member of the General Library Committee of London University, he was requested in 1833 to draw up a scheme for a catalogue, which he did within three days ;[2] and the Reform Club, of which he was a member until 1873, also appealed to his professional knowledge, and committed the cataloguing of its library to his care. Panizzi's connection with the Reform Club is an interesting one. His great friend, the Rt. Hon. Edward Ellice, was its founder in 1836, and its purpose was to promote social intercourse among the Reformers of the United Kingdom. It was determined from the beginning to form a library which should be notable, and very soon subscriptions to buy books and gifts of books made the collection worthy of a systematic classification. Naturally, Panizzi, who was one of their own members, was asked to advise the Library Sub-Committee, along with Vardon, the Librarian of the House of Commons. Panizzi and two other members prepared a list of the most necessary books to procure, and when the increased collection had to be catalogued, the expert advice of the Keeper of the Printed Books at the British Museum was sought. The help was willingly given, and seven rules drawn up for the compiling of the catalogue. Knowing Panizzi's principles, it is unnecessary to add that the plan

[1] Fagan, I., p. 173.
[2] University of London. Minutes of General Library Committee, Oct. 28th, 1833, quoted by Brooks, p. 49.

L

provided for a written catalogue, and the printed catalogue followed only in 1883.[1]

One of the finest collections of books in the country was the library brought together by the Rt. Hon. Thomas Grenville in the course of years of discriminating purchase. The enjoyment of a sinecure office had made it possible for him to expend a large fortune on the formation of his library, which he generously made available to any scholars who wished to consult it. Panizzi's connection with Grenville was fostered by, if it did not originate in, the former's study of Bojardo, of whom Grenville had several rare editions. On the conclusion of the publication of his major work in 1834, Panizzi was inspired to issue a special edition of only fifty copies of the sonnets of Bojardo, which appeared in 1835 under the title *Sonetti e Canzone del Poeta Clarissimo, Matteo Maria Bojardo, Conte di Scandiano*, and which he dedicated in gratitude, *all' onorevolissimo signor Tommaso Grenville, Consiglier privato di S.M.* As he said in the dedicatory epistle prefixed to the edition, no occupation had ever been dearer to him than that one, which had rescued the works of the Count of Scandiano from oblivion, and at the same time had guided him in memory, by its allusions, to his native province of Modena, which he never expected to see again.[2] With exquisite tact Grenville had ventured to forward to Panizzi, in the letter expressing his pleasure that the edition, of which he had just received a proof copy, was to be dedicated to him, a draft on Coutts' bank for £100.[3] Panizzi appreciated the kind thought, but returned the draft. One feels that he had a feeling of peculiar tenderness towards this edition of Bojardo, and an artist's love of a thing of beauty. Grenville's letter of thanks when the volume reached him is interesting in that it expresses his point of view regarding the usefulness of his own library.[4] Personally Grenville was a man of singular charm and delighted in the society of friends. The dinners in his house to which a few chosen friends were invited, followed by quiet games of whist, must have done much to impress Panizzi with the dignity and peaceful happiness that attended his declining years. Grenville conceived a strong liking for his young Italian friend and encouraged him in every way in his new office. He

---

[1] *Catalogue of the Library of the Reform Club, with revised historical introduction.* Printed for the Members. London, 2nd edit., 1894.

[2] From the copy of the work, No. 21, presented with an autograph inscription to the British Museum by Panizzi himself.

[3] Panizzi Correspondence, Vol. I., fol. 353. B.M., Add. MSS. 36714.

[4] *ibid.*, fol. 384. See App. III.D.

was one of the Trustees of the Museum and took pride in being the first to announce to Panizzi any decision which affected his well-being.   Panizzi's natural curiosity as to the ultimate destination of Grenville's marvellous library could not be altogether hidden, and his opinion of the value to the community of the National Collection was unquestionably a strong factor in deciding Grenville to alter the will he had made bequeathing his collection to his nephew, the Duke of Buckingham, and to leave it to the Trustees of the British Museum.   One Sunday in November 1845, Panizzi called to pay his respects to Grenville, and the old gentleman, who was then ninety years of age, confided to him what he had done.   Curiously enough Panizzi wrote down on his return home, as far as he could, a verbatim report of the conversation, and deposited the document with W. R. Hamilton, the antiquary, one of the Trustees of the Museum, who opened it two years later on the day following Grenville's death.   Two wishes Grenville expressed to Panizzi, that his collection should be kept unbroken and that the remainder of the catalogue, which was incomplete, should be printed ; and Panizzi lost no time in recommending the best means for their observance.   He superintended the removal of the books to the Museum and took what measures he could to insure their preservation, although it was some three years before the Trustees were persuaded to provide adequate accommodation or even protection for them.[1]   The loss of his old friends, those whose kindly, almost fatherly interest in him, had removed much of the bitterness of his exile, affected Panizzi the more as he had no ties but those of friendship.   Five days after Grenville's death, he wrote a long letter to Mrs. Rutherfurd,[2] wife of his great friend, the Lord Advocate of Scotland, and told her of his sorrow.   " A man alone in the world—a foreigner—without any other ties of affection or of blood concentrates all his feelings in his friends & to lose one of them is a greater loss to him than it is to others whose heart is filled by other objects." [3]

The period of Panizzi's life between 1837 and 1848, was one of the

[1] Fagan, I., pp. 267–79.

[2] Not to Lord Rutherfurd, as Fagan states on p. 280 of his work, where he quotes this portion of the letter with some slight inaccuracies.

[3] From the Panizzi letters among the Rutherfurd papers in the keeping of the Faculty of Advocates, Edinburgh, to whom I am indebted for permission to examine the correspondence.   This passage is from the letter referred to in note 2, above.   A number of letters were lent by Lord Rutherfurd's nephew to Louis Fagan for the purpose of his biography of Panizzi.

greatest industry. Fagan records his working sixteen hours a day. No detail in the working of his department was too small for his attention. His large circle of friends made an exacting call on time for social duties, and the prominent position of most of them in the world of politics increased his natural tendency to follow enthusiastically not only the affairs of the Continent, affecting his native Italy, but also the domestic affairs of Britain. He was constantly being appealed to, to use his influence in finding posts for others, to procure introductions, in fact to give help in countless ways. His official duties brought him into contact with many interesting people, who often interrupted unwittingly his more serious work, which he had to make up afterwards. His correspondence was enormous, but one feels that it was a source of great pleasure to him rather than a labour, and that letter-writing was a substitute for interchanging visits, when distance made that impossible. It is a great tribute to Panizzi's personal attractions and to his adaptability, that he was able to take his place as an equal among the leaders of the social and political world of his day. His tastes were innately aristocratic, and the formality and stateliness of English society made a strong appeal to him. As a diner-out he became notorious, and he had himself great gifts as a host. His epicurean tendencies were no secret, and good wine was a joy to him that not even the gout which attacked him in his early fifties could destroy. Mérimée often added the excellent wine of the south to the inducements that France could offer, to tempt the great librarian to a well-earned holiday. Panizzi's holidays were certainly well-earned but they were also well spent. The Continent often claimed him[1] and he made several journeys to Germany in the earlier days, combining duty with his pleasure by examining famous libraries. In June of 1845 the longed-for permission to enter Austrian territory unmolested was granted him, and an extended leave of three months enabled him to visit Vienna in addition to leading German towns, before proceeding to Italy. In Vienna he met his old persecutor, Francis IV., Duke of Modena, and had an interview with him, when they settled old scores.[2] An attempt to extract permission to visit Modena, unrestricted and unfettered, proved vain, and Panizzi was forced to see his old friends at Mantua and then approach Parma by a circuitous route to avoid his native duchy. The tour, in spite of hindrances, was a delightful one, and he wrote enthusiastically to Rutherfurd of the kindness of his friends, and of the beauty of the country through which he had passed. He was greeted effusively on

[1] See App III.E, 2.   [2] Fagan, II., p. 191.

his return home, for his London friends had suffered no small anxiety on his account. Most often he travelled north and many were the happy holidays he spent with friends in Scotland. The letters which he wrote to the Rutherfurds tell of delightful visits to Craigie Hall and later, after 1846,[1] to Lauriston Castle, Rutherfurd's beautiful home near Cramond on the Firth of Forth. There was much in common between the two men, and the letters hint at a love of even boisterous fun, which we know never quite left Panizzi. One joke Panizzi kept up against his Scottish friend all his life. We imagine that on several occasions Rutherfurd had been guilty of posting letters to Panizzi on Saturday, expecting that they would be delivered the following day. What serious inconvenience had been caused by their non-delivery in London before Monday we cannot tell, but from quite early days the joke finds a place in the letters. It is quite evident that bound up with it, is a sly hit at Scottish Sabbatarianism, as a Sunday delivery was then in force in the north. Panizzi sends reminders as to the posting of letters on Saturdays in letters to Mrs. Rutherfurd, to be passed on to her husband. When Andrew Rutherfurd, nephew, wrote in November 1854, giving him news of his uncle's illness, Panizzi replied—

Of course you will write to-day so that I may get the letter by the early post of Monday & that of to-morrow in the afternoon of that day. I am, however, sure, whatever he may boast of now, that your uncle did not know that letters are not delivered in London on Sundays. It is a point in which I have always found him very dull. Please report to him the information.[2]

And again, writing to his friend's nephew he says :

My dear Andrew, A thousand thanks for your regular & *favorable* reports. I got this morg., that of Saturday, and this afternoon that of yesterday. You wrote on Saturday probably not knowing that letters are not delivered in London on Sundays. I have often reminded of this His Lordship,[3] your uncle—a clever & well informed man in other respects, but who never seemed to recollect this simple fact. And had he not neglected your education most shamefully he would have told you of that : but he is most perverse on that subject of non-delivery of Sunday letters : he neither knows it nor will he tell others. I luckily never forget it, but if I had he never would have reminded me of it.

[1] Date of purchase of Lauriston.
[2] Rutherfurd Correspondence—Letter to A. R., nephew, dated Nov. 25th, 1854.
[3] Rutherfurd took his seat on the bench as Lord Rutherfurd in 1851.

I beg you will give [him] these few lines to read & remain, Yours ever affy. A. PANIZZI.

N.B.—Letters are not delivered in London, but in the Country & provinces—at Edinburgh for instance—they are delivered *in a sort of way*.[1]

To Lord Rutherfurd himself he wrote in August of 1854 on the same subject, " Damn it ! don't you know it yet after having been told so often, ye thick-skulled mon ! " after stating the fact in a previous letter as one " wherein we show our religious feeling—of which you Scots have no notion ".[2]

The earliest letters to Rutherfurd were written in Italian, but as they grew more intimate it was superseded by English. Rutherfurd apparently mapped out one of Panizzi's first tours to the Highlands during a visit he paid to Craigie Hall, and Panizzi wrote from Dunkeld a letter of thanks for the hospitality he had received, and intimating his intention of visiting Inverness.[3] One regrets that Panizzi kept no diary, for the tale of his wanderings would have been an interesting one. At one time he projected a tour with Rutherfurd to Sutherland-shire, and probably paid many country-house visits with him. Craigie Hall and Lauriston were always a great attraction, and Panizzi looked forward eagerly to the peaches and dry champagne of the former, and, announcing a visit to Edinburgh after a short stay in Liverpool, said, " One of the reasons of my hastening my arrival is the hearing the progress made by the peaches and apricots which might be poached if I don't come to watch them." [4] During these visits Panizzi would meet the legal luminaries of Scotland, and there are many passing references in his letters to prove this. One of the subjects frequently discussed seems to have been that of the Scottish kirk, and Panizzi took a whole-hearted interest in a matter which affected individual freedom. He mingled a certain amount of good-natured banter with it of course, and once wrote to Mrs. Rutherfurd, *à propos* of a mistaken reference, " I was thinking of the Kirk as I always do when I write to Scotland." [5] He alluded in one letter to a plan he had of writing an article on the " Kirk question ! ! ! which will appear on the first of October—not caring a damn for the parsons but a great deal for the laymen who have taken an interest in that question ".[6] It must have been a joke among the friends at Lauriston

---

[1] Rutherfurd Correspondence—dated ' Monday '.
[2] *ibid.* Letters to Lord Rutherfurd.   [3] *ibid.* See App. III.E, 1.
[4] *ibid.*, dated ' Wed., August 6th '.   [5] *ibid.*, dated ' Nov. 11th '
[6] *ibid.*, dated ' Wed., Aug. 16th '—no year, but anterior to 1846.

to teach Panizzi the local dialect and he wrote once to Rutherfurd, endeavouring to persuade him to come to London to take part in a certain Parliamentary discussion, " Altho' not a Scotchman—altho' I speak wonderfully well the Scottish language—I take no small interest in this matter as I feel that, seriously, you are the boy to knock these fellows down & do yourself no small good ; and who the devil could, should or would enjoy it more than your *Tognetto* ? " [1] Scottish words occur every now and then in the letters. He speaks of young Andrew Rutherfurd's ' bairn ' for example. His love of Scotland was sufficient to make him employ in after years a ' Scotchman ' as a servant.[2]

At an early stage in the friendship between Rutherfurd and Panizzi, at least we infer that the letter is early as it is written in Italian, Panizzi felt that he could invite himself to Craigie Hall without fear of being misunderstood. " Se siete certo di esser a Londra il 19 Agosto ci vedremo dopo ; ma se per caso accadesse che non veniste son mezzo tentato esser da voi circa il nove Agosto e restar con voi otto o dieci giorni. Vengo a posto per veder voi e non per altro, e m' invito a Craigie Hall. Non ho mai osato far tanto in vita mia con altri amici in Gran Bretagna. Che ve ne pare ? " [3] There was a warm sympathy between Panizzi and Mrs. Rutherfurd, whom he calls " the best of the two inhabitants of St. Colme St.",[4] and quite a considerable number of letters in the family correspondence are addressed to her. He sent her anecdotes and jokes from time to time, and announced that " Brougham and Leader have bought a forest of 600 acres for £1300 near Cannes with plenty of boars in it", with the comment, "Bores in London are to be had for nothing ".[5] One note is characteristically to the point : " Dear Mrs. Rutherfurd, A friend asked Lord Stanley how he felt with regard to his late colleagues ?—Your question reminds me of a story I heard once, said his Lordship.—On examining some girls at a charity school the question was put : Where do good people go after death ? They go to Heaven. And what do they do there ? They rejoice at seeing the bad ones burn. In haste, Yours truly A.P." [6]

No reference has been made to the long letters containing news of contemporary politics and criticisms of various new cabinets. Fagan

---

[1] *ibid.*, dated ' Tuesday '.
[2] *ibid.*, to Andrew Rutherfurd, nephew, dated ' Mar. 30th, 1864 '.
[3] *ibid.*, to Lord Rutherfurd, dated ' lunedì, 26 luglio '.
[4] *ibid.*, to Mrs. Rutherfurd. Reference to 9 St. Colme Street, the Rutherfurds' town house.
[5] *ibid.*   [6] *ibid.*, dated ' Tuesday ', probably 1846.

has quoted most of them in full and at this date they are perhaps less interesting than the more personal letters, once their existence has indicated Panizzi's constant and living interest in the government of his adopted country. Those referring to the Royal Commission of 1847–9, however, demand a little attention. Rutherfurd was a member of the commission, and therefore Panizzi appealed to him for information as to whether the question of the catalogue was to be considered first, or the Secretary's department, in order that he might prepare his papers.[1] The letter is sixteen pages long and contains a number of criticisms. The ending " Adieu, my dearest friend ", shows clearly Panizzi's feelings towards Rutherfurd, and it is doubly painful therefore to read the later letter after the enquiry is finished, in which he wrote of Rutherfurd's change of manner towards him : " I should not have had so strong an affection for you nor should I have deserved yours had I not felt the great change which has taken place in your manner towards me : I avoided speaking of it, not thro' pride, because I cannot have any with such a friend, but thro' heaviness of heart & because such things do not bear either arguing or remonstrating—they are to be felt." [2] He had burnt Rutherfurd's letter to him and suggested that the same fate should meet this expression of his feelings, and that the matter should then be no more discussed between them. The tremendous ordeal which he had just undergone, although he had emerged from it victorious, had worn him out, and probably made him super-sensitive as regards the attitude of others towards him. The difference seems to have been cleared up satisfactorily, however, for in a later note, repeating his demand merely for justice, he wrote, " It is a great comfort to find that all my friends have not turned against me—above all others you." [3]

A memorial addressed by some eminent scientists who were dissatisfied with the constitution of the governing body, to the Prime Minister on March 10th, 1847, was the cause of a Royal Commission being appointed to enquire into the grievances. The Commission met three times in 1847, and in 1848 it was found necessary for a more expeditious despatch of business, to alter its conditions. Lord Ellesmere presided and among the members were Lord Seymour, Lord Canning and Andrew Rutherfurd, Lord Advocate of Scotland. As Fagan points out, Panizzi's own ideals of what a national library should be, had so spread since his appointment to the Keepership eleven years before, ' that he was tried by a standard created by

---

[1] Rutherford Correspondence dated ' Jan. 11th '.
[2] ibid., dated ' Sunday ' (1849 ?).   [3] ibid., note undated.

himself'. The chief points of attack were the Secretaryship, an office formed some nineteen years before, and which had proved in the working to be rather destructive than otherwise of the authority of the Principal Librarian ; and the library itself. The duties of the secretary seemed to be so light as to be capable of being performed as before the creation of the office, by the Principal Librarian ; although by a spirit of contradiction not uncommon, an assistant secretary had recently been appointed. The recommendation of the Commissioners in regard to this point were obvious. The enquiry into the state of the library was directed mainly to the delay in the preparation of the new printed catalogue, which we know was a piece of work that Panizzi regarded as useless and wasteful of time and money. Contradictory instructions from the committee had in great measure nullified the usefulness of Panizzi's carefully drawn-up rules, sanctioned by Parliament in 1839. He was only too glad to be given an opportunity of proving the superiority in simplicity of preparation and capability of expansion of a manuscript catalogue, over a printed catalogue prepared alphabetically. The plan of movable slips pasted on the leaf was suggested and adopted later.[1] Panizzi's antagonism to a printed catalogue neglected its value to other libraries as a book of reference, but after all his aim was first to set his own house in order. The last word in library cataloguing has not yet been said, and the twentieth century has seen the spread of the Dewey system of decimal classification and the system of card indexing. The press had been the medium of a fairly persistent attack on Panizzi in the course of years, and the official enquiry gave his assailants a chance to voice their grievances. Cowtan reports Panizzi's own words of challenge, " I have a request to make of the Commissioners ", he said, " which is, that they will examine the complainers. I have had the honour of laying before the Commissioners the names of parties complaining. I want those gentlemen who make complaints anonymously to *come to this table, and state the facts that they have to complain of, and I pledge myself to answer their complaints.* I shall be very sorry if they do not make their complaints here." [2] The challenge was widely accepted, and yet Panizzi was able to refute or explain all the charges made against him. He had the warm support of a number of men of standing, however, John Wilson Croker, Dr. Maitland, Librarian at Lambeth Palace, Hallam, de Morgan, Cureton, the Royal Trustee and others.

[1] Fagan, II., Ch. VIII., ' The Royal Commission, 1847–9 '.
[2] Cowtan, p. 40.

The report of the Commissioners was a vindication of Panizzi, and they recorded their opinion that, " Whatever be the judgment formed on points at issue, the minutes of evidence must be admitted to contain frequent proofs of the acquirements and abilities, the manifestation of which in subordinate office led to Mr. Panizzi's promotion to that which he now holds under circumstances which, in our opinion, founded on documentary evidence, did credit to the Trustees of the day ".[1]

It is an interesting and significant fact that in the many tributes to Panizzi from eminent men at the time of his appointment as Principal Librarian in 1856, two qualities are mentioned time and again, in addition to the tribute to his great talents and stupendous energy, and these are his unusual administrative powers and his strict discipline. " I have never known any one in authority so strict and precise in maintaining order and discipline, so rigid and exact in requiring the full amount of duties to be performed, who, at the same time, had the singular happiness of gaining the respect and esteem, and receiving the warm attachment and affection of all those placed under his authority," said Dr. Cureton [2] ; and W. R. Hamilton spoke of his " most happy mode of extracting from all under him the greatest amount of efficient service, and of exacting the strictest regularity of attendance, great impartiality, a deep sense of moral justice, and an honest devotion of his whole time to the public service ".[3] He had a very strong sense of justice, which was at the root of his devotion to duty and his loyalty to his subordinates. It was only natural that so strict a disciplinarian should have enemies, even within his own house. Unswerving obedience to rules for the common good is not attained without arousing a certain antagonism in those who are lazy or indifferent to their duty. Among these Panizzi was not popular, but for that he cared little. No desire for popularity ever kept him from expressing his opinion where correction was needed. The resentment felt by those who came under the lash of his tongue was probably all the greater as he was a ' foreigner '. It is more galling to be brought to book in one's own land by a native of another. On the other hand the real workers valued his example, and realized that their services were appreciated. Enthusiasm begets enthusiasm. Panizzi's quick temper, of which so much has been made, was recognized by his friends, but they loved him in spite of it, knowing the warm heart of the man. In the early days in London he stamped his letters with a seal bearing the device of a harp with the motto *je réponds à qui me touche*, which

[1] Cowtan, p. 44.   [2] ibid., p. 63.   [3] ibid., p. 64.

expressed him well in more ways than one. He was too ready to rush into print when attacked. Letters to *The Times* only produced an impression of irascibility in the minds of his new fellow citizens, which is not yet obliterated. Lady Dacre suggested tactfully the unwisdom of this tendency, while acknowledging a copy of his reply to Keightley's attack in the *Foreign Quarterly Review*. She speaks of

your very clever & spirited ansr. to your *defamer*, whose name I have forgot, having sent the paper on to Mrs. Lawrence, who speaks of it in a letter I recd. yesterday with equal admiration—& astonishment at the elegance & correctness of your English, (putting us natives all to the blush !). She agrees however with us in the only critique we should presume to make—that the *Defamer* did not deserve anything so well written. You had the right so completely on your side, that, had I been at your elbow, I should have tried to check your pen, & to have induced you, if you honor'd him with any reply at all, to state the simple facts in the fewest words possible, with most contemptuous civility. [1]

With this readiness to take fire at the slightest fancied insult, however, Panizzi had an astonishing modesty where honours to himself were concerned. He wrote to the Warden of London University in September 1828, before he began his work there, " never mind *doctoring* me when you write. I now am divorced from Justinian, and so mine is but an empty title, like that of King of Cyprus and Jerusalem taken by so many Sovereigns, at whom I take the liberty to laugh." [2] He liked to be ' Panizzi ' *tout court*, to his friends ; Signor on no account, and preferably not Mr. Panizzi. When Napoleon III. decorated him in Paris with the cross of the Legion of Honour, on his return from Naples in 1851, he wrote to Rutherfurd and to Haywood, and said that it made him miserable. In 1855 Victor Emmanuel presented him with the Order of St. Maurice and Lazarus of Sardinia ; and he would not ask the necessary permission to accept either.[3] We know that he twice refused a knighthood, before the Queen finally made him a K.C.B. in 1869.

The more one studies the life and work of Antonio Panizzi, the more clearly do his lovable qualities emerge. There are constant evidences of his generosity, always quietly and tactfully shown. His care for his subordinates was unceasing, and he worked continuously until he obtained better conditions for them and an adequate scale of salary. The hot-headedness which was characteristic of him in his

[1] Panizzi Correspondence, Vol. I., fols. 416–17. B.M., Add. MSS. 36714.
[2] University College MSS., No. 940.   [3] Fagan, II., p. 113.

youth, and which aroused so many antipathies in later years, never stood between him and his real friends. His love for children and talent for winning their confidence is revealed in many little allusions in his correspondence. One of his earliest child friends in London was Jane Frances Bickersteth, Lord Langdale's daughter, who kept in touch with him and stayed at his house in after years, when she was the Countess Teleki. Lady Dacre's letters abound with messages about her grandchildren, and Panizzi went to see them when their parents and grandparents were in Ireland. We shrewdly suspect that Panizzi was the donor of the spade without which Frankie could not be induced to bathe [1] ; and he is considered a suitable guest to accompany the Dacres on a picnic to Greenwich with a party of children. " Tuesday is my granddaughter's birthday and Grandpapa insists upon your being one of his *convives* to celebrate the anniversary." [2] He was a good friend to the two Fagans, whose parents were in Naples, and Louis Fagan seem to have been a frequent visitor at his house during his school holidays. He took the boy back to Naples with him in 1851 and they appear to have made excursions together there. Fagan even visited the prisons with him. That he was a favourite with the Prince Imperial we gather from his letters from Mérimée ; and in the earliest days of his friendship with Gladstone, the latter's little boy was an attraction in the invitation.[3] When local schools refused to admit Settembrini's son, Panizzi brought him back with him to England, undertook all the responsibility of a guardian to the young Raffaele and even arranged to take him to Lauriston on holiday. After finding a suitable school for him in Yorkshire, it was a great disappointment that the boy was so wild as to necessitate his withdrawal.[4] Nothing would content him but to go to sea, and the story of his rescue of his father and the other Neapolitan prisoners in 1859, is too well known to require repetition. Sir James Lacaita's son attracted Panizzi's attention, and he was glad to hear they won a certain cricket match, although he disapproved of the importance attached to cricket and other games in the English schools.[5] When Garibaldi came to London and was fêted as few men have ever been in England, Panizzi included his young sons in the invitation he gave him to dine with him.[6]

Panizzi's literary output during his tenure of the Keepership of the

---

[1] Panizzi Correspondence, Vol. XIII., fol. 39. B.M., Add. MSS. 36726.

[2] *ibid.*, Vol. II., fol. 31. , B.M., Add. MSS. 36715.

[3] Brooks, p. 69. [4] See App. III.E, 4 and 5.

[5] Brooks, p. 158. [6] *ibid.*, p. 152.

Printed Books was naturally considerably less than in the previous years. He published a report *On the Supply of Printed Books from the Library to the Reading-room* in 1846 for private circulation, and in 1851 *A Short Guide to that Portion of the Printed Books now open to the Public.* A number of articles were written for periodicals, mostly dealing with topics of the day. In 1838 he wrote on the " Congress of Verona " for the *British and Foreign Review*, five years later two articles appeared in the same review, one on the " Spanish Question ", and the other on " Amari's History of Sicily and the Sicilian Vespers ". Amari had used his works as a vehicle for attack against the Neapolitan Government and in consequence had to go into exile. He lived in Paris from 1842 till 1848, and returned to take part in the Sicilian Revolution. A letter from Panizzi to a friend in Paris, containing a criticism and appreciation of Amari's History, and a kindly offer of pecuniary assistance, was passed on to the author and formed the beginning of their friendship. Amari was a man of great independence of character and purity of motives, and he refused Panizzi's offer of help, willing rather to stint himself of almost the necessaries of life, than be a burden on others. His first letter expressed his gratitude, and gave a very full account of the state of things in Sicily and of the oppression which stifled her youth.[1] Later he wrote seeking Panizzi's help in finding him a post in England which would leave him time to devote to his beloved history of Sicily, and thus to exercise an influence over his compatriots. In Paris there was no sale for anything but dramas and novels. Malta attracted him more than England on account of the climate.[2] Panizzi's review of his book was taken to Naples and Sicily by a friend, that it might extend its influence. Amari was sincerely grateful for the encouragement Panizzi had given him, and for the work he had obtained for him in the purchasing of Sicilian books and pamphlets for the British Museum. In passing, it is interesting to note that Panizzi formed a valuable collection of pamphlets dealing chiefly with Italian affairs, but also with English Education, economics, banking and other topics, for himself, which he either gave or bequeathed to Fagan. On the completion of his biography of his old friend and protector, Fagan presented these, some 430 in all in 24 volumes, to the Reform Club, in 1880. They were catalogued fully for the first time in 1920.[3] For a time the *North British Review* accepted a considerable number of articles from Panizzi, and there is an interesting letter to the editor, containing

---

[1] *Lettere ad A. P.*, p. 140.   [2] *ibid.*, p. 146.
[3] Reform Club. *Catalogue of Panizzi Pamphlets, 1880.*

suggestions for future numbers, among the letters to the Rutherfurd family in the Scottish National Library. The remarks and criticisms show a wonderful understanding of public wants in the matter of periodic literature ; but one wonders what Panizzi would have thought to-day when he stigmatized the 'forties as ' this age of light reading ' ! The most important of his contributions to this review was the article on the Post Office, dealing with the opening of Mazzini's letters in transit in 1844. The echoes of the storm that the violation of the trust placed in the postal service roused have not died away entirely yet. Carlyle took the matter up and wrote an indignant letter to *The Times*. We shall discuss later in connection with Mazzini this question which was so burning at the time.

A matter that aroused European interest for some four years was the one known as the ' Spanish Marriages ', in connection with which an underhand policy was pursued by Guizot, minister of France, which had less serious consequences than were anticipated at the time. The intrigues centred round the child queen of Spain and her sister, and the influence their eventual marriages would have on the balance of power in Europe. France feared the position that the choice of any but a Spanish or French consort for the queen would create ; and insisted on the descendants of the Bourbon Philip V. being the only eligible candidates. To please the other countries in Western Europe, however, the French king's sons were excluded. Britain's position was clearly stated to Guizot by Lord Aberdeen, then Foreign Secretary, as being that of not wishing to interfere in a matter which concerned Spain alone, unless the balance of power in Europe should be threatened by the choice of a French prince. It is a question whether British interference at the time might have been sufficient to prevent France from pursuing her underhand policy. Britain was accused of supporting the candidature of Prince Leopold of Saxe-Coburg, although it seems without real foundation. The candidates were finally limited to the queen's cousins, Don Francis d' Assise, Duke of Cadiz, and his brother Dón Enrique, Duke of Seville. As it turned out, the choice fell on Don Francis for the queen, and by intrigue the Duc de Montpensier for the Infanta. A promise was given to Britain that the marriage of the Infanta should not take place until the queen had given birth to several children, thus making sure that the balance of power would not be upset by any accession to the throne of Spain of a member of the French Royal House. By a trick the letter of the law was adhered to, in that the marriages were not simultaneous, but the spirit was disregarded, for they both took place on the same day, October 10th, 1846. Panizzi had been a friend of Thiers since 1840, and in 1845 had been his cicerone in England, and an unofficial advocate of this country's cause. He had brought about a meeting between him and Lord Palmerston ; it was therefore not surprising that both sides turned to Panizzi for inside information during the controversy that raged on this question of the Spanish Marriages. Panizzi's correspondence with Thiers was voluminous, and he seems to have been provided with the necessary documents to make clear the British position to Thiers, who could use his information to counteract the effect of Guizot's policy, which he in turn expounded in detail to Panizzi. Fagan has gone into the matter very fully and has quoted all Thiers' letters, so that this short reference suffices, to show that Panizzi played an important though unofficial part between Britain and the French opposition.

Various abortive risings in different parts of Italy had shown that the country as a whole was not yet ready for revolution ; but the election of a new Pope in June 1846, a man of mild temperament and kindly disposition, roused popular enthusiasm for the Papacy, which was crowned by his granting of a general amnesty a month after he was proclaimed Pope. His weakness showed itself, however, in the pledge attached to the pardon, to abstain for the future from political action. Hundreds of prisoners and exiles returned home, and there was a chance that the Pope might have the honour of bringing about the unity of Italy ; but though he loved the popularity, he was too timid to break as a temporal ruler with the Austrian Empire, and the chance was lost. In Piedmont the anti-Austrian feeling was spreading. Charles Albert permitted free discussion in the Scientific Congress which met at Genoa in 1846, and expression was given to the desire for independence and for the driving out of the foreign power from Italian territory. The Austrian occupation of Ferrara in 1847 united Italians of all provinces in a resolve to defend the Pope's dominions, and Metternich was obliged to withdraw his troops, yielding to the signs of the times and to strong pressure from the British Government. The Sicilian revolution in January of 1848, which was primarily a separatist movement, and resulted in hard fighting for a constitution, was followed by the rising in Naples which forced Ferdinand to grant a constitution at the end of the same month. The French revolution in February restored the republic, and revolts in Prussia and Hungary showed that the whole of Europe was seething with agitation. The Chartist riots in England were another expression of the same spirit, although the particular methods of attack that the Chartists adopted necessitated Panizzi's organizing the defence force of the British Museum. The other Italian states followed Naples, and Piedmont received Charles Albert's promise on February 8th. A few days later was Tuscany's turn and even the Pope, who was not unkindly disposed to the new movement, so long as it involved no bloodshed, was forced to grant concessions and appoint a cabinet with a majority of laymen.[1] The Cardinals adopted a constitution of their own devising and took the tricolour for the national flag. The next move in the great game was war with Austria. Hopes were high, and Austria was warned by Palmerston of the danger of her invading the free Italian states which France and Britain would protect. The Tobacco Riots in Milan the previous year had shown the temper of the people, and the Milanese prepared for a struggle but kept themselves well in hand. There were conflicts with the Austrian authorities in some of the smaller towns, and the Austrian general saw that war was inevitable and sent to Vienna for reinforcements. The Hungarian insurrection gave the Milanese their opportunity and they rose suddenly. A crowd of 20,000 citizens marched to the office of the Vice-Governor, demanded the disbanding of the police and the formation of a citizen guard. The leaders would have nothing but absolute independence. Barricades were thrown up, desperate fighting took place in the streets and the Austrians were driven out. The Five Days of Milan showed of what the Italians were capable. Panizzi kept in close touch with the movement in Italy, and, his hatred of the Austrians being in no wise diminished by his long residence in England, he took as active a part in affairs as he could. By keeping the Italian point of view always before the British statesmen with whom he was on terms of great intimacy, he was able to prevent any leanings towards Austria, which the Crown already favoured. Panizzi's old friend Giovanni Berchet was a member of the provisional government in Milan, and throughout the momentous year of 1848 they kept up a vigorous correspondence. They were of one mind in refusing to countenance a republic, and although the idea of Italy free and undivided was their ultimate goal, the time was not yet. The immediate necessity was a consolidation of their forces in the north, the fusion of Lombardy and Piedmont; and, as a constitutional monarchy was their ideal, Berchet overcame his old personal enmity to Charles Albert, and accepted him as the king who would be the best for his country. Panizzi's share in the great work was to influence English opinion in favour of a new state, which would compensate for the disintegration of Austria, and also provide

[1] Bolton King, *History of Italian Unity*, I., Ch. X.

a certain support against France in case of need.[1] Venice had proclaimed a republic under Daniele Manin, but had turned to Lombardy for help, which the imminent fusion with Piedmont was likely to make possible. The hesitation on the part of some of the Milanese to seek this necessary fusion was attributed to the malign influence of Mazzini and his supporters, many of whom were returned exiles. Berchet only voices the opposition that was spread in certain circles to Mazzini's doctrines. It is we who can judge of his great work, when the unity of Italy is complete, and prejudices are dead. Berchet was too near, and saw too clearly the dangers of schism. The help of republican France was scorned by the Constitutionalists.[2] *Italia farà da sè*, was the motto. Panizzi's replies to Berchet were long and detailed, and were passed on to the government. The work involved in the writing of such letters was enormous, and they were frequent, daily at times. The fusion with Piedmont hung fire for a while. The Milanese Government had not learned to sink their differences and delay was caused by a plebiscite. Berchet blamed republican propaganda for the opposition to Charles Albert in England, and admitted that he himself had buried the past.[3] Meanwhile Palmerston had refused the Austrian envoy any mediation, so long as the Austrians remained in either Lombardy or Venetia. The question of the future capital of the North Italian Kingdom was agitating a section of the Milanese people, although a matter of indifference to those who had a broad outlook. Curiously enough, Berchet asked Panizzi's opinion on the cession of Savoy to France as a means of preventing her invading Italian territory. He had great vision and some of his words could well be applied to the state of things to-day. He talked of the petty minds that followed an old policy with old methods, " e non s' accorgono che un' Europa nuova si prepara, la quale vuole vedute nuove di diplomazia, di politica, di relazioni internazionali ".[4]

Meanwhile the enthusiasm for the war was gaining daily in Piedmont. The Five Days of Milan decided the king. Cavour proclaimed that the supreme hour for the Sardinian monarchy had struck. He saw that the moment had come when the House of Savoy must take the lead. The people went into the war like the Crusaders of old, and the king gave them their flag, the tricolour with the cross of Savoy.[5]

> " Il verde, la speme tant' anni pasciuta ;
> Il roseo, la gioia d' averla compiuta ;
> Il bianco, la fede fraterna d' amor." [6]

---

[1] *Lettere ad A. P.*, p. 154.   [2] *ibid.*, p. 160.   [3] *ibid.*, p. 162.
[4] *ibid.*, p. 167.   [5] Solmi, *The Making of Modern Italy*.   [6] Berchet.

It is not for us here to go into the details of that disastrous campaign of 1848-9 which opened so gloriously, and for lack of good generalship ended in such disaster. The petty jealousies between the states, the lack of unity of command, the fatal indecision of the king, and many more causes contributed to the failure ; but out of the ashes of the sacrifice there rose a people that had learned a lesson, and when the next time came they found the strength that is in union.

Panizzi had come through great trials in these years. He had built up a tremendous organization at the British Museum, he had sustained a great ordeal in the enquiry of the Royal Commission and he had strained every nerve to help his native land, for which his affection never diminished. His unusual strength and energy had carried him through, but he was weary. The next fifteen years were to bring him yet more work, the building of the new reading room at the British Museum, but also great honours, the Principal Librarianship of the Museum, and at last his well-earned rest. Many of his old friends passed away but he made new friendships, with Prosper Mérimée, with William Ewart Gladstone and others, which compensated him in a measure for the loss. And he was to live, one of the very few of the early patriots, to see the consummation of their great desire, the independence of a united Italy. We leave him however, at the end of the first big Italian revolution, in a despondent mood and worn with the labours of the past years and the strain of his long ordeal. His wrist was troubling him in spite of a visit to Ems for treatment, and he wrote sadly to Mrs. Rutherfurd :

I feel a great disinclination to do anything. I have learnt so well at my expense that all my troubles & vexations have been caused by my own foolish notion of doing energetically & honestly my duty, that I have become apathetic. I hate books, and writing and reading : above all things I am disgusted with the Library and my place. Do not pity me however ; I am not unhappy : on the contrary I never was happier than I am idling away my time, musing over the fire with the poker in my hand, and going to bed delighted at the thought that the day is over. [1]

---

[1] Rutherfurd Correspondence. Letter dated ' Nov. 11th '.

CHAPTER SIX

ROSSETTI, THE PISTRUCCI FAMILY, PEPOLI, GALLENGA, GAMBARDELLA

ROSSETTI really belongs to the earlier refugees of 1820 and 1821, but as it is precisely of those early years of his exile that little is known, we venture to place him among the later exiles where he heads a small band of professors of London University. There is little that we can add to the knowledge of Rossetti, as he had the advantage of a literary son who was able, as far as his memory went, to elucidate anything that Rossetti's own autobiography had left unclear.[1] The period of his exile of which we would fain know more is doomed to remain somewhat in the dark, perhaps because there seemed little to tell. " For some years after settling in London he went a good deal into society, and was welcomed in several houses," [2] said William Michael Rossetti, but which families he visited and in what society he moved is left largely to our imagination. Looking back over the history of the refugees, one is struck again and again by the apparent triviality of the cause of capital sentences and of lifelong exile, and Rossetti holds a unique position. No accusation of having taken part in conspiracies, no leading share in insurrection, only the singing of his country's freedom drove him out to seek the shelter of a foreign land. Gabriele Pasquale Giuseppe Rossetti was born on February 28th, 1783, in Vasto in Abruzzo, on the Adriatic coast of the Kingdom of Naples. His father was a blacksmith and locksmith, vassal of the Marchese del Vasto, but the family seems to have been of some importance and even to have owned property some generations back, before they fell into low estate. Gabriele went to school at Vasto, and was guided in his

---

[1] Mr. R. D. Waller in *The Rossetti Family, 1824–54* (1932), has dealt in even greater fullness with Rossetti's life in London, and particularly with his *Dante* studies.

[2] *Dante Gabriel Rossetti*. Memoir by W. M. Rossetti (London, 1895), p. 11.

first literary studies by his brothers, two of whom acquired a considerable position and reputation, and by a local priest, Padre Vincenzo Gaetani. His early poems and drawings, for he had a talent for fine draughtsmanship, came into the hands of the marquis, who in 1804 sent for his vassal to be educated at the university of Naples. Unfortunately the French invasion cut short his studies after a year and a month, by sending the marquis, a fugitive, to Sicily with the king. The Bonaparte régime was hailed as the advent of freedom by the people, although a few, and among them Rossetti, saw in it only a change of despotism, since Napoleon had assumed the Imperial crown. The arrival of Joseph Bonaparte, however, won over even Rossetti to his side and in 1807 he published his first volume of poems, which dealt partly with the great changes that had taken place. It happened that Rossetti had unusual opportunity of meeting members of the Bonaparte family in later years. He himself told that in London he was well acquainted with Joseph Bonaparte after his return from America in 1831, and that he found him kind-hearted and cultivated in mind, although he had been a bad king. In his house in London Rossetti also met Lucien Bonaparte and his son, the future Emperor Napoleon III., the former " a republican, but with many prejudices ", but the latter " of a character all puffed up with ambition " who never gave utterance to " a single word indicating a liberal spirit ".[1] Lucien's daughter, Lady Dudley Stuart, was Christina Rossetti's godmother ; and Prince Pierre Bonaparte was frequently in the Rossettis' house. The success of Rossetti's first poems, which looked to the freedom of Naples, was due in part to the enthusiasm they awakened among the young people who heard him recite his verses in his beautiful, melodious voice. He was made poet of the Theatre of San Carlo where his work was to supply libretti for the operas ; but the quarrels among the singers and composers and managers decided him to seek other work, and he was appointed to a subordinate post in the Royal Museum at a commencing salary of some £31 2s. 6d. per annum. Joseph was removed to Spain and succeeded by his brother-in-law, Joachim Murat, a good king as Rossetti calls him, but a victim to the restoration after Napoleon's fall. Through all these changes Rossetti kept his post, and under Joachim had been secretary for Public Instruction and the Fine Arts during the provisional government in Rome. When the dreaded Ferdinand returned, chastened by years of exile, and without his hated consort who had died in Sicily on the eve of his departure, he hailed the milder rule in verse. The king's illness and recovery

[1] *Gabriele Rossetti*, by W. M. Rossetti, p. 15.

gave him another theme and brought him Ferdinand's favour. The old evils of Bourbon rule soon returned, however, and the result was the Revolution of 1820 and the establishment of the constitution. Rossetti greeted the dawn of freedom in several odes of which two, the *Aurora del 21 Luglio del 1820*, ' *Sei pur bella cogli astri sul crine* ' and *Fratelli all' armi, all' armi !* spread his fame all over Italy. Porro brought the latter to Zaita for Arrivabene to read, and one of the accusations that Arrivabene had afterwards to refute was that he had spread the song in Lombardy as an incitement to insurrection. Ferdinand's treachery placed all the friends of the constitution and with them Rossetti in the gravest danger. Rossetti had become a Carbonaro towards the end of 1820, before it was a crime to be a member, and throughout this time was 'a warm friend of General Pepe. It is difficult to determine what part he took in the subsequent events and the battle of Rieti, but from various chance references to him as the Tirtæus of his country, and from a letter received in 1847 from a certain Dr. Costanza, recalling a meeting at Montecassino, " when you were returning from the gorges of Antrodoco after the hapless result of that first passage of arms ", William Michael Rossetti infers that his father had accompanied the Constitutionalist forces, at least as the bard to stir them to deeds of heroism, if not as an important combatant. Be his share what it may, the defeat of the Constitutionalists made his flight imperative ; and after living in hiding for three months until General Fardella, then Minister for War, warned him that his life was in danger, he was aided by the British Admiral, Sir Graham Moore, whose wife had been attracted to the poet by his songs. Wearing the uniform of a British subaltern, Rossetti was driven through the streets of Naples to the man-of-war which was to bear him away for ever from his native land. He called down the thunderbolts of God on the *rè fellon*, and said good-bye to Italy in his *Addio alla Patria*.

> Addio, terra sventurata ! . . .
> Ma la terra era celata.
> Ei nel duol che l' aggravò
> Chinò 'l capo e singhiozzò.
> Ahi l' amor della sua terra,
> Ahi qual guerra—in sen gli fà !
> Infelice ! il cor gli dice
> Che mai più non tornerà ! [1]

On June 24th, 1821, Rossetti left Naples, and for the next two and a half years made his home in Malta. His fame had preceded him and

[1] *Gabriele Rossetti*, by W. M. Rossetti, p. 185.

he found English society in the island anxious to receive him. Some eleven years before, Rossetti had essayed his talent as an *improvvisatore*, under the influence and guidance of a famous extempore poet, Luigi Quattromani. He had quickly become known, and was soon in great demand on all festive occasions, both in Naples and in Rome. On his arrival in Malta a desire was expressed that he should display his power, to which he willingly agreed. At a great reception, where the flower of society was met together, Rossetti improvised no fewer than six poems, and aroused the wonder of his audience, among whom was John Hookham Frere. From that time dated the friendship between Frere and Rossetti which was one of the greatest inspirations of the exile's life. In his rhyming autobiography the poet praises the famous Englishman's talents, his immense learning, his modesty and generous courtesy ; and Frere's death in 1846 was a deep and heartfelt grief to him. In Malta Rossetti's life was spent in study and in teaching, but in his case teaching was no hardship.

> " Many, I know find teaching wearisome,
> Whereas to me 'twas profit and repute." [1]

It was not his first experience as a pedagogue, for in 1817 when Ferdinand withheld the appointment to the Chair of Rhetoric at Naples which Rossetti had won in competition, the disappointed candidate opened private classes for the students who refused to attend the lectures of his supplanter. Malta was not to shelter the exiles for long, however, for the Neapolitan consul was instrumental in having some turned away, and made it obvious to Rossetti that he could hope for no peace unless in England itself. He had been one of the thirteen Neapolitans excluded from the amnesty of September 28th, 1822. Once more Admiral Sir Graham Moore came to the rescue, and, in spite of the king's demand to deliver him up, conveyed Rossetti to England, where he landed sometime in April 1824.

From this moment until his marriage in April 1826, we can only surmise what his life was. He must have received a number of introductions to London people from his English acquaintances in Malta, and certainly John Hookham Frere would not be likely to let him arrive in London unheralded. Here the scholarship he had acquired in Malta stood him in good stead ; and he seems to have met with fairly speedy success as a teacher, for he was able to devote much of his time to the study of Dante and the preparation of his *Comento Analitico*, dedicated to Frere, of which the first volume was published by sub-

[1] *Gabriele Rossetti*, p. 73.

scription in 1825, with the date 1826. During this time he must have had some intercourse with his fellow exiles, although there is no evidence of his mixing with the Lombard-Piedmontese circle that surrounded Foscolo, and W. M. Rossetti states that he barely knew Foscolo personally. In his memoir of Dante Gabriel, W. M. Rossetti speaks of their father's old friendship with General Pepe, kept up by correspondence to the end, and states that Pepe, so far as he knew, never came to England,[1] a statement which he must have had cause to modify before translating his father's autobiography, for he there refers to the General's *Memoirs*, in which an account is given of the nine years spent, with some interruptions, in London. William Michael Rossetti was too young when Pepe left in 1830, to know or remember about him. That every Italian staying in or passing through London of a liberal mode of political opinion sought out his father to make or renew acquaintance with him, refers also to a period within his memory, and was certainly not true of the earliest years. One of the first families, however, with which Rossetti became intimate was that of Gaetano Polidori, who had been for a time Alfieri's secretary, and on February 17th, 1826, he announced to Charles Lyell his approaching marriage to Polidori's second daughter Frances, seventeen years younger than himself and of whom he was sincerely fond, although to Lyell he gives the rather curiously practical reason, that " era necessario prendere un più regolare sistema di vita per attendere ai miei studj, e ciò ha contribuito a farmi fare una tal risoluzione ".[2] Whatever the motives for his marriage, it brought him great happiness, and it would be difficult to imagine a more united family circle than the Rossettis', where the individuality of each member was allowed full development in an atmosphere of sympathy and love.

The publication of the *Comento Analitico* brought Rossetti the friendship of Charles Lyell of Kinnordy, a most enthusiastic and devoted student of Dante, and they conducted a lively correspondence for a number of years from which one gleans much information about the progress of Rossetti's studies. The publication of the *Comento* by subscription left Rossetti with a debt of £280, which was a heavy burden on him until he had cleared it off. Lyell tactfully offered to finance the next work *Lo Spirito Antipapale che produsse la Riforma*, which was to be dedicated and made over to him, a suggestion evidently designed to free Rossetti from any sense of pecuniary obligation to him. The book was published in 1832. Lyell seems also to have supported

[1] *Dante Gabriel Rossetti*, p. 54.
[2] Correspondence with Charles Lyell of Kinnordy, referred to above.

him in the publication of the *Mistero dell' Amor Platonico del Medio Evo derivato dai Misteri Antichi*, a work in five volumes which was printed in 1840 but was withheld from publication in this country owing to its handling of religious themes, which would probably have endangered the author's position as a teacher. Frere sent him £150 and later a further sum towards the cost of printing this lengthy work. Lyell, who had suggested the theme originally, had contributed £400 and in the end all but a relatively small number of copies were consigned to the flames. *La Beatrice di Dante*, published in 1842, in which Rossetti reasoned that Beatrice was not a real woman but an embodiment of philosophy,[1] was also inspired by Lyell who thought of it as an introduction to the new edition of his translations of Dante, and for a time supported it ; but Lyell refused to accept it when the length of the treatise became clear to him. Rossetti undertook the expense of publication himself, but only the first part appeared. One is appalled at Rossetti's labours in connection with his prose works. All of these develop the same theory of the existence of a secret society, akin to free-masonry, to which Dante and other great poets of the Middle Ages belonged who masked their opinions from the gaze of the vulgar by making use of a highly symbolized and allegorical language, which he interprets with most ingenious and painstaking detail. During all this time of intense study Rossetti was kept very much occupied with his teaching work, at one time having as many lessons to give as forty-five per week. The wonder is less that he lost the sight of an eye as the result of his excessive work, than that his health did not give way utterly under the strain. We know very few of Rossetti's many pupils, but among them was the family of Sir Isaac Lyon Goldsmid, the famous financier and philanthropist, one of the founders of University College ; and also a member of the family of Leigh, among whose papers there is an attractive letter from an obviously cheerful and willing Italian master,[2] and later a note of thanks for a gift of partridges and a hare.

William Michael Rossetti remarks with great impartiality, " when a man says that Beatrice did not exist, and that Dante was a sort of Freemason, he must expect that people who are of a contrary opinion will express themselves forcibly ",[3] and Rossetti's works called forth

[1] Mr. Waller deals with Rossetti's writings and examines his theories in detail.

[2] Correspondence of the Family of Leigh, 1651–1837. B.M., Add. MSS. 36663. See App. IV.B.

[3] *Gabriele Rossetti*, p. 99.

each in its turn a considerable amount of adverse as well as favourable criticism. Such daring theories, so carefully elaborated, were liable to be condemned wholesale by those who were not convinced, even though the author's ingenuity and talent were recognized. Lyell had to warn him against extending his theories to Chaucer, whose Patient Griselda was to have been elucidated, and to Spenser and even Cromwell. His *Dante* was sarcastically criticized in the *Quarterly* by a man he afterwards discovered to be a clergyman called Blount or Blunt, and, deeply hurt, he made every effort to obtain reparation. The article on Foscolo's *Dante* which had appeared in the *Westminster Review* of 1826 had referred to the " strange fancies " of Rossetti in the first volume of his commentary, words which wounded him sorely. Having heard that Foscolo had handed the article to Bowring, Rossetti supposed he had been the author of the panegyric on his own work. It was perhaps as well that he remained in ignorance of the fact that Panizzi had written it to help the unhappy poet. The style alone might have caused him to doubt Foscolo's authorship, for it is poor even for Panizzi in his early days. Rossetti's second volume, two years later, was greeted by an article in the *Foreign Review* which roused his wrath against Ravina, until he found seven years later that Panizzi was its author. Rossetti had chosen for himself in literature a thorny path, but it must be admitted that he trod it bravely.

The desire for the certainty of a fixed income was not the least of the considerations which induced Rossetti in December 1827 to apply for the professorship of Italian in the newly constituted University of London. He had the support of well-known Dante scholars, William Stewart Rose, Cary, Davenport and others,[1] and probably considered he had as good a chance as any of the candidates. His chagrin, therefore, can be imagined when the council of the University " per influenza di Mr. Brougham ", as he wrote to his friend, Charles Lyell, " ha preferito a me un uomo ignoto che non ha prodotto al mondo neppure un alfabeto, un certo Panizzi, che per la prima volta suona nell' orecchio degli uomini ".[2] He might have felt still more outraged had he known that his successful rival was the man who had accused him of " strane fantasie ", although it would have comforted him to hear that Thomas Campbell regarded authorship, for the holders of some, at least, of the Chairs, as a positive disqualification. Research,

[1] Correspondence with Charles Lyell of Kinnordy. Letter dated ' Dec. 11th, 1827 '.
[2] *ibid.* Letter dated ' Feb. 20th, 1828 '.

according to him, was no part of the duty of a teacher.[1]   It is interesting to notice that Gaetano Polidori was also a candidate for the
Chair.[2] From this time dated Rossetti's animosity to Panizzi; it
was founded on no personal grounds, but was due rather to Rossetti's
own self-esteem which admitted no rival.   His reward came in 1831
when he was appointed to the Chair of Italian at King's College,[3]
which had been founded in opposition to the dissenting Whig tendencies
of University College, to educate youth " according to the duties they
owe their God and King " [4]—a curiously anomalous position for a
professed free-thinker.   The post was not arduous, for Rossetti's
students were hardly more numerous than Panizzi's, the first year only
two ; and Rossetti held it, with an interval in 1843 on account of
serious illness, until his failing health and sight made him renounce it
in 1847.[5]

The great compensation for his exile was to Rossetti his home life.
No pining for the land he had left escaped him, and he cheerfully
shouldered his responsibilities and denied himself that his children
might not want.   The four children were all born in the early years of
his married life, and he bore with patience their childish games, allowing them " to litter and rollick about the room while he plodded
through some laborious matter of literary composition ".[6]   His letters
to Lyell constantly refer to Dante Charles Gabriel, Lyell's godchild,
and no baby trick passes unnoticed.   It is good to think that he lived
to see some of the work of his famous children, and to delight in their
prowess.   William Michael Rossetti draws delightful pictures of the
home at 50 Charlotte Street, of his father coming in wearied after a
long day's teaching, lying down on the hearthrug in front of a roaring
fire and falling into a sound sleep.   The cat would sit beside him, her
fore-paws stuck into the wire of the fender, warming herself, " the cat
making the Y ", Rossetti said.[7]   At other times some of the innumer-
able Italian friends would come in for a talk, " chiefly on political
topics, mingled at moments with a little literature, and constantly with
a liberal sprinkling of my father's poems, which were received with

---

[1] *University College London, 1826–1926*, by H. Hale Bellot, 1929, p. 51.
[2] *ibid.*, p. 46.
[3] Correspondence in the possession of King's College, London, made
available to me by the kindness of the Secretary. See App. IV.A.
[4] *The Centenary History of King's College, London, 1828–1928*, by
F. J. C. Hearnshaw.
[5] See note 3, above.
[6] *Dante Gabriel Rossetti*, p. 12.   [7] *ibid.*

sonorous eulogy, founded at least as much on political or national as on literary considerations ".[1] The visitors received tea or coffee and bread and butter, modest hospitality as suited their host's means, but dispensed with kindness and friendliness. The whole family was present at these gatherings, the " signora Francesca " presiding with quiet dignity and the children busy with their particular hobbies or playing with the cat. The visitors were worthy Italians ; the Rossettis had few English friends. Italian was the language spoken in the home, and although Rossetti had learned English during his stay in Malta, and could speak and read it fairly well, his pronunciation was very Italian. He never became naturalized and was of all the refugees perhaps the one who remained most purely Italian, even after long residence in England. To discuss all the exiles and others who frequented the Rossetti home circle would be pointless when W. M. Rossetti has already done so from actual experience, but some must be mentioned here. Angeloni was one, the literary purist who became blind in his old age and died in penury ; then General Michele Carrascosa, the Rossettis spell his name so, who was one of William Michael's godfathers ; Filippo Pistrucci of whom we shall have more to say ; Sangiovanni, a picturesque figure who made a living by modelling in clay, an exile from Naples after the suppression of the constitution, with a life of wild adventure behind him ; Ciciloni who taught Italian and replaced Rossetti at King's during his illness in 1843 ; Rolandi, the bookseller, who knew everyone of his compatriots, and probably most of their affairs ; Gallenga ; Count Giuseppe Ricciardi, a South Neapolitan and ardent patriot of a revolutionary-republican type ; Janer-Nardini, born in Tuscany of Spanish descent, a fairly constant visitor, and Count Carlo Pepoli, ' a good-looking, cultivated Bolognese of high honour and ancient family ', a friend of Leopardi who dedicated a poem to him, regarded by the Rossettis as ' rather a dandy ', of whom too the tale is not yet told. With Mazzini, the greatest of them all, Rossetti had some intercourse, though never of a very intimate kind. The divergence in their political opinions precluded that. They were both devoted to the cause of Italian Freedom and Unity, but not agreed as to the means of attaining them. After 1849 Rossetti held Mazzini responsible in great measure for the republican agitation which 'did much to bring about the defeat of the Italian forces. In his age and partial blindness Rossetti returned to the poetry of his younger days. As long as life endured he hoped to war against Tyranny in verse ; and in prophetic

[1] *ibid.*, p. 46.

vein, even after the disasters of 1849, he foretold ' more favourable days '—

> " All the less possible the victory seems,
> So much the greater is the glory of God ! " [1]

With Berchet, Rossetti shared the honour of being the singer of the *Risorgimento* and of the two was perhaps the more inspired. In common with the rest of his countrymen in exile, Poland's struggle for independence, even for existence, claimed his sympathy, and after the fall of the republic of Cracow an interesting little collection of verses, *1846, Cracovia, Carmi di Gabriele Rossetti, Nardini, Pepoli, Ricciardi* [2] and others, found its way with Mazzini's help [3] to Lausanne, where it was published in 1847. The songs were an offering from some of the exiled sons of Italy to their Polish brothers, but the introduction was an exhortation to the Italians themselves. " Noi moviamo al conquisto della perduta nazionalità politica. E come potremo ottenerla, se pria non sentiamo in noi la coscienza nostra, se pria non possediamo intiera-mente l' antica nazionalità morale, che si rivela nel culto delle arti e della poesia ? " and at the last " ricordi Tirteo, si rinfiammi nell' ira dell' Alighieri, e tuoni ! E sarà venerata, obbedita dai popoli ".[4]

Rossetti's last years were clouded by ill-health and suffering, and his family helped willingly to keep the home without too great a restriction of their modest comforts. His wife made heroic though unsuccessful efforts by starting a small school in town, followed by one in Somerset where they lived for some time. In 1854 they returned to the house in London which William Michael had prepared for them, and on April 26th ' the wearied traveller ' sank to the rest he had longed for.

In 1847 Rossetti was succeeded in the Chair of Italian by Valerio Pistrucci, of whom we know nothing more than can be gleaned from his application for the professorship : that he was a Roman married to an Englishwoman, that he had taught Italian for the preceding ten years,[5] and that he ' adhered to the creed of the reformed church '. The testimonials which he enclosed with his letter would have given some indication of his connections, but they were probably submitted in the original and returned to him after the appointment. Pistrucci's reference to his ten years' teaching experience make it hardly possible

---

[1] *Gabriele Rossetti*, p. 104.

[2] Published by S. Bonamici e Comp., Lausanne, 1847.

[3] *Gabriele Rossetti*. Letters from Mazzini, pp. 163–4.

[4] *1846, Cracovia*, p. 9 *et seq.*

[5] Correspondence in the possession of King's College, London. See App. IV.c.

that it was to him that Panizzi referred, when considering the choice of an assistant at University College, but it was most likely one of the same family. From his friendship with Mazzini we know perhaps most about Filippo Pistrucci, although the references to him by Jane Welsh Carlyle and Jessie White Mario are so confused as to make an account of his work difficult. We know that he was a brother of the famous medallist and gem-engraver, Benedetto Pistrucci, who modelled the St. George and the Dragon on our gold coinage, and who came to London in 1815, not as a refugee. Filippo was a Roman, an engraver like his brother, and a famous *improvvisatore*. He was a great friend of Gabriele Rossetti's, and Rossetti refers to him in a letter to his wife during her absence in Buckinghamshire in 1832. On May 29th he gave news of Pistrucci who had been run over in the streets of London. " Yesterday poor Pistrucci wrote me a letter which is really fit to make one weep," he wrote. " He says he is suffering horrible torments, and it has been discovered that his thigh was broken in three parts, so that he is crippled." [1] W. M. Rossetti said that he remained lame, though active, for the rest of his life. There is a charming water-colour sketch by him of Dante Gabriel and William Rossetti, done about the year 1838, inserted in the translation of the versified autobiography of Gabriele Rossetti. The study is of head and shoulders, and shows Dante Gabriel in full face, with bright flashing eyes, sensitive mouth and a certain air of confidence. William looks out over Dante Gabriel's left shoulder, his head slightly turned to the right of the picture, and seems to shelter behind his big brother. His expression is more childishly serious, shy and less assured. In Cyrus Redding's *Recollections* (Vol. II., page 196) there is a letter from Foscolo, undated and in excellent English, apologizing for having dictated his letter, because he was sitting for his portrait " before M. Pistrucchi, poet and painter ", and he added, " If you wish to hear his *improvisations*, you must come this evening to tea at eight o'clock." In spite of the mistake in name this is obviously the same man. Later when Mazzini founded his school for poor organ boys, Filippo Pistrucci was secretary and teacher in it. He afterwards published his lectures.[2] Jane Welsh Carlyle called him *Petrucci*, and a foot-note to one of her letters explains that he was " an Italian exile of Mazzini's circle, whose gloom earned him the nickname of Heraclitus, the weeping philosopher ".[3] After the anniversary dinner of the

[1] *Gabriele Rossetti*, pp. 123, 125.
[2] *Epistolario di Giuseppe Mazzini*, II., p. 415.
[3] *Jane Welsh Carlyle : Letters to her Family*, ed. by L. Huxley, p. 22.

Italian school in 1842, to which she had been invited but had not gone, owing to Carlyle's momentary objection to what he called " a nest of young conspirators ", she wrote a long account of it to her cousin. Thirteen pounds had been collected, " from which deduct the expenses and there would remain, I am afraid zero, or perhaps a *deficit*—the *supper* of itself must have gone with a half—*forty-five* gallons of beer, *fifty* pounds of macaroni, and beef of unascertained quantity ! " After this sumptuous repast the distribution of prizes took place and speeches were made. " You may be sure that old Petrucci would not let slip so fine an occasion of gratifying his melo-dramatic propensities and accordingly a series of *scenes* were most unexpectedly introduced." After Mazzini's speech to the boys exhorting them to be good " learners and patriots ", a pupil read a sonnet to him and presented him with a bouquet. " Nor had Petrucci forgotten himself—when the company were about to disperse one of the pupils again stepped forth, and declared that it would make their enjoyment perfect if Mr. Petrucci would favour them with an *improvis-ation*. ' Oh ! *impossible, impossible* ! '—with all sorts of coyish grim-acing—at length he allowed himself to be so far prevailed upon that he would read them a composed poem of his own—which he thereupon drew *all ready* from his pocket—and calling to him ' the Dr. Rossetti ' the two old fools proceeded to deliver in horrible recitative a dramatized poem written for the occasion ! " [1] The description is unkind but vivid. Rossetti evidently took an interest in the school. In October 1845, Mazzini seconded Pistrucci's invitation to him to allow his voice to be heard in one way or other at the Anniversary of the School on November 10th, and his son William, who went with him, remembered both Mazzini and his father speaking. In 1845 and again in 1848 Rossetti mentioned Pistrucci in connection with concerts to raise funds for the school. Jessie White Mario, speaking of the 1843 anniversary, said that the old teacher Pistrucci improvised. The same evening roughs tried to break up the proceedings at the insti-gation of the agents of the Sardinian embassy and ' poor old Pistrucci even feared for his own life '.[2] In referring to the designing of the medals presented to Duncombe in 1845 she says, " Exquisite works of art, they had been designed by old Scipione Pistrucci, sculptor, painter, and teacher in Mazzini's school ",[3] obviously confusing Filippo with his son. Scipione is described as a Milanese, though the son of a

[1] *Jane Welsh Carlyle : Letters to her Family*, p. 50, letter 23.
[2] *The Birth of Modern Italy*, by Jessie White Mario, p. 64.
[3] *ibid.*, p. 85.

Roman. He too was an artist. " Congiungeva al patriotismo e alla devozione per Mazzini, ispirazione e maestria non comune nell' arte del disegno e della pittura, ingegno coltissimo, austero costume e rara gentilezza d' affetti." [1] Scipione was the painter of a portrait of Mazzini which the latter sent to his mother.[2] In 1837 Filippo invited Mazzini and the Ruffinis, who shared his lodgings, to spend their first Christmas Day in England at his house. Mazzini wrote to his mother of the invitation and spoke of the " improvvisatore Pistrucci, padre del giovane che m' ha fatto il ritratto ", and continued, " egli ha, oltre il pittore, ch' io amo molto, un altro figlio, e questi due vengono ogni sera in casa nostra, talora anche a pranzo, perchè abbiamo tanta confidenza con essi da trattarli come ci trattiamo ".[3] This other son was Emilio Pistrucci. Mrs. Carlyle wrote to her cousin in 1842 of a sum of £41 that Mazzini had to pay " for that thriftless Scipione Petrucci ", and which he had to borrow at high interest from money-lenders [4] ; and on July 15th, 1843, he announced to her the death of Scipione Pistrucci's wife.[5] Scipione had suffered persecution in Piedmont and in Switzerland, which aggravated the disease from which he suffered and led to his early death, at less than forty years of age, in 1854. Filippo Pistrucci survived his son by three years. The ' Miss Pistrucci ' who carved the onyx cameo of his wife for Lord Rutherfurd was more probably a daughter of Benedetto. .

If the revolutions of 1820–1 were the work chiefly of the army, the revolution of 1831 was led by the professors of the University of Bologna. The events in France had brought to a head the seething discontent in Central Italy and the Carbonari had prepared a network of insurrection in the north and centre. After Francis of Modena's treacherous desertion of the rising he had pretended to lead, Bologna rose in revolt in February 1831, and was immediately supported by all with liberal sympathies. In less than three weeks the Central Provinces had cast off Papal rule, and with a quietness and order that was almost unprecedented. Delegates were chosen for " the Assembly of Deputies of the Five Provinces of Italy ". Of this provisional government Carlo Pepoli, professor of Philosophy at the University and of an old Bolognese family, was a member. France broke her promise to help the revolutionaries if Austria should intervene, and Austria, having been secretly notified of France's abstention, soon

[1] *Epistolario di Giuseppe Mazzini*, I., p. 415.
[2] *ibid.*, I., p. 484. [3] *ibid.*, I., pp. 581–2.
[4] *Jane Welsh Carlyle : Letters to her Family*, p. 47.
[5] Jessie White Mario, p. 61.

swept through the Central Provinces : the government, having withdrawn from Bologna, capitulated to avoid useless bloodshed, on the promise of an amnesty from the Pope. In spite of the promise the leaders were arrested, and fresh exiles made their way to safety. Count Carlo Pepoli, after suffering imprisonment in Venice, emigrated and settled in London. We know very little about his first years there, but he was one of the frequenters of the Rossetti household. With the Carlyles he became very intimate and they give us the most vivid picture of him. Jane Welsh Carlyle, writing to Mrs. Aitken in August of 1835 of the new friends she had made in Chelsea, spoke of their Italian acquaintances, among whom was the ' Count de Pepoli ', and Carlyle himself added the footnote, " Il conte ' Pepoli ' was from Bologna, exile and dilettante, a very pretty man ".[1] He was the only one of their Italian friends who found favour with Mrs. Carlyle's mother, and their Scottish maid, Anna, " instead of calling him ' a fley-some body ' any longer ", came round to the opinion that he was " a real fine man, and nane that comes can ever be mentioned in ae day with him ! "[2] and was rewarded for putting on her best cap by his " I weesh you good-day ", when she let him out. Some time after, although exactly when it is difficult to determine, Pepoli gave Mrs. Carlyle Italian lessons. He wrote a letter, unfortunately undated, to his ' Cara Signora Jane e Scuolara *Modello* ', which has found its way into the correspondence of Leigh Hunt,[3] who at one time did some kindness for which Pepoli wrote him a most grateful letter.[4]

When Panizzi's appointment to the British Museum necessitated his retiring from the Chair of Italian at University College, Pepoli was prevailed upon by his friends to apply for it. He submitted testimonials from the Duke of Sutherland, Dr. J. Belluomini, Dr. W. Gairdner, J. S. Mill and the Rev. William Turner. The letters were first sent to Carlyle, and in his absence forwarded to the secretary by Erasmus Darwin. His " high literary attainments ", his " great learning and perfect acquaintance with the language and literature of Italy ", his zeal in " his undertakings and his very gentlemanly deportment and nice sense of honour " were all stressed, and Dr. Belluomini, after admitting the equal claims of the other candidates as regards

[1] *Letters and Memorials of Jane Welsh Carlyle*, by Thomas Carlyle, ed. by J. A. Froude, I., p. 33.

[2] *ibid.*, letter 11.

[3] Leigh Hunt Correspondence, Vol. II., 1825–41. B.M., Add. MSS. 38109, fol. 149. See App. IV.D.

[4] *ibid.* fol. 191. Add. MSS. 38524.

merely the language teaching, added " mais pour un professeur d'université qui à mon avis doit aussi être homme de lettre [sic] bon juge des ouvrages d'autrui, et bon compositeur et filologue lui-même, vous vous persuadez, j'espere, [sic] après avoir lu ses titres, qu'aucun autre peut lui être comparé ".[1] Pepoli was appointed, two of the other candidates being Janer-Nardini and G. B. Nicolini. In the history of University College, Pepoli is referred to as being " undistinguished as a scholar ", although Professor Gardner states that he " enjoyed some reputation as a poet of the classical school. He translated the gospel of St. Matthew into the Bolognese dialect. If his prose essays have not left any mark on Italian scholarship, his *epigrafi* and memorial discourses were highly esteemed ".[2] He published a book *On the language & literature of Italy* in 1838, the year of his appointment to University College, and was also the author of *I puritani e i cavalieri, a serious opera*, in conjunction with Bellini. He wrote also the libretto of *Norma*, which was likewise composed by Bellini and was the opera performed on April 14th, 1864, with the singers Mario and Grisi, on the occasion of Garibaldi's visit to the Italian opera in London. It was evidently well known to both Mazzini and Mrs. Carlyle, for Mazzini said that Mrs. Carlyle, when lying with a stiff neck and wearing a black scarf round her head, had the effect of the priestess in *Norma*.[3] Pepoli held the Chair until 1847.

In 1839 Pepoli married Elizabeth Fergus of Kirkcaldy, " elderly, moneyed and fallen in love with the romantic in distress " as Carlyle wrote of her.[4] Mrs. Carlyle was delighted to have an old friend so near to her in Chelsea. Some people predicted doubtful happiness as the outcome of the disparity in age, which was considered very great, although it seems to have been seven years, but at the beginning Mrs. Carlyle wrote, " they both look well content, if the romance of the thing could but hold out ! "[5] As a matter of fact the happiness lasted. When Carlyle was in Scotsbrig in October 1845, Mrs. Carlyle sent him a charming account of a visit she had paid the Pepolis with Darwin. ' The dinner at the Pepolis ', she said, ' " went off with effect ", well-cooked, well-served, and well-eaten, it was really a little

---

[1] Testimonials and other correspondence relating to Carlo Pepoli in the possession of University College, London, for the perusal of which I am indebted to the Librarian. See App. IV.E.
[2] H. Hale Bellot, pp. 123–4.
[3] *Jane Welsh Carlyle : Letters to her Family*, p. 226.
[4] *Letters and Memorials of Jane Welsh Carlyle*, I., p. 33.
[5] *Jane Welsh Carlyle : Letters to her Family*, p. 3.

" work of art " the whole thing—no incongruities, no verfailed attempts. Never did a new house bring a more marked blessing with it. Elizabeth in her new atmosphere of order and cleanliness, looks herself again ; even Pietro has bloomed up into a Christian waiter ! I do not pretend to get much " good joy " from witnessing " the happiness of others " but it was really a sort of pleasure for me to see the light and order which Elizabeth has managed to bring out of the chaos given her to rule, and to hear her innocent genuine thankfulness for her small mercies ! Darwin remarked as we drove home, that " things seemed to be going on very nicely indeed—a little too much disparity in the ages still ; but as Pepoli was growing regularly older and Madame younger, even that *too* would come right at last ! " ' [1] Pepoli was then forty-nine. In 1849 he was a deputy in the Roman Republic and in 1859 returned to Bologna after the liberation of Romagna and Emilia. His wife's illness recalled him hastily to London in 1862, and he remained constantly with her until she died some days after his arrival. He returned to Bologna, became a senator of the Italian Kingdom and died in 1881 at the age of eighty-five. Although beyond the limit of this study, we are tempted to refer to a most interesting account of the state of Bologna in 1860 at the time of the elections, which Pepoli sent to Sir Henry Layard. The goal they had all striven for was in sight at last and even the clerics joined in the general rejoicing.[2]

Antonio Carlo Napoleone Gallenga, who succeeded Pepoli at University College in 1847, was the most unacademic of professors, a picturesque figure more suited to the world of romance than the rostrum of a lecture hall. He told his own story in *Episodes of my Second Life* (1884), and in an autobiographical sketch *Castellamonte* (1854), both written in admirable, fluent English. He was born in Parma in 1810, of Piedmontese family. As a youth he had the reputation of being a genius and he certainly was versatile to a remarkable degree. In 1831 he had been a conspirator, a State prisoner, a combatant, a fugitive and, for five years after, an exile. He then ventured to return to Italy under the name of Luigi Mariotti, and as he said ' smuggled his way from state to state till he reached Naples and embarked for Malta.' In 1836 he went to the United States and became lecturer in Italian at Boston. At Cambridge, Mass., he met James Russell Lowell, Oliver Wendell Holmes and many other famous people. He also knew Longfellow, who made him publish his first book of poems. He lectured

---

[1] *New Letters and Memorials of Jane Welsh Carlyle*, by Thomas Carlyle and edited by Alexander Carlyle, p. 181.

[2] *Layard Papers*. B.M., Add. MSS. 39068, fol. 76. See App. IV.F.

in English but found difficulty with the pronunciation. *W* and *wh*, and *ths* in *months*, *truths*, and similar words gave him trouble ; and even after fifty years' practice he admitted that he could hardly open his lips without betraying his foreign accent. In spite of this he aimed at more than mere correctness of style. He wished his English to be as much as possible like that of his favourite authors, Lytton, Disraeli, Carlyle, and Washington Irving—no mean ambition. At the house of Lorenzo da Ponte, an exile whose memories went back to pre-Napoleonic times, he met his exiled compatriots. In the spring of 1839 he came to England and remained for about two years, occupying himself with teaching and literary works. He called himself a " Tinker of Books ", and predicted that what he wrote was so soon dead and buried that not a line of it would ever rise to bear witness against him. His judgment of himself is hard, for his works, if light reading, are entertaining. After two years in Nova Scotia, he returned to England and became naturalized in 1846. His first important work was *Italy : General Views of its History and Literature in reference to its present state*, published in 1841. While still known as Mariotti, he wrote a complaint to Panizzi that unscrupulous compatriots in distress had preyed upon his generosity and had caused him to give them money he could ill afford. Hearing afterwards that they were dishonest, he hastened to protest against any abuse they might make of his name and to disavow any connection with them.[1] Another time he wrote to Panizzi in Italian, presumably shortly after his arrival in London, requesting permission to use his name as a reference in his quest for pupils.[2] His connection with Panizzi was probably closer in later years, for there is a number of letters from him among Panizzi's correspondence, and a long one dealing with the case against the scholar Libri, who was accused of appropriating public manuscripts. Gallenga was such a bird of passage that he wrote from London, Manchester and Wales, then wandered away from England again on one of his journeys to the Continent or America. His life was full of change. In 1833 he had met Mazzini at Geneva and heard the story of Jacopo Ruffini, who had killed himself in prison, thinking that his friend had betrayed him. Gallenga had then undertaken to assassinate Carlo Alberto, whom he thought the cause of all their troubles, and Mazzini had in the end given his consent. Nothing had come of it, but in 1856 a letter of Mazzini's had revealed the old plot. Clumsy

[1] Panizzi Correspondence, Vol. XIV., fol. 258. B.M., Add. MSS. 36727.
[2] *ibid.*, fol. 260.

newspaper articles had accused Gallenga of being a regicide and had caused him to give up his seat in the Chamber of Deputies in Turin and his cross of St. Maurice. He accused Carlo Arrivabene, his substitute at University College (wrongly as he afterwards discovered) of trying to stir up the Senate to dismiss him. He told his tale to Panizzi, asking his help and support.[1] In 1848 Gallenga went back with Mazzini to Italy at the outbreak of the revolution and volunteered in the Piedmontese army. The remainder of his life was as full of change and travel as the beginning. He was foreign correspondent of various newspapers and for seven years leader-writer for *The Times*. He too died full of years, in 1895.

In America Gallenga had become acquainted with a Neapolitan refugee, a man of great diversity of talents and abundant vitality. His own account is so vivid that we give it in full.

My other friend [he says] was a Neapolitan, though a native of Zante or Corfu, by name Spiridione Gambardella, who had come out with the Operatic body, as a first-rate tenor ; but either because he had lost his voice, or was tired of a singer's calling, he took to portrait painting ; and, though he had never had any regular drawing lessons at home, he had here made himself a master in oil-colours, had achieved great means and established very profitable connections among the wealthiest New York families. Gambardella was in the prime of youth, had the advantage of a tall and elegant figure, fine Grecian features, and wonderful animal spirits ; withal a great versatility of talent which enabled him to take up anything he had a fancy to and become familiar with subjects from which his utter want of elementary studies might be expected to have utterly debarred him. It is thus he dabbled, not without success, in astronomy, and about three years later I found him in London, where he had set up an observatory, and put himself into communication with Lord Rosse, from whom he received some points about the construction of a great telescope intended to rival his Lordship's own world-famous instrument.[2]

Among the letters of Charles Babbage, the mathematician, there is one from Gambardella referring to a meeting with Lord Rosse, which Babbage was apparently to arrange for him.[3] This curious man was introduced to Carlyle in October 1841 by R. W. Emerson, and he was a frequent visitor at his house. Carlyle sat to him for his portrait,

[1] Panizzi Correspondence, Vol. V., fols. 468, 67. B.M., Add. MSS. 36718. See App. IV.G.
[2] *Episodes of my Second Life*, I., pp. 374-5.
[3] Correspondence of C. Babbage, Vol. XIX., fol. 253. B.M., Add. MSS. 37200. See App. IVH.

but it was a failure, a result that a number of Gambardella's works attained, although the portrait of Mrs. Carlyle, painted by him as a gift for her cousin, Jeanie Welsh, was a remarkable success. Perhaps the subject pleased him. Darwin said that his portrait of Jeanie Welsh herself was the only picture of Gambardella's he had seen that gave him any idea he could ever become a good artist.[1] He seemed however to receive many commissions and to make a small fortune. In 1842 he went to Liverpool, duly provided with introductions by Mrs. Carlyle, to Geraldine Jewsbury among others; but he returned for a time to London the following year, when he painted the picture of Mrs. Carlyle referred to above. In 1844 Mrs. Carlyle visited her uncle in Liverpool and wrote a very entertaining account of a picnic she had enjoyed with Gambardella and her cousin. They had crossed to New Brighton and were there supplied with donkeys by their original host. They picnicked at a lovely place, all wild thyme and white roses, and Gambardella sang Italian songs and proposed the healths. " He is far best in the open air ", she added, " being, in fact, a sort of savage." [2] For some years they do not seem to have seen much of him, but in November 1849, Mrs. Carlyle reported to her cousin that " Mr. C. actually went with Gambardella one day on the same velocipede to Wimbledon ! " [3] And one day the artist appeared at the door with a " phaeton and white pony and laced-hatted tiger, all as small as might have suited Queen Titania and in it the loveliest—child ! about 3 dressed like a miniature Garibaldi— another Spiridione ".[4] His after history we do not know, whether his country claimed him, or whether he lived and died a voluntary exile.

[1] *Jane Welsh Carlyle : Letters to her Family*, p. 104.
[2] *New Letters and Memorials*, letter 51.
[3] *Jane Welsh Carlyle : Letters to her Family*, p. 337.
[4] *ibid.*

CHAPTER SEVEN

GIUSEPPE MAZZINI

IT is with the utmost diffidence that one turns to the contemplation of the greatest among the many brave and beautiful lives that were laid upon the altar of Italy's unity and freedom. When so many great scholars have devoted themselves to the study of the life and influence of Giuseppe Mazzini, it is presumption to attempt to add anything to what is already written about him ; but the gallery of portraits would not be complete, if the one man were omitted whose work extended beyond the disasters that succeeded the great rising of 1848, and who never ceased to prepare his country for the consummation of the effort of over fifty years of struggle and suffering on the part of her noblest sons.

Mazzini was born in Genoa on June 22nd, 1805, the son of a doctor who was also professor of Anatomy at the University, a man of strong democratic principles. His mother was a woman of fine character whose interests exceeded the bounds of her domestic duties. The boy had poor health in the first years, although he gave early signs of a remarkable intelligence. Although confined almost entirely to a little chair-bed in his mother's room, he had the sunny disposition of a child in all the enjoyment of health and strength. This imprisonment in one room was but a foretaste of his experience in after years, and he seemed to be able to overcome always the feeling of the restriction imposed by necessity, and to concentrate on others rather than on himself. The beauty of the boy's character made him beloved by his parents and three sisters, and he grew up in an atmosphere of happiness and affection. His democratic tendencies were fostered by seeing his father's care for his poor patients, by the spirit of sympathy for all sufferers which both of his parents showed, and probably by a sense of shame when the old Genoese republic was handed over to Piedmont after the downfall of Napoleon. After the failure of the Revolution of 1821, when the Piedmontese refugees passed through Genoa before the city surrendered, the youthful Mazzini was so touched at the sight of their misery that he gave them the money he had in his pockets, and thenceforth dressed in black for the sorrows of his country. After his preparatory studies he went to the university at the age of fourteen, and studied law, medicine having proved too trying for his sensitive nature. He was happy as a student, an omnivorous reader, fond of gymnastics, fencing and walking, and a favourite with his fellows. There are some men in whose presence all unclean words and thoughts are banished, and Mazzini was one. This influence he kept throughout his life, and his purity of mind and character, and the beauty of his nature gave him a position which is unassailed among the makers of modern Italy.

Although law was his profession, Mazzini's tastes were literary. And the great poets of Italy, Dante and Alfieri, both singers of their country's freedom, Shakespeare, Shelley and above all Byron, for whom he had a deep and lasting admiration, Goethe and Schiller, all claimed his study ; but he put all thought of devoting himself to literature aside, at the inner call to rise up and play a part in Italy's struggle for life. Two journals with which he was connected and in which he expressed his views were suppressed, but he had three articles accepted by the *Antologia* while still in the early twenties. About this time he joined the Carbonari, and the accusation that he had enrolled a new member, added to what was already known of his opinions from his writings, was sufficient to cause his arrest. He was kept for six months in the fortress of Savona on the Riviera, where, instead of fretting at the captivity, he spent his time working out his ideas for the future of Italy, and planning the association afterwards so widely known as Young Italy. His ideas of Unity and Liberty for Italy did not stop there, but from the unity of the Italian people were extended to embrace the whole of God's people in a universal brotherhood which should make this life a step in the great ladder leading up to perfection. As a preliminary to the attaining of this progress, the recognition of each nation's existence was essential and hence the aim of Independence was joined to the other two. No other Italian had gone beyond the idea of freedom, independence and unity for Italy, and many not even so far ; but Mazzini looked upon Italy as leader in the far wider scheme which sought to bind earth to Heaven. His imprisonment ceased, only to give place to banishment, and then began those years of sorrow, which with all their suffering only served to make the spirit within him burn more bright.

After a short sojourn in Geneva, where he made the acquaintance of

Sismondi and of some of the Italian exiles there, who however disappointed him by the narrowness of their views, he was advised to join the exiles at Lyons instead of proceeding to Paris as he had at first intended. Mazzini made his way there and found the plans far advanced for a raid on Savoy, with the semi-official help of the French. The withdrawal of French aid, as the spirit of the July Revolution came under the influence of the king's changed policy, made the raid an impossibility. An attempt to send a party from Corsica to the help of Romagna, which was the outcome of the failure of the larger plans, was foiled by the collapse of the rising in the Central Provinces. From Corsica Mazzini went to Marseilles, where he remained for two years until 1833, stupendously active in the propagation of his republican doctrines, and finding the greatest happiness of his life in the consciousness of performing the task he had set himself. The six months' imprisonment at Savona had given him the necessary quiet for working out his theories. His study of Byron, Dante and the Bible, reading which the governor of the prison thought quite innocuous, fixed his ideas, and he left with his policy already defined and his watchword of *Dio e il Popolo* already on his lips. In Marseilles some nine or ten young men banded themselves together with Mazzini at their head, fired with enthusiasm, and determined to work until they had achieved their end. Mazzini saw the cause of failure of the previous revolutions in their leadership, the hesitation and over-caution born of aims that were political rather than social ; and in the neglect to use the power of the masses. He looked to the young to assume the task of lifting the ideals of the people to a higher plane, and of giving them an inspiration that would carry them on to the greatest sacrifices in face of defeat. That youth counts not the cost was a truth which he realized and turned to account. The next revolution was to be a rising of the people as a whole, not of a mere section of the leaders and thinkers, and the great work of preparation was in the hands of the young. The necessity for some organization to direct the movement led to the formation of the society of Young Italy, which combined with the making of a new Italy the social uplifting of the masses. The organ of the society was the *Giovine Italia*, which appeared at irregular intervals between 1832 and 1834 and which was directed, and to a great extent written, by Mazzini himself. The work of writing articles, printing, distributing and even smuggling the journal into Italy devolved upon the little group in Marseilles, and all over Italy their efforts met with a response which astonished even themselves. In 1833 plans were laid for a revolt which Mazzini at first hoped Carlo Alberto, who had recently ascended the throne, would lead. The discovery of the plot caused the Piedmontese Government to pursue the conspirators with incredible cruelty, and the king was too terrified to stay their hand. Among the leaders in Genoa was Mazzini's dearest friend, Jacopo Ruffini, who was imprisoned, and who, rather than betray his friends, took his own life. Mazzini's sorrow at the death of his friend was so great that he almost lost his reason. He was only saved by the love of Giuditta Sidoli, a young widow with fervently patriotic sympathies, to whom he was engaged to be married, and by the faith and continued affection of the Signora Ruffini, whose soul was big enough not to hold him accountable for her son's death. During this time Mazzini lived in hiding, refusing to leave France in spite of the Government's decree. For a whole year he eluded the grasp of the police, and only twice went outside the house and then in disguise. In July 1833 he went to Geneva, and, convinced that the moment had come to strike, organized an insurrection which was to start in Savoy. Unfortunately the choice of General Ramorino as the military leader dispelled what little chance of success the revolutionaries had ; and delay and the absence of the general in Paris frittered away the forces of the volunteers, until it was the mere ghost of the original band that met at the frontier. As the expedition seemed foredoomed to failure, Ramorino disbanded the men ; and the funds collected with so much difficulty, and the energy and enthusiasm were wasted. Mazzini himself, worn out with overwork, passed through a period of collapse and serious illness, physical and mental, before he could take courage to rise up again and carry on his self-appointed task. From that time forth his creed of Duty took root in his mind, and he set out alone with God's help to achieve his aim, putting aside all hope of joy or reward, and seeking only to give and to serve.

From Mazzini's letters to his mother, which were very frequent and written as from niece to aunt to avoid detection, we can gather the details of his daily life in Switzerland. His companions in exile were Giovanni and Agostino Ruffini, the two brothers of his dead friend. Giuditta Sidoli remained near him too, until in September 1833, she left for Italy, to Mazzini's great alarm, with the intention of seeing her two children, who were being brought up by her father-in-law in Reggio. The duke forbade her to see them, and the attempts to do so, which she never ceased to make, were fraught with the greatest danger to herself. After the ill-fated Savoy raid, the exiles were forced to leave Geneva, and Mazzini and his two friends betook themselves to Lausanne, whence after a short time they went to Berne. Mazzini's enthusiasm made him seize the opportunity, when exiles from many countries gathered round him after the raid, to found the Association of Young Europe, which should spread his teaching all over Europe. The Powers brought pressure to bear on the Swiss Government, and after various attempts to withstand it, the Swiss too ordered the exiles to leave the country. That the idea of England as a refuge was gradually forming in Mazzini's mind is evident from his letters to his mother. She had already begged him in June 1833, to go to London, but he had replied, " Non vi starò a dire che s' io m' allontanassi di troppo dall' Italia, morrei " [1] ; and Giuditta had supported him by writing, after a report on Mazzini's health, " Non crederia però mai che il clima d' Inghilterra potesse convenirgli—anzi lo crederia dannosissimo —pel fisico e pel morale." [2]   In April of the following year he wrote to his mother that the aim of the Government was to drive all exiles to London or to America, and the Swiss would grant no other passports. The sufferings of the refugees forced to go to England without means of providing for their needs, evidently aroused the Signora Mazzini's compassion, and half in answer and half as an argument in favour of himself remaining in Switzerland, her son wrote her in May, that London for the penniless was *un vero inferno*, and that " In Inghilterra non v' è simpatia, non v' è soccorso, non v' è nulla—in Inghilterra, in mezzo a gente che parla una lingua diversa, cosa faranno ? " [3]   The police made frequent changes of abode necessary, Berne, Soleure, Grenchen, and finally the poor hunted exiles were obliged to live for months without daring to set foot beyond the doorstep of the house that sheltered them.   During the whole of this time Mazzini's energy never slackened, and he studied and wrote articles and letters, found time to interest himself in Swiss politics and to found a society of Young Switzerland, with a paper to voice its aims, and to watch the trend of affairs in England.   His only joys were the affection of his dear ones at home and of Giuditta, and the sight of the Alps from his window, his beloved Alps with their snowy peaks and their strength, beyond which lay all he held dearest and had left for conscience' sake. The close confinement which Mazzini had some peculiar strength to endure told sadly on the health of his two friends, and, yielding at last to necessity, he decided to leave for England.   He hated change of any kind and one can gauge the depth of his affection for the Ruffinis, when he was prepared to go so far away for their sakes, and to leave the Alps which he loved.   His last letters to his mother from Switzerland

---

[1] *Epistolario di Giuseppe Mazzini*, I., p. 61.
[2] *ibid.*   [3] *ibid.*, p. 195.

are written to *carissima madre* and signed with his own name. Henceforth subterfuge would be unnecessary and letters could be addressed openly to him. The arrangements for the journey were made with care, and Mazzini was able to give his mother a London address for letters, care of Mr. Hick, 24 Goodge Street, Tottenham Court Road. Some feeling that the impending change might be good after all and would open out new avenues of usefulness was a compensation. Mazzini had always a certain sympathy with northern peoples and he hoped soon to grow accustomed to the new life. " Io mi avvezzerò ben presto alla vita inglese e alle abitudini ", he wrote, " Anzi ho in me molti punti di contatto con quegli uomini. I miei compagni faranno lo stesso : e quanto alla vita materiale, il solo sagrificio che mi pesa pèr essi, è quello di non bevere più vino. Io non ne bevo mai, e in conseguenza perdo nulla." [1] A last long letter was written to his mother on December 31st, 1836, and on January 2nd the travellers set off *via* France. Mazzini's description of the journey through France and of the crossing from Calais to London was graphic if not wholly encouraging. Of all times of the year to arrive in London from abroad, surely the worst is January ; and it required the unquenchable optimism of a Mazzini to write on the day after a bad crossing, in spite of the " fango per le strade che spaventa " and the " cielo piovoso, nebbioso ", that the city with its dark, smoky brick houses appeared to him a " cosa fantasmagorica " which pleased him and reminded him of Ossian and his poems.[2] The little party that had travelled together, the two Ruffinis, Angelo Usiglio [3] and Mazzini wished to remain together, which increased the difficulty of finding suitable accommodation within their very scanty means. The day after their arrival they met Scipione Pistrucci, who was one of the devoted friends who had carried Mazzini into safety after his collapse from fatigue on the night of the Savoy raid ; and Giovanni Battista Ruffini, a Modenese, whom he had known in Marseilles. They found temporary lodgings with Ruffini, but of a kind not calculated to impress them with the comforts of London. Seven days after his arrival Mazzini began to make enquiries about the *Edinburgh Review*, with a view to submitting an article on Guerrazzi's *Assedio di Firenze*, and thereby to relieve the pressing financial needs of the moment, and to start his work of making known the conditions and intellectual tendencies of contemporary Italy. This article did not appear in any English periodical, but henceforth no efforts were spared to find editors who

[1] *ibid.*, II., p. 405.   [2] *ibid.*, pp. 414–15.
[3] Mazzini also spells the name *Usilio.*

would accept others. Mazzini seems at once to have got into touch with Fortunato Prandi, and their common interest in Foscolo and acquaintance with Enrico Mayer drew them together. The first months in London were very hard to bear. Living was more costly than Mazzini had even anticipated, memories of the mountains filled him with longing for the beautiful country he had left, real loneliness of soul increased as the petty irritations of their daily life destroyed the harmony between himself and the Ruffinis which alone could have made existence possible. The promise given to the Signora Ruffini not to part from her sons made it impossible for Mazzini to leave London in quest of literary work elsewhere, and they themselves had first to learn the language, before they could hope to maintain themselves. To add to Mazzini's distresses he had letters from a young girl in Switzerland, which increased his already morbid belief that he was doomed to bring unhappiness into the lives of others. The girl had apparently loved him secretly for three years and was wasting away, unable to conquer her passion. Her friends besought him to come back and save her life, but the only result was to make Mazzini unhappy, for he had long decided that all other love must be sacrified to Italy, if his life-work were to succeed. At that moment he even decided to allow no new affections to enter his life, although fortunately for himself and his mission, he afterwards revised his decision. His manner of living differed very little from the days of his Swiss exile, when it was imperative to remain indoors to avoid discovery. In London he went out for meals and then returned to his books and his papers. Before three weeks had elapsed, he realized the impracticability of continuing to live in lodgings, and the decision was made to rent a cottage, where they would share a reception room, and have a private room each. The initial expenditure for furnishing would soon be made up for by the economy effected in living. Mazzini outlined the plans in a letter to his mother dated January 28th,[1] and subsequent letters contain further details, requests for bed-linen, cutlery of a modest kind, white curtains for the ' stanza di ricevimento ' —without measurements, be it noted, for the cottage had not yet been found—salame, a ham and a cheese. Angelo Usiglio seemed to be the most active in house-hunting, and in the third week of March the little company moved into their new quarters at 9 George Street, New Road, where a maid-servant, and a boy of fourteen called David ministered to their needs. At long last Mazzini's books arrived from France and he settled down to a life of study and literary work. His

[1] *Epistolario*, II., p. 426.

letters to his mother give minute details of their housekeeping, evidently in answer to her anxious enquiries, and he is forced to own to the servant's limitations in the art of cooking, roast beef and fried potatoes being apparently her only accomplishments.

His determination to continue as far as possible the cloistered habits of his life in Switzerland, made Mazzini avoid all acquaintances at first. Panizzi he refused to seek out, preferring to trust to meeting him at the British Museum ; the recommendations that his mother sent him to Italian merchants in business in London, he either passed on to others or neglected, and the exiles he already knew he avoided. The introductions he hoped for were to Englishmen who would help him in his work, and not limit their attentions to invitations to dinner. On the 11th of February he announced that he had a letter for Thomas Campbell, and reported that he had already met a lady several times, whom we know to have been Mrs. Archibald Fletcher, for whom he had had an introduction from Filippo Ugoni. Mazzini was then in the depths of despondency, and unfortunately by talking of his beloved *Chatterton* alarmed Mrs. Fletcher for his safety to such an extent that she wrote to him, but was reassured in a long letter that he had no thoughts of suicide. She noted in her diary in April 1845, during another visit to London, that she saw Mazzini frequently, and that his eloquence and power of expressing himself in good English was appreciated by all.[1] Mazzini had an aversion to teaching Italian as a means of earning a livelihood, that was shared by a good many of his unfortunate compatriots, and looked to the reviews to provide him with his daily bread. It is interesting to find him explaining to his mother, in words strangely reminiscent of Foscolo, that ' qui nelle riviste scrivono i membri del Parlamento e gli uomini i più indipendenti e distinti '.[2] He trusted to find acquaintances who could help to dispose of his articles. Meanwhile the struggle to obtain the barest means of subsistence involved him in debt, and forced him to pledge some of his books and maps, and even his mother's ring. The remittances which he received from home might have kept him alone, but he shared everything with his friends, even his clothing. The privations of the early years in London were aggravated by his loneliness, and the lack of news from Giuditta. He felt a stranger in London even after nine months and longed for the beauties of nature that he could not afford time or money to seek. He met J. S. Mill in September and received promise from him that some articles would be accepted for his review, and his hopes were raised ;

[1] *Autobiography of Mrs. Fletcher*, p. 256.
[2] *Epistolario*, II., p. 436.

but years elapsed before journalism brought him in a reasonable return and at no time did it bring him sufficient to keep him without subsidies from his mother, who never failed him.

Some prospect of a better outlet for his labours seems to have induced Mazzini in July 1837 to visit Edinburgh. His friend Giuseppe Giglioli had been there since 1833, teaching,[1] and he had had a frequent correspondence with him since his own arrival in London. Giglioli seemed to think that the north offered him better chances and Mazzini would have joined him but for the Ruffinis. For the expenses for the sojourn in Edinburgh, Mazzini was obliged to exhaust the fund which had been placed to his credit by his parents.[2] He expected to be away for three weeks, but returned within ten days, comparing Edinburgh very unfavourably with London. The city was less beautiful, and to see the beauties of nature one had to leave Edinburgh and spend longer in Scotland than he was prepared to do. The only thing which made an impression on him was Holyrood Palace and that because of Queen Mary's rooms. It is curious that in the long letter that he wrote to his mother on his return there is no mention of the friend he had gone to see. On the contrary he speaks of his own loneliness. The truth was that he hated travelling and only found pleasure in familiar places. When once he knew London he loved it, and it had taken time for his love of Switzerland to grow. He had no sooner returned to London, than his homesickness expressed itself in plans to meet his mother and sisters somewhere in Switzerland or France. The Ruffinis were also to be there with their mother, and they would spend happy days together. One marvels at the dread of travelling which was sufficient to keep the Signora Mazzini from her son for so many years, when she might have joined him for a short while. The passport difficulties cannot have been insurmountable.

In November 1837 Mazzini made the acquaintance of Thomas Carlyle, although it was not until 1839 that he really began to see him frequently ; and he found a joy in the resulting friendship which

[1] Giglioli matriculated as a student of medicine at the University of Edinburgh on April 27th, 1838, and in the three following years. He graduated M.D. in 1841.

[2] *Epistolario*, II., p. 500. It is interesting to note that the fact of Mazzini's visit to Edinburgh is questioned by Professor Mario Menghini, editor of the *Edizione Nazionale degli Scritti Editi e inediti di Giuseppe Mazzini*, pub. by Paolo Galeati, Imola. (Vol. VI., p. 32) ; although it is difficult to see what purpose could be served by Mazzini's making a misleading statement of his movements after the journey was supposed to have been completed.

brightened his life, until the divergence of their opinions estranged them. Mazzini's review of the *French Revolution* in the *Monthly Chronicle*, in spite of differences in opinion which he did not hesitate to express, caused Carlyle to call upon him. Mazzini returned the call, met Mrs. Carlyle and was invited to dinner. During 1840 the admiration that Mazzini and Carlyle felt for each other led to very frequent visits, and Mazzini wrote full accounts to his mother of the arguments that took place ; for the intense individualism of the one, and the doctrine of salvation through and by the masses of the other, had not yet assumed a form which made continued friendly intercourse between them impossible. They presented a united front in attacking utilitarianism, which was always a subject to open the flood-gates of Mazzini's eloquence. He never ceased to twit his great friend Emilie Ashurst for her utilitarian sympathies. Mrs. Carlyle at once awakened a response in his affections and their friendship endured through all the years of her life, in spite of the breach between himself and Carlyle. In 1840 the decision was made to break up the little household at George Street, which had gradually become such a centre of discord, that its continuance could only increase the unhappiness of all its members. Agostino Ruffini seems to have been the chief cause of the dissension and to have had an uncontrolled temper which made constant bickerings and quarrelling the prevailing atmosphere. Mazzini had hinted at the necessity for separation at various periods, in his letters to his ' second mother ', the Signora Ruffini, but she was unwilling to consent to her sons' being removed from his protecting care. It is very curious to compare the unanimity of Mazzini's various biographers in condemning Agostino, his shallowness and ingratitude, and above all, his treachery in spreading calumnious reports about the friend whose only fault was his too great generosity to his brother men, with the eulogy which David Masson wrote of him. Masson spoke of his courtesy, his gentleness and his unconscious magnetism. " One of Italy's best, finest and gentlest ", he wrote, "—a man to be known on and on, ever more subtly and intimately, and yet never to be exhausted or known enough ; to be found wise, true, honourable and good by even the most delicate tests that could be applied." [1] One can only explain the apparent contradiction by the supposition that Mazzini, in spite of old association, worked as an irritant on the nerves of Ruffini whose never very strong character had been unable to bear up against the effects of continuous exile, confinement and privation, and who lacked the higher inspiration of Mazzini's faith. It is difficult to excuse his part in turning his

[1] *Memories of Two Cities*, by David Masson, p. 125.

mother from the man she had loved as a son, when the two brothers met her in Paris later.   When Agostino went to Edinburgh in 1840, well provided with letters of introduction by the Carlyles and one from Mazzini to Mrs. Archibald Fletcher, he had little difficulty in making his way, and was soon able to furnish rooms for himself in George Street, where he lived in comfort if not in luxury.   Masson speaks of his singular tolerance of all the varieties of speculative Italian patriotism, republican, monarchical or theocratic, although the underlying idea of Italian unity was fixed [1] ; and this tolerance was unquestionably one rock on which his friendship with Mazzini was shattered.   Giovanni continued to live with Mazzini for a year longer until, after a quarrel, he removed to Paris.

The Carlyles persuaded Mazzini to settle in Chelsea, and after a few months in Clarendon Square he found a house quite near them at 4 York Buildings, King's Road, which he rented for an English-woman whom he had saved from starvation some years before, and her Italian husband, an exiled artisan from Perugia.   The Tanciones agreed to board Mazzini and Giovanni Ruffini for the modest sum of £40 each per annum.   Mazzini remained for three years, finding in his constant companionship with the Carlyles, and especially with Mrs. Carlyle, a solace for his loneliness.   Mrs. Carlyle has been frequently criticized for the flippant tone of her references to Mazzini in her corres-pondence ; but it is not difficult to read between the lines, and to dis-cover the depth of her affection for him, which showed itself in impatient irritation when he refused to attend to his health, or to cease sacrificing himself for others whom Mrs. Carlyle, with greater worldly wisdom, saw to be not altogether worthy of his goodness.   She confessed her-self, after taking the prospect of his departure in 1848 with surprising calmness, that all her affection for him ' waked up ' when she knew him in jeopardy during the siege of Rome and so gallantly fulfilling his destiny.[2]   Mazzini was her frequent companion on little excursions and her confidant in the distressing years when she tormented herself with unreasonable jealousy of her husband's friendship with Lady Harriet Baring.   The fun she makes of his little oddities in speech was affectionate and kindly, and she seems unfeeling only when roused to anger at his making himself into ' " minced meat " for the universe '. When Mazzini was ill in the summer of 1843 and developed the abscess on his face which owing to neglect threatened to affect the bone, Mrs. Carlyle took matters into her own hands and wrote to Dr. Toynbee,

[1] *Memories of Two Cities*, p. 130.
[2] *Jane Welsh Carlyle : Letters to her Family*, p. 327.

who had already shown his interest in him. She was distressed by
the lack of comfort in the Tancione household, and longed to be able
to bring him home and nurse him ; and her words are full of tenderness
when he calls to see her after the wound had been probed by the surgeon
and a tooth had been drawn to help the discharge. " I could not help
crying half the time he stayed ", she wrote to her cousin, Jeanie Welsh,
"—he looks so emaciated and so calm ! if his mother were near or
any human being to nurse him I should not mind so much, but he has
nobody but poor helpless me——" [1] She cannot always be blamed
for not seeing eye to eye with him in his schemes for the regeneration
of Italy, and if her criticism of his support of the inventor of dirigible
balloons seems unkind, she was not alone in condemning the notion
as highly fantastic. One day in October 1842, Mazzini had come to her

radiant over an " aviso interessante " which he produced from his
pocket, setting forth that one Mussi or some such name, had discovered
—a power for regulating balloons as perfectly as a steamboat or railway
carriage, in confirmation whereof behold certificates from the *Grand
Duke of Tuscany* and the heads of the *Academy of Science at Florence*,
etc. etc., before whom his model had been displayed.[2]

The man was penniless but was willing to sell his secret for the ' trifling
sum of *two thousand* pounds ! '

If Mazzini can find him work in the interim [she continued] the man
may be induced not to part with it ! till some member of *the Association*
in Italy may be found to make the purchase. " Then ", says Mazzini,
" the power of directing balloons *ours* ; all is ours ! " " You mean
that you would invade Italy in balloons ?—that the *Association* would
descend on the Austrians out of the skies ! " " Exactly ! and I confess
to you—you may think it childish—but there is something of romance,
something which flatters my imagination in the idea of *starting up a
big nation* in a manner never before heard tell of ! " " *A la bonne
heure*, my Dear ! but if it be decided that we are to begin the war by
personating the fallen angels, adieu to *my share* in the expedition."
" Now, why so ? (with a look of the most grave astonishment). It was
just in reference to *you* that I felt the greatest preference to *this means*
—to think that you could go without incurring the physical suffering
of a sea-voyage, and all the dangers—what shall I say ?—of being sunk
perhaps by a volley of cannon from the shore ! and then there would
be something so new and so—what shall I say ?—*suitable* for *you* in
descending as it were out of Heaven to redeem a suffering people ! " [3]

One may be pardoned for wondering what rôle was assigned to
Mrs. Carlyle in the coming invasion, for her physique hardly fitted

[1] *Jane Welsh Carlyle : Letters to her Family*, p. 139.
[2] *ibid.*, p. 34.   [3] *ibid.*, p. 34.

her for the work afterwards so heroically performed by Jessie White Mario, in nursing Garibaldi's wounded. There is no doubt that her increasing disbelief in Mazzini's schemes was due as much to lack of imagination as to the possibilities, as to an uncertainty regarding their practicability. He seemed to have implicit faith in her and told her, she says, all his secret operations—even names, although she considered no amount of confidence in a friend could justify him for making such dangerous disclosures concerning others. She proved her own inability to keep the secret confided to her, by writing to her cousin at the end of January 1844, with due warning to ' keep this from the knowledge of Gambardella of course ', that Mazzini was going to have a ' new " Savoy's expedition " into Italy as early as the end of this February ! ! ! ' [1] In spite of everything her affection for him endured, and in 1847 she wrote that he had a power of identifying himself with those he loved—at least in their sorrows, which she never saw equalled. She too spoke of his looking almost ' dazzlingly beautiful ' on one inspired occasion, for few of his friends failed to describe his lovely clear olive complexion, his delicately fine regular features, and the extraordinary sweetness of his expression, which the splendid brow and bright flashing eyes redeemed from any trace of effeminacy.

Mazzini's attention was soon drawn to the little organ boys and terra cotta figure vendors who frequented the London streets. As early as 1820 the Sardinian Consul General reported to the Home Office that some hundreds of Sardinian subjects, mostly Genoese, were wandering about London and the provinces, begging, ' which they practice with impunity under pretence of exhibiting monkeys, tortoises and other animals '. These men used to bring over boys if they had no children of their own, and they brought them up to earn money for them.[2] The report was inspired however not by humanitarian reasons, but because it was thought that these men might be bearers of correspondence between the disaffected in France and Italy and those in England. Mazzini tracked some of the masters and brought them to justice in court for their cruelty to the poor little children. The thought of building up some nobler citizens for Italy induced him to open a free school for the boys in 1841, where from 9 o'clock every evening they might learn the rudiments of education and something of the duties and rights of citizens. Lord Ashley, Joseph Toynbee, William Shaen and Harriet Martineau were among the earliest helpers, and Filippo Pistrucci was the secretary. Mazzini

[1] *Jane Welsh Carlyle : Letters to her Family*, p. 183
[2] Records Office. H.O. 5. Alien Office Reports.

himself undertook part of the teaching and all the responsibility of raising funds for the maintenance of the school. Concerts and bazaars and subscriptions were the sources of income, and every year an annual anniversary dinner and prize-giving was held for the boys, to which well-wishers and friends contributed. Mrs. Carlyle often refers to these functions in her letters, and Gabriele Rossetti was an annual visitor. The school lasted until the events of 1848 called Mazzini back to Italy. About two hundred boys attended it and some Italian workmen. The latter formed an association with national aims ; and Mazzini started a journal for them, the *Apostolato Popolare*, to which he contributed. This had the honour of being the first Italian association of working men. Later, in his second exile, Mazzini conceived the idea of a shilling ' subscription for European Freedom ', chiefly with the aim of arousing the interest of the English working classes and thus encouraging the Italians who had struggled.[1] Among Panizzi's correspondence there is a statement dated August 15th, 1847, of the aims of the *Associazione Nazionale*, signed by Mazzini, Giglioli, who seems to have left Edinburgh, Gallenga and W. J. Linton.[2] The latter throughout took the keenest interest in Mazzini's plans, and the committee met weekly at his house in Hatton Garden.

The event in the course of Mazzini's first period of exile in England which brought him most into public notice was the opening of his letters in transit, by order of the Home Secretary, Sir James Graham, acting for Lord Aberdeen, who wished to prevent the hatching of plots in England for Italian insurrections. Mazzini suspected the tampering with his letters from the double dates and times of posting on the official stamp, and applied a long series of tests, with hairs and sand in the envelopes, and marked seals and wafers, before putting the matter into the hands of Thomas Duncombe, the member for Finsbury, who brought it up in the House. Mrs. Carlyle had known of Mazzini's suspicions from the first and delighted in adding messages to her notes, addressed to the Austrian Embassy, requesting that they be not delayed. The indignation that swept the country at the violation of common honesty was voiced in the press, and Thomas Carlyle wrote an eloquent protest against a practice which he classed with the picking of men's pockets. It was found necessary to appoint committees of investigation, and public opinion was still further roused by both committees, of the House of Lords and of the House of Com-

[1] Leigh Hunt's Correspondence, Vol. IV., fol. 190. B.M., Add. MSS. 38111.
[2] Vol. II. B.M., Add. MSS. 36715. See App. V.

mons, meeting in secret. It is unnecessary here to go into the details of the enquiries, and it is sufficient to note two of the articles that appeared in the reviews on a topic so present to men's minds. Panizzi wrote a lengthy article in the *North British Review* in which he went into details of the legal aspect of the matter, criticized the appointment of the members and contrasted the reports of the two committees. The writer of the article in the *Westminster Review* made the reports the text for a strongly worded indictment of English academical and university education, which, by encouraging the study of the ' transformations of Ovid and the history of the Punic Wars ', left no place for the decalogue or any sound interpretation of its meaning, and bred a generation of statesmen whose moral creed was to " steal, to lie, to commit forgery, treachery and tyrannous injustice ". Lord Aberdeen to his shame denied handing over to the Austrian Embassy the information gained from the correspondence, but it was shown to have been done ; although later researches seem to prove that the British Government was not guilty of giving information about the Bandieras and their raid, and hence of causing their death ; or shall we say that their information was already known to the Austrians ?

The outcry against the opening of the letters by the Post Office brought Mazzini the solace of much personal sympathy and was the beginning of the greatest friendships of his exile. William Henry Ashurst, an enthusiastic Radical and supporter of Rowland Hill's postal scheme, sent his son and eldest daughter, Eliza, to call on him and invite him to their house. To their surprise Mazzini accepted the invitation and thenceforth took possession of them once and for ever, as the youngest daughter Emilie expressed it. He quickly found himself at home in the household, which was entirely free from the convention now associated with the middle of the Victorian era. The married daughters, Caroline wife of James Stansfeld, Matilda wife of Joseph Biggs of Leicester, and Emilie married then to Sydney Hawkes and later to Carlo Venturi, were as great friends as the others. Emilie, whose utilitarianism he so often attacked, was perhaps as ' man to man ' his greatest friend, Caroline his ideal of womanhood. Their wide interests and progressive minds made them keen supporters of Mazzini's schemes. The most intimate knowledge of their relations with him is gained from his published letters to the family.[1] The more formal terms of the first soon give place to a familiar friendliness,

---

[1] *Mazzini's Letters to an English Family*, ed. by E. F. Richards. 3 Vols., 1920.

and there are countless touches of kindly wit and revelations of his sense of humour. His friendship with the Ashursts brought back something of natural fun into his life and kept him from the morbid depression which had so often overwhelmed him in the earlier years. Speaking of his sadness once to Eliza Ashurst, in a letter of December 18th, 1846, he wrote : " Mine is a matter of course ; and it is only a sign that, in spite of all the efforts of my philosophy, there is still an *excédant* of life within me revolting occasionally and reasserting its rights,"[1] perhaps a not unhealthy sign when all is said and done, for it kept his sympathies warm for his fellow men. In 1846 the Ashursts proposed that Mazzini should live with them at Muswell Hill, but he felt for several reasons the advantage of his independence, and refused. " You forget what I am and upon what an undertaking I am bent," he wrote to Eliza. " Next year, most likely, I will vanish out of England into space ; perhaps to come back, perhaps to never more come back."[2]

Of Mazzini's extraordinary power of attracting birds all his biographers speak. At Savona his companion was a wild finch which flew in and made friends with him, and in London he had canaries and linnets which flew about his room and perched fearlessly on his head. He even had wire netting put over the window, that they might have the freedom of the room without cages. In the first house his friend was a cat of which he was very fond, while Usiglio had a Newfoundland dog, which however died after a short time. Mazzini's one vice, if it can be so called, was smoking. " I smoke whilst reading or writing," he wrote, " never dominated, but dominating ; transforming, not assimilating substances ; producing, not consuming ; perhaps looking unconsciously for a symbol, alas ! to my thoughts and schemes, ending in smoke " ![3]

When the great call came in 1848, Mazzini was ready. He went to Paris immediately on the downfall of Louis Philippe, and after a few days in London again set out, and this time for Milan. Of the part he played there in arousing the enthusiasm of the crowd, but opposed by the Provisional Government who regarded his republicanism as the greatest barrier to the achievement of their own aims, it is hardly our province to speak here. Some scapegoat must always be found and his antagonists accused him of causing the split in the Italian ranks that brought about the defeat of the Lombard-Piedmontese army. His chance came when in 1849 Rome was left without a ruler. The Pope having fled, a republic seemed the natural successor,

[1] *ibid.*, Vol. I., p. 45.   [2] *ibid.*, p. 37.   [3] *ibid.*, p. 41.

and Mazzini was called, first as a deputy and then as Triumvir. His great work in the city, and his inspiring of the people during the shameful siege which their sister republic, France, laid to Rome, gave him the leadership he had dreamt of. That it ended with the entry of the French troops and led to a second exile was just another of the cruel blows that Fate dealt him through the course of his life. The following years in London brought him more friendships, greater activity in plotting and scheming, greater intensity of his republican ideals and also greater opposition. For Mazzini there was no middle way, but one right and one truth. Moderates had no place in his theories and absolutists were to be overcome, not won. His beauty of character kept round him a circle of supporters who idolized him and accepted his teaching without question ; and even if his republicanism did not win through in the end, his influence in spreading among the people the doctrine of unity upon which freedom and independence are based, is incalculable, immeasurable, the purest inspiration of the rise of Modern Italy.

APPENDIX I.A

1. *Mr. S. E. Cook to Mr. Sicard.*

BERNE—11*th Aug[t]*, 1816.

DEAR MR. SICARD

I am sure you will excuse the trouble I am giving you, in asking you to be so good as to assist my Friend Col. Foscolo, who will give you this & who is now on his way to London to establish himself for some time —He has no acquaintance whatever & it being his first visit to England if you can help him in procuring lodgings and in giving him such directions as a stranger wants in such case, I shall feel particularly obliged to you—Col. Foscolo is a native of Zante, now under protection, & is a man of letters, of great & extensive knowledge. Should he find you, he will explain his wants to you. I have rather recommended him the new part of the town, between Portland Place and Baker Street, as *genteel, cheap & healthy* but you know the town better than I can pretend to do & a good deal depends on the Colonel himself on his arrival— I have heard nothing from Howman, nor of him. I hope to do so on my arrival in Italy in October—as I am anxious to do so— Accept my best wishes for Mrs. Sicard & your circle and believe me

Your obed[t] Servt

SAML. ED. COOK.

Address : Mr. Sicard, Prs. of Wales's Apartments, Kensington Palace.

[MSS. Lab., Vol. XLII., Sec. A.]

2. *William Stewart Rose to Foscolo. Undated.*

CARISSIMO,

Non rispondo a certe vostre domande, sperando di poter rispondervi qui a voce. Vi prego di passarci più presto che potrete. La mia casupola è distante, lo confesso, ma in Inghilterra il trasporto è facile e non caro. Mettendovi in diligenza la mattina un quarto avanti le otto capiterete a casa di mio padre dentro della giornata, ed indi a casa mia in un paio d' ore. Vi consiglio di prendere un posto in diligenza, qualche giorno avanti, e quelle che mi sembrano più commode, sono *the Telegraph* e l' *Union*. La prima alberga al White Horse Cellar e l' altro al *White Bear*, tutti e due in *Piccadilly*. In una di codeste carozze passerete

fino a *Southampton* ed ivi troverete un mio servo con un legnetto che vi trasporterà a casa di mio padre.
Addio! sono impazientissimo di vedervi.

Wm STEWART ROSE.

Il mio cameriere manda le istruzioni riguardo alla diligenza in Inglese. Il viaggio costa trenta scellini. Ci è poi una mancia di due scellini e mezzo per il cocchiere. Un posto di fuori si paga una lira.
[*Ibid.*]

3. *From William Stewart Rose to Foscolo. Undated.*

CARO MIO AMICO
Rilevo da una lettera ricevuta oggi dal Sotto Segretario, che l' Alien Act non frappone alcuno ostacolo al passar voi da me in campagna o in altro luogo. Anche vi aspetterò impazientemente.

Per ora addio.
Il vostro amico
W. S. ROSE.

[*Ibid.*]

4. *From William Stewart Rose to Foscolo. Undated.*

CARO MIO AMICO,
Mi rincresce assaissimo della vostra disgrazia, la quale però non deve durare molto tempo in questo paese, dove le febbri non sono da temersi come in Italia.
. . . Allorche [che] potrete viaggiare senza incommodo avrò gran piacere abbracciandovi quì, dove l' aria che è perfetta, seconderà la vostra convalescenza, e dove potrete pigliare, occorrendo i bagni tepidi o freddi di mare— Il Conte Matexà mi ha mandata la sua commendatizia ed io l' ho invitato a venir passare qualche tempo quì inteso che questi contorni offrono più cose da vedersi cioè *Portsmouth*, l' isola di *Wight ecc.*
Se voi guarite presto, come spero, potrete forse combinare il viaggetto insieme con lui. . . .
Vi prego de' miei complimenti a Lord e Lady Holland, e mandatemi, vi congiuro, notizie delle vostra salute.

Il vostro amico
W. S. ROSE.

[*Ibid.*]

5. *From William Stewart Rose to William Frere. Undated.*

MY DEAR FRERE
I proposed two *Spring* Lyons to you from Italy. I now send you, to stay your appetite, two from Greece. One of them you know by reputation, Foscolo. . . . Now, be a good Polito, and carry them to Caius, if you can, with my best regard to Davy. Foscolo has some English and as much Greek & Latin as you like. The other roars admirably in English.

Yours most affectionately
W. S. ROSE.

Address : To the Master of Downing Coll. Cambridge.
by favour of the Signor Foscolo.
[*Ibid.*]

6. *Minutes of a letter to Wm. Stewart Rose from the Sigr^a Magiotti.
Undated.*

SIGNORE

Se la fata galante finta un giorno sentimento per M. Peers non per
questo è [   ] di sentir davvero la forza dell' amicizia e ricomparira
come fata galante non più a Peers ma anche a Lei—Sign^e Rose per
comunicarle alcuna mia idea sul prossimo avvicinamente alla gran-
d'Isola del Sig. Foscolo, mio dolcissimo amico. Egli non ha di mestieri
che io glie lo raccomandi poiche essendogli stato vero amico un giorno
è impossibile non esserglelo [*sic*] per tutta la vita, e [*sic*] vero pur troppo
che le fù dura Madrigna l' Italia e che lo trasse a volontario esilio nel
quale ebbe tribolati giorni—Ho desiderato mille volte che altro cielo e
più adagio [?] lo accogliesse e le fosse più clemente e scegliendo Londra
per sua dimora parmi che abbia fatto cosa degna del suo genio potendo
così impiegare i giorni presenti alla celebrità del suo avvenire, ed avere
distrattazione [*sic*] e piaceri onde rianima e il suo ingegno immaginoso e
independente—le conoscenze con i Dotti Inglesi, e farle ala presso i
librai e stampatori, gente iniqua dapertutta Italia.

[MSS. Foscoliani, Vol. X., B, 6. Bib. Naz., Florence.]
Catalogued by Chiarini, 1885.

7. *From William Stewart Rose to Foscolo.*

[MUDIFORD, *Ott.* 1816]

CARISSIMO,

Rilevo dalle due lettere che mi avete mandate che vi si pressa molto
di starvene a *Holland House* ed io desidererei piuttosto di raffermarvi
in codesto progetto che di sollecitarvi di tornare in Hampshire. Nella
detta casa troverete chi possano secondare i vostri progetti molto meglio
che non io, libri e società, laddove da me, che vivo *mihi* ET UNDIS, non ci
è che il mare e la quiete. Poi le spese del viaggio, per non dir nulla
degl' incommodi della strada non sono cosa lieve, ed, in quanto al giro
che facevamo conto di fare nell' isola di Wight, quantunque il tempo
adesso sia bellissimo, per quando voi foste di ritorno, sarebbe forse
tale da escludere i viaggi.

·Gli animali* stanno a ruminare. Buffo vi lecca la mano.

Addio e dall' anima

W. S. ROSE.

P.S.—Ho scritto poco, chè ho una penna che vuol scrivere a modo suo.
Compatitela.

[MSS. Lab., Vol. XLII., Sec. A.]

8. *From William Stewart Rose to Foscolo.* [*Undated—Probably
October* 1816]

CARISSIMO

Che voi vi siate intanato, deliberatissimo di non isbuccare, mi pare
una risoluzione maggior d' ogni eccezzione, ma non posso dir lo stesso
del resto della lettera, poichè nè voi siete inglese nè noi siamo ancora di
Novembre, mese nel quale, secondo un autor francese, ogni inglese si
crede in diritto d' ammazzarsi. . . .

In somma, caro voi *non vi lasciate uccidere Dal morte melancolies.*

Che quantunque i vostri affari possano riuscir male, niente di ciò che mi avete detto mi desta un' opinion simile.

Ditemi come v' accoglie *Murray* e credetemi sempre
Vostro amico e servitore
W. S. ROSE.

[*Ibid.*]

9. *From Lord Holland to Foscolo.*

[*Note on back :* Holland House Ottobre—1816 Lord Holland]

[*No heading*]

J'espère que votre absence ne sera pas longue—et que vous viendres ici à votre retour passer quelques jours à faire quelques connaissancez qui vous seront utiles aussi bien qu'agréables pour vos projets de literature —J'y joings une lettre pour Mr. Longman qui imprime mon petit livre a cette heure, qui est un très honnête homme et le plus considerable, quoiqu' *il n'est pas* le plus *entreprenant* de tous nos *publishers*—Car il faut savoir que nous avons ici, outre les éditeurs des livres—le *publisher* qui fait le fraix [*sic*] de l'édition, l'imprimeur qui imprime les livres sous ces [*sic*] ordres et le libraire qui les vend en détail—Le *Publisher* le plus à la mode et certainement le plus entreprenant c'est *Murray*, Albemarle Street.   Je ne le connais pas personellement [*sic*] mais j'écris deux mots pour vous y presenter si vous le preferez aux *publishers* plus longtems etablis & a quelques egards plus froids de la cité tels que *Longman & Rees* ou Cadell & Davies—Je viens de traduire la lettre interessante du voyageur—[Evidently the first of the letters on the customs of England and Italy, which Murray undertook to publish.   Lord Holland speaks of the publication of the letter and the changes necessary to make it appear written by an Englishman.]

Venez donc je vous prie—Milady aussi bien que moi est desolée de ne plus vous voir.

V^{ll} HOLLAND.

[This letter is entirely in Lord Holland's hand-writing.]

[*Ibid.*]

9A. *From Lord Holland to Longman, enclosed in above letter.   Undated.*

DEAR SIR,

This letter will be delivered to you by Mr. Foscolo—His high & merited literary reputation is known to you & as I understand from him that he wishes either to republish some of his works or to print some new ones in England, I thought you would feel obliged to me for procuring you his acquaintance, & I am at the same time anxious from the interest I take in all that concerns a man of his genius that he should receive the best advice & assistance in giving his works to the English publick—I have therefore referred him to you for all information necessary to his undertaking.

I am Sir
truly your obliged
VASSALL HOLLAND.

[*Ibid.*]

10. *Draft of a letter from the Signora Quirina Magiotti to Wm. S. Rose.*

FIRENZE 21 *Marzo* 1817.

SIGNORE

Inaspettati al certo le giungeranno i miei caratteri seppure la memoria
della *fata* galante non le facesse supporre ricordare che le fate giungano
improvvise e mai inopportune ; con questo breve preambulo io entro
in materia con voi Signore per domandarvi novelle del vostro e mio
amico Sig. Ugo Foscolo che delle quali ne sono affatto priva fino dal
sette novembre (nel qual giorno ricevida Londra) e con grandissimo dolore
mio e de' parenti suoi che privi di sue lettere viviano [?] nella continua
angoscia dell' incertezza. Io non ho mancato dirigerli le mie lettere a
Londra Soho Square N⁰ 11 ove dimorava ma il suo ostinato silenzio e
per me il colpo il più crudele che potra mai arrivarmi. Io sono legata
con esso da strettissima e —— amizia [*sic*], il suo bene, e il suo male
riverbera sulla mia anima, e il non saper cosa mi pensava di Lui mi
angoscia maggiormente, tanto più che nei calamitosi tempi del 1813 e
1814 trovandoli nell' alta Italia, le sue finanze soffrirono molti cangia-
menti, ond' è che io temo che le sue entrate non possino corrispondere
alle spese necessarie, e che viva una vita troppo ristretta e forse—
    Io vi prego, Signore di prestarli tutta la vostra asistenza [*sic*] in qual-
unque genera per mio conto—farete cosa gratissima a me ed a' parenti
suoi se curete la—[*unfinished*]

WILLIAM ——

[MSS. Foscoliani, Vol. X., B.   Bib. Naz., Florence.]

11. *From William Stewart Rose to the Signora Quirina Magiotti.*
Undated.

PREGIATISSIMA SIGNORA,

Io ho rilevato da Foscolo che Ella non ha ricevuto una mia lettera
scritta in risposta alla Sua de' venti due Marzo, la quale và [*sic*] ugualmente della fata Morgana e della fata galante di Firenze. In quella
mia smarrita, io le partecipava d' aver somministrato quaranta lire
sterline al nostro amico, col patto che egli, potendo, me ne rifarebbe in
fine di questo anno (1817) e non potendo, io ricorrerei a Lei, a secondo
della promessa contenuta nella sopradetta sua de' 22.—Stia sicura che gli
avrei somministrato per 40 lire sterline, senza la di Lei malleveria,
quando io non restassi molto, & bilanciato nella mia economia domestica
per aver dovuta rinunziare, a cagion della cattiva salute, ad un impiego,
che mi fruttava il doppio di quello che io posseggo in adesso.
    Io ho l' onor di rassegnarmi
        Di Lei
            Signora Quirini
                L'ubbid^{mo} e divot^{mo} [*sic*] servitore
                    GUGLIELMO STEWART ROSE.

Address : Madame Quirini Magiotti, Poste Restante à Florence.
[*Ibid.*]

12. *From William Stewart Rose to the Signora Quirina Magiotti.*

VENEZIA *a'* 12 *dec^{re}* 1817.

PREGIATISSIMA SIGNORA,

La sua, in risposta alla mia di Londra, dopo di aver visitato codesta
città e poi tornato qui in Italia, mi è finalmente capitata in Venezia.

Le sono tenutissimo della proposizione fattami in essa, ma devo aspettare una lettera da Foscolo prima di valermene ; poichè volendo egli incaricarsi del ripagamento dei noti denari, piuttosto che indossarla un tale incommodo, mi pregò di dargli tempo sino alla Natività, inteso che allora io ricorrerei a Lei, caso lui non mi potesse rimborsare. In conseguenza dunque della sua ultima, gli ho scritto, che così farei quando egli non potesse adempire le nostre condizioni. Io dunque sospendo d' indicarle la maniera di rifarmi delle 40 lire sterline somministrategli, fino all' epoca di cui ci eramo convenuti ; cioè sino alla natività.

Dovrei aggiungere che non ho avuto notizie di Foscolo dacchè io son partito di Londra, ma il Cav. Cicognara, il di lei gran panegirista, m' ha informato che ha ottenuto, o spera d' ottenere una qualche carica nelle isole Ioniche.

Desiderando le sue notizie,

Io mi dò l' onor d' essere

suo ubb^{mo} servitore

W. S. ROSE.

Address : Poste Restante, Florence.

[*Ibid.*]

[This letter and Number 13 have been quoted in full by Del Cerro in his *Epistolario, compreso quello amoroso di Ugo Foscolo e di Mocenni-Magiotti Quirina,* p. 246. They have been included here to complete the correspondence between William Stewart Rose and Quirina Magiotti.]

13. *From William Stewart Rose to the Signora Quirina Magiotti.*

PREGIATISSIMA SIGNORA,

Per caro che avrei il carteggiar con Lei su degli altri argomenti mi rincresce assai di doverlo fare sopra quello tristissimo de' denari. Però siccome parebbe, a seconda della sua ultima, che io non mi sia bene spiegato nelle mie, mi è forza di tornarci. Eccole dunque, in ristretto, come è andata la faccenda tra me e Foscolo. Somministrandogli le note 40 lire sterline, gli dissi che io ricorrerei a la Signora Quirini pel ripagamento ; ma egli mi pregò di dargli tempo fino al Natale, sperando di poterle restituire avanti di codest' epoca. Passato però il natale, e non avendo ricevuto alcuna lettera da lui, quantunque io gli abbia scritto, e che io sia sicurissimo che la mia lettera (rinchiusa in una, addirizzata ad un mio amico), gli sia pervenuta, mi trovo in necessità di valermi della di lei promessa di spedirmi essa somma, somministrato a Foscolo, onde io soddisfaccia alle pretese d' un amico in Inghilterra, dal quale l' ho presa in prestito. La prego dunque, o Signora, di mandarla al Signor Colalto Niccolò, Salizzada San Samuel, Venezia, di attribuire questa mia premura al vero mottivo e di credermi sempre con tutta stima dovuta

Suo umillissimo [*sic*]

servo ed amico

WILLIAM STEWART ROSE.

P.S.—Dimenticava di dire che ho fatto la sua ambasciata in là Cicognara.

a' 4 febbrajo, 1818. VENEZIA.

Address : Poste Restante, Florence.

[*Ibid.*]

14. *From Samuel Rogers to Foscolo.*

May 21st.

[*No heading*]

I have read what you have written, & am at a loss what to say to You. *Praise from the Praised* is such sweet music, that none can resist it. *Me*, I will confess, it has in this instance overcome altogether. I was before, I fear, a vain man. Now I am in great danger of becoming a proud one.

Ever your obliged & affect^e
Friend
SAM^L ROGERS.

Pray, pray forgive my impatience.

[MSS. Lab., Vol. XLII., Sec. A.]

15. *From Lady Charlotte Campbell to Foscolo.*

GLOUCESTER PLACE
17 *May* 1817

[*No heading*]

You are very good and I am very grateful. No person can more highly value your gift ; few perhaps have paid Ortis a more sincere tribute of feeling, than myself. It is all that I have to bestow, but you will not despise, for your work, this homage of a woman's heart.

When shall I see you, my Dear Sir to thank you in person & assure you that I am most sincerely

Your obliged
CHARLOTTE MARIA CAMPBELL.

[*Ibid.*]

16. *From Serafino Buonaiuti to Foscolo.*

HOLLAND HOUSE.
Sabato sera 18 *Gen.* 1817.

STIMATIS^MO SIG. UGO

Miledi Holland avrebbe voluto oggi scriverle di propria mano, ma un doloroso mal di testa l' à tenuta confinata tutta la giornata nel letto.

Era per dirle, che l' altro giorno il celebre Mr. Knight venne a vederla, e ch' essa lo incoraggì a venirle a fare una visita come a compagno letterato, e vicino : e ch' egli accettò l' incoraggimento con piacere. Perciò Miledi spera, che non sara stata, o non sarà sorpresa di essa visita.

Miledi dice parimente, ch' ella à accettato da Mr. Knight un invito a desinare per subito che sarà stabilita nella casa di Londra, e ch' ella vi sarà pare invitato, perchè il Sig. Knight desidera farla conoscere a degli Ellenisti ; e spera ch' ella lo gradirà ; ed intanto Miledi la prega di far con esso conoscenza, come anco per vedere le sue celebri collezioni.

Mr. Knight ha incontrato Calvo, ma non è molto innamorato del suo *classicismo* ed opinione sulla scienza degli antichi Greci.

Mi permetta di dirmi con moltissimo stimo
Suo
U^mo Dev^mo Servitore
SERAFINO BUONAIUTI.

P.S.—Batocchi scrive bene ! ma è un poco parolaio ; lo stile del Casti è più vernacolo, ma è men fecondo : vi son bellissimi tratti nuovi !

[Addressed to No. 10 instead of No. 11 Soho Square.]

[*Ibid.*]

17. *From Roger Wilbraham to Foscolo.*

IN STRATTON STREET No. 11
ai 30 *di Marzo.*

Nel rammentare il Sig^re Ugo Foscolo della sua graziosa promessa di pigliar a zuppa martedì venturo dopo le sei ore in casa di Ruggiero Wilbraham, si rassegna nello stesso tempo il suo umilissimo servitore & lo prega di ricevere le sue grazie distinte per la lettura dei suoi preziosi libretti.—La sua eloquenza veramente incanta ; ed avendo ella avuto quell' effetto sopra il cuore d' un ignorante ma pure affettuoso Dilettante della lingua seduttrice d' Italia, si puol [?] giudicare quanto maggiore effetto deve produrre su' i sensi di quei che l' intendono perfettamente.

[The remainder of the letter asks Foscolo's help regarding a sonnet to Genoa by Pastorini in the 18th century.]

[*Ibid.*]

18. *From Foscolo to John C. Hobhouse.*

WOODSTOCK ST. *decemb^r* 28, 1818.

MONSIEUR—
Ayez la bonté de faire arriver par l'entremise de votre Banquier la lettre ci-jointe, et le bill de £200 Livr. sterl. aux Îles Ioniennes à Mr. Dennys Bulzo de Zante sur lequel je lève pour le payement de cette somme. Lorsque la lettre de change sera payée, votre banquier prelèvera la somme de cent-vingt cinque livres sterl. que vous me prêtez, et il disposera des autre soixante-quinze livres selon les indications que je donnerai. Dans le cas (ce que je ne crains point) que la lettre de change ne soit pas accepté, je la retirerai ici en payant les cent vingt-cinq livres, et en tout cas les fraîs, huit jours après que l'on me presenterà la lettre de change protestée. Pour éviter autant qu'il est possible tout incon-venient, veuillez bien prévenir vôtre banquier de n'epedier [*sic*] la lettre de change que d'ici a huit jours à fin de donner le tems d'arriver aux Îles à un autre lettre d'avis que j'ai dejà fait précéder depuis le *20* de ce mois. Malheureusement il n'y a pas de postes regulières jusque a Zante, et il faut souvent dependre du moyen des barques de sabotage. J'ose esperer que vous me pardonnerez tant de peines, ce que vous serai [*sic*] convaincu que je vous les donne pour combiner mon devoir et ma reconnaissance avec vôtre delicatesse et votre interêt. Aussi je vous prie de laisser cette lettre chez mon banquier pour *memorandum.*

J'ai l'honneur d'être
Monsieur
Vôtre tres-obeissant serviteur
HUGUES FOSCOLO.

To John Hobhouse Esqr

[*Address :* John Hobhouse, Esqre, 43 Clarges Street.]

[Broughton Correspondence, Vol. II. B.M., Add. MSS. 36457.]

19. *From Ugo Foscolo to Lord John Russell.*
[*Almost illegible.*]

MILORD
Avant de vous presenter mes remerciments j'ai jugé de cõmuniquer votre Lettre aux Pargiotes et le secours que vous avez bien voulu leur donner avec tant de générosité. Ils avaient souvent malgré leurs mal-heurs et leur *imperieuse* pauvreté, [externé ?] de la renitence a solliciter

et accepter de l'argent,—mais cette raison n'existe plus aussitôt qu'ils savent que ce bienfait vient de vous, et que vôtre [sic] liberalité doit servir autant à reparer leurs besoins imminents, qu'à me rembourser en partie de l'argent que j'ai avancé pour eux au delà de mes propres moyens. Au rest, Milord, vous pouvez être sure [sic] que leur discretion sera égale à leur reconnaissance ; et que le secret demeurera entre nous, au moins tant que le Tems qui cache et decouvre les secrets des hommes à son gré, ne le manifeste. Aussitôt que je aurais apris de quelle manière rediger leur Petition et quelles sont les formalités à remplir et les expedients à prendre pour qu'ils s'adressent au Parlement sans frôler les regles de la Diplomatie, je ecrirai leur papier, et ils vous le presenteront eux-mêmes. Et dans ce cas, Milord, j'ose vous prier d'accepter l'homage qu'ils vous offriront de leur gratitude. Agréez en attendant le mien ; et je vous le dois autant et plus que les Pargiotes.

Je suis,
Milord
Votre devoué recoñaissant serviteur
U. Foscolo.

N. Bond St. 27 April 1820.

[Correspondence of Lord John Russell, 1819–60, fol. 6. B.M.]

20. From Ugo Foscolo to John Cam Hobhouse.

Date on postmark—Aug. 11, 1819

Mon cher Monsieur—

Ce discours d'Aquisgrana que l'on m'attribue, me parait une sotte declamation ; il y a deja deux mois que etant chez Dulau a Soho Sq. et ne me connaissant pas, il m'offrit son Aquisgrana en me la raccomandant, car disait-il c'est un écrit de Mr. F.—— J'en ai parcouru une demie page et je lui ai dit que c'etait une bêtise de quelque' [sic] inconnu, et une forgerie des libraires. Les bonnes gens qui ecrivent l'Ape, m'ont demandé des articles ; je leur ai repondu que mes vaticines leur seraient beaucoup plus utiles ; aussi je leur ai prophetizé que l'Ape finirait en Palabroné.—Vous presumez l'affaire de Parga naive ;—et moi j'y vois très clairement au milieu des ombres les crimes de ses executeurs, et le sang des victimes—mais il faut dissimuler jusque'au jour que je puisse convincre (sic) les criminels de ma vive [voix] que s'ils echaperont à vos bouraux [sic], il [sic] n'echapperont pas à l'ignominie.—En attendant j'ai tout-à-fait fini l'article sur Parga pour l'Edinb. Review : et je viens de l'envoyer. Je me suis strictement, froidement, stoiquement contenu entre les limites de la narration ; mais les faits suffiront pour faire croire même les incredules ; et j'ai evité de leur faire soupçonner quelque interêt de ma part. J'ai toujours appuyé les faits importants à des documents, et aux mots ecrits par les Agents de cette conspiration. Je vous ai cité une fois, je vous ai refuté une autre ;—je vous l'avais predit : Le New-Times vient de reimprimer et commenter avec du poison tout ce que vous avez ecrit precipitamment dans votre ouvrage sur l'Albanie contre le charactere [sic] des Pargiotes—Mon article est de 42 pages d'impression ; car je doit [sic] me servir d'imprimeur au lieu de copiste, et j'en fait tirer deux copies. Comme mes pages sont un peu plus-longues que' celles de l'Edinb. Rev. il est probable que Mr. Jeffrey trouvera l'article trop long ; et il est possible que'il desirera de suprimer quelques faits trop criantes [sic] contre le Gen. Maitland ;—quoique je hoñore Mr. Jeffrey comme le plus independant dans cette caste. Au reste nous verrons ;—et j'attende [sic] de jour en jour sa reponse.—Mais si il y fera trop de mutilations, j'ai deja pris le parti de publier à la fin de l'année ici avec mon nom une *Histoire de Parga* en forme, en italien, et divisé en trois livres, en suivant tant que j'en serai capable la maniere des historiens grecs.—J'en ferai executé la traduction anglaise contemporannément dans un style *Signorile asciutto*, e *assoluto* ; et je suis certain que votre langue, malgre son verbiage moderne, saura facilement s'y prêter. J'ajouterai aux deux editions Anglaise et italienne tous les documents en appendix, et je ferai en même tems publié [sic] un [sic] traduction de l'ouvrage en français par un ecrivain qui vient de publier une nouvelle traduction de l'Ortis ou il a admirablement saisi les characteristics [sic] de mon style.—En attendant si vous me donnerai [sic] un moyen sûre [sic], mais très-sure de vous expedier la seule copie imprimée qui me reste de mon article, vous l'aurez tout-de-suite à Hastings, mais je vous le repète, il faut que je puisse l'envoyer avec pleine confiance qu'il ne s'egarera pas ;—je me servirais de la poste comme le moyen le plus sure ;—mais cela couterai [sic] trop de fraix [sic]—je me porte beaucoup mieux de ma jambe ;—mais la convalescence ; le long travail ; la solitude, car il n'y a plus d'amis en ville ; et milles [sic] petits soins et afflictions de la vie humaine me rendent si faible et si triste a ne pouvoir pas marcher pendant un quart d'heure de suite, et a ne pas jouir de rien.—Cependant la raison me servira de force et de gaieté—En attendant une reponse—Adieu de tout mon cœur

Tout à vous
U. Foscolo.

Mercredì, 11 *Août* 1819.

Address : John Hobhouse, Esqre, 6 Wellington Place, Hastings.

[Broughton Correspondence, Vol. IV. B.M., MSS.]

21. *From Lord John Russell to Foscolo.*

[1824 (?) Placed among the Nov. letters]

Dear Foscolo,

I think you are quite right to adopt the plan of your friends of giving lectures—it is not in this country any way degrading—Campbell & Sydney Smith have done so very lately—As to your houses you have a long lease of them, have you not ? I wish to ask you how you get books to consult upon any subject on which you are not writing for the booksellers—on what you are writing for me for instance—pray answer this forthwith—

My father thought your house very pretty—pray come & see me when you come to town—

Yrs. truly,
J. Russell.

66 South Audley Street. *Monday.*

[MSS. Lab., Vol. XLVI.]

22. *From William Stewart Rose to Foscolo.*

Giovedì Mattina [1824]

Caro Foscolo,

Mi pare, ripensando al vostro progetto che il solo modo in cui potrebbe riuscire sarebbe di contar sopra di questo solamente come una via di

guadagnarsi *il vitto attuale*, e di ricorrere a qualche altro metodo per
mettere a parte qua, che somma, che vi serviste [?] in caso di bisogno ; e
se, a quest' effetto vorreste seguire l' antico mio progetto di pubblicar
Dante ossia altra opera classica Italiana *by subscription*, siate sicuro che
io farei ogni mio sforzo di secondarlo quando voi conveniste della cosa.
. . . Poi non v' ha niente in questo progetto che potesse offendere la
vostra *proper pride*, inteso che Pope e molti altri hanno fatto la medesima
cosa.   Parlate con Hallam, ossia con chi volete di questo, ma per amor
di Dio cacciatevi di testa l' idea che si possa guadagnar dippiù di 200
lire per anno, faccendo da Maestro.   Forse che io non abbia ben calco-
lato i profitti di codesto mestiere ; ma chi, tranne Zotti e Paranti faccen-
dolo, hanno potuto metter qualcosa à parte . . . vi vedrei mille volte
più volontieri tornare in Zante, che faccendo la vita che temo che farete
quando voi non pensaste ad altri mezzi da guadagnare il vitto.

In fretta e furia
Il vostro
W. S. Rose.

[*Ibid.*]

23. *From William Roscoe to Foscolo.*

Lodge Lane, nr. Liverpool.
10th May 1824.

My Dear Sir,
   I shall be happy to become a subscriber to your great work of Dante
say after the first 20 or 30 names ; not however upon the terms which
your liberality & friendship leads you to propose, but upon such as
one author may offer to another, viz. to repay you in works of my own—
in which case I shall be happy to possess a copy of yours ; & with the
sincerest wishes for your success, am
Your truly obliged & faithful friend,
W. Roscoe.

[*Ibid.*]

24. *From J. Hatfield to Foscolo.*

Dear Foscolo
   Though you are unfortunately in my debt I do not see exactly why
I shd. lose my friend as well as my money.   There are still many points
in which we might associate, and tho I was very much hurt at the manner
in which you carelessly passed over the promised day of payment *without
letting me know anything about it*, all resentment, if I ever felt any, is
past and absorbed in the sympathy which I feel for your distresses.
Our venerable friend Mr. Roscoe before he left town, enquired particularly after you and desired me to tell you that if an old edit[n] of Dante
(1379) now in his possession, wd. be of any use to you in your researches,
it is much at your service ; his address you are aware is W.R. Lodge
Lane n[r] Liverpool.   Hoping to see you before quitting town
I remain d[r] Sir truly yrs
J. Hatfield.

5 St. Albany.   *Sunday 27 June.*
   Address : U. Foscolo, Esq., D. Cottage, South Bank, Regent's Park.

[*Ibid.*]

P

25. *From Lady Charlotte Bury to Foscolo.*

CLIFTON, *October the 9th.*
1824.

You have probably forgotten, My Dear Sir, that there is such a Being in the world as Her who is now about to recall herself to your remembrance, by the strange, and it may be somewhat abrupt measure, of requesting a favor at your hands—And yet if Ugo Foscolo be the same Ugo Foscolo I had the pleasure of seeing so often at my House in Gloucester Place in 1817, I feel assured He will not only forgive my request but [if in his power] will comply with it.

It is for one of your unhappy Countrymen that I solicit a word of recommendation from you.   One of those unfortunate men who have suffered in the good and great cause of liberty—Signor Radici has become known to my husband and myself lately. . . .   Signor Radici is now endeavouring to obtain the vacancy in the Dublin University of Professor of the Spanish, and Italian Languages, and a letter from you in his behalf . . .

Mr. Bury will have great pleasure in receiving an old friend of mine, and you will find us both equally glad to have the advantage and pleasure of cultivating your society.—

I remain Dear Sir
With every good wish
Yours sincerely
Charlotte Maria Bury.

[*Ibid.*]

26. *From William Pickering to Foscolo.*

LONDON, *Nov.* 30. 1824.

DEAR SIR,
Mr. White has not, neither have I made the least disclosure to your gardener *this you may rely upon,* & I am persuaded he DOES NOT know where you are—I think he knows only the first address, where you was [*sic*] for a week.   Unless he has watched Miss Hamilton to your present dwelling which we dt. think likely—at all events keep as much in the house as possible—lest you are seen & take the chance—I will do any thing to farther your wishes that I am able.   Remain
With much respect
Yrs.
W. PICKERING.

[*Ibid.*]

27. *From C. Sinclair Cullen to Foscolo.*

July 14th [1826]

DEAR F.
Ly. Charlotte Bury lives at 6 New Cavendish Sq.—Wilmot Horton at 4 Richmond Terrace.

I saw Hallam yesterday—He told me Lady Dacre is anxious about the publication of your *Homer.*   How much have you translated ?   I told him your scheme about publishing the Dante and Homer.   He said he would talk to Murray.   I shall at all events on Sunday & will see you on Monday.

Yours
C. SINCLAIR CULLEN.

[MSS. Lab., Vol. XLVII.]

28. From Mrs. Sarah Austin to Foscolo.

Mrs. Austin presents her compliments to Mr. Foscolo & her thanks for his corrections and suggestions—She will make a point of keeping as near to them as possible in an endeavour to give a perfectly English dress to his meaning. Mr. Foscolo is aware that there are terms of expression wh. without being grammatically wrong, offend—one hardly knows how—against national habits of speaking and thinking—These for a popular journal it is desirable to avoid. It is not therefore that she imagines her own casting of a sentence better—perhaps not so good as that in the original but that she knows it to be more English that she ventures to change it. Nevertheless wherever in this process the *meaning* is at all obscured or changed Mr. F. will have the goodness to correct it. Mrs. Austin thanks Mr. Foscolo for the honour he intends her & hopes his health may soon be sufficiently restored to put his design in execution.

1 LITTLE GEORGE ST. WEST^R *Nov.* 17. [1826]
Mrs. A. will send more MS. in a day or two.

[MSS. Lab., Vol. XLVI.]

29. From C. Sinclair Cullen to John Cam Hobhouse.

[dated by J. C. H. 1830]

MY DEAR HOBHOUSE

If you can make up your mind or purse to give 100£ for the Foscolo papers which you saw—they shall forthwith become your property—& you be irresponsible for the use you make of them.

Pray answer me as soon as you can

Yrs. truly
C. SINCLAIR CULLEN.

May 6th DERBY ST. PARL^T SQ.

Address : J. C. Hobhouse, Esq., M.P., Charles St., Berkeley Sq.
[Broughton Correspondence, Vol. X., fol. 106. B.M. MSS]

APPENDIX I.B

1. ALIEN OFFICE REPORTS, SECRET FILE DEALING WITH GENERAL PEPE

(1) *General Pepe.* 1822.

Reports on G. P.'s movements. (Alien Office.)

CHARTER—in water-colour, with designs of sun with face, 3 nails, cross and battle-axes, crown of thorns, spear and sponge on rod, cloth, and red cap of liberty, fire, full moon, lictor, four-leaved shamrocks and palm, gold jug—house, basket, beehive, blue, gray and pink ribbon, ladder, etc., and sealed with seal and three ribbons, blue, gray and pink—seal represents crown struck by two flashes of lightning, heart pierced by dagger held in a hand, and broken instrument and motto " Sotto il titolo li seguaci di Louvel all o. di Cerignola Lar. V." round.
A . . . G . . . D . . . G . . . M . . . D . . . S(?) . . . E . . .
D . . . L . . . J . . . N . . . V . . . T . . . M . . . E . . . S . . .
G . . . A . . . D . . . S . . . M . . . D . . . Divina Trinnita [*sic*]
S . . . F . . . V . . .

Noi G . . . M . . . Dignitari della ᴁ¹ᵉ . . . V . . . sotto il [drawing of seal.] T . . . li Seguaci
di Louvel regolarmente sostituiti all' o . . . di Cerignola certi si chiamo, attestiamo
e dichiariamo che il ᴁ¹¹ᵉ N . . . ℰ . . . Maggiori di Cavalleria appartiene a questa ᴁ
V . . . come membro onorario, essendo stato per tale proclamato regolarmente a ciò in attestato
della stima dovutagli pel sincero attacamento all' ordine e per le sue nobili e raffinate
facolta cosi morali che intellettuali.
Investiamo tutte le ᴍ . . . regolarmente costituite e tutti si [?] N.
N . . . ℰℰ . . . regolari sparsi
sulla superfissa della terra per tale riconoscerlo e pr·stargli tutti le ajiuti e soccorsi
che potesse aver bisogno dichiarando di fare noi lo stesso a tutti quelli che si
presenteranno nel nostro O . . . in fede di che gli abbiamo rilasciato il presente breve
O . . . di Cerignola li 20 primo mese anno 1° Costituzionale.
G . . . B . . . S . . . 1° assisᵉ Gen . . . M . . . L. Oratore 2° assisᵉ Segretario F. Demestini (?) Vin° Carassi Stati Giuseppe J. Taruzzi F. Chiomenti Luigi Peroz

[*All reports unsigned.*]

(2) Report. 20 *May* 1822.

Macerone has last week been to Chatham to take up a vessel or vessels for Gen¹ Pepe's Expedition. . . . Pepe is going in about 10 days to Madrid. The Spanish Ambassador has conferences with Pepe and Macerone almost daily and furnishes money ; they have also received remittances from Naples, from Mad. Murat. 1000 stand. of arms are ordered on a peculiar construction according to a plan shewn me ; from Brander & Potts & 1000 more from the House of Lacy & Co. The Copy of the Diploma, similar to the Society of the Carbonari, which I have obtained, has been sent over from Naples & distributed to 32 Persons here including 6 Members of Parliament—My Informant has a Commission drawn out by Macerone empowering him to be *Ordonnateur* & director for managing the Shipment of all the stores, after the departure of Pepe—when he will be enabled to give a fuller detail—

Florestini [*sic*] Pepe the brother is to command an Expedition at the same time from Sicily where he now is.

(Enclosed in this letter is a sheet with drawings in water colour of a musket of the type ordered, of a grenade, and of a lance with a pink, blue and gray pennant.)

(3) ALIEN OFFICE. 4 *June* 1822.

Macerone was yesterday introduced by Cap. Johnston (the Smuggler) to Bernardi No. 33 Thayer St Manchester Square the principal of a foreign Gambling house ; to raise the sum of £2000 for the payment of his stores, of Arms & accoutrements ; the Security offered was Johnston's Pension of £200 p.ann. from the Government ; till the repayment of the same—Johnston also proposed to assist M—with a vessel of his own, built on a new Construction, to accompany the expedition. Tomorrow is fixed for settling the arrangement of the same.

(4) Report. 1 *May* 1822.

Pisa the Aide de Camp to General Pepe has lately procured a Passport from the Portuguese & Spanish Ministers, under an assumed name & proceeded to Spain . . . [Maj. Baldwin going to Ireland to raise men.]

[*Passages in italic are marked in pencil in original.*]

(5) Secret Report. 29 *April* 1822.

General Pepe & Macerone have now engaged *two Vessells* in the river to proceed with Arms and Powder they are now purchasing. On Saturday Macerone & another *were at Brander & Potts Gunmakers* in the Minories for the purpose of purchasing of Arms & Belts and To-morrow or next day, *Pepe & Macerone* are to go to Woolwich to purchase some old Brass Cannon to be recast in small ones, supposed by Galloway who has a foundry in Holborn & who has also contracted with them for small arms.

Major Baldwin who was lately arrested in Paris and arrived from thence is to be Colonel of a Reg^t and he is going *to Ireland* to engage men and Officers under the pretext of emigrating to the Cape or America ; this is the same person who raised men for Devereux—A Mr. McDermott is also to raise men and officers in Scotland each are to have the Sale of a certain number of Commissions to defray their own expences [sic]. Macerone has lately remitted a considerable Sum of Money from the Stock of the Society to a General Commanding the French Army near the Pyrenees. Santa Rosa is now the Corresponding Agent in Paris

(6)   Secret Report. 6 *May* 1822.
[Gives Pepe's plans for operation in Dalmatia]

. . . It appears to be the object of the Revolutionists to make a Diversion pretending to aid the Cause of the Greeks against the Turks, & having thereby rose a Thousand Montenegrinos with their Means of Warfare, to then embark in a number of small Vessells ; pass the Adratic [sic] during the Night and land in *Calabria* being the Southernmost part of the Neapolitan territory where the other Divisions will land according to the plan reported in former notes—
                                        [First paper initialled] B.P.C.

(7) *The following six papers are numbered No. 1 to No. 6 and headed on back—" Report of General Pepe's Movements " and dated— all unsigned and in different handwriting from the preceding.*

No. 1
Information dated 29*th January* 1822.

Sir Robert Wilson, Wood, Waithman, assisted by Maceroni [sic] and foreigners who resort to England are at the head of a Society who call themselves " The Confederation of European Constitutionalists ". Their present object is accomplishing a complete revolution in the whole of Italy, and under the sanction of the Portuguese and Spanish Governments. Sir R. W. is at present at Paris organizing the same with Benj. Constant, Peyronnet & others . . . [mentions vessel proceeding with arms from London to Lisbon whence after embarking troops it will sail for Italy.]

The Informant has been appointed Gen[1] of Artillery for this Expedition and is the bosom friend of Maceroni, who will in a few days depart for Paris——

No. 2
April 29*th* 1822.
Gen[1] Pepe & Macerone have now engaged two vessels in the river to proceed with Arms & Powder ; they are now purchasing . . .
[Maj. Baldwin to go to Ireland to engage men. Same information as in (5). Santa Rosa is now their Agent in Paris.]

No. 3
May 6*th* 1822.
[Plan of operations in Dalmatia drawn up. Repetition of (6).]

No. 4
2*nd May* 1822.
Pisa the Aide de Camp to Gen[1] Pepe has embarked some time since under the assumed name of Pozza, & having Passports from the Portuguese & Spanish Ambassadors in London—but his departure does not appear on the Alien Registry.

No. 5

20 *May* 1822.
[Practically a repetition of No. (2).—Explains that the drawings are a plan of design of arms ordered from Brander & Potts.]

No. 6

Report.   4 *June* 1822.
[Practically a repetition of No. (3).]
[Records Office, H. O. 5.]

2. Two letters from Giovanni Arrivabene to Antonio Panizzi

(*a*)   Bruxelles 4 *dec.* 1836.
                                         Rue Pépinière 8.
Carissimo Amico
    Vi raccomando il Sigr. Maro [*illegible*] emigrato veneziano.
Egli si reca a Londra per dar lezioni di matematica.   Ha professato qui questa scienza per due o tre anni, e con buon successo.
    Scrivetemi, e poscia io vi risponderò, e manderò notizie mie e di Scalvini.   Ora non ho il tempo se non di dirvi che siamo a Bruxelles, io in buona egli in non troppo buona salute.   Fate ci un' altra visita, & vi festeggieram perchè vi scriviamo ed uniamo.
                                         Affe. amico
                                         G. Arrivabene.
(*b*)
Mio ottimo amico
    Ricorro a voi per un favore.   Molti anni sono depositai presso quella buona anima di Obicini una carta, segnata Bonjour, molto importante per me.   Due anni fà trovandomi in Londra la cercai in Size Lane, No. 12, presso un Sigr. Coxhead depositario delle carte di Obicini. Egli era assente.   Mi scrisse in data del 20 Aprile 1835 che aveva ritrovato la carta che io gli aveva poscia domandata per lettera e me l' avrebbe mandata, da Mr. Senior pr. la picciola posta.   Io, temendo che non andasse smarrita, e non avendone allora bisogno immediato, pensai bene lasciarla ov' era.   Oggi mi è necessaria.   Vi prego quindi recarvi un giorno in Size Lane, presentare al Sigr. Coxhead il qui accluso biglietto, e ritirare la carta sud^a. . . .
                          Di cuore mi dico
                               aff. amico
                               G. Arrivabene.
Bruxelles.   11 *Giugno* 1837
   Rue Pépinière 8.
[Panizzi Correspondence.   B.M.   Add.   MSS.   36714, fol.   448, and 36715, fol.   14.]

3.   Letters from Dal Pozzo to Ugo Foscolo and Others
(*a*)
Mio caro Foscolo,
    Se non avete più bisogno dell' *Uso e de' pregi della lingua italiana*, che ebbi il piacere di prestarvi, vi prego a rimandarmelo—poichè ho bisogno di rinfrescarmi certe notizie non di lingua, ma di storia patria, di cui abbisogno per un certo lavoro. . . .
    Il voto del mio cuore è che siate, o divenghiate tranquillo, e felice—

Molto con Bossi, che va a partir per Messico—molto con Cimitile abbiam parlato di voi, coll' interresse [sic] dell' amicizia.

Vi prego di consacrarmi la vostra, e state sano

FERD. DAL POZZO.

LONDRA. 31 ALPHA ROAD
REGENT'S PARK.
12 *Marzo* 1825.

[MSS. Lab., Vol. XLVI.]

(b)
Lady A. M. Elliot.
Elliot (Murray Kynynmond de Minto) Anna Maria, sorella del conte Gilberto più noto con il titolo di lord Minto. [p. 124, Bollea].
[*MS. p. 30. Not published.*]

Vendi. 23 Sept. 1831.

ELLIOT (LADY A. M.) La lettre, que vous m'avez fait l'honneur de m'adresser du 6 de ce mois, ne m'est parvenue qu'avant hier et j'y réponds aussitôt. La famille Viaris est dans le plus affreux besoin, et Madame est très dangereusement malade ; elle peut cependant durer encore quelque temps. Je sais leurs besoins par moi-même, qui, sous la couleur de prêt, donnai à cette pauvre et intéressante dame 300 fr., il y a environ un mois ; je les sais encore plus en détail par l'avocat Demarchi que vous avez connu, Miladi, à Edimbourg, et qui a passé quelque temp [sic] des vacances à Paris et qui n'a pu s'empêcher de lui faire remettre par une tierce personne 120 fr.

C'est de l'argent, et puis encore de l'argent, et toujours argent, et aussi de quelques bons conseils donnés avec une certaine autorité que cette famille a besoin ; sur le système dans lequel est cette maison ne peut se soutenir [sic] aux visites, et les attentions que pourrait avoir pour eux ma femme, qui d' ailleurs n'a pas les qualités propres pour cela ne peuvent soulager leurs infortunes.

Si vous voulez que je vous parle franchement, il faudrait, si vous en avez le loisir, que vous veniez à Paris vous-même, qu'avant de venir, vous faisiez une bonne souscription à Brighton et Londres, que vous en faisiez faire une autre à Edimbourg, où Mad. de Viaris fut si respectée et aimée ; vous avez tant de parens et tant d'amis que les deux ensemble peuvent produire une bonne somme ; vous vous trouverez ici, quand il sera décidé si Gaetan est admis ou non à l'école polytechnique ; s'il l'est, il faut faire la dépense de l'équipement, et songer à la pension de 1200 fr., je crois, qu'il y a à payer pendant 2 ou 3 ans avant qu'il soit placé, s'il ne l'est pas il faudra songer à quelqu'autre établissement pour ce garçon qui, au dire de Demarchi et de ceux qui le connaissent plus que moi a beaucoup de mérite ; il faudra placer les filles ou à S. Denis, ou dans quelque autre établissement, la mère dans une maison de santé et fermer la maison ; car ce qui les ruine, ce sont les deux établissement (sic), l'un pour le mari, l'autre pour le reste de la famille.—Si Mr. Viaris, au lieu d'être en activité, eût une bonne retraite, ou une place fixe de commandant de quelque place, vous concevez, que la dépense serait infiniment moindre. Le même logement, à peu près, servirait pour les deux ; et ce que Mr. Viaris depense pour son ordinaire, suffirait aussi à sa femme. Je trace à la hâte ces projets, qui sont susceptibles certainement de modifications, et altérations suivant les circonstances. Mais il faut un *système* et de *l'ordre* même lorsqu'on a très peu et précisément parce qu'on a peu.

Si vous faites cette oeuvre celeste de venir à Paris, vous apporterez un remède à tous les désastres de cette famille, et ce sera fait pour toujours. Avec vous à la tête, qui trouverez encore à faire peut-être une bonne souscription à Paris parmi le grand nombre d'anglais qui est ici,—avec vous à la tête, dis-je, je ferai aussi moi de mon mieux ; je vous seconderai de toutes mes forces.

Je vous demande une infinité de pardons de la liberté que je prends et en vous retournant les complimens de mon épouse très-respectueux, j'ai l'honneur de me dire avec un grand dévouement——

(c)
[*MS. p. 32. Not published.*]

Lunedi, 26 *Sett.* 1831.

ELLIOT—
Eh bien, Miledi, la pauvre Madame Viaris a succombé à ses souf-frances le jour après que j'ai eu l'honneur de vous écrire, c'est à dire le 24 du c^t.

Mr. de Viaris est à son régiment ; on lui a appris le cours de la maladie, et dernièrement la mort. Je ne sais, s'il viendra à Paris dans cette circonstance ; les intimes de la famille, qui ont soigné la malade ; et soignent à présent les enfans, sont d'opinion qu'il ferait une dépense inutile à venir et retourner à sa destination, et qu'on peut s'entendre sur les arrangemens à prendre et les dispositions à donner, même par lettre. Quant à moi, cela me paraît difficile.

L'évenement douloureux, qui a eu lieu, simplifie ces arrangemens et ces dispositions. Mais il ne serait pas moins à désirer, que votre intérêt vous portât à faire tout ce dont j'ai parlé dans ma précédente du 23 ainsi " je m'y réfère et j'ai l'honneur. . . ."

(Viarigi, barone, capitano di battaglione al 50° regg. di linea in
     Francia.)

(d)
[*MS. p. 38.* (to London)]

Vendi. 7 *oct* 1831

ELLIOT (LADY)
J'ai reçu la lettre que vous me fîtes l'honneur de m'adresser en date du 28 du mois dernier.

Mr. Viaris, qui est venu à Paris, consent que les deux demoiselles plus agées aillent à Genève avec Madlle. Cheypière, et c'est là le meilleur parti à prendre. Quant à Sophie, il faut essayer si on peut la faire recevoir à S. Denis pour une place gratuite ; elle est au dessous de 12 ans, condition strictement requise. Deux dames sont interessées pour cela ; Mad^e de Flahault à qui j'en ai parlé, et Mad^e Andryanne, dame que je ne connais pas, mais que je me propose de voir pour cet objet. Mad. de Flahault dit que Sophie pourrait, en attendant, entrer comme pensionnaire (la pension est 1000 francs), qu'assurément, en fin [*sic*] de mois, elle aurait la place *gratuite* ; moi je ne sais voir cette connexion si facile. Qui sait quand la vacance d'une place gratuite se fera, et lorsqu'elle se fera, s'il n'y aura pas d'autres qui l'emporteront ? Je tâcherai d'éclaircir cela, non pas avec Mad. de Flahault, qui est trop haut personnage pour descendre à de tels détails, et à qui, au surplus la pension de 1000 fr. paraît une chose de rien, mais avec Mad. Andryanne et d'autres personnes. Si en attendant Flauhault [*sic*], qui est en chemin pour Paris, mais qui est retardé par des quarantaines, arrivait ce serait un grand bonheur.

A l'égard de Gaetan, Mad. de Flahault est très-disposée de le recommander vivement au Gl. Bertrand qui est le directeur de l'école polytechnique, pour la bourse. Et moi, je n'ai pas laissé à l'égard des professeurs de faire quelques démarches. . . .

Quant à l'argent nécessaire pour payer les marchands, le loyer, et tout ce qui est requis pour pouvoir fermer la maison, etc., sur la foi de la souscription que vous faites, j'ai dit à Madlle. Irma Gray (vous savez qui c'est, j'imagine) que j'en aurai avancé une portion, si besoin était, mais que je ne pouvais qu'avancer, vu qu'il n'y a qu'un mois que j'ai donné 300 fr., et qu'il m'était impossible de faire de plus. J'ai pensé que j'aurais revu cette demoiselle Irma avant que cette lettre partît, mais ne la voyant pas venir, il faut que je la ferme, et que je vous prie instamment de me faire savoir au plutôt sur quoi je puis compter par rapport à l'argent—qui est l'article le plus essentiel.

Afin d'avoir une réponse plus vite, j'envoie celle-ci par l'estafette, et je vous prie de faire de même à l'égard de v^e réponse.

J'ai l'honneur, etc.

Quand j'étais pour cacheter celle-ci j'ai reçu votre lettre du 2 du courant mois. Je n'ai rien à ajouter d'essentiel hormis que je parlerai avec Mad. Andryanne, avec Mad. de Flahault, et je reverrai Mad. la Duchesse de Broglie, enfin vous pouvez compter sur mon activité, ma vigilance pour éviter les dépenses inutiles—mais non sur ma bourse, qui suffit à peine aux dépenses de ma maison.

(e)
[*MS.*, *p.* 44.]

                                                    Samedi 15 oct. 1831.
BROGLIE (DUCHESSE). Lady Anna Maria Elliot (sœur de Lord Minto) doit vous avoir écrit pour vous interesser à procurer au jeune Gaetan Viaris, fils du Baron Viaris, chef de bataillon au 56me regiment de ligne, une bourse ou demi-bourse dans le cas qu'il soit nommé comme l'on espère, élève à l'école polytechnique. La concession de cette faveur dépend, l'on me dit, entièrement du Ministre de la Guerre.

. . . [Request to assure his nomination by speaking of him to the examiner. While realizing that merit alone decides—other things being equal, it is sometimes necessary to choose according to age or circumstances.] . . .

Enfin l'arbitre dans ceci, comme dans toute autre chose humaine, se glisse et l'emporte. Le pauvre jeune homme, dont je parle, est dans une position tout-à-fait digne du plus grand intérêt ; il vient de perdre sa respectable mère (qui fut une grande amie de Lady Anna Maria Elliot) et sa famille se trouve dans les circonstances les plus difficiles. On me dit que ce jeune homme a subi son examen d'une manière très distinguée. Mais l'arbitre, la faveur . . . il faudrait, Madame, s'emparer aussi de ces chances. Si vous, ou Mr. le Duc votre époux, pouvez faire quelque choses [*sic*] pour lui assurer le vote favorable de *Mr. Dinet*, de grace, daignez le faire,—et le plutôt possible ! Il n'y a pas un moment à perdre, me dit-on. Excusez mes pressentes, et peut-être importunes sollicitations. Mais c'est une chose si décisive pour cet intéressant jeune Viaris, dont certainement, ou du moins de sa famille, vous avez dû entendre parler à Genève, où ils ont longtems vécu, et furent si respectés. Les bons Sismondis les aimaient entre autres, beaucoup, beaucoup, comme aiment les Sismondi.

(f)
[MS., p. 129.]

Mardi 31 *Janvier* 1832.

ELLIOT (LADY A. M.) J'ai tardé à répondre aux deux lettres, dont vous m'avez dernièrement honoré, Miledi, parceque je n'ai pas été trop bien en santé, que j'ai été occupé de quelques affaires personnelles, et qu'enfin il n'y avait rien d'urgent à répondre.   Ce que j'ai fait presqu'immédiatement, ç'a été de remettre à Mr. Boffani les deux cent francs que j'avais reçu du Général Flahault et nous fûmes convenus, Mr. Boffani et moi, que cette somme aurait servi pour solder la dette envers Mr. Fazy, ce qui entrait aussi, me dit-il, dans les vues de Mr. Viaris.

D'après le contenu de votre seconde lettre, il reste inutile de parler de la convenance ou du désavantage du choix que Gaetan a fait de sa carrière future.   Mon opinion est qu'il a bien fait ; les carrières civiles sont longues, et d'un succès plus incertain.   Son éducation ne l'avait pas preparé, ce me semble, pour un civil quelconque.   Etranger, sans fortune, sans parens en France, il est plus aisé qu'il parvienne aux premiers grades dans le militaire, que dans toute autre profession.   A l'égard de ses sœurs, jamais elles ne pourront vivre avec lui ; il faut qu'elles deviennent capables d'être de bonnes mères de famille, et qu'elles se marient.   Même sans dot, avec une figure agréable, ou non désagréable du moins, et des qualités,—voulant descendre à un rang inférieur,—toute fille, en général, qui *veut* se marier,—trouve, un jour ou l'autre, un époux.—Je le leur souhaite du tout mon cœur. . . .

Ma femmé a été très sensible à vos souhaits, et à vos complimens. Elle vous offre ses respects.   Nous nourrissons l'espoir que nous ne tarderons pas beaucoup à vous voir sur le continent.   Comptez, en attendant sur notre bonne volonté à vous être utiles si l'occasion s'en offre, . . .

P.S.—J'ai plaisir d'entendre que M. Pecchio soit bien portant.   Vous m'obligerez beaucoup si en le voyant, soit lui, soit son excellente femme, vous me rappelerez [*sic*] à leur aimable souvenir.

[Florence, Biblioteca Nazionale.   MS. Copialettere dal di 24 ag., 1821. N.14.   83 letters of F. Dal Pozzo.]

4. ALIEN OFFICE REPORTS

Return of Persons natives of Piedmont who obtained Passports from the Sardinian Minister to depart for the Continent, to embark for Greece—and received a Visé on their Passports from the French Minister in London to pass through France landing at Calais . . . but after being detained at Calais for a month were sent back to Dover—by order of the Minister at Paris—

Names :

Amb. Tito, Surgeon   —detained 31 days.
Jos. Cornaglia, Musician   —detained 30 days.
Fra. Casali, Naval officer. —detained 25 days.
Domin. Gualchi, Gen¹   —detained 24 days.
Jean Berra, Gen¹   —detained 24 days.
Jos. Rosetti, Gen¹   —detained 21 days.

They all referred to Gen¹ Mina.

[*On back of Report.*]

Return of certain Natives of Piedmont who recd. Sardinian Passports to depart for the Continent, etc.

Copy to Foreign Office. *8th Mar.* 1823.
[Home Office Records. H.O. 5.]

5. LETTERS TO FORTUNATO PRANDI, AND FROM SARAH AUSTIN TO FRANCIS PLACE CONCERNING HIM

(*a*)   (*From Mrs. Sarah Austin to F. Place, Esq.*)

26 PARK ROAD. REGTS. PARK.
Dec. 31 1828.

MY DEAR MR. PLACE,

After maturely deliberating which of my friends or acquaintances I had better apply to to help a very excellent fellow through unmerited difficulties & sufferings I came to the decision that you are the man. First, because if you undertake it you will *do it* with energy & promptitude, as well as kindness ; & secondly, because if you do not find it convenient or agreable to undertake it, you will say it at once. As you & I are not fond of long preambles I shall tell you the facts. Prandi, whom you have seen with me I think, & of whom you may hear from many as a man of *the most* exact probity & honour, is thus situated. Three years ago his father, who is an opulent man in Piedmont, thought fit to withdraw his small allowance, partly because he refused to call on the Ambassador with letters of recommendation from the War Minister of Piedmont ;—(a friend of his father's) partly, there seems too much reason to suppose, from some base intrigue of his eldest brother's. About the same time or rather sooner he was drawn in by one of the bubble companies—composed of soi disant merchants, part French, part English, part Italian (not one of whom had a shilling). Under a promise of a place of £600 a year he gave them the active labour of 7 months, incurred debts for stationery, &c. &c, & finally got not a farthing.—He was then taken by Southern (the Ed^r of the Westminster) as an assistant. *He* of course cheated him as he did me & every body.—At last he took to giving lessons which he has done very successfully & is still doing. He had however, during the short season of London masters, not only to live, but to work against nearly £150 of debt. To meet these he applied to Bertolini, the Proprietor of Newton's Hotel, St. Martin's Street to lend or borrow him money. The latter B. did, but at such a rate of interest that as he last night told me, he has paid within 2 years £40 for interest, which £40 would now completely set him through. It is to prevent his having recourse to such ruinous means again that I have taken in hand to write to you.

He wants to borrow £50 at 5 p^r cent. And now as to the prospect of his repaying.

1st. His character—Not only has he never received one farthing directly or indirectly of any of the sums subscribed for the Refugees, but he has never been prevailed on to accept the slightest obligation from any of the many people who respect & esteem him. On the contrary he has been always giving, time, books, clothes, anything he had to the most miserable of his countrymen. I could refer you to John Mill, Eyton Tooke, my Brothers, John, Richard or Edward, Mr. Lyell, Hon. Sec^y to the Geol. Socy., Mr. Empson, Law Professor of

Haileybury Coll. &c. &c. So much for his intentions—Now as to his means—He has books to that amount or very nearly, which I have only stopped him from selling because I knew he would sell them extremely ill in such haste. His teaching is now good, & will enable him to repay the whole within a year, if it keeps up. Last year he did actually pay £60 of debt besides that monstrous interest.

3rd. If he were to die, there is, besides the books above mentioned, the certainty (as he thinks) that his father, who is a proud man, would not suffer his son's debts to go unpaid. But you will say why does he not apply to any of these numerous friends I speak of—Because he never will ask anything of anybody—He has not the least idea of my making this application to you. I begged him when I discovered the straits he was in to ask my Brothers to lend him the money. He said he would not—that he was quite determined not to borrow of his friends & that his only wish was to find somebody who would trust him with the money at a moderate rate of interest.

Now I have thought of Mr. I. L. Goldsmid. He knows Prandi & likes him & he can satisfy himself of his high character by speaking to Mr. Mill, John or Richᵈ or Mr. Lyell all of whom he knows. It cannot put him to the least inconvenience & he is extremely disposed to do kind things, as I know. Do you know him? Is he the man to apply to? I thought of writing to Mr. Mill because I know he takes an interest in this poor fellow but I recollected how much he is engaged. Nevertheless if you like to tell him the purport of this, you can. He & you are not people to accuse me of *indelicacy* for trying to help a worthy man—

If you think you can see him through, call on him. I have enclosed a note entreating him to lay aside pride & false delicacy & to be as frank with you as he was yesterday with me. You are not a person to afflict any honourable poor man with shame. I am perfectly confident you would feel hearty respect for & interest in him did you know half the instances of scrupulous probity I have seen in him through such difficulties as, (to a man bred in affluence) are enough to shake the finest resolution.

As all people are not like you & Mr. Mill I would thank you not to mention to anybody else that I took upon myself this business.

Have the kindness to give me a line in answer or, (better still) a call— I am always at home in an evening & generally in a morning. We dine at 3, at 4 I am sure to be found. I make no apologies. I am sure they wd. only annoy you.

> Believe me, dear Sir,
> always very sincerely yrs.
> SARAH AUSTIN.

Address : Francis Place, Esqʳᵉ, Charing Cross.

[Reply from Mr. Place, stating his own inability to help, but assurance of Goldsmid's suitability.]

[Letters to F. Place, Vol. I., fols. 217–19. B.M., Add. MSS. 37949.

(b) *From Mde. Andryane to Monsieur Prandi. Postmarks :* 19 Juin, 1840. Franc (*illeg.*) and Paris, 20 Juin. 40.

J'ai reçu Monsieur, avec une bien agréable surprise et avec un vif sentiment de gratitude, les deux volumes que vous avez bien voulu m'adresser pour mon frère, j'éprouve le besoin de vous en remercier.

Me voilà plus que jamais bien confuse de mon ignorance : j'ai voulu il y a quelques années apprendre l'anglais et le manque absolu de mémoire, résultat d'une pauvre tête trop longtems fatiguée, m'a forcée d'y renoncer. Je ne pourrai donc vous lire Monsieur, c'est pour moi un vif regret. Mais au moins ma fille, celle que vous avez sans doute appelée *la petite Louise*, vous lira avec une bien vive satisfaction et s'en promet de véritables jouissances, quoiqu'elle aye [*sic*] juré de ne plus jamais ouvrir les mémoires d'un prisonnier, tant ils lui avaient couté de larmes, en réveillant de cruels et chers souvenirs.

Mon beau frère a été bien heureux de me dire Monsieur, tout le plaisir qu'il a eu à vous connaître, et la réception si parfaite qu'il a reçue de vous : je vous remercie pour ma part ! tout italien qui l'aime et sait l'aprécier [*sic*] a droit à ma reconnaissance ! il a tant souffert pour eux ! pourquoi vous [?] l'ont-ils si peu senti ! . . . Si je vais en Angleterre, je serai bien empréssée [*sic*] Monsieur, de chercher à vous exprimer de vive voix, tous les sentiments distingués dont je vous supplie de trouver ici l'assurance.

19 *juin* 1840.   PAULINE ANDRYANE.

Address : Monsieur Prandi, Berneer's Street, Oxford' Street, Angleterre, London.

(*c*)   *From A. Andryane to Prandi.*   *No postmark.*

MON CHER PRANDI,   AMIENS 1ᵉʳ *Juin* 1840.

Je ne veux pas quitter Amiens, sans vous dire combien j'ai regretté d'avoir du [*sic*] quitter Londres si vite, et sans vous exprimer tout [*sic*] ma reconaissance pour votre bon et cordial accueil. Je vous l'ai dit en nous separant, et je vous le repete [*sic*] aujourd'hui, mon voyage d'Angleterre m'est cher, puisqu'il m'a donné en vous un ami. Cela seul suffit pour que je m'en applaudisse chaque jour.

Je conte à Mde. Andryane toutes vos amabilités, toutes vos prévenances : elle veut que je vous en remercie pour elle : elle me prie aussi de vous dire qu'elle sera heureuse de vous voir à Paris. J'ai si bien parlé des bons momens que j'ai passés en Angleterre, que nous y serions retournés immédiatement, si ce maudit procès qui m'a rappelé de Londres ne me retenoit pas en France. Je pars ce soir pour Paris, pour être de retour ici dans quelques jours, puis repartir, et toujours ainsi pendant deux mois encore. C'est un triste metier que celui de Plaideur. Sallandronge sera à Londres mardi, c'est à dire demain. Je vous dirai que j'ai été si malade dans la traversée que j'en étois réduit à ne plus être qu'une masse de chair. Le mal de mer est une vilaine chose, et cependant, je suis prêt à l'affronter de gaieté de cœur pour retourner vous voir.

La tentative d'assassinat contre la reine d'Angleterre, fait ici une grande sensation. On y porte un intérêt extreme, et ce m'est une preuve de plus que le deux nations se rapprochent et mettent de coté leurs anciens préjugés. Veuillez dire a votre cher ami Patti [?] que je conserve un souvenir de cœur de toutes ses aimables attentions. Il est impossible d'être meilleur qu'il ne l'a été pour moi. Pourrai-je [?] etre aussi heureux pour lui prouver qu'il n'a pas affaire à un ingrat.

J'ai retrouvé mon petit Frederic plus éveillé que jamais. Qu'est ce que tu m'as rapporté s'est-il écrié !? ou est mon cheval . . . mon petit

cheval . . . et mes petits amis ; viendront-ils me voir ? J'ai dit que
le petit cheval n'avoit pas voulu passer la mer, et que les petits amis
viendraient l'année prochaine . . . oh bon, nous jouerons bien . . .
dites leur à ces chers enfans que je répondrai [*illegible*] à leurs gentilles
lettres. Chargez vous aussi mon cher ami, de toute l'expression de ma
reconnaissance pour les personnes qui sous vos auspices, m'ont accueilli
avec tant de bienveillance. Ne perdez pas de vue la Brochure de M.
Horner. Veuillez me rappeler a son bon souvenir. Mille amities a
notre tres bon et tres cher ami Patti [?] . . . et croyez bien mon cher
Prandi a tout mon devouement.

A. ANDRYANE.

Madame Andryane me charge spécialement de vous exprimer combien
elle est sensible du don que vous lui avez fait de la traduction des
mémoires elle destine vos livres à sa bibliothèque intime. C'est en les
faisant lire à Frederic, qu'elle compte lui apprendre l'anglais.
Je serai à ma campagne dans huit ou dix jours. Voilà mon adresse.

à Monsieur Andryane,
au Chateau de Coye
par Luzarches.

dept. de l'Oise, France.
[Letters to F. Prandi lent to the author by the late Mrs. Janet Ross.]

APPENDIX II.A

LETTERS FROM SANTA ROSA TO MRS. AUSTIN

1. (*Postmark :* 26 Dec.)

Thursday morning.

DEAR MADAM,

I like you because you are good, and because your gentle face express faithfully your goodness. I should not easily close the list of *because* —— but I won't omit this : I like you because you are most affection- ate in the world to your fire side. Let, let foolish people open a large yawning when they must remain at home one whole day. I pity them, almost I despise. I know a country man of mine, gentle and pretty creature who one day tell so to his friend ; " Alas ! I give handsome presents to people who will be able to learn me to use the twenty four hours of every day. Shocking ! 24 hours in every day ! This Gentle- man however is presently a outlaw ; Who would guess it ?

I am a little tired of the dinner I was present to, yesterday : yet that meeting was much pleasing to me. I was sitting near to *Ugoni* and at left side sweet *Arrivabene* stood with much calmness. The first don't forget to talk of your *radicalism*. The second increased very much in my favour. *Il entre de plus en plus en grace auprès de moi*, telling scriptur- ally, et for useful interpretations of my bad English.

I received yesterday a very dear letter from one my friend, whom I like heartily from where we were yet at ninetenth year of life. He is a physician ; very fond of his profession ; humane, disinterested towards his sicks ; perseverant, prudent friend ; he likes children of mine as well as they should be proper things of him. His letter gives me a diligent account of those unfortunate children ; diligent, and favourable, much favourable, you know. I wish only two things in the world. My country's deliverance ; and obscure, private life amongst my wife, my tender wife, and my children. A glory : I think it vaporous dream. Affections enjoyed in peace ; dream, perhaps, but clear and delicious dream.—

I hope to see you to-morrow at two hours afternoon. Let you remem- ber that I will be very much angry with you, if you shall wait for me only one minute.

Let forgive my outlandish English, and believe me

Your faithful friend

S. S. R.

Address : Mrs Sarah Austin, 18 Queen Square, Westminster.

2. (*Postmark* : 30 Dec., 1822.)

Sunday morning.

MY DEAR MADAM,

You are the most good-natured woman in the world, to be sure.—You like my *Italian English* ! I promise you many and many letters, and all wrote as well as the heart could suggest them. Perhaps this way out is better for improving. But I beg you to consider I cannot be introduced in another way. You must then leave me to writing carelessly, and therefore joyfully. I shall amend by degrees my present incorrections.

My last *Soirée* was more numerous than usually. Beyond Charles S. Marsan, a Savoie fellow, and a big Piedmontese outlaw, the Logician, and a Napolitan Lawyer given me the pleasure of their society : Welcoming Logician, I will say, because I like him, and because he bestows to me the agreable news of you, and hopes, which I don't dare expect the cheerful reality. I shall tell you something about Napolitan Lawyer ; unhappy man indeed. In year 1799 he took some places in revolution, and was banished. In 1820 he fancied to perform a second revolution after the July's revolution, aiming, I think, to overthrown the Regent's government, in hope to safe his country from treacherous and coward rulers of it. I don't know either lawyer and his friends are in their possessions the means on purpose, or not : but it is true that these conspirers charged to invite the people to the anarchy, even in mind to favour the Austrian's political views, have been cast in the jail threated in their life and, worst thing indeed, in their reputation. It is said that the depravate rulers made the infamous scheme to throw off the conspirers, in secrecy, and is added that Napolitan people having some suspicion about it tumultuously requested the lawful judgement of these poor fellows. The result of which was their absolution. Now the lawyer is outlaw, formally excepted from the late amnesty, and the object of the greatest abhorrence from actual rulers.

He have his wife and four children of him to Naples. No connexion, no friend are so bold as to visite such family. The name of Paladini, only to pronounce, is a guilt. O Italy ! o my unhappy mother ! It appears that a cruel destiny have told to italians so ; " Either vile ; either distressful ; Let make the choice."

Marquis de Priè is arrived to London. I shall see him this evening with very much pleasure. Courtier as to manners ; patriot as to principles, and as to the honour of persecution suffered from the King Charles. But I must retract my expression of courtier. It is true that this Gentleman was *maître de cérémonies at St. Cloud*. But he was then very young. The court of Napoleon was more a Wolf's crowd, than fox's one. And my gentle friend don't have been the time of improving as Wolf.

Monday morn.

I have just finished to write these words, when the same little Wolf knocked at my door. I must confess to you I trust myself into the Wolf's paws much heartily. Charles S. M. was with him. Words followed words between the Wolf and the *Man*. Never was a Wolf better combed than this, to be sure. It is right to add for the Wolf the praise of cheerful friendship.

In the last evening the toast to English people was bring from me among Italian fellows and accepted with much earliness—*The Times* of this morning give up the notion of Montmorency's dismission. We must see if the Minister De Villète wiser of ultras will adopt in the home's business constitutional views. In this way only the Bourbons have some possibility to conserve a crown illegaly acquired in years 1814 and 1815. I don't like the Bourbons. But I dislike very much the Bonapartist. French people has not enough prepared and disposed about republican institutions. To make a second unhappy essay of republican government and after little time to abase itself under the yoke of a soldier will be the greatest calamity and retard, perhaps run away the hopes the liberty's friend in Europa.

I hope to see you to-morrow, or Wednesday. I am very better. The Ct. Ugoni told me yesterday evening that Miss Smith was ill. I beg you to send to me news of her.—How delightful shall be to me to cross St. James Park and take my way towards Queen Square! I will find you in perfect health, and in your usual serenity. I will? It is bold word indeed. No matter. It is true, that I will.

In my next letter I shall describe you my countryhouse near Savigliano. Don't you allow me to soften my griefs with recollect my dearest remembrances, and to speak about these cheerful things to gentle-natured Woman, as you are. I have certainly find the only way existing for me to learn English. My wise and good mistress, Farewell, I am heartily
Your sincere and affectionate friend
S. S. R

Address : Mrs. Sarah Austin, 18 Queen Sq., Westminster.

3. (*Postmark :* 21 Ja. 1823.) [*Inscribed :* + Jany 20th 1823]
Lundi soir, 20 *Jan.*

M. Mill devoit vous apporter une petite lettre, mais elle n'était pas finie lorsqu'il revint la prendre & je fus réduit à vous envoyer verbalement de mes nouvelles. Celles que je vous donne ce soir sont meilleures. Je passe une partie de la journée sur mon canapé, et j'espère marcher d'un pas sûr sinon rapide vers mon parfait rétablissement. Je suis très content des soins affectueux de mon médecin, il paroît mettre plus d'intérêt que moi-même à la promptitude de ma guérison.

Votre dernière lettre m'a fait un bien grand plaisir surtout parce qu'il m'a paru y trouver plus que jamais l'expression de l'heureuse sérénité de votre existence. Je vous félicite des faveurs du philosophe, et beaucoup plus encore du retour de M. Austin ; j'espère qu'il aura fait un bon voyage ; & que sa santé se trouve aussi bonne que peuvent le désirer ses amis, au nombre desquels vous ne refuserez pas de me placer, et non des derniers, quoique *dernier venu.*

La société de mes amis et la lecture me préservent de l'ennui, mais les atteintes de la tristesse ne se repoussent pas aussi facilement. Peu accoutumé à être malade, doué d'une imagination qui s'empare quelque fois de mon avenir d'une manière bien funeste, qui même se plaît à répandre sur le présent quelques images sombres je dois passer des momens accablans . . . vous le concevez, Madame. Mais c'est pour moi un véritable soulagement que de vous en parler. Je crois être si bien compris. La Philosophie de Bentham vous a laissé un excellent cœur. Mais que dis-je? on calomnie cette philosophie quand on l'entend d'une autre manière que vous & moi. Ne le pensez-vous pas ?

J'ai tout-à fait encore l'air d'un malade et ne suis point établi dans

mon *sitting room* d'une manière pro [*paper torn*] à recevoir la visite d'une
Dame Anglaise. Ainsi ne venez pas me voir : mais daignez m'écrire
un peu souvent. Quelque sûr que je sois de votre bonne amitié il m'est
toujours très doux d'en recevoir de nouveaux témoignages.
A'dieu, Madame ; je lis peu d'anglais. Les livres que vous m'avez
envoyés sont tous commencés, mais je ne sais si je pourrai aller jusqu'au
bout.—Vous savez que je n'aime pas Cobbett. Aussi le *Times* de ce
matin sous ce rapport m'a fait plaisir. V⁵ incorrigible Whig.
Address : Mrs. John Austin, 18 Queen Square, Westminster.

4. (*Postmark :* Even. 30 Ja. 1823.)   [*Inscribed :* Janᵞ 28th + 1823]
                                                    Mardi 28 *Janvier.*
    Voici, Madame, une partie de vos livres. J'ai remis Berwick à St.
Marsan, qui vous en tiendra compte. Je vous avoue que de tous les
ouvrages que vous m'avez prêté [*sic*] c'est celui dont la lecture m'a le
plus attaché. J'ai passé avec lui dans les vallées des Alpes des heures
qui suspendirent entièrement chez moi ce que ma situation me donne
de tristesse.
    Je crois que je passerai tout le reste de la semaine au coin de mon feu.
Ce ne sera que Lundi ou Mardi que je ferai une course à Queen Square.
Ai-je besoin de vous dire avec quel plaisir ? Jamais je ne me suis trouvé
dans un état moral aussi décourageant, et je sens que la société d'une
amie aussi éclairée & aussi bienveillante que vous me fera beaucoup de
bien. Il est vrai que j'ai peu d'espoir de jouir de cette société habituelle-
ment & c'est ce qu'il me faudrait. Voilà une des impossibilités qui
ajoutent infiniment aux peines de ma situation.
    Je suis tout-à fait sans nouvelles de ma famille, et mon cœur est
rempli d'inquiétude. Je suis aussi très mécontent de la guerre d'Espagne
que je vois imminente, et dont les résultats me paroissent à craindre.
Je ne vois pas encore que les Espagnols aient une véritable armée, et
sans une armée on ne se défend pas.
    Si vous lisiez le *Times* aussi assidument que moi vous serez frappée
comme moi de ce cri général qui s'élève en Angleterre pour la réforme
du Parlement. Après ma patrie l'Angleterre est le pays auquel je suis
le plus attaché, et je prends un intérêt très vif à sa prosperité, à la conser-
vation de sa liberté, au perfectionnement de ses institutions.—Ces *meetings* sont une chose admirable. Y-a t'il [*sic*] une autre contrée où l'on
puisse s'assembler, délibérer sur un sujet que le gouvernement ne con-
sidère qu'avec effroy et qu'avec répugnance. On n'abdique pas une
patrie malheureuse, sans quoi je voudrois être Anglais.
    Miss Smith a quitté Park Street ! Je n'ai pas eu de ses nouvelles depuis
très longtemps. Elle n'a répondu à une lettre que je lui ai écrite
pour m'excuser de ne pas avoir reçu un de ses parens, célèbre Docteur,
qui avoit la bonté de venir me demander des nouvelles de ma santé.
Ce jour-là j'étais souffrant, abattu. Il m'était pénible de voir d'autres
personnes que mes intimes amis. Malgré ma bonne raison, je crains
que ma sauvagerie ne m'aie [*sic*] fait un pas de tort auprès de votre amie.
J'en serois réellement affligé—   .
    Bien des amitiés à M. Austin, et bien des caresses à Lucy.—Pourquoi
ne suis-je pas logé dans le quartier de We [*covered by seal*] Jamais je ne
l'ai tant regretté.—Mon anglais va horriblement, malgré ma lecture
assidue. Mes amis désespèrent de m'entendre jamais prononcer cor-
rectement un quart de phrase. Je suis trop vieux pour l'Angleterre.—

Adieu, Madame, n'oubliez pas de me donner de vos nouvelles, à moins que vous ne vouliez ajouter au sombre de mon humeur. Gai, triste, inquiet, tranquille je ne cesserai jamais de vous honorer et de vous aimer dans toute la sincerité de mon cœur.

Vᵉ dévoué sr. & ami
SANCTOR S.R.

Address : To Mistr. John Austin, 18 Queen Square, Westminster

5. (*No postmark.*) [*Inscribed :* 1823 + War in Spain]

Friday morning

Voici le saint de M. Butler ou ma tolérance est si douce, si universelle si sincère que j'aurais lu la vie et les merveilles d'un pauvre petit moine de St. François sans me permettre un sourire de mépris. Mais un archevêque persécuteur ! Le sang me bouillonne dans les veines. Les Catholiques Anglais qui appelent [*sic*] la tolérance à grands cris devraient-ils rappeler la mémoire d'un Giovanni de Ribera ? Lisez-le, si vous voulez. Moi, je l'ai tout lu ; et j'y ai découvert à la fin que Benoit XIV, ce pape si renommé par sa tolérance a declaré que le conseil donné par Giovanni di R. d'exiler les maures, peres, femmes, enfans, n'était opposé ni à la *charité*, ni à la *prudence* et ne devoit pas mettre d'obstacle à la béatificationde l'archevêque (pag. 154).

Laissons-là les persécuteurs. Je les abhorre de quelque masque qu'ils se couvrent. Le bonnet rouge du Jacobin, et la mitre d'un archevêque Espagnol, le manteau noir du ministre presbytérien, l'habit brodé d'un Inspecteur de police de Bonaparte . . . anathème sur tout ce qui attente à la liberté,—mais non anathème . . . n'imitons pas leur langage, tolérons-les eux-mêmes ; mais ôtons leur le moyen de nuire & couvrons-les de notre mépris.

—Passons à une autre scène—Je viens de lire le *meeting* du Yorkshire, ou plutôt de le parcourir—Un pauvre homme, Mr. Wortley, je crois, a parlé, a voté seul contre la réforme. Quelle imposante unanimité ! C'est véritablement le peuple Anglais qui répudie la Chambre des Communes. Je suis fâché que Norfolf [*sic*] se soit souillé du vieux Cobbett.—On croirait quelquefois que ces misérables brouillons sont à la solde des ennemis de la réforme parlementaire. Il n'y a que la crainte de voir de telles gens en crédit qui puisse donner à nos adversaires quelques partisans de bonne foi.

Ma santé va bien, mais il me faut aller doucement. Mon Docteur vient de me l'annoncer de la manière la plus positive. J'avais reçu une invitation pour mercredi prochain à 6 milles d'ici. Le Docteur consulté a dit *Non*. Je passerai, je pense, toute la semaine prochaine dans mon petit réduit. Mes soirées sont quelquefois brillantes ; j'avais sept à huit personnes avt. hier ; et quelquefois solitaires ; hier à soir, par exemple, je n'ai eu que l'Archevêque de Valence.

J'ai commencé comme je vous l'ai dit la memʳᵉ sur la Rⁿᵉ Elizabeth, mais mon ame n'est pas montée sur un ton à pouvoir s'occuper de pareilles époques de l'histoire. Je lis volontiers dix ouvrages sur votre grande Révolution, et sur la Révolution Française, mais pour votre Elizabeth, le cœur ne m'en dit point. J'ai commencé un Roman anglais et je le continue avec plaisir, il me fait du délassement aux lectures politiques françaises que je ne discontinue pas.

Je n'ai aucunes nouvelles de ma famille depuis fort longtemps ; et

cela ajoute à ma tristesse.   Je vous avoue que la guerre contre l'Espagne,
qui paraît inévitable me donne beaucoup plus d'inquiétude que d'espoir.
Mes pensées ne sont pas plus riantes que l'hyver de Londres—Ceci me
ramè [*paper torn*] a votre sérénité, mon excellente amie.   J'en crois
précise [ment] ce que vous en croyez, ce que vous m'en dites.   Il y a
tant de vérité dans votre existence morale que je pense vous avoir deviné,
et vous connoître beaucoup quoique notre liaison ne date que de quelques
mois.
     Vous aimez si passionnément votre Lucy que cela m'encouragera à
vous parler de mes enfans vivans et morts sans craindre de vous ennuyer.
—Que je hais la distance qui nous sépare ! et cette fâcheuse maladie !
et les formalités anglaises !—Adieu, madame.   Rappelez-moi au souvenir
de M. A.—quant à Lucy, elle doit m'avoir entièrement oublié.
               Votre bien sincère et bien aff^d ami
                                             S. S. R.

Address : Mrs. John Austin, 18, Queen Square, Westminster.
With 3 books.

          6. (*No postmark*) [*Inscribed :* 1823.   About Feb^y]
                                        Vendredi soir.
     Pourquoi donc du Français, mon aimable amie ?—Ne vous ai-je pas
dit combien vos lettres Anglaises me faisoient de plaisir ?   Et s'il s'agit
d'un exercice utile n'est-ce pas à l'Italien que vous vouliez le consacrer ?
—Avez-vous voulu me faire votre cour ?   Ce serait plutôt un reproche
à ma faiblesse.   Mais ne voilà t-il pas que j'ai commencé ma lettre en
français—fâcheuse habitude ! Je veux m'en défaire une seconde fois
quoi qu'il m'en puisse coûter.
     Se avessi avuto prima d' oggi notizie circostanziate dell' accidente del
nostro Radice, prima d' oggi ve le avrei mandate.   Novamente il povero
giovane ebbe a soffrire cinque giorni di angoscioso stato.   La nave
usciva felicemente dal Canale Britanno quando il vento si mestò e la
spinse ad occidente.   Il Capitano inesperto, disanimato si abbandonò al
furore del mare imperversato.   Non sapeva dove si fosse, dove s' andasse ;
un albero della nave si ruppe il quarto giorno della tempesta e colpì il
mastro in 2do che per più ore non fu capace chi di velare disperatamente.
E il Capitano si giudicava perduto e lo annunziava a' smarriti passeggieri ;
quella notte si passò nell' aspettazione di perire ad ogni momento.   Il
mattino seguente il mare scarnò, ma crebbe di nuovo alla sera, e rinnovò le
orribili angoscie di prima.   Alla fine si scopre una terra, ma scogli e
isolette rendevano l' approdare pieno di perigli.   Sopravvenne la notte,
e tutti si credevano che sarebbe l' ultima ; chi potea credere che la nave
mezzo sdruscita [*sic*] e spinta dai corse delle onde, e dal rabbioso vento
contro a que' scogli non dovesse rompere miseramente ?   Il loro scampo
fu davvero una maravigliosa cosa.   Allo spuntar del giorno il mare si
rappacificò.   La nave lungheggiò il lido e si provò di entrare nel porto
di Cork, ma i venti ne la respingevano.   Allora appunto fu che Radice
e un altro passeggiere, inglese, incontrata una picciol nave pescareccia
vi si gittarono e approdarono a King's Sail,[1] d' onde si recarono a Cork.
Della nave lasciata Radice non avea udito nulla ancora nell' ora in cui
scrisse.   Chi sa se avrà potuto reggere al malvagio tempo della notte
seguente ?   E se giunge in porto non sarà atta a far viaggio per più e

----
[1] Kinsale.

più dì. L' Inglese compagno di Radice se ne prende molta cura. Io voglio ridire che sia propria tra i gloriosi Inglesi e gli infelici Italiani una dolce simpatia.

Porro al quale Radice ha diritto la sua lettera ha subito scritto per raccomandarlo ad una sua intima conoscenza in Irlanda. Se voi ne fate altrettanto spero che il nostro amico ricéverà nella sua sventura ogni più desiderabile conforto. E a lui, e a noi, e spezialmente a me sarà caro di esserne debitori al vostro ottimo e benevolo cuore. Radice indugierà di poco a scrivere una seconda lettera di cui voi risaprete il contenuto tosto che mi sia noto..

Ora vi parlerò di me, e sarà per darvi nuove poco buone della mia salute. Ho lo stomaco dissestato a segno, che non posso a meno di prendermene molto cruccio. Ma probabilmente la mia immaginazione cresce il male. Soffro con meno pazienza da alcuni dì. Per mia buona ventura ho libri che mi occupano moltissimo : *Las Casas e Montholm.* Più leggo, e più mi persuado che il trionfo della fazione di Buonaparte non sarebbe favorevole alla via pratica, e meno alla libertà dell' Europa. I Buonapartisti sono più incorreggibili che i Borbonisti. Vorrei che gli udiste scusare Buonaparte, quasi lodarlo e dei legislato [ri (*paper torn*)] fatto muti [?], e dei Senatori docilmente servi, e dei tolti Tribuni ; e dar vanto alla dolcezza della sua polizia, alla popolarità de' suoi principii ! . . . O Sarah Austin ! Quanti quanti sono gli uomini arruolati sotto la bandiera liberale che non anelano ad altro che a godere gli onori, gli agi, e la facoltà dell' opprimere altrui passata ora ad un altra aristocrazia !

Ho riletto la vostra lettera. . Che mai mi dite intorno alla precedente ? Di che vi volete scusare ? a chi scrivete ? Non sono io quel vostro amico, già amico vecchio, che nello scrivervi, nel parlarvi si abbandona sempre ai primi suoi movimenti ? Ve ne scongiuro e prego, recordatevi che io non sarò mai sì lieto che nello scorgere voi lieta e contenta, e condotta al faceziare, il che non potete fare se non gentilmente.—Vi do la buona sera, e mi auguro una buona notte.

V. aff. amico

S. S. R.

Address : To Mistr. John Austin, 19 [*sic*] Queen Square, Westminster.

7. (*Postmark incompl.*12.ii.1823.) [*Marked in fem. hand* "1823 Lent +"]

Thursday [2] *evening.*

I have received with much pleasure your very amiable letter, from which I am informed of yours ki..dly attentions with regard to our friend Radice. Blessings, thousand blessings upon you, my gentle mistress !

Today G[1] Pepe paid to me a visit, a tall and well looking gentleman indeed. He seems to love much his country ; and, you know, his country is also mine, and will be for ever.

Welcome this Thursday,[2] which brings to me a letter from my friend Cousin, with good news of his health.

My possibility to see you at next Sunday evening is now uncertain ; but Thursday morning I will write to you about that. I will be earnest to communicate to my friend C. Porro your obliging invitation.

Yesterday I was, and quite alone, at Drury Lane to see King Lear. Ken affords to me much, very much delight. He plays warmly but naturally, variously, but ever distinctly, and with beautiful evidence.

[2] Tuesday ?

I had in my hands the book of play and lost few words when Ken played.
The actress *Cordelia* sobs yery well, but ever sobs, and tired me at last.
That work of *sauvage ivre*, how the friend of your brother-in-law calls
him irreverently, has some beauties who reach the bottom of heart, but
has some lenghts, and trivial and odd fancies from which the coldness
make its way into the soul of spectators.

To-morrow is called in my country *Ashes's day*. This evening is the
last of the merriments. Two years ago, these days were awful days.
Amongst the foolish pleasure of the world devoted friends of the liberty
are preparing a blow from which the hope of happiness beams throughout
the whole Italy. But she was a beam which cloud of the traitors and of
the cowards dimmed and perhaps for ever.

My friend Porro had lend to me a sister of Carmagnola. We shall
read it together.

The news you have given to me about Miss Smith are very melancholy.
I fear indeed that her health should be not little altered. I want myself
to make some abode in the country. But now I am so circumstanced
as to do it quite impossible. Farewell my young and wise mistress.
I wish you good Quaresima. Will you come with me at the Saint Andrea's
church to receive the holy ashes on the forehead ? and to hear a minister
preach over the pulpit ? After it to walk a little. Look at the harmless
splendor of the sun ! Look at snowy Alpes which draw themselves
majestically on the blue sky ! Alpes ! useless bulwark of my country !
—Farewell again.

Address : To Mistr. John Austin, 18 Queen Sq., Westminster.

8. (*Postmark :* FE. 24, 1823)

LONDRA 2 GREAT MARYLEBONE STR.,
PORTLAND PLACE,
a' 23 di Febbo 1823.

Appena mi giunse il vostro mestissimo biglietto io vi scrissi una lettera
breve per pregarvi di mandarmi le vostre nuove. Non sapendo il vostro
indirizzo costì, scrissi *alla Sig^a John Austin-Taylor* senz' altra indicazione.
Mi avvedo che non mi sono ingannato sulla bontà del vostro cuore.
Voi mi avete scritto in mezzo alle vostre sollecitudini. Non vi posso dire
quanto io ve ne sia grato : nè anco potrei abbastanza vivamente mostrarvi
la mia letizia per le migliori novelle che mi date della madre vostra, e
della vostra tornata in Londra fra pochi dì. Il dolore che avete provato
nel vedere la madre fra i spasimi, e i pericoli di morte, io lo capisco,
mia ottima amica, ed io lo divido. E così divido il piacere dolcissimo che v' ha inondato il cuore nello scorgere la cara infirma tornare
alla vita dai confini della terribile e indefinibile eternità. Dio ve la serbi
lungotempo ancora. Non vi pare che sia dolce il pregare, o piuttosto
l' innalzare l' anima nostra verso il suo principio quando abbiamo il cuore
pieno di consolazione e di speranza ?—Nella sventura, io sono molto
meno religioso che nella prosperità. Ma veramente sono stato sì rare
volte felice, che potrei a 40 anni annoverare i pochi momenti in cui ebbi
a pagare al mio fattore un tributo di soave riconoscenza.

La mia salute è migliorata. La compagnia di Luigi Porro, eccellente
amico, il metodo più regolato del vivere, l' aver passeggiato un poco,
queste cose tutte insieme mi hanno tornato non ancora nel mio primo
vigore corporale, ma almeno ad una condizione di salute discretamente

buona. Ho una cameretta che mi piace assai, dove c' è un sito per lavorare molto ben disposto. Vi passerò gran parte del mio tempo.—Leggo per la 2da volta il Caino di Byron, intendendolo a mezzo ; e forse lo leggerò una terza volta : Fossi ivi con voi ! Ho una voglia pazza di proferire l' inglese a dovere, e mi provo di declamare i versi del Caino. Ma guai se S. Marsano mi sente : egli vi adira. Persino Priè che farebbe, in una conversazione di *Country Gentlemen* quella figura che John Bull all' Accademia di Parigi, si piglia la libertà di ridere quando proferisco l' inglese. Toccherà a voi, mia buona e dolce maestra, a pormi a segno di ridere a suo tempo di chi ride ora di me.

Ho veduto ieri il Duca di S. Lorenzo. È un vecchietto che mi par savio e gentile : Il vostro Governo ha rinviato ieri la proibizione del vendere armi e munizioni da guerra ai sudditi di Spagna, manifesto e primo segno della sua amicizia. Vedremo si i frutti secondi saranno sani. Molti ne dubitano. I giornali *ultra* ci narrano che Bessières e Mérinoy uniti sono alla testa di 10^{m} uomini e minacciano Madrid. Ma i fondi di Francia tuttavia declinano, e ciò fa sperare che quella notizia sia invenzione o esagerazione fortissima. Il Portogallo, secondo i fogli di questa mattina, manda 30^{m} uomini per ajutare i Spagnuoli, e già i primi corpi sono entrati nel territorio dell' alleato. Questa è ottima, e sostanziale notizia. Tutto contato e pesato, le mie speranze non sono però uguali ai miei timori.

Ho veduto sovente il G^{le} Pepe. Ve ne dir [*letter torn*] quando saremo nel cantuccio del Camminetto a [*letter torn*] Ieri S. Marsano mi ha dato il vostro indirizzo, e mi ha detto che tornereste fra due o tre giorni in città. Non lascio di mandare a Norwich questa lettera : se vi trova partita di quivi, che monta ? Io avrò sempre speso una mezz' ora molto caramente, conversando con voi.

Subito giunta qui, vi piaccia scrivermelo, che io verro andar tosto a felicitarvi della madre riavuta e del vostro piacere di riveder Lucietta vostra.—Ho sempre il vivo desiderio di passar la Primavera in campagna, ma è incertissimo che io vi possa riuscire.

Notizia de' miei, nessuna. Ho mille pensieri inquieti che mi tengono assidua compagnia.—Il Cte Porro che si prometteva assai piacere, dal passare una sera con voi mi commette di ossequiarvi, e si consola del vostro tornare in Londra col cuore riposato dopo tanta angoscia. Abbiate cura della vostra salute, e vogliatemi un poco di bene, se non volete aver taccia d' ingratissima.

V. sincero amico,

S. S. R.

Address : To Mistr. John Austin, at Mistress Reeve's St. Martin's, at Palace, Norwich.

9. (*No address, no postmark*)

Ce 1. mars.

Plus de vos nouvelles, mon aimable amie. Votre dernière lettre annonçait un prochain retour à Londres, ce qui ne m'empêche pas de vous écrire une seconde lettre à Norwich. Je pense que si vous étiez dejà à Queen Square j'aurais reçu un mot de vous. St. Marsan m'a dit hier qu'il n'avait pas reçu de vos nouvelles non plus. J'ai donc un juste sujet d'inquiétude ; je vais aujourd'hui à Queen Square où je laisserai ma lettre si je ne vous y trouve pas.

J'ai eu quelque ennuis ces jours-ci. Ma santé va passablement bien.

Que de plaisir j'aurai à vous voir ! Mais quel chagrin pour moi, si votre retour était retardé par de tristes circonstances !

Adieu, mon excellente amie. Je n'ai pas besoin de vous assurer de la vivacité de mon attachement.

SANCTOR DE S. R.

Comment oubliois-je de vous dire que j'ai reçu des nouvelles de ma famille ? Cela prouve que j'étois bien occupé de vous—Ces nouvelles sont bonnes, tout-à fait bonnes. Ma femme se porte bien. Elle pense toujours à m'envoyer mon fils aîné, & à se réunir à moi. Non, je ne méritois pas qu'une femme aussi courageuse & aussi tendre s'associât à ma destinée.—et à une aussi triste destinée.

10. (*Postmark* : Mr. 19. 1823)

LONDRA 19 *Marzo.*

Ho letto due volte la vostra ultima lettera. Mestissima veramente, e tale che non posso rispondervi altro se non che intendo e divido il vostro dolore. Agevol cosa il dire altrui " rassegnati, soffri costantemente ". Ma io non amo di dare alle persone i consigli che non potrei io medesimo seguire. Il vostro è contrasto dolorosissimo di affetti e di doveri. Chi potrebbe non averne lacerato il cuore ? Voi prendete per norma il vostro dovere, e ne giudicate saviamente. Questo sta in voi ; ma il non soffrire in tal situazione, e il non soffrire molto e duramente sarebbe da superba filosofessa, e non da ottima e benevolente donna qual voi siete, e sempre sarete per la consolazione e il diletto di coloro che vi amano, tra' quali io non intendo esser l' ultimo, mia buona amica. Io vi vedrò Lunedì prossimo 24 del mese. Mi auguro, ma non oso sperare di trovarvi soletta nel vostro cantuccio. Comunque, anche il solo vedervi me fara contentissimo.

I have thought all society even his wife was indifferent, almost burthensome to him . . . Queste sono le vostre parole. E voi vedete quanto eravate ingiusta. Ve ne voglio sgridare. È vero che le creature più gentili meno conoscono la propria gentilezza. Questa sia la vostra scusa. Ma io sempre ho creduto che voi facevate principalissima parte della felicità anzi della esistenza di vostro marito. Siatene superba e lieta. Chi sa meglio di voi che il vostro marito non è uom volgare ? E che se i tempi favorissero lo slancio e la prova degli ingegni e delle nature egli si troverebbe ben tosto nella prima fila ?—In quanto a me, vi confesso che il contristare un uomo della sua tempra me parrebbe doppia colpa ; e il renderlo felice opera sublime perchè difficile, ardua, e richiedente una tenerissima perseveranza.

Io sono in sullo sgridare. Il mio compagno e amico Porro non vi è noto. Io non acconsento che voi gli diate il soprannome di *lieto*, perchè temo che non vi siate formata un idea giusta della sua natura. Non è di quelli che considerino la vita umana come un giuoco di fanciulli. La felicità degli uomini e quella de' suoi concittadini più particolarmente è lo scopo di tutti i suoi pensieri. Egli risente vivamente la soddisfazione di aver sagrificato gli agi e le dolcezze della vita alla professione pubblica dei suoi principi ; ama con singolar tenerezza i suoi amici e compagni d' infortunio, e preferisce la loro società a qualunque altro diletto : Confronta talora il suo viver qui frugale, temperato sì, ma liberissimo colla miserabile e inquieta vita dei Lombardi che non hanno abbandonato la patria, e non hanno ancora venduto l' anima loro al Diavolo, ossia a Francesco Imperadore : Non si può intendere abbastanza quanto sia cocente, rabbioso il dolore di vivere tra padroni che vi abborrono, vi scherniscono, vi disprezzano, e si studiano di ferirvi nei punti più delicati della vostra esistenza sociale e domestica. Porro sgombro di qual doloroso peso, superbo dei figli constanti nell' amor filiale, pieno dellas peranza di vedere il risorgimento della patria: Porro *sotto l' usbergo del sentirsi puro* è un uomo lieto, sì. Ma questa letizia e una conseguenza della altezza de' suoi principii, della forza del suo carattere. Ho io detto sufficientemente per convincervi che l' amico mio non è lieto perchè leggiero, ma lieto perchè forte ? Da questa mia lunga diceria voi dovete conchiudere in qual pregio io tenga i vostri giudizii, gentilissima amica.

Sono anche un poco di cattivo umore, e sapete il perchè ? Tra le altre cose mi è di molto disappunto l' essere per Venerdì invitato ad una volta in tre luoghi dove mi piacerebbe quasi ugualmente l' andare. Fossi Sant' Antonio da Padova ! Egli avea tal segreto di essere in più siti ad un tempo.—Volete voi tradurre la sua vita, delizia di Butler ?— Sono invitato da Mistriss Grote, in città. L' ho conosciuta in casa vostra in quella sera che io tormentai dalla tosse avea più voglia di tacere che di parlare.—e da Mistriss Parry mia conoscenza sin dal 9mbre scorso e che intimissima di Mistr. Opie mi scrive ch' ella sarebbe da lei quella sera. Pensate che disgusto è il mio di mancare tal occasione ! [*paper torn*] da un' altra figura conoscenza del mio Cte Porro ; e vi si legge una Tragedia d' Alfieri. Tutto questo lo stesso Venerdì. Sono impegnato da Mistriss Grote che fu la prima ad invitarmi. Il G^{le} Pepe vi si troverà con me, ma ciò non mi consola niente affatto. Domani sarò a visitare Mistriss Opie : S. Marsano ha molti impegni, e credo che non potrà. Egli vi si raccomanda, e dice che ha risposto alla vostra lettera tanto mesta, di cui mi scrivete " he must forgive it ".

Ieri sera Canning ha detto in Parlamento che l' Inghilterra conserverebbesi neutrale. Sir Fr. Burdett ha parlato caldamente. I miei Whighs sono poco contenti, e spero che se non altro faranno de' bei discorsi. Domani a sera conoscerò uno dei capi di quella parte : il Mr. Landsdowne. Ho riveduto Sir MacKintosh. Un' ora di ragionamento con lui soddisfa assai l' intelletto ; ma non si può dire ugualmente che la sua società sia confidente e amorevole. Egli ha un non so che di gelato nei suoi modi che non si confà colla mia natura. Sono stato con Porro Lunedì sera in villa dal Sig. Fry, il quaker. Ho conosciuto la sua numerosa e lieta famiglia. Vi assicuro che quella visita mi ha fatto un' impressione di piacere e di mestizia indefinibile. Nel suo complesso era però dolce, e mi parvero brevi troppo le ore che passai nella compagnia dei buoni quakeri.

Addio. Io spero e desidero che nel vostro lasciare Norwich la vostra madre si trovi meno aggravata, onde l' angoscia della dipartenza vi sia scemata un poco. Cucchi mi ha scritto, e di voi con grandissime lodi. Se io potessi io non vorrei che le persone vi lodassero se non colla mia licenza, e non la darei che ad alcuni pochi eletti. Ma questa non è cosa da dire al Maestro delle trentadue scolare. Farewell.

Yours for ever,
S. SANTA ROSA.

Address : To Mistr. Austin, at Mistr. Reeves, St. Martins Palace, Gildengate Street, Norwich.

11. (*No postmark*) [*Inscribed :* Feby. 1823. *altered to* April 1823]

Dimanche.

Voici la dernière lettre que je vous écrirai depuis Marylebone Street.
Demain à 2 heures je serai à *South Banke.* Ce sera le commencement
d'une vie nouvelle ; mais vous, mon excellente amie, serez toujours
pour beaucoup dans mon existence. Ai-je besoin de dire à quel point
je vous aime et je vous estime ? J'ajouterai à cela que j'espère être
connu de vous ; chose qui ne m'arrive pas avec tous mes amis ; chose
qui me paraît la plus désirable, la plus essentielle. J'ai l'orgueil de
croire qu'avec tous mes défauts je vaux la peine d'être aimé si l'on me
connaît bien. N'allez pas sourire de la solennité de cette lettre " Ne
dirait-on pas que ce sont des adieux en partant pour les Indes ? " Ma
chere amie, un changement dans la manière d'exister vaut bien un grand
voyage. Ne souriez donc pas, où je me fâcherai.
J'ai vu l'autre jour Othello pour la 2ᵈᵉ fois avec Charles S. M. l'homme
terrible qui a fait peur à Miss Smith. Keen a joué à faire trembler,
c'est à dire admirablement ; mais je ne voudrais pas le voir une
troisième fois dans cette piece.
Savez vous que je suis très impatient de voir Lucy que je n'ai plus
vu [*sic*] depuis bien longtemps ? Je crains cependant que ce ne soit
pas Jeudi prochain. Vous aurez de mes nouvelles et peutêtre des l
[*paper torn*—(livres)] anglais.
Je vous renvoye le parapluie que j'ai pris chez vous à défaut du mien.
Car si le mien est perdu ce n'est pas une raison pour que je retienne
celui-ci qui ne m'appartient pas. Je ne desespere point au reste de
ravoir le mien lorsque vous aurez le loisir d'y penser.
Je vous souhaite du loisir et du repos. Je n'aime point votre frère
s'il vous donne trop de besogne. Un travail réglé, tant qu'il voudra,
mais qu'il ne vous accable pas de son fatras scientifique.
Ricordatemi al vostro caro marito e vogliatemi un poco di bene.

V. affᵐᵒ amico,
Santorre S. R.

Address : Mistr. John Austin, 1 Henrietta Street, Brunswick Square.

12. (*No postmark*) [*Inscribed :* June 2ᵈ 1823]

Green Cottage,
Southbank,
Regent Park.

Lundi, le 2 Juin.

Mon aimable amie, je comptois aller vous voir aujourd'hui, et voilà
que Berchet m'apprend que vous allez entendre des *Speeches* a *Freemason's Hall.* A Dieu ne plaise que je vous y accompagne. Pour la
première fois je m'ennuierais avec vous. Ne me faudrait-il pas écouter
dans un religieux silence au moins une douzaine d'orateurs sans com-
prendre la moitié de ce qu'ils disent ? Et n'y a-t-il pas là de quoi
s'impatienter outre mesure ? Demeurer assis cinq ou six mortelles
heures à côté d'une chère et aimable personne avec laquelle on
causerait volontiers, sans pouvoir lui dire plus de quatre mots pendant
tout ce temps-là, retenir à toute force des bâillements impérieux pour
ne pas scandaliser l'assemblée, et avoir pour toute consolation le plaisir
de trépigner des pieds à la fin de chaque discours et d'épanouir la face
de quelque Gentleman, voire même de quelques doyens ou demi

prélats *hérétiques* !—Et ne me dites pas qu'il y a de l'exagération dans
mes craintes. J'ai été a Freemason's Hall dans une autre occasion.
Au lieu d'un Duc de Gloucester, il y avait un Duc de Sussex. Mais
moi, qui malgré toute ma reputation aristocratique, ou plutôt parceque
j'ai un certain genre d'aristocratie, ne me soucie guère de contempler
le visage d'un Duc, j'abandonne aux enfans de la bonne Angleterre
ma quotepart des compliments que sa Royale *Highness* débitera à
l'assemblée avec une grace toute particulière, et un charme indéfinissable,
comme tout ce que font ces gens-là.

Je me reproche beaucoup, mon excellente amie, la lettre que je vous
ai écrite dernièrement. Ne m'en veuillez pas. C'est peut être une
maussade preuve d'amitié, mais ce n'en est pas moins une preuve que
de se laisser aller en écrivant au premier mouvement de son ame. Il
y a de la confiance à se montrer à un ami tout à fait tel qu'on est. C'est
comme un amant qui ose se présenter à sa maîtresse avec un habit
mal fait, et les cheveux mal peignés. Ça n'est pas bon pour tous les
jours, j'en conviens, dans les deux cas mais quand ce n'est pas trop
souvent, je crois que la personne qu'on traite de cette manière ne doit
pas s'en plaindre. Ne croyez-vous pas que les hommes toujours
sereins, toujours rians, toujours prévenans sont des créatures trop
parfaites, que les romans nous montrent quelquefois, mais que la vie
réelle ne nous donne jamais sans une triste et lourde compensation ?
Véritables [. . .] dormantes! Adieu, mon aimable amie, j'irai vous voir
dans la semaine et j'espère prendre bien mon temps.

V^{re} dévoué ami
S. S. Rosa.

P.S.—Je vous renvoye les billets que Berchet m'a fait remettre.—
Quand irons nous voir Shakespear ?

13. (*No postmark*) [*Inscribed :* June 1823]

Lunedì mattina.[1]

Invece di una mia visita eccovi una mia letterina e con essa il libro
di Berchet. L' ho letto con piacere grandissimo. Molti italiani gli
daranno taccia di prosaico, perchè avvezzi a contentarsi di suoni
vuotissimi di pensieri. Certo, Berchet s'è lasciato sfuggire dei versi
troppo negletti, ma il colore del suo stile e del suo verseggiare io lo
tengo il vero e proprio per lo scopo che egli se è prefisso. L' ultima
parte mi è sembrata la migliore. La delicatezza e la forza del sentire
vi lampeggiano.

Spero di vedervi prima di Domenica, anzi ne son certo, se la mia
malvagia fortuna non vi fa uscir di casa nell' ora in cui vi capiterò.

Porro è stato contentissimo della sua passata ad Henrietta Street, e
quasi non pensa ad altro che al mattino di Domenica ventura. Mi è
parso che il vostro marito abbia ricevuto con piacere l' invito che io
gli feci non senza timore di gelata risposta. Ieri sera egli fu davvero
un' amabile persona.

Il conversar con giovani francesi non vi riempie il cuore di speranza

---

[1] If the inscribed date ' June 1823 ' is correct, this letter was probably written
on the 9th. It was evidently written before the letter of 12th June and may
have been left by Santa Rosa himself when he called at Henrietta Street on
the 10th.

non vi ravviva il desiderio di libertà ? A me non manca mai di far quelli effetti.

Ricordate Santorre a Lucy.

Il vostro sincerissimo amico

S. S. R.

[No address on outside—but signs of its having been erased.]

14. (*Postmark* : 13 Ju. 1823, Night)

GREEN COTTAGE, SOUTH BANK,
REGENT PARK, *ce 12 Juin.*

J'ai été avant-hier à Henrietta Street dans l'espoir d'y trouver votre mari e d'avoir de vos nouvelles. C'était l'heure de son dîner, et je l'avais choisie exprès. Mais malheureusement pour moi Mr. Austin dînait chez un de ses amis et il a fallu me contenter d'une petite conversation avec la bonne de Lucy. On vous attend mardi prochain, m'a-t-elle dit. Bien certainement dans la matinée de Mercredi j'irai vous voir. Je ne saurais, ma chère et bonne amie vous adresser des paroles de consolation. Partager votre douleur est tout ce que je puisse et vous dire et vous répéter dans la sincérité de mon cœur que vous avez en moi un ami bien affectionné qui a besoin de vous voir sinon heureuse, au moins paisible et résignée aux souffrances de la destinée humaine. Je ne saurais vous parler de bonheur dans ce triste moment, mais pensez à Lucy, à tout ce qu'elle vous promet. Votre visite aura fait beaucoup de bien à votre pauvre père. Je vous assure que mon amitié pour vous et tout ce que vous m'avez dit de son ame [*sic*] si tendre, si douce, et si élevée me fait prendre un vif intérèt à lui.

S. Marsan vous a écrit, et vous avez dû recevoir sa lettre. Nous parlerons ensemble de son voyage. J'ai dîné avec lui la veille de son départ.

Je n'ai rien à vous dire de moi si ce n'est que je suis peu, bien peu content de mon train de vie. Je n'ai pas encore pu par le concours de diverses circonstances commencer la tâche que je me suis imposée. Il m'est arrivé un ami de Suisse, un ami de 48 ans, docte jurisconsulte, homme aimable, ayant beaucoup de jugement, de l'esprit et du caractère. Son nom est le Chevalier Dal Pozzo. Il a été Pr. Président à Gènes sous l'Empire, et Ministre de l'Intérieur à Turin lors de notre révolution

Porro me charge de vous dire combien il a pris de part à votre chagrin. Je suis toujours plus content de sa société intime.

Adieu ma chère amie. Je suis impatient de vous voir, et cependant je crains le moment parce qu'il pourra renouveller [*sic*] votre peine ; mais n'y a t'il pas quelque secrète douceur de céder à son affliction à la présence d'une personne qui la comprend et la partage ? Si vous ne retournez pas Lundi ou Mardi, daignez m'écrire un mot pour que j'aie di vos nouvelles. Adieu encore.

Votre affectionné et sincère ami,

SANCTOR DE STA. ROSA.

Address : To Mistr^{ss} John Austin, (Taylor) Norwich.

15.

GREEN COTTAGE 19 *agosto*

Se non vi ho scritto prima incolpatene la mia smemoraggine. Io non sapeva poi dove si fosse Dorking e mi toccò andare a *Henrietta Street* per pigliare una lezione di Geografia inglese dalla v^a cameriera ; e vero che io pensava di aver da lei il vostro indirizzo più sicuro e più esatte. Ho incontrato vostro marito in quell' occasione ; stava per partire alla volta a Dorking, e mi promise di ricordarmivi. Radice vi ha scritto. Almeno io credo. Egli sta bene, salvo che è diventato nero come un *Bedoino*. Non ritornerà a Norwich, ma spero che potrà esser allocato bene per qualche mese, e in modo da potersi acquistar amici e riputazione, il che nella vostra Inghilterra è una gravissima cosa. Il regaluccio per la mia Santorrina passerà il mare e l' alpi alla pma. buona occorrenza. Vene ringrazio proprio di cuore. Voi sapete trovare i veri modi di farmi sorridere l' animo, almeno per qualche minuto. Ho anch' io un presente da farvi, ma fo certo di capitare la vostra tornata.

Intanto vi dico che abbiamo avuto lettere del Viaggiatore. Alcune di data anteriore a quella che vi è nota ; una sola più fresca. Le nuove che egli ci da della sua situazione non sono tali da farci sperare che gli arrivi lo scopo che s'era prefisso. Del resto pare che non abbia inciampi o ostacoli da temere nel corso del suo viaggio.—Quelle prime sue lettere scritteci non arrivarono a loro tempo a cagion di uno sbaglio che fu fatto nell' indirizzo.

Mi è riuscito di gran piacere il veder Collegno. Ci racconta mestissime cose della Spagna. Sembra che l' edifizio vada crollando e rovinando sempre più. Per me non crederò mai che si possa fondare stabilmente lo stato senza il consenso della maggiorità di una nazione.

Ho buone notizie di Porro, mi scrive sovente, e sempre c' è una o due righe per voi.

Leggo Shakespear con mediocre assiduità. Ho letto La lettera d'Eloïse di Pope. Toglietene alcun antitesi che non appartengono al linguaggio della passione, e rimarrà una cosa soavissima. Io l' ho letto con una commozione di cuore ; la conosceva prima, ma in francese. Il vostro inglese mi va propriamente a sangue. Fra 4 anni al più, io credo che lo leggerò e scriverò, e *apprezzerò* meglio di qualunque altro forestiere. Sono orgoglioso troppo, forse—ma io credo di riuscire nelle cose che m' interessano molto, e dipendono da me solo.

Priè ha lasciato Southbank. Il Colonnello parte domani. Rimarrò solo con Pecchio.—Non so che cosa farò giunto che io sia a mezzo settembre.

Quando tornate voi da Dorking ? Spero che ivi sarà fra due settimane al più al più—Certo, Mistriss Mill vi riterrà per le falde della veste— Si capisce troppo bene. E voi siete una buona creatura, onde calcolate male, assai sovente e ne sono contentissimo.

La mia lettera è orribilmente scritta. Temo che non mi possiate diciferare. Ma non posso scrivere adagio quando scrivo così come l' animo mi detta. E non saprei, scrivendovi, far' in altro modo.

Il Portogallo non è tranquillo. Forse vi toccherà di badarci un poco, onde i francesi non vi preoccupino il luogo di pacificatori. La Spagna a mio senso è quasi impossibile a pacificarsi : vi vorrebbe un re forte savio, fors' anche non vi riuscirebbe. Con Ferdinando non ci vedo modo.—Addio, radicalissima e carissima amica. Vogliatemi un poco di bene, e date a Lucy per conto mio, due o tre teneri baci.

SANTORRE S. R.

(*No address*)

16. (*No postmark*) [*Inscribed* : Aug^st 30 1823 +]

GREEN COTTAGE *ce* 30 *Août*.

Lisez mon Postscriptum avant la lettre.

Je n'en ai pas pu déchiffrer plus de la moitié, ma chère amie, & je vous la renvoye cette lettre, qui pour être écrite par un auteur de romans n'en est pas plus romanesque. Vous sentez bien que je n'en ai pas dit un mot à Radice de peur d'avoir une scène de transgression [?]. D'ailleurs notre cher Chevalier errant désappointé, notre pauvre maître d'école en disgrace est, je l'espère, sur le point de partir pour Bath où il aura pour quelque temps une existence sinon aisée, au moins assurée, avec l'espoir de consoler et d'améliorer sa situation.   Cucchi demeurera donc en pleine possession du bénéfice de Norwich.   Radice doit l'avoir tranquillisé à cet égard, et je n'ai pas manqué de l'y engager.

⸴ Voici trois lettres pour vous.   Deux sont arrivées depuis assez longtemps, & ont été écrites dès le commencement du voyage ; je vous ai dit, je crois, comment elles s'étaient égarées en route.   La troisième est d'une date plus récente ; lors qu'elle m'est arrivée je vous attendais de jour en jour.   Votre dernière lettre m'ayant ensuite appris que vous ne reviendriez pas d'un mois j'ai été sur le point de faire une course à Dorking et de vous remettre moi même les dépêches en question ; mais vous l'avouerai-je ?   Je me suis arrêté dans l'incertitude de savoir si ma chère amie, jeune femme vivant seule dans un petit cottage, pouvait recevoir ma visite sans que Son Seigneur & Maître y trouvat [*sic*] de l'inconvenance.   Si mon scrupule est un peu bête, c'est cependant le scrupule d'un ami, et d'un ami qui ne met jamais son propre plaisir au premier rang.

Mardi prochain je vais chez Mr. Fry, et j'y demeure jusqu'à Vendredi matin.   Cette famille paraît me vouloir tant de bien, que je n'ai su comment me refuser à son aimable invitation.   Elle m'a toutefois un peu contrecarré car je vais commencer à travailler après demain 1^r 7bre.   C'est une résolution prise, et fermement prise.   Félicitez-m'en, et préparez-vous à être patient auditeur de mes cahiers.   Quelles heureuses matinées je vais passer ma chère amie !   Elles commenceront Lundi, et ne discontinueront point à Plasket chez Mr. Fry ; j'y suis en famille, et je porterai avec moi tout ce qu'il me faut pour travailler.

Avec votre permission, vous n'aurez pas un mot de politique. Lorsqu'on est aussi étranger, que je le suis maintenant, aux affaires, et qu'on est bien décidé à ne pas se repaître d'illusions à quoi bon se tourmenter, et se fatiguer l'esprit ?   Mais, un moment . . . pourrai-je ne rien vous dire sur la mort du pape ?   On prétend que l'Autriche désire la Thiare pour un de ses archiducs que est Cardinal, mais qu'elle le désire ou non, qu'elle intrigue ou non, jamais le sacré ' Collège ' ne fera un pape étranger.   Si le Cardinal Spina était choisi on aurait un homme d'esprit et de tact à la tête de l'Eglise Romaine.   Savez-vous qu'un pape habile homme aurait un beau rôle à jouer dans les circonstances où nous nous trouvons ?   On a si peur en Europe de la Ste. Alliance qu'un pape, qui n'en serait pas l'esclave et qui le prouverait par des actes solennels, deviendrait infiniment populaire.

A votre retour je vous présenterai le Ch. Dal Pozzo mon ami, et son livre.   Il vient de faire plutôt une bonne action qu'un bon ouvrage en faisant imprimer ici ses Observations sur la nouvelle organisation judiciaire du Piémont. C'est une bonne action parce que l'auteur a écrit dans des vues d'utilité très positive mais presqu'entièrement locale ; et c'est precisément par là que l'ouvrage est peu intéressant pour la plupart des classes de lecteurs, qui s'ennuyent bientôt des questions de jurisprudence et d'administration judiciaire si elles ne se rattachent pas à des considérations politiques ou morales, & cela d'une manière directe & évidente. Vous êtes, au reste, bien faite pour apprécier le courage et la persevérance d'un homme qui n'a pas cessé depuis neuf ans de combattre avec toutes les ressources de sa logique et de sa doctrine légale les déplorables fautes des Ministres ou plutôt du gouvernement de son pays.

Encore un mot sur le voyageur. Nous avons su qu'il a donné de grandes inquiétudes chez lui par la direction de son voyage. Je n'espère rien d'avantageux de ces inquiétudes ; rien qui puisse entrer en balance avec les dangers qu'il a courus. Je voudrais le voir en deça du détroit. L'Angleterre est véritablement la patrie d'adoption que les italiens doivent se donner. Le Comité espagnol s'occupe avec bienveillance de ceux de nos compatriotes qui sont arrivés tout récemment de la péninsule dénués de moyens d'exister. Puissent nos petits enfans payer un jour notre dette, mais que ce ne soit pas en pareille occasion ! Marchez à l'amélioration sociale sans révolution. Peut-être, cela vous est-il possible. Pour sortir d'une révolution avec la liberté il faut des vertus dont les doctrines de notre siècle ont altéré les sources.

Adieu, mon excellente amie. Je vous remercie des bonnes nouvelles que vous me donnez de Lucy & je la remercie elle-même de ne pas m'avoir oublié. J'attends de vos lettres, et je n'ai pas besoin de vous dire avec quel plaisir je les reçois toujours.

Vtre. dévoué e sincère ami,
Santor Santa Rosa.

P.S.—Je vous envoye une autre lettre qui vient de m'arriver Ch^{les} lui-même arrive Jeudi. Il me la mande d'Amsterdam le 29 du mois . . . [?]
Lundi soir, 1er 7bre.

17. (*Postmark :* Se(pt). 3, 1823)

Green Cottage, *ce 2 7bre.*

J'avois une bien longue lettre à vous envoyer, mon excellente amie. Un caprice, peut être, me l'a fait condamner et vous n'aurez que deux mots de moi. Je vous renvoye la lettre de Mrs. Opie. M. Cucchi est bien heureux . . . Radice part pour Bath sous peu de jours. Il y aura une existence sinon aisée du moins assurée.

Charles S. arrive Jeudi matin. Je ne le verrai que Vendredi : je pars demain pour une course à la campagne, que je ne peux pas différer.

Je suis effrayé de l'aspect que prend le ciel, ce soir. Je comptais sur un beau Septembre. Nous avons eu trois jours délicieux. Me permettrez-vous de vous aller donner un bonjour ? Vous ne revenez qu'au mois d'Octobre à ce que j'en ai appris chez vous où j'ai été aujourd'hui pour avoir de vos nouvelles.

Adieu, bien des choses de ma part à M. Austin si ma lettre le trouve encore à Dorking, ainsi que je le pense. Je suis tout à fait heureux du retour de St. Marsan.

Ne m'en veuillez pas pour ma sotte et courte lettre. Croyez que rien ne saurait altérer les sentiments d'amitié que je vous ai voués.

Vtre. sincère ami,

S. SANTA ROSA.

Address : To Mistriss Austin, at Mr. Gough's, Holmswood, Dorking, Surrey.

18. *(No postmark : letter unsigned)*

91 ALPHA ROAD   3 *octobre* 1823.

Me voici établi dans mon nouvel hermitage, véritable hermitage puisque j'y suis seul. J'y suis assez bien. J'espère que j'y aurai votre visite et que Green Cottage ne m'aura pas été seul heureux.

J'ai été hier dîner à la campagne où j'ai rencontré le Cte de Joreno, plus Européen qu'Espagnol, instruit, causant bien. Il croit impossible la pacification de sa patrie sans l'établissement d'institutions sagement libérales. Je l'ai fait convenir qu'après ce qui s'est passé & avec un roi comme le leur même le [. . .] de pacification sera très difficile sinon impraticable, à moins de l'appuyer par l'occupation étrangère, qu'il regarde cependant comme un obstacle à ce qui peut se faire de bien en Espagne.—Je vous avoue que si j'étais Ferdinand je me mettrais plutôt dans la poche du Duc d'Angoulême et je partagerai avec lui plutôt que de rester en Espagne sans l'appui d'une armée française, surtout si par un établissement constitutionel quelconque il perd l'appui du *parti de la foi*, minorité plus faible que la minorité constitutionelle, mais qui a cependant plus de forces que le parti qui soutiendrait un systême intermédiaire.—Que faire donc ? Rien ne peut-être fait sans de graves inconvénients. Toutes ces difficultés seront le désespoir du [. . .] & peuvent amener de nouveaux événements.

Vous voilà une page de politique. Encore un mot. Riégo a tenté une chose fort grande, et l'a fait avec courage. L'odieux Ballasteros demeurera la honte de l'Espagne. Son rival, son ennemi va peut-être mourir, mais ce sera comme un homme d'honneur et en bon patriote. Il ne mourra pas tout entier.

J'ai de très bonnes nouvelles de Porro, qui s'amuse de tout son cœur. Il a entendu de la musique délicieuse à York. Sa lettre est presque un hymne, mais elle paraît griffonnée par le diable.

Vous serez donc ici le onze. J'aurai l'honneur de vous présenter le cher Dal Pozzo et le cher de Collegno. Vous voyez que je me sers des grands mots en temps et lieu.

Ce matin en revenant de Clapham, j'ai trouvé chez M. Obicini une lettre de Mad. de Ste Rose. Elle me donne d'excellentes nouvelles de mes enfans et de tous mes amis. Sa lettre est d'une tendresse réellement touchante. Je n'ai pas à me plaindre de mon lot. Je n'ai jamais été aimé que d'une femme au monde, et cette femme est ma femme.

Le bon Radice m'écrit de Bath. Il se plaint de vous, de votre silence. Envoyez moi une lettre pour lui, ma chère amie. Il est un peu triste.

Cucchi m'écrit de Norwich et m'y attend. Je vais le détromper. Je suis comme collé à Londres. Ne pourrai-je pas devenir un officier de la Paroisse ? Je ne m'amuserais pas mal aussi d'être quelques uns de ces bons *Gentlemen* redresseurs de torts.

Muschietti va partir pour Manchester et s'y établir. Il me prie de vous dire de sa part les choses les plus aimables.

(No signature and no address ; probably incomplete)

R

19. (*Postmark* : 12 Noon 22 De. 1823)
31 ALPHA COTTAGES *le* 20 *Xmbre*.
Mon aimable amie, Je tarde bien à vous donner de mes nouvelles,
mais S. Marsan, j'en suis sûr, n'aura pas manqué de suppléer à mon
silence. Je voulais au lieu de vous écrire vous aller faire une visite,
& vous dire toute la déplorable histoire de notre article. Il se trouve
que tout en me portant mieux, si j'en dois croire à mon Docteur, jamais
je n'ai éprouvé plus de malaise. C'est au point que la seule pensée
de m'éloigner pour quelques heures de ma retraite m'effraye. Je
voudrais bien m'endormir et pour longtemps. La vie me paraît insipide
ou douloureuse. J'ai reçu des nouvelles de ma femme et de mes enfans.
Ils se portent bien & pensent à moi ; et moi je ne pense à eux que
pour me tourmenter de la sombre destinée qui les attend.
J'ai vu Bowring chez mon voisin le Col. Jones mercredi dernier. J'ai
évité de lui parler de mon article, parce que ma lettre était assez positive
pour rendre inutile toute explication ultérieure ; cependant d'après
quelques mots qu'il m'a dit [*sic*] en me quittant je crois qu'il faudra
encore que je lui écrive ou que je lui parle à ce sujet. Je dois beaucoup
d'égards à Bowring et pour l'amitié qu'il m'a toujours témoignée
personellement, et pour l'intérêt dont il a donné tant de preuves à
mes compatriotes. Cela retient ma mauvaise humeur qui n'est pas
petite. Elle va jusqu'à me donner envie de vous gronder, quoique je
vous doive de bien humbles excuses pour vous avoir fait employer si
mal & inutilement huit à dix jours de votre temps ; et comment y
a-t-il sujet à gronderie, me direz-vous ? Avez-vous donc oublié que
mon article a été lu par S.A. le Prince Héréditaire John Mill ? Ce
qui n'entrait pas du tout dans mes vues ;—*Ma quel che è fatto è fatto.*
Le retour de S. Marsan m'a fait un des plus grands plaisirs que je
puisse éprouver dans mon apathie actuelle. J'espère que vous en aurez
eu aussi beaucoup à le revoir. Votre attachement & votre estime pour
lui ne sont pas le seul des titres que vous avez à les [*sic*] mêmes sentimens de ma part, mais c'est un de ceux qui me sont les plus chers.
Porro va venir. Il viendra beaucoup trop gai pour moi : cependant
le moment de son arrivée m'en donnera quelques-uns de joie. Je ne
sais pas encore ses projets pour l'hyver ; et je suis également incertain
pour les miens.
Vous trouverez ma lettre fort triste ; et cependant je l'écris en sortant
d'une longue conversation avec le gnle Vaudoncourt, qui m'a beaucoup
et agréablement occupé ! Adieu, mon excellente amie !—Je n'irai vous
voir que lorsque je suis un peu plus *moi* ;—si vous avez quelques soirées,
n'oubliez pas le Président, Maître des requêtes,[1] Jermyn's Street, St.
James. 94 *late* 100.
(No signature)
Address : Mistress Austin, 1 Henrietta St., Brunswick Square
(Dated by S. R. on p. 4, 31 Alpha Cottages ; 20 Xme).

20. (*No postmark*) [*Inscribed* : Dec. 22nd 1823 + *but this seems to be
scored out. If Dec. is correct,* ' *Wednesday* ' *is either the 18th or the
25th, probably the latter, although there is no mention of Christmas*]
Wednesday.
Bonnes nouvelles.—Le *fragment* par sa taille et son habit ressembloit
comme deux gouttes d'eau à un *Quaker*, qui ne vous appartient pas &
[1] Dal Pozzo.

vous m'auriez ri au nez si je vous eûsse envoyé un tel personnage, V^{tre} mari ne s'en seroit pas trouvé plus content. Je ne voyois que *Quakers* ce matin-là, car j'ai encore cru que les hymnes de votre père étaient de la famille. J'étais pressé lorsqu'on est venu prendre les livres, j'ai jugé par l'habit des gens sans leur demander leur nom, et voilà la cause de toutes nos inquiétudes.

J'ai donc et vous enverrai tout de suite le fragment de Blackstone *item* le fragment aussi de M. Bentham adressé à Mrs. Austin and *to all* & *item* les *hymnes* de votre père. Êtes-vous contente ? J'espère que oui : mais je n'en mérite pas moins d'être bien grondé! et je suis au reste sérieusement affligé que ma précipitation vous ait causé de l'ennui.—

Si je l'eusse pu prevoir, ma chère amie, j'aurais passé en revue toute ma bibliothèque depuis Bonald jusqu'à Mill, depuis Rousseau jusqu'à La Mennais, depuis Shakespear jusqu'aux anacréontiques di *Francesco Saverio di Rogati*.

Hier un anglais venu d'Italie m'a remis des lettres qui m'ont fait du bien au delà de tout ce que vous sauriez imaginer. Ç'a été réellement une *providence*.

Ce que vous me proposez, mon amie, me prouve combien vous prenez intérêt à ma situation—mais vous ne sauriez croire à quel point je suis incapable de contracter de nouveaux attachements : et je suis entouré de soins affectueux et se sentir dans l'impossibilité d'y répondre par ce qui seul peut les payer seroit en vérité ajouter à ma tristesse—mais cette tristesse, mon aimable amie, s'est adoucie. Les lettres d'hier sont pour moi un trésor de consolation. Adieu ; pardonnez-moi mon griffonnage. Un mot sur John Mill—Jamais il ne m'est venu dans l'idée qu'il eût pu influer sur la mauvaise fortune de mon article, jamais.—J'ai voulu seulement vous dire que j'avais été un peu ennuyé de voir ma pauvre prose exposée à sa censure. Au fond c'était plutôt par plaisanterie qu'autrement que je vous en ai parlé. Adieu.

V^{re}

dévoué ami

S. S. R.

(*No address*).

21. (*No postmark*) [*Inscribed :* June 1823, *altered to* 1824]

31 ALPHA COTTAGES, *Mardi.*

J'écris à Radice qui a tous les droits possibles de se plaindre de moi. Je n'aurai rien à lui dire pour mon apologie, et cependant il y a un détestable orgueil à n'en point faire, et à croire qu'on doive vous pardonner lorsque vous avez eu la bonté de dire " j'ai tort ".—Je n'aurai jamais cet orgueil, et je suis d'avis qu'il faut se résigner aux conséquences de nos torts, et les réparer si l'on peut.

Il est assez probable que je m'éloigne de Londres dans quinze jours. Je n'oserai point aller vous faire mes adieux cette semaine-ci où vous me marquez être accablée de travail, mais vous me permettrez bien de vous voir la semaine prochaine.

St Marsan vous aura dit que ma santé était de nouveau dérangée. Je suis tout-à-fait une pauvre créature au physique et au moral. J'avois toujours appréhendé le terrible moment où je me survivrais. Il est arrivé. Ce qui reste de moi ne vaut plus la peine d'y penser.

Porro, qui m'écrit très ponctuellement, me prie de le rappeler à votre souvenir. Il est si bon qu'il éprouve le besoin de voir ses amis tranquilles et heureux, et qu'il feroit le tour des trois royaumes pour la satisfaction des personnes qui lui sont chères ; avec cela une aimable facilité de caractère, et celle de se plier aux mœurs, aux usages de tous les pays où il est appelé à vivre ; l'esprit entreprenant ; aucun préjugé, à part celui de n'en vouloir pas tolérer chez les autres ; raisonnant bien et juste si on l'arrête à temps dans sa course un peu vagabonde ; le cœur susceptible de longues adorations . . . mais ne voilà-t-il pas que je vous fais un portrait à la mode de Made de la Fayette . . . notre ami ne seroit pas cependant un héros de roman malgré ses longues adorations. Il rit et parle trop.

Je vous quitte pour écrire au chevalier de la douce et triste figure. Il voudroit que j'allasse vivre avec lui. Je prends trop d'intérêt à son bonheur pour lui donner un camarade de mon espèce.

Adieu, Madame. Vous auriez tort à votre tour si vous doutiez de la sincérité de mon dévouement et de mon amitié.

S. S. R.

(*No address*)

22. (*Postmark torn :* Night 20 – 18) [*Inscribed :* 1824 Confalonieri]

31 ALPHA ROAD, *Lundi.*

J'ai reçu hier, votre aimable lettre, à Brighton. Elle m'a fait d'autant plus de plaisir que j'étais dans une véritable inquiétude pour votre *Baby.*—J'arrive. J'ai trouvé un paquet de Radice : il vous est destiné, je vous l'apporterai, ou vous l'enverrai le plutôt possible. C'est un article sur *Dante* : je l'ai parcouru à la hâte ; je ne suis pas de son avis quant à sa manière de juger la vie politique de Dante, & je crois d'ailleurs qu'il ne faut parler des temps anciens que pour en tirer des leçons pour les modernes en rapprochant les uns aux autres.—Sous ce rapport l'article de notre ami, qui est écrit avec élégance & douceur, ne me satisfait point assez. Je suis fort triste et mal disposé à l'indulgence. Ce n'est pas de Brighton que j'ai apporté ma tristesse.—Je l'ai trouvée ici. Confalonieri est condamné à mort, et l'on ignore si la grace [*sic*] demandée à l'Empr. François par la noblesse de Milan sera accordée & si d'ailleurs on est à temps, car le jugement capital a été prononcé & approuvé par l'Empereur.—Cet infortuné patriote est très malade dans sa prison. Sa femme est à Vienne.—

J'ai eu de bonnes nouvelles de Porro. Adieu, ma chère amie, ma santé est fort bonne, j'ai trouvé l'air de Brighton excellent, et j'y ai été entouré des soins de la plus franche amitié.

Vre aff. ami

SANTOR S. R.

Address : Mistress John Austin, 1 Henrietta Street, Brunswick Sq.

23. (*No postmark*) [*Inscribed :* May 9th 1824.]

NOTTINGHAM, *le* 9 *mai* 1824.

5252 PARLIAMENT STREET.

Il y a longtemps que je ne vous ai donné de mes nouvelles, & je suis si sûr de votre attachement que je me crois obligé de vous demander pardon d'un silence dont je ne saurais donner d'autre raison qu'une certaine indolence apathique qui n'est pas la meilleure de mes qualités, je l'avoue. Mais il faut aimer nos amis tels qu'ils sont ; et je le répète encore, je ne doute pas un seul instant de votre amitié. Si cette confiance me fait être trop indulgent envers mes propres défauts, songez aussi, mon aimable amie, que sans elle il n'y a pas de solide attachement. Voilà mon preambule achevé. Je m'en vais maintenant vous féliciter de votre dernier Dimanche. M. Henri Enfield a écrit à sa mère qu'il y avait foule chez vous. Je vous somme de m'en rendre compte ; anglais, Italiens, français, si vous en aviez, ce que je ne crois cependant pas. Je sais bon gré à S. Marsan d'avoir bien voulu être aimable avec le jeune Enfield. Remerciez-l'en de ma part en attendant que je lui écrive une bonne et longue lettre. Vous ne sauriez vous imaginer à quel point la famille Enfield est bonne pour moi. Ce sont les soins d'une ancienne amitié. Je passe quelquefois des moments assez gais avec trois aimables enfans de 6 à 10 ans. Je leur fais des Evêques, des Jacobins, des Moines, des Religieuses, des Valaisannes, croquis dignes de Raphaël ou peu s'en faut, quoique mes amis ne rendent pas justice à mes talents. J'en appelle à ma petite Anna dont le sourire & l'enjouement, avec un certain air franc, con *un poco di gentile baldanza*, me conviennent beaucoup.— Mistr. Enfield la belle mère est partie le matin pour Norwich, je l'ai priée de me rappeler au souvenir de votre excellent père.—Si je m'amuse avec des enfans de 8 à 10 ans, je suis sûr en revanche d'ennuyer les jeunes personnes de 16 à 20 ans, à qui je donne des leçons d'Italien, et que dans ma mauvaise humeur j'oblige souvent à me répéter dix fois des Subjonctifs, des Impératifs, des Optatifs, et tout le reste de cette anath [. . .] lignée. Si St Marsan voyait ceci, ma *mauvaise humeur* le ferait rire, & il en appréhenderait d'autres suites, dont je ne vous parlerai pas, et pour cause.

Ma santé n'est pas bien, mais j'espère que je me porterai beaucoup mieux dans quelques semaines. Je n'étais pas entièrement rétabli lorsque j'ai quitté Londres, et il y a eu de l'étourderie à venir m'isoler ici, d'autant plus que la vie que je fais n'est pas des plus favorables à mon parfait rétablissement. Je suis cependant beaucoup mieux que dans les premiers mois, et ma prochaine lettre vous donnera d'excellentes nouvelles d'une santé à laquelle vous avez toujours pris tant d'intérêt.

J'ai toujours cru dans les beaux jours de ma jeunesse que ma 40e année serait une époque de décadence. Je l'éprouve à présent à l'égard de ma memoire, et à tel point que je suis obligé de renoncer à l'espoir d'apprendre l'anglais. J'apprends, et j'oublie. Quelquefois, s'il m'arrive de soutenir une conversation de cinq minutes sans de mortelles angoisses, je me crois avancé : le lendemain je ne sais plus trouver deux phrases. Il est clair à mes yeux que je ne saurais plus rien apprendre. J'avoue que je me crois encore capable de tirer parti du peu que je sais. Lorsque j'*ose raisonner*, je ne manque pas de vigueur, et mon imagination donne de temps à autre des signes de vie. Mais pour apprendre, serviteur ; Il n'y a pas moyen. Le moment de travailler est donc venu, et je n'aurai pas de temps à perdre. C'est ma pensée habituelle ; mais mon apathique indolence est là. Le souvenir de mes fautes politiques m'accable. *Il desiderio della patria* (français : vous n'avez pas le [ce ?] mot là !) me poursuit. Il faudrait que j'eusse toujours à mes côtés un ami. La violence qu'il exercerait sur moi pourrait seule me sauver. V. Cousin seroit un ami. César di Balbo, dont vous nous avez entendu parler, S. Marsan et moi, le seroit aussi. Quant à St. Marsan lui-même c'est une autre espèce d'influence qu'il exercerait sur moi, si je commençais à travailler. Le désir de mériter son suffrage doublerait ma force, j'*oserais raisonner* pour la lui montrer toute entière—Nous sommes tous les deux si orgueilleux ! chacun à notre façon ; car nous ne nous ressemblons guère que par la sincérité de notre caractère.

J'attends de vos lettres avec impatience. L'intérêt que je prends à vous, à tout ce qui vous regarde est bien loin d'être diminué. L'absence n'y peut rien. J'épreuve un sensible plaisir lorsque j'entends parler de vous par les Enfield, ou chez M. Needham dont la famille intéressante & nombreuse me témoigne aussi beaucoup d'amitié. M. Needham a six filles, trois d'entr'elles de l'âge de 18 à 22, sont très jolies, et ont la bonté de s'ennuyer avec moi une fois la semaine pendant deux heures ainsi que leur frère aîné. Elles savent le français, et un peu d'Italien, mais elles ne parlent qu'anglais à votre pauvre ami, qui est très embarrassé de sa personne au milieu de cette aimable jeunesse.

Je passerai très probablement l'Eté et l'automne ici sans interruption. J'espère que notre correspondance ne discontinuera pas. Donnez-moi des nouvelles de Radice. Parlez-moi de mes amis, et de tout ce que vous savez pouvoir m'intéresser.

J'oubliais de vous parler de la Westminster Review. Mr. Southern [1] n'aurait-t-il [sic] pas dû m'envoyer un exemplaire du dernier cahier si mon article s'y trouve ? Cet oubli, ou cette négligence ne répond guère au portrait que vous m'avez fait de lui. Croyez-vous pouvoir convenablement lui rappeler ce devoir de convenance ?—J'ai vu M. Bowring à son passage ici ; il y a été très goûté.

Adieu, mon aimable amie. Rappelez-moi au souvenir de M. Austin, et à celui de Lucy qui pourrait très bien m'oublier sans cette précaution, —Voyez-vous quelquefois le C. Porro, & Bercesio ? [2] Avez-vous fait de nouvelles connaissances parmi mes compatriotes ? J'attends de vous une lettre remplie de détails, une charmante lettre en un mot comme vous savez écrire. Adieu encore.

V^{re} affectionné et sincère ami

SANCTOR S. R.

24. (*Postmark* : Nottingham MY 25 : C. 27 MY 1824)

NOTTINGHAM 5252 PARLIAMENT STR. *Ce 24 de mai.*

J'ai reçu les 4 portraits et votre aimable lettre. Théodore est frappant de ressemblance. C'est absolument lui, et c'est aussi *moi*, à 9 ans. J'ai cru voir ma propre figure telle qu'elle se trouve dans un tableau de famille peint il y a trente ans. Eugène le second de mes fils, ressemble aussi beaucoup, c'est bien là sa physionomie, bonne, ouverte, qui respire la joie, et le besoin de la répandre autour de lui. Quant à Théodore ses traits n'annoncent-ils pas comme les miens un conspirateur ? Puisse-t-il l'être un jour et avec plus de bonheur que son père !—Ma fille aînée n'est pas arrivée, je m'en plains vivement à sa mère. Ma fille cadette ne me convient point et je la renvoye. Il m'est impossible de croire que le peintre ait rendu fidèlement dans la miniature qu'on m'a envoyée, ma pauvre petite Pauline, que je veux . . . le dirai-je, presqu'aimée d'un amour de préférence. Vous voyez, ma chère amie, par les détails que je vous fais combien je suis persuadé de votre tendre amitié pour moi.

Votre longue lettre m'a bien intéressé. Je vous remercie de tous les détails qu'elle contient. Je reconnais Dal Pozzo à toutes ses courses, à tous ses billets, à toute son impatience, mais je ne le reconnoitrais pas

---

[1] Founder and Editor of the *Retrospective Review*.
[2] Berchet.

au moindre symptôme d'ingratitude. Si vous l'en avez soupçonné, ma chère amie, sachez que vous avez grand tort. Dans la lettre que j'ai reçue de lui il y a huit jours il y a une demie page pour vous seule. Il me parle des peines que vous vous êtes données pour lui comme un homme qui en est pénétré. Ainsi donc, lorsque vous verrez notre président " Serena i tuoi bei rai ". J'espère que ma galanterie ne m'attirera pas une [. . .] de votre part. Notre cher ami de Clifton est tout à fait plaisant avec ses comparaisons. Je suis très platonicien. mais je ne vais pas si loin, et une belle femme sera toujours pour moi une belle femme.

Je suis très fâché de ne pas vous avoir envoyé ma réponse à votre seconde grande lettre puisque mon retard à vous écrire a pu alarmer votre amitié. Mais je l'ai conservée et vous la verrez si vous me témoignerez le désir de connaître le fond de ma pensée. Nous sommes persuadés tous les deux que la plus grande franchise est le devoir d'un cœur droit et délicat dans les rapports d'une véritable amitié.

Revenons à Rad. J'ai lu sa lettre avec un vif intérêt. Ce ne sont que des complaintes mais elle partent d'un excellent et noble cœur. Plût à Dieu que ma patrie eût un grand nombre de jeunes gens d'un tel caractère.—Qu'il trouve la destinée triste, je le conçois. Qu'il songe cependant qu'il y a une grande satisfaction intérieure à avoir rendu témoignage au culte de notre première jeunesse. Ceux qui professant *la réligion de la patrie et de la liberté* au fond de leur cœur ont laissé passer l'occasion de lui *rendre gloire*, c'est à dire d'agir et de souffrir pour elle, auront toute leur vie un ver rongeur dans leur sein. Notre ami voudrait-il à tel prix être à Turin entouré d'amis, voire même de jolies femmes qui le cajolassent (le cher enfant aime assez à être cajolé) ? Ecrivez-lui cela de ma part, et qu'il ne regimbe plus contre la destinée qu'il s'est faite. L'enseignement l'ennuie, mais par Dieu, s'il était dans un donjon à Fenestrelle s'amuserait-il davantage ? Je vous renvoye les lettres par une occasion qui m'est procurée par les Enfield. Cette famille m'inspire toujours plus d'attachement et la reconnaissance que je lui dois ne m'est plus à charge : j'ai payé ma dette par un sentiment que je ne me croyais plus capable d'éprouver pour de nouvelles connaissances—les Needham me montrent aussi beaucoup d'amitié. Ce que vous me dites de leur froide réserve n'est pas du tout applicable à mes rapports avec eux. Les D^lles Needham parlent très peu, mais leur silence est plutôt une habitude de timidité que l'expression d'un sentiment moins aimable.

J'ai reçu la brochure de Dal Pozzo et les p^res pages m'ont un peu impatienté. J'aime les rapprochements, mais il ne faut pas les multiplier, et surtout les accompagner d'interminables citations. La fin de cet écrit est beaucoup mieux. Ne trouvez-vous pas comme nous que Dal Pozzo a fait très bien de publier sa brochure ? Elle honore son caractère et sa carrière. Quant à l'effet, il ne pouvait être considérable. Il faut connaître les Anglais bien à fond pour arriver jusqu'à eux.—Je commence seulement à savoir comment on n'y arrive pas.

J'écris à S. Marsan. Ce que vous me dites de sa santé me donne beaucoup de tristesse, mais je ne veux pas m'avouer que ce soit de l'inquiétude. Grand merci de vos détails sur le 2^d num. de la *Westminster Review*. Ils m'ont fait plaisir.—J'ai trouvé dans l'épreuve qu'on m'a envoyée de mon article quelques pensées qui ne sont pas les miennes et qui sont même l'opposé des miennes.—D'ailleurs le retard exige des ch..ngements. Je vais voir si j'en suis capable. Mon métier actuel me fatigue la poitrine, & dans l'intervalle de mes leçons, dans mes jours de repos, je voudrais n'avoir rien à faire qu'à lire, prendre du thé & écrire à mes amis.—Cependant, j'essayerai.—Je comprends parfaitement M. Austin dans sa manière de travailler et dans le besoin impérieux de faire bien.—Je vois avec une grande satisfaction par plusieurs phrases de vtre. lettre que je conserve ma place dans son souvenir. Que je le reverrai avec plaisir !—Puissé-je le voir un jour où il doit être ! ce qu'il doit être. Je ne lui désire pas moins que la place du Grand Inquisiteur d'Angleterre ; vous savez de qui je veux parler.[1] Cet homme figureroit mieux dans le Conseil aulique ou à l'archevêché de Paris que sur le sac de laine.

P.S.—Vous trouverez avec la lettre de Radice un rouleau de papiers pour Bercesio, et une petite lettre pour Porro ; n'envoyez pas celle-ci par la petite poste ; faites-la-lui parvenir autrement. Adieu. Il me reste bien des choses à vous dire, mais je veux que ma lettre parte demain. Je vous quitte pour dévorer dans dix minutes mon dîner après quoi je prendrai le chemin de Lenton msn. de campagne de M. Needham. Nous parlerons de vous. Ecrivez-moi, et de longues lettres. Songez que je suis à Nottingham. Adieu, encore. V^re affectionné ami

SANTOR S. R.

Address : Mrs. J. Austin, 1, Henrietta Str., Brunswick Square.

25. (*Postmarks :* Nottingham JY 29 1824, *and* Paid JY 30 1824)

NOTTINGHAM *le* 28 *juillet* 1824.

Ma bien chère amie, j'ai reçu et votre lettre, et votre dernier billet. Je vous avoue que votre silence m'a peiné. Mais je ne vous l'avoue qu'à une condition & c'est de ne pas m'en écrire une ligne de plus lorsque vous n'en aurez pas le loisir.—Je suis une étrange créature : moi si inexact à répondre à mes amis, je souffre beaucoup s'ils ne me répondent pas : mon imagination me tourmente ; je les crois fâchés contre moi : je les accuse d'indifférence, et je me vois déjà un motif de moins d'être attaché à la vie.—Il faut cependant que je me corrige de ce défaut, ou plutôt de ce malheur. Quant à ce qui vous regarde, ma chère amie, je vous déclare que je crois en vous, c'est à dire à votre amitié, et que je repousserai toujours comme des tentations du *malin esprit* toute pensée contraire à cette foi.

S. Marsan nous a quitté hier ; Castiglione nous est arrivé Dimanche matin, et ils sont partis ensemble pour Manchester, d'où ils se dirigeront vers le Cumberland. Porro me reste et pour plusieurs semaines. Muschietti seulement un jour ou deux.

Je suis pénétré de votre bienfaisante activité pour mes compatriotes, et je vous envoye le *Statement* que vous me demandez, ou plutôt des matériaux pour celui que vous ferez vous-même. Vous trouverez peut-être ce que j'ai écrit trop long, mais il m'a paru que bien des personnes savent si peu et si mal nos affaires que c'est un soin nécessaire que de leur en donner une idée juste et nette si on veut avoir leur intérêt. Au reste, raccourcissez, ajoutez à votre gré d'après la connaissance que vous avez des circonstances, et des dispositions de la plus grande partie des personnes à qui on adresse la circulaire. J'observe relativement à

[1] John Scott, Lord Eldon.

Mistriss Fry que les Quakers se feroient un scrupule de concourir à envoyer en Amérique des gens qui y vont pour se battre. J'ai tâché dans mon esquisse d'écarter au moins en partie cette difficulté. Vous me ferez part de la réponse de Mistriss Fry, à qui j'écrirai. Ainsi que Porro, si cela sera convenable ou utile d'après sa réponse. Dieu vous bénisse, ma chère amie, pour tous vos soins, pour votre touchante sollicitude, pour cette activité de bienveillance qui est un si bel attribut de votre sexe ! J'oubliais de vous dire que quant à Nottingham, je ne vois pas d'inconvénient à ce que vous vous y adressiez à vos amis même dans d'autres villes, on m'en parlera et je tâcherai de trouver quelques mots d'anglais pour ajouter mes sollicitations aux vôtres.

Je suis très fâché que S. Marsan e Porro ne soient pas à Londres pour contribuer à la réussite de votre projet—Muschietti me dit que vous en avez parlé à Floresi. Je crois qu'il est inutile que je vous répète que ce jeune homme est un de ceux sur lesquels on peut compter pour la sagesse des vues et pour la discrétion.

Adieu, ma chère amie, vous recevez bientôt une autre lettre de moi. Mes amitiés à M. Austin et à v^{re} beau-frère.

V^{re} dévoué ami,
S. SANTA ROSA.

Je viens de recevoir une lettre de ma femme et de mes enfans.—elle est du 12 de ce mois—cette fraîche date me rend la lettre très précieuse. Leurs nouvelles sont excellentes. Tous mes enfans m'ont écrit quelques lignes, excepté la petite Pauline, que ne peut pas encore tenir la plume dans sa main.—J'aime beaucoup la lettre de César Germanicus. " Io sono il vostro Cesare che vi ama tanto."—Adieu, je suis sûr que vous partagez le plaisir que j'éprouve dans cet instant. Porro e Muschietti veulent que je les rappelle à votre souvenir. Nous avons beaucoup parlé de vous, lui, S. Marsan, et moi.—Les oreilles ne vous ont-elles pas corné ?

Address : Mrs. Austin, 1 Henrietta Street, Brunswick Square.

26. (*No postmark*) [*Inscribed :* July 29, 1824]

Ce 29 Juillet.

Vous recevrez ci-jointe les lettres de Radice que vous m'avez envoyées —Il est bien que vous sachiez, ma belle Dame, que c'est pour la seconde fois que deux d'entr'elles font le voyage de Nottingham.—Vous voulez donc que je les apprenne par cœur.

Vous aurez déjà reçu à l'heure qu'il est ma réponse à votre lettre du 26. Celle-ci ne vous parviendra que par la première occasion des Enfield.

La famille Needhame a comblé de politesses tous mes amis.—Ç'a été une suite d'attentions auxquelles je n'avois pas le moindre titre, et qui me pénètrent de reconnaissance. Un des enfans de Mrs. Enfield est malade à la campagne où ils sont tous.—Il se porte mieux à present. J'ai réellement partagé les inquiétudes d'une mère excessivement tendre. Miss Enfield que S. Marsan a vu ici à un souper—l'on soupe à Nottingham comme à Paris au temps de Louis XV.—a enchanté mon ami par la douceur de sa physionomie et la grace de son maintien.

J'ai trouvé Charles assez bien—Je crois que le voyage d'Ecosse sera très utile à sa santé—Toutes les *tristizie* de certains individus de l'émigration l'avaient beaucoup affecté, malgré tout le mépris qu'il ressent pour eux. Il a tort quand ses mépris se généralisent ; et le tort peut modifier à son insu les principes qui font sa gloire.—C'est un des facheux résultats des tracasseries de l'émigration, c'est un de ceux qui me chagrinent le plus. *Modifier à son insu ?* me direz-vous. Qu'est-ce que cela signifie ? Pensez-y et vous verrez que le phénomène arrive chez les hommes qui sentent vivement et ont de l'impétuosité dans le caractère.

Je me porte assez bien et j'ai grande envie de travailler. Mon métier continue à me profiter, mais je soupire après le moment où je pourrai le quitter sans imprudence. Ce moment sera une grande époque de ma vie.

Adieu, mon excellente amie, je vous aime réellement beaucoup, et j'espère que vous ne prendrez pas les mots pour une formule.

(No address and no signature)

27. *(Postmark :* C 7 AU 1824)

NOTTINGHAM *le* 5 *août* 1824.

Ma chère amie, je n'ai pas répondu à votre lettre du deux de ce mois à poste courante parce que j'étois bien aise de pouvoir vous mander ce que Porro écrivait au G[1] De Meistre dont il attendoit aujourd'hui une lettre. Cette lettre est arrivée et mon ami lui répond par le courrier de demain. Voici la substance de sa réponse : " il croit que l'on doit présenter au Comité Anglais les comptes du Comité Italien à chaque fois où ils seront demandés et avec tous les éclaircissements qu'on peut désirer ; que si le comité anglais, ou quelques-uns des membres veulent communiquer les comptes à d'autres personnes, soit émigrés italiens ou autres, Porro pense que le comité Italien ne doit point s'en occuper.—Il pense aussi que les comptes doivent être présentés à tout comité de l'émigration italienne qui soit formé légalement. Il ne peut reconnaître cette légalité dans un comité qui a été formé dans une convocation partielle des émigrés." Ne trouvez-vous pas, ma bonne amie, que l'opinion de Porro est raisonnable, et ne vous semble-t-il pas aussi qu'elle tranche la difficulté puisque rien ne s'oppose à ce que Bowring comme membre du comité anglais communique les comptes qui seront remis par le G[1] De Meistre à qui bon lui semble, et fasse ensuite à ses collègues les observations qui peuvent résulter de cette communication.—Quant à la réunion de l'émigration italienne je la désire plus que je ne la peux espérer au point où en sont les choses.—S'il[s'] agissait d'un grand but je me jetterois au feu pour tâcher de l'obtenir, mais comme ce n'est point ici le cas je ne crois pas devoir prendre une part active à des affaires auxquelles je suis demeuré entièrement étranger depuis mon départ de Londres au commencement de mars dernier.—Je suis loin de regarder comme de méchantes gens tous les italiens qui se sont rangés du parti opposé au comité dont j'ai fait partie : la plupart ne sont que des têtes échauffées dont on pourroit se servir utilement au besoin et que je vois avec douleur conduites ou influencées par quelques hommes ou brouillons, par caractère, ou peut-être payées par nos ennemis pour entretenir la discorde parmi nous.—Le mal est fait ; si nous étions sur une scène d'activité, je vous le répète, je chercherais à le réparer dût-il m'en couter le repos et toute espèce de chagrin. Mais dans notre situation, ne pouvant rien offrir pour calmer les inquiétudes, et alimenter l'activité d'esprit de mes malheureux compatriotes, je dois me borner maintenant à faire tout le bien que je pourrai aux individus.

Le G[1] Demeistre est un honnête homme, un homme ferme, un homme droit ; mais il n'a rien de conciliant ni dans le caractère, ni dans les manières. Peu d'hommes sont moins aisés à persuader.

Il se peut que Porro aille faire une course à Londres si le G^l De Meistre l'en presse de nouveau, mais il ne voit guère la possibilité de faire maintenant le bien, c'est à dire de rétablir la concorde dans l'émigration. Mon amie, ne vous laissez pas aller à un sentiment de mépris pour le caractère italien parce que vous voyez de près la turbulence et les passions d'un certain nombre d'individus. Songez à l'amertume que donnent les malheurs de l'émigration, et réfléchissez que cette pauvre Italie se trouve depuis cinq siècles soumise à des gouvernements où la bassesse et l'intrigue étaient à la fois presque les seuls moyens d'ambition et de défense. Je n'écrirai point à Bowring. Je suis fâché qu'il ait l'air de soutenir un des deux partis qui divisent l'émigration. Je serai cependant toujours très heureux de tout le bien qu'il fera à des Italiens. Si quelques beaux parleurs l'ont trompé, il les connaîtra bientôt.

Souvenez-vous que l'esquisse que je vous ai envoyée doit être modifiée tout-à-fait à votre gré, si vous jugez convenable de vous en servir. Votre cœur vous recompensera de tout le bien que vous tâcherez de faire à mes malheureux compatriotes ; doublement malheureux de n'avoir pas pu éviter la plus terrible des calamités de l'émigration : la discorde.—Vous recevrez par la p^{re} occasion un paquet que je vous prie de faire parvenir au Chev. Baromi par la voie de Floresi, ou de Dal Pozzo. Ce sont des certificats relatifs au service militaire d'un certain nombre d'officiers Piémontais. Veuillez bien le dire à la personne que vous chargerez de remettre le paquet à son adresse. Adieu, ma chère amie,—écrivez-moi souvent et parlez-moi de vous et de tout ce qui vous intéresse. Porro vous dit mille choses aimables. Adieu encore.

V^{re} aff. ami
Santor S. R.

Address : Mrs. John Austin, 1 Henrietta Str., Brunswick Square.

28. (Postmark : C/30 Au. 30/1824)

Nottingham le 28 août.

Votre longue lettre m'a fait grand plaisir ; ou plutôt elle a fait cesser [?] cette peine que j'éprouve à chaque fois que je suis un peu longtemps sans recevoir de vos nouvelles. C'est bien pour moi que tous les plaisirs ne sont qu'une cessation de souffrance ou de malaise.

Vous avez très bien fait, mon amie, de ne pas me transcrire ce que Ch. S. M. vous a mandé au sujet de certaines craintes ; ces craintes j'ai peut-être eu le tort de les concevoir légèrement & j'ai eu certainement celui de vous en parler. Attaché de cœur et d'esprit à ce malheureux parti de la liberté qui tombe en ruines de tous côtés mon inquiète sollicitude devoit s'éveiller à la seule apparence d'un danger qui touchait de plus près à cette religion de la patrie dont je suis le disciple enthousiaste.—Je suis satisfait de voir que le danger n'a existé que dans mon imagination ; j'apprends même avec plaisir que S. M. s'indigne à la seule pensée. Mais je ne veux point savoir, ou je veux oublier qu'il se soit servi d'expressions amères envers un ami dont personne ne connaît plus que lui le caractère, & les sentimens. N'en parlez donc plus.

J'ai vu v. lettre à Mr. Enfield. Il est absent, sa santé l'oblige à prendre des bains de mer. La famille Enfield & ses amis partagent votre sympathie pour nos malheurs & j'espère qu'ils pourront contribuer à les adoucir.

Quant à la distribution des secours, à leur emploi, il faudra voir ce qui

sera réglé à Londres.   Porro s'y trouve & pourra donner des services.
Je ne peux d'ici offrir que des vœux & quelques guinées de temps à autre.
Si quelques personnes bienfaisantes vous demandent à qui elles doivent
adresser l'argent qu'elles destinent aux émigrés italiens indiquez le Gl. De
Meistre ou Porro.—Quant à Carlini, j'y penserai moi-même ; je sens, à y
bien réfléchir, que je ne dois diriger la bienfaisance d'autrui sur mes
sensations individuelles.

Vous me donnez une nouvelle qui me feroit grand plaisir si elle n'était
pas accompagnée de réflexions bien tristes, bien sombres en vérité.—Je
n'y répondrai qu'un seul mot : *Sarah Austin*, vous aurez un être de plus
qui vous chérira, qui puisera son bonheur dans le vôtre—vous serez
toujours une mère adorée.   Je désire vivement pour v. bonheur domes-
tique que M. Austin prenne dans sa carrière la place qui lui appartient
de droit.   C'est là le but où il faut tendre avec une persévérance qui ne
s'altère pas un instant.   Cette année-ci est-il réellement moins avancé que
l'année dernière ?   Cela m'effrayerait.   Que le progrès soit lent, rien
n'est plus naturel ; mais s'il s'arrêtoit, il faudroit voir où en est la cause &
lui faire franche & vive guerre.—Je vous rappelle la nécessité, le devoir de
faire à M. Austin père, une cour honnête.   Je crois que vous lui convencz ;
il vous estime.   Tirez parti de v. heureuses dispositions.   Tournez de ce
côté là l'activité, l'amabilité de votre caractère.

Vous me pardonnerez ces details ; vous les autorisez par votre charmante confiance.—J'ajouterai encore : travaillez, & beaucoup.   Point
de découragement.   Les résultats sont incalculables si l'on fait un peu de
temps la même ligne avec des moyens intellectuels tels que les vôtres.

Deux mots de moi.   Je vois le monde de mes écoliers s'augmenter
sensiblement & je vais gagner le mois qui vient plusieurs guinées au delà
de ce que je dépense.   Mais mon existence intérieure est telle qu'il faut
que je change un peu violemment de situation.—

Je vous parle en mystique, mon amie.—L'explication arrivera avec le
temps.—Aimez-moi avec tous mes défauts ; Je vous aime bien, moi,
quoique je ne vous reconnaisse [?] *presque* point.

Adieu, mon excellente amie—

                                                                    S. S. R.

Address : Mrs. John Austin, Dorking, Surrey.

29. (*Postmark :* Nottingham, 20 OC. 1824)

NOTTINGHAM, *le* 19 *octobre.*

Je vous adresse cette lettre-ci à votre maison de Londres parceque je
crois que vous y serez à cette heure ou que vos lettres y seront retirées
pour vous être envoyées.—J'ai lu celle que vous m'avez écrite il y a
quelques jours avec toute l'attention avec tout l'intérêt de l'amitié ; je n'y
répondrai point avec détail, ma chère amie, et sans parler d'autres
raisons en voici une que vaut toutes les autres : je serai à Londres le 24 ou
le 25 de ce mois pour y passer une semaine.

Je remets à notre premier entretien ce que j'ai à vous dire de mes
projets.   Mon langage vous a paru mystérieux.   Il l'était parceque
j'étais dans le doute sur ce que je ferai, et sur l'issue [*sic*] de certaines
démarches ; ce doute est presque dissipé ; je vais à Londres pour
pouvoir me décider avec parfaite connaissance de camp, il me sera doux,
mon amie, de vous parler de ma future destinée.   Quelle lettre vaut un
entretien quand on n'a rien à se cacher ?

Pour ne plus avoir à parler de ce triste professorat de Dublin je vous donnerai dans ma lettre deux mots d'explication sur le terme de mépris qui me paraît vous étonner lorsque je l'applique à un sentiment de Radice envers moi.—Il a cru que je lui ai préféré Pecchio parceque Pecchio est noble, & que lui ne l'est pas. Or un homme capable de se décider sur un pareil motif est un homme digne de mépris à mes yeux, surtout si cet homme professe mes opinions.—Croyez, ma chere amie, que jamais je ne me sers d'une expression forte sans une raison grave.

J'ai reçu une lettre de S. Marsan qui m'a fait grand plaisir. Je lui ai répondu hier. Il est à Edimbourgh, et ne parle pas d'un prochain retour à Londres. Aucun détail sur sa santé, il me dit seulement qu'il n'a pas été toujours bien. J'en conclus qu'il est mieux à present. Sa lettre m'est une nouvelle preuve que lorsque j'ai jugé son cœur, je l'ai bien jugé. Je vois plus que jamais que ses attachemens sont sérieux & qu'on ne le verra dans aucune occasion négliger les devoirs qu'inspirent les véritables affections à un cœur aussi délicat que le sien.

J'ai soulagé le mien en lui disant que j'avais eu tort dans cette certaine supposition, ou plutôt dans cette crainte malfondée d'un changement dans ses opinions politiques.

Adieu, ma chere amie, je ne vous écrirai plus puisque j'espère vous voir Lundi ou Mardi si vous êtes arrivée à Londres.

V^e affectionné ami
SANCTOR S. R.

Address : Mrs. Austin, 1 Henrietta Str., Brunswick Sq., Russell Sq.

30. (*Postmark :* 25 OC. 1824)

LONDRES *lundi* 25 *october*
à 5 *heures du soir.*

Je vous écris de chez Dal Pozzo qui m'apprend que vous n'êtes pas à Londres, & que vous n'arrivez que dans 5 ou 6 jours—Et cela quand vous m'avez écrit il y a dix jours environ que vous alliez partir pour Londres.

Jugez de mon chagrin quand je vous apprends que Jeudi soir je m'embarque pour la Grèce. Je ne vous en ai jamais parlé parceque la chose était encore douteuse.—J'ai appris à la fois la décision de l'affaire & l'accélération du départ.

J'ose à peine espérer de vous voir. Il y a impossibilité matérielle que j'aille à Dorking. J'ai mille choses indispensables à faire ici avant de partir.—Je suis arrivé ce matin de Nottingham, où j'ai passé les trois derniers jours accablé de besogne & plus encore par le chagrin de quitter d'excellens de tendres amis.

Je suis peut-être l'ennemi de mon bonheur. J'ai peut-être eu tort de quitter un séjour de paix & de tranquillité où j'ai été entouré de soins, d'amitié.—Dieu la récompense !

Si vous pouvez venir me dire adieu, mon amie, faites-le-moi savoir à l'instant. Je suis logé 13 Air Street, Piccadilly.

Mon amie, je vous écris dans un moment d'abattement singulier pour un homme qui se jette de plein gré dans une vie active. Mais avec mon imagination ou mon cœur il est impossible de n'avoir pas de ces heures tristes. Je quitte mes meilleurs amis. J'ignore si je vous verrai encore, vous que tant de confiance tant d'amitié me rendent si chère.

Adieu plaignez-moi, & si je ne vous revois plus, mon amie,—prenez soin de votre bonheur ;—Adieu encore. Il faut que je finisse lorsque j'ai tant de choses à vous dire—Faut-il donc que ceci soit mon dernier mot ? Non si je pars avant votre arrivée vous aurez une autre lettre de moi.

SANCTOR S. R.

Address : Mistress Austin, Dorking, Surrey, to be forwarded WITH SPEED.

31.   (*Postmark :* 28 OC. 1824)

Notre départ est retardé de 36 ou 48 heures—Je vous reverrai donc, ma chere amie—quant au moment il est de toute impossibilité que je le sache ayant plusieurs affaires à expédier assez peu importantes, mais qui n'en exigent pas moins que j'arpente Londres d'un bout à l'autre.

Les explications que j'ai eues relativement à Radice prouvent qu'il y a eu dans sa conduite une grande *force de logique*, mais j'ai le cœur soulagé de ce que je peux peut-être excuser sa conduite en sacrifiant tout-à-fait la perspicacité de son jugement.   Mon galimathias, tout galimathias qu'il est vous fera plaisir j'en suis sûr.—Adieu, mon excellente amie.—Je vous reverrai avec plus de plaisir que je ne saurai vous l'exprimer.

[*No signature*]

Jeudi matin.

Address : Mistriss Austin, 1 Henrietta Street, Brunswick Square.

32.   (*No postmark*)   [*Erroneously inscribed in another hand :* " Oct. 30, 1824 "]

Lundi à 3 heures

Dans une heure nous partons, ma chère amie—adieu.   Soyez heureuse. Pensez quelquefois à ce que je vous ai écrit avec le zèle de l'amitié.— Ne m'oubliez pas, & écrivez-moi souvent aussi souvent que vous le pourrez.

Adieu, ma chère amie.

V^{re} dévoué ami
S. SR.

Malgré vos déclarations je vous reccomande [*sic*] une personne que St. Marsan va vous reccomander aussi de la manière la plus vive.   C'est M. Ferraro, Piémontais.—Il s'agit toujours des mines & vous êtes priée, humblement priée d'en parler à votre frère—C'est un digne officier, un homme rempli d'honneur.   Il est appuyé ' au Comité '—Ou je me trompe ou St. Marsan vous le reccomandera avec plus de chaleur que la dernière dont il vous a parlé !

Address : Mrs. Austin, 1 Henrietta Street, Brunswick Square.

[See p. 95, footnote 1.]

APPENDIX II.B

LETTERS FROM SANTA ROSA TO THE ENFIELD FAMILY.

1.

TO THE AMIABLE GIFTERS

I received with the greatest pleasure, my dear friends, all your presents. Your Thompson, Maria, the old delightful companion of my walks in the purest and happiest time of my life, will enlive many days of my declining age by a double power of associations. I will try your Cowper, my dear Anna, for your sake, and also I am very much attracted by the prints of the book, principally by a poor, unhappy creature of your blessed sex barefooted, wandering, as it appears, in a dark night. I like besides, your letter, Anna, and I thank you very heartily for it, & for the book. But I am aware just now of my forgetting your uppermost valuable present. I allude to the penwiper, however I fear that something pert is hiden under it. Your very eloquent but a little [illegible] style my pretty friend Harriet, pleased me very much. Your present instantly put in a full show, and you will see as it looks well, this very day. As to you, my good Dick, I promise you to keep very carefully your pencil if you promise me on your side of employing your pen, in the due time in the same glorious way as your grandfather did.[1] Nor [Now ?] from the youngest to the eldest. I will read Goldsmiths Poems with great delight, and think always of the kind gifter of them. I have, my dear friends, many things more to say, but I am indeed urged by the late hours. I could not [?] up early, having been awaked at 4 o'clock, by my neapolitan friend to whom I gave a bed—so farewell. I will see you at half past four, and you will see better by my looks, than by my words as I feel the kindness which you have showed to me in my birth day.

Your very affectionate friend
SANTORRE DEROSSI DI SANTA ROSA.

October 19th.
To Maria, Henry, Anna, Richard, Harriet.

2. *To Mrs. Enfield, Nottingham*

LONDON 6 AIR ST. PICCADILLY.
Samedi 30 *Octobre.*

MADAME ET TRÈS CHÈRE AMIE,

Enfin le jour de notre depart est fixé. Je crois que nous irons nous embarquer à Gravesend Lundi matin. Depuis le moment de mon arrivée je n'ai pas eu un moment de tranquillité, car il s'agissoit presque

[1] Doubtless a reference to William Enfield, LL.D., author of *Enfield's Speaker*, and other works.

tous les jours de partir le lendemain.   Ma santé est assez bien, mais je suis fort triste.   Point de nouvelle de Piémont & plus que l'apparence d'avoir en Grèce de grandes difficultés à faire quelque bien.   Porro pourra vous donner des détails à ce sujet.   Notre batiment est anglais [*illegible*] presque sert mon ami Collegno & moi & tout nous fait espérer un voyage heureux.

Mr. Hart m'a écrit & me demande ma silhouette, il la recevra par Porro, que je charge aussi de vous en remettre une.   En verité mon excellente amie, mon cœur est rempli de souvenirs de Nottingham, il a eprouvé en vous quittant des émotions douces & amères à la fois, dont je ne me croirai [croyais ?] plus susceptible.

Je voudrais vous écrire une longue lettre et je ne puis, je suis inter- rompu à chaque instant par des visites.   Mais voici une interruption bien agréable.   Porro entre et me donne la lettre qu'il a reçue de Henri. Vous voyez que j'avais prévenu votre désir relativement à la silhouette.

Il faut que je vous quitte.   Puisse Dieu vous recompenser dans l'amour [?] de vos chers enfants de tous les bonheurs que vous avez répandus sur mon existence pendant huit mois.

Je vous donnerai de mes nouvelles à mon arrivée en Grèce.   Je prévois qu'elles seront d'un genre assez triste.—Adieu.   Mes tendres amitiés à M. Enfield et Henri à William à notre chère Maria à Anna à Edward.   J'embrasse de tout mon cœur Dick & Harriet—Veuillez être mon interprète auprès des Needham.

J'ai espéré pouvoir envoyer quelque poètes italiens à chacun [?] de mes [*illegible*] intimes de Lenton mais je n'ai pu trouver à ma fantaisie que les Bassevilliennes ¹ pour Miss Anna, veuillez lire [*illegible*] l'édition n'est pas belle, c'est pourtant celle qui lui convient le plus parce qu'il s'y trouve des notes, et d'autres pièces de poésie bonne à connaître.   Rappelez-moi au souvenir de Mr. Taylor, & de sa famille.   J'oubliais celui qui en fera [?] partie, le Dr. Carpenter.   J'écris deux mots à Mr. Hart.

Adieu, ma chère amie
Votre dévoué
SANCTOIRE DE SAINTE ROSA.

3 ·

April 6th, 1825.

MY DEAR & EXCELLENT FRIEND,

Your kind letter reached me the 10th of March on my arrival here from Athens, where I was detained by fever.   I did not suffer very much, but in this country that kind of indisposition leaves a man in such a state of weakness which is not easy to describe.   I feel now perfectly well.   The month which I spent here with Porro & Collegno restored me also to a comfortable state of mind.   I am just starting from this place ; I shall not tell you where I go, because neither you, neither Mr. Enfield will approve it.   But, my dear friends, you must think that the circumstances which surround a man, are sometime powerful.   As to my hope of being useful to this worthy people you know that they were reduced almost to a nothing when I left England.   They are very little in this moment.   I shall see after this campaign ; but as all my feelings are strongly inclined towards England, and as I do not find in the manners & in the character of the ruling classes in Greece any attractive nor any simpathy with my

¹ *Basvilliana*, Monti's poem.

own nature, I think, my dear friends, that I will salute again those blessed and hospitable shores which I left altered [?] by feelings I am not ashamed of, but with perhaps some inconsideration.—In my letter to Mr. Hart I give him a sketch of the situation of the Greek affairs. I prefer with you, my good friend, speak only of me ; I write to you in English, but to you alone, as I am aware of the incorrectness of my language & style. It is just that I should conquer my *amour propre* in order to spare to you the trouble of reading french I write rapidly as I think.

I received many letters from home, but all of an ancient date. My dear wife is well and she hopes we shall be soon reunited, however her affairs are not yet concluded. I am very impatient to receive from her a letter. Writing after she had received the news of my journey to Greece I confess to you that I am not without some apprehension on that point. I have again received the portrait of my second daughter and now they are all five settled in a little box which shall follow me for ever until the moment in which I will embrace the originals. I dare not gaze on them but very seldom. My heart could not bear it—I assure you, my excellent friend, that the letters of your dear children were all of them heartily welcome. If according to my wishes, I will see Edward, Anna, Harriet, Richard at the end of this year, with what sweet pleasure it will find them improved in every respect. Tell them I expect to find them so nor will I be disappointed—but—I say—improved—yes—but keeping their own kind of childish amability—As to Maria, I don't know if I wish her improved, I hope to find her as she was. It is not enough ? Do you not think so yourself, happy mother, only I think that her progress in the [Italian ?]. But I will not remember of having been her master nor master of anybody in Nottingham, I will think only of you as of the kindest friends that I could find anywhere in this world. Of how you and yours should be sadly impressed by the sight of Greece ! The women look so unhappy, and they are so, as I can judge by every information I have collected ; children in the common [?] people are bred up with so little attention to their health—Sick persons are so often abandoned to their wretched destiny, so much superstition is mixed with religion overclouding the best part of it—and nevertheless the only classes of the nation which I heartily esteem are those who are ruled by the religion, [corrupted ?] as *she* is— In the highest with few exceptions, you shall find more the corruption than the light of civilisation. I think indeed that the mixture of the oriental manner which [with ?] the european wickedness is one of the worse which can exist. With all this, if Greece will be able to withstand hard by herself against the Mussulman (who in this year redouble their efforts & dispose them better than in the former campaigns) I hope that the spreading of knowledge will help the good disposition of the Greek people and make them happy. If the events should draw them under a Government which should forbid the liberty of the press and of discussion, and prevent consequently the influence of morals & enlightened visitors of Greece, this country will be a wretched one.

I know by Porro that C. Pecchio had established himself in Nottingham & [—?] in Derby. I cant have the single doubt of the good success of the latter having the patronage of Mr. Higginson and being a very clever man himself and far superior to the common set of Italian masters. His pupils will be soon aware of it. About Pecchio I fear only that his amability will have put in a very unfavourable light & the oddities and the eventual sadness of his predecessor. I want to think of the moment of my last taking leave from my Nottingham friends in order to find some counterbalance to my fears.   How I could doubt a single instant of living in your benevolent hearts !   I hope to receive a long letter from you and I beg to be informed of every thing which interest your family—Be so good also as to give me the news of Mr. Turners family & of D. Carpenter. Remember me to them & tell them that I shall never forget the evenings which I spent in their company.   I wish also to be remembered by you to M. Attenburrows family to Mrs. Turner, & to Mr. Smith Carpenter —My departure seemed to be settled for tomorrow in the afternoon.   I am sure that your prayers and those of your family will follow me and protect me.   It shall be rather an hard way of living for some months but I ought to give a good example.   I could not remain idly here in those moments out of danger but of renovated & serious struggle for Greece.   The last news which are spread today in this place are quite favourable.   We must hope on the help of providence as well as in the courage of Greek, and as a necessary supplement to their want of good order and ability.   You know perhaps my good friend, that Mr. Hart thinking that I could be exposed here to some difficulties in money matters caused 30 pounds to be paid to the Greek Deputies in London for my account.   I received them and I ought to say that in the present circumstances such kind and friendly solicitude of Mr. Hart is very useful to me.   I hope that on the settlement of my familys affairs at home I will be able to pay that little debt to my friend.   I do not want to express to you my feelings of gratitude towards him.   You know my heart enough—I wish that my letter should be read by you only and those who are one with you, as your husband and your son and daughter— God bless you all.   May he grant that I shall see you again, and in the same state of cheerful prosperity.   Farewell.

Yours for ever
Sanctor Santa Rosa.

4. EXCERPTS FROM ' MEMORIES OF LENTON '.   *M.C.M.*   *Arden Press,*
Letchworth.   1910.   *Private Circulation*
(*Page* 13)

We now come to that eventful year of 1824, the year of our interesting intercourse with the Italian refugees.   The Piedmontese revolution of 1820 (or rather, the unsuccessful attempt at a revolution) had flooded England with political refugees, Mrs. Austin (*née* Sarah Taylor) wrote to ask my father if there was an opening for one of them as a teacher in Nottingham.   The result was that Count Santa Rosa settled there, lodging in Parliament S^t.   We & Mr. Henry Enfield's family saw a very great deal of him, and had the greatest affection & admiration for him.   Maria Enfield and I especially worshipped him.   On our way to school Ellen & I often went round by his lodgings to leave flowers, eggs or books &c, and felt it was an honour if we got a sight of him, or a word from him.   He was a great deal at Lenton during the summer of 1824, and I and my sisters had great enjoyment singing with him his favourite national songs, sitting in the verandah, or collecting round the drawing-room window ; Henry and Maria Enfield, and I remember once Richard Martineau being of the party.   My sister Hester sat at an open window upstairs to listen, and my mother was sometimes with her, sometimes with us.   Santa Rosa used often to have his fellow-exiles to visit him, and he generally brought them with him to Lenton.   Amongst them I remember Mr. Radice, Count Arrivabene, Marquis San Marsan (whom we admired extremely), Count Porro, Count Pecchio, &c. Santa Rosa was a very domestic, affectionate, character, and he used to tell us a great deal about his children. He had their portraits, & used to lay them on his table by turns, as his companions during his breakfast. It was a dreadful grief to us all when he left to take part in the struggle for liberty in Greece (in which Lord Byron also took part, and died at Missolonghi) ; and when nearly a year afterwards, I saw in the paper the news of his death, at the battle of Navarino, I felt it a very great blow, and the determination to meet him hereafter was a sort of crisis in my religious life.

Anne Needham (afterwards Mrs. William Enfield) to Miss Mitchell

Not a day passes just now without some peculiar interest. I allude principally to the frequent visitations we have lately had from Santa's illustrious compatriots. On Monday evening the garden contained a singular and interesting assemblage. There were Santa Rosa, the Marquis Charles de San Marsan, and Count Porro and Castiglione, wandering about the garden and distributing amongst us the favour of their rare conversation. . . . Whoever else we see, Santa must always stand at the head of our affections and admirations. We always love him with a peculiar love, when we see him with his friends. . . . We find ourselves already on exceedingly intimate terms with the merry little Porro ; indeed in his week's residence with Santa he has already made nine meals here. . . . One morning we took him for a walk. . . . He is a most entertaining little man, always brings laughter to the house, and leaves still more behind him. He is a Unitarian, Santa a reforming Catholic, and the first time they were here together they had a most spirited conversation on the subject of Catholicism. He will attend our pew on Sunday. He has told us all his private family history, and made himself acquainted with ours. He is a widower aged forty-two with a Catholic family in Milan, had been voted dead and alive again, banished and his estates confiscated ; nevertheless he is always happy & merry, and cares for nothing. . . . San Marsan personifies all you can imagine of grace and nobleness of deportment. He is tall and thin, with brown waving hair and wild restless eyes, right hand fingerless almost, having been shot away in Russia, when he was aide-de-camp to Napoleon, and he is now but thirty ! He has been here three times, and perhaps in a month or two may be here again. His manners are perfect. . . .
Probably Muschietti is in Nottingham again now, on his road from London to Manchester.

Anne Needham to Miss Mitchell

November 1824.

MY DEAR BISHOP
The very day you were last written to, we heard news that has made me pass a fortnight so sorrowfully and tearfully that it has not twice been equalled in my twenty-three years. Our dear, glorious Santa has left Nottingham and England probably for ever. We knew that this might take place in a month or two, but were little prepared to hear from him that morning, that it was his last visit to us. Oh, it was so sad ! . . . He had long had it in contemplation to turn his talents to

the assistance of the Greeks, and was going for a few days to London to settle finally whether he should go to them or not. But on that day, October 21, he received letters telling him that the ship in which he was to go was on the point of sailing. He told us that only his friend Collegno was to accompany him—a noble pair ! He came from France to join Santa. Santa does not expect to be actively employed this winter, except in examining into the state of the country, the character of the people the language, &c. He was very unhappy at being obliged to go so suddenly, with many dear friends at such a distance that it was impossible for him to see them, especially San Marsan. He said that Nottingham was the heart of England to him, and that if ever he returned to England it would be to Nottingham. He seemed beautifully kind to us all that miserable evening. He staid till eleven next day, and then promised to see us again at Nottingham on Sunday. He afterwards told Papa that he left Lenton with a broken heart, and I am sure each of us could answer for those that he left behind. William walked with him, and was delighted with his conversation the whole way, telling him how he could not bear to feel himself growing old in uselessness and inactivity and speaking of his future plans. Indeed, it could not be that a mind like his should be meant to waste its strength in so limited a sphere. If there had been any probability that his family could have joined him here, he would have given up everything for a domestic life, but there was none. Porro and Muschietti came to him directly which must have been a great comfort to him. Poor Muschietti was obliged to return to Manchester on Monday ; Porro went with him to London, and is still there ; but as he meant to return in a day or two after the vessel sailed he will soon be with us, for she was to sail yesterday. He will tell us much of Santa's last days in England and will bring some book & perhaps letter from him. We did see him on Sunday, just before he left Nottingham, but only for a few minutes. (Our blessed mother gave up this last farewell to one whom she loves as well as we do, because she knew it would keep one of us at home ; the fact needs no comment) What added most to his unhappiness in leaving England was that he had passed several months without hearing from his family. However, on Tuesday the 31st [1] a letter from Turin came here for him which was sent on to him by a private hand, and I hope it might reach him in time to lighten his heart before his departure.

[See p. 110, footnote 2.]

[1] Tuesday, 26th ?   This letter was acknowledged on Saturday 30th.

APPENDIX II.C

1. *San Marzano to Mrs. Austin* (*Postmark* : Aug. 5. 1824)

EDIMBURGH *le* 5 *Août* 1824.

Lorsque notre ami S.R. vous parlera de la philosophie de Platon écoutez le avec attention si cela vous amuse, il vous en dira à cet égard plus que Platon n'a jamais pensé, mais quant à ce qui concerne la connaissance des hommes et la manière véritable d'envisager the best intercourse between the individuals is the community alors, ma chère amie, priez-le d'aller se coucher et vous pouvez hardiment lui dire qu'il n'y entend mot. Ce qu'il vous a dit à mon égard est un des plus parfaits nonsenses qu'il ait jamais dit dans cette matière. Je le plains. S'il peut seulement lui venir dans l'esprit que quelques individus dont ni le nombre, ni les talens, ni les actions ni les richesses, ni la position sociale ne rendent d'aucune importance pour leur pays soient capables par leur bassesse d'altérer les principes qui ont dirigé ma conduite politique. Je dis que je le plains si cela est, pour cette raison que lors même qu'il n'aurait pas une haute idée de mon caractère il devrait en avoir assez de mon sens commun pour savoir que ce n'est pas la conduite d'un petit nombre de brigands qui pourroit changer mes opinions à l'égard de l'humanité toute entière. Il y a des gens, en fait de *principes* qui aiment le *simple* et d'autres le *composé* ; Moi je préfère le premier genre ; le principe qui m'a fait agir est celui-ci ; *j'aime le bonheur de mon pays* Cela est peut-être trop court pour ceux qui aiment les dédales des abstractions méthaphisiques [*sic*]. j'irai plus loin, j'aime *le bonheur* uniquement parceque je l'aime et je ne connais pas d'autre raison à cela.—Mon ami S.R. trouvera cela bien *vulgaire* et moi je pense pour me dédomager [*sic*] de son opinion que c'est précisément la simplicité de mes principes qui en fait la force essentielle et que des opinions fondées sur la base aérienne des abstractions sont plus sujettes à vaciller que celles qui s'appuient sur des raisonnemens solides et sur l'analyse toute simple des mouvemens d'un cœur que la nature a d'elle meme incliné à la bénévolence [*sic*].

Non seulement je vous authorise mais vous m'obligerez meme en lui communiquant cette partie de ma lettre telle qu'elle est ; · je n'accuse pas son cœur en m'ayant mal jugé ! Mais j'accuse son étourderie et sa manie de phra [*paper torn*].

Remerciez bien Mr. Austin de la complaisance qu'il a eu d'assister de ses conseils Sig^{re} Demestre ; celui-ci a quelques raisons bonnes pour ne pas montrer les comptes à ces gens, cependant je pense comme vous qu'il faut éviter les polémiques de [   ] en cette affaire ; si on l'attaque par quelques nouveaux articles auquel [*sic*] il soit *absolument* nécessaire de riposter je lui conseillerais de faire encore mention de la lettre de T. Smith et de declarer qu'après cela il traitera avec le plus parfait mépris toute attaque ultérieure et qu'il se croit dispensé d'en ennuyer le public davantage—*Il serait du dernier ridicule de montrer à des gens qui sont —— iés au mois de mai les comptes de l'argent qui a été distribué en Décembre et qui ne les regarde nullement—Vous dites fort bien que je suis mieux en me trouvant loin de ces ordures. Je m'en félicite de tout mon cœur.

Maintenant chère amie laissez moi vous parler de vous dont l'excellent caractère serait seul capable de ramener à l'amour de l'humanité même ceux que les rires (?) des hommes en auraient éloignés davantage. Je vous remercie du tendre intéret que vous prenez à ma santé ; puisque vous voulez bien vous en occuper je vous décris (?) que je me sens beaucoup mieux ; l'air d'ici est plus vif et peut-etre cela me fait-il du bien. Je ne manquerai pas de voir le Dr. dont vous me parlez si le cas se presente [   ] d'en avoir besoin.

Comme je n'aime guère à perdre le sens d'une partie ——————— de vos lettres je vous prie, surtout quand vous écrivez de travers de soigner un peu plus votre écriture. Sta R. etait chargé de vous envoyer une lettre de moi par les Enfields J'ignore si c'est celle dont vous me parlez.

Continuez encore de m'écrire a Edimburgh car quoique je quitte cette ville dans peu j'y ferai chercher mes lettres à la poste et me les ferai envoyer. Je vous souhaite à votre cottage un meilleur tems que nous n'avons ici.

Adieu ne manquez pas de me donner de vos nouvelles quand vous n'aurez rien de mieux à faire car je n'ai pas besoin de vous répéter que ce qui vient de vous m'est bien cher.

(*Unsigned*)

(This whole letter is particularly illegible, and from * written ' de travers '.)

2. *San Marzano to Mrs. Austin.* (*Postmark* : Glasgow, 26 Aug. 1824)

GLASCOW *le* 26 *Août* 1824.

Ce n'est que hier ma chere Dame que j'ai recu [*sic*] votre lettre du 11 à la vérité il n'y a la rien d'étonant [*sic*] vu la vie errante que j'ai menée ces jours ci. J'ai poussé ma course jusqu'à Inverness et de là par le Canal Calédonien et l'Ouest de l'Ecosse sono capitato quì. Pour un homme qui a comme moi une espece de culte pour le grandiose des Alpes je dois avouer que je n'ai rien trouvé de merveilleux dans ces Highlands, malgré cela j'ai été touché de la Mélancolie de ces Solitudes ; elles ne sont pas sans charmes mais c'est celui du Désert ; point d'arbres point de maisons pas d'habitans, un silence solemnel [*sic*] une Nature languissante, des ruines et des souvenirs romanesques voila les montagnes de l'Ecosse ; avec de l'imagination on peut s'y plaire—On passe près de la foret de Birnam et l'on se figure les sorcières de Macbeth, au fort St. George on montre le lit ou Duncan fut assassiné. Je vous fais grace ma chere amie d'une serie d'autres souvenirs résultats des lectures de votre Walter Scott—Il est de fait que cet auteur et Mr. Bell l'inventeur des batimens à vapeur ont créé de nouvelles valeurs pour l'Ecosse qui est maintenant bien plus *visible* (?) qu'elle n'était il y a quelques années. Ce fameux canal qui unit la mer d'Allemagne à l'Atlantique est une fort belle chose mais n'est pas fort utile quoi qu'en dise [sic] les Ecossais. Je crois que l'année passée son revenu a à peine suffi à l'entretien des Digues ; C'est une affaire de Luxe à la *Romaine* et vous faites bien car vous etes des peuples modernes celui qui ressemble le plus à ces Messieurs et par surcroit vous avez beaucoup d'argent. Vous savez ma chere amie que l'etat de ma santé à Londres aggravoit [sic] encore les peines de mon exil, il paroit comme si de telles impressions m'avaient suivi dans ma course. Je me figurais retrouver des lieux semblables à ceux de mon pays j'ai cru voir Asti [?] et Turin et le chateau d'Inverary d'une grande ressemblance avec notre chateau de Cortiole ; j'avais le cœur bien serré en le voyant en pensant à ns. chers petits—on continue de m'ecrire beaucoup de bien de ma fille mais tout cela est loin ! Mr. A. a très fort raison. N'allez pas vous imbrattare avec cette engeance ; ne me demandez pas des renseignemens car je m'en lave les mains, si Dal Pozzo vous a reccommandé [sic] quelqu'un apparemment il sait ce qu'il fait mais je ne m'en veut [sic] pas meler. Je crois vous avoir déjà dit qu'à peu près tous ces gens n'ont rien a faire avec la révolution et qu'il y a parmi eux un bon nombre de véritables brigands.

Je vois que mon ami Sta Rosa m'attaque par terre et par mer au public comme au *privé*, mais je suis bon chrétien et lui pardonne. Si au milieu de vous délices champêtres vous vous rappelez de moi et m'ecrivez continuez encore d'adresser vos lettres à Edimburgh.

Je ne sais pas si j'irai en Irlande de cette année et à proprement parler je n'ai pas de plan fixe mais je crois que je ferai quelque séjour en Ecosse —Adieu ma belle et chère Dame Croyez-moi [?] vot. dévoué S^t M.

Address : Mrs. Austin, Post Office, Dorking, Surrey or Sussex.

3. (*Postmark :* Sep. 18. 1824)

EDIMBURGH *le* 18 7bre 1824.

La défense doit etre proportionée à l'attaque. Ce n'est pas la première fois ma chere amie que vous m'attaquez avec une pareille chaleur *sur les* [illegible] les sentimens d'orgueil qu'on se plait à m'attribuer ; je m'apperçois [sic] qu'on vous *travaille* à ce sujet car je ne pense pas avoir donné moi-même des raisons suffisantes d'avoir ces sortes de craintes à l'égard de mes opinions. Je crois déja vous avoir observé plus d'une fois que l'etat de notre pays est si différent du votre sous tous les rapports que sans y avoir été il vous est difficile d'avoir une juste idée de la réalité des choses et vous etes d'autant plus exposée à tomber dans des erreurs qu'on se sert dans le langage ordinaire de mots semblables pour exprimer des choses qui dans nos deux pays diffèrent fortement pour le fond. Je ne veux paroître ni plus ni moins populaire que je ne suis. Je suis satisfait de mes sentimens car si je ne l'étais pas je les changerais—à mes yeux etre le *flatteur* d'un peuple ou d'un Roi est la meme chose ; tout le monde ne pense pas ainsi ; aussi y a-t-il des tribuns et des Chambellans ; la farce est la meme et bassesse pour bassesse des lambris dorés sont plus agréables à mes sens que des carrefours fangeux ; voilà pour mes [ ] mais en vérité il est peu nécessaire d'insister la-dessus car le peuple le *véritable peuple* c'est-à-dire la Majorité d'une Nation demande du *bonheur* et non pas de la *flatterie*. Cette expression de *véritable peuple* implique la supposition qu'il y ait un *faux peuple* et c'est le cas dans notre pays ; je crois bien que chez d'autres nations aussi il y a une classe de gens qui sans etre mus [?] par aucune vue de bien public declament par esprit de pure jalousie contre les hautes classes. Mais ces gens doivent etre bien moins nombreux en proportion que l'Etat de civilisation du pays est plus avancé, tant de motifs grands et utiles d'excitement existent alors qu'il est naturel de voir paroître moins les bas sentimens. Voilà pourquoi vous ne pouv [*paper torn*] avoir une idée exacte de ce *faux peuple* de chez nous qui est si injuste dans ses accusations contre un ordre de gens qui loin d'avoir à se reprocher la jouissance d'aucun privilege ou d'exercer aucune vexation [?] envers le peuple n'a fait que paroitre [?] depuis nombre d'années en tete de tout ce qui paroissait avoir une tendance propre à reveiller la nation de son long asservissement. Lorsque un individu ou une classe est accusé d'orgueil il faut faire bien attention que l'accusation peut egalement etre l'effet de l'orgueil réel de l'accusé ou d'un orgueil existant dans l'accusateur lui meme. Que chez nous on ait malheureusement rencontré [vu *crossed out*] trop souvent le cas de gens accusant à faux l'orgueil des Nobles tandis qu'ils en offroient euxmemes un exemple dégoutant c'est une vérité que les faits ont prouvée ; La plupart des soidisans republicains de la première révolution sont devenus des voteurs [?] serviles ; Je me rappelle qu'à Turin lorsqu'on fit un projet pour amalgamer la société dans différentes classes, la chose échoua parcequ'il n'y avait pas moyen de faire un choix de personnes qui satisfit ou ne blessat [*sic*] pas l'orgueil de l'aristocratie bourgeoise. Ma *défense* a été un peu longue mais je tiens fortement à l'estime de mes amis et d'une amie telle que vous surtout ; je suis d'ailleurs profondément affecté de l'injustice de certains hommes ; qu'il me jette la première pierre celui qui a pour le bien du peuple mis *at a stake* [*sic*] plus que moi ; Croyez-le chere Amie la civilisation est bien arriérée chez nous C'est la conséquence de notre servitude mais tel qui porte des habits de gentelman [*sic*] est souvent moins policé [?] que des hommes des basses classes qui chez nous sont plus vertueuses que les classes moyennes. Richement vous m'avez fait de la peine parceque vous méditez à ce sujet ; Ces fausses inculpations à mon égard en sont un peu accréditées par ma negligence et mon mépris à les riposter ; Là je suis en général très fier mais auprès de vous je ne veux pas etre méconnu et j'exige une réparation—Allez demander a nos paysans si je suis orgueilleux et vous verrez ce qu'ils en pensent. J'ignore ce qui est survenu à notre ami S^a R ma [*sic*] je m'en informerai.

Votre lettre m'a fait un grand plaisir je l'attendois avec impatience —De gré ou de force je veux que vous m'aimiez car votre amitié m'est d'un grand charme. J'oubliois de vous dire que parmi ceux que j'ai appelés canaille il y a un Comte et un Chevalier. Donnez moi des nouvelles de notre ami Dalpozzo. Vous en savez sans doute quelque chose ; il est décidément a great admirer of yours. Quand serez-vous à Londres ? Je n'ai encore rien décidé sur mon départ d'ici ; il me reste encore quelques visites à faire.

[*No signature*]

[S M° *written on address in another hand*]
Address : Mrs. Austin, Post Office, Dorking, Surrey.

4. *San Marzano to Mrs. Austin?* (*No postmark nor address*)
Sabato.

Ho letto ieri sera l' articolo *government.* Havvi nel metodo dell'autore un procedere lumeggiante di chiarezza e tutto geometrico. Non si possono contrastare i vantaggi di un simil metodo, non vi ha dubbio che quel camminare seduti sopra privilegij con tanta cautela fondati deve rischiarire assai la digressione, ma convienci pare badare al non eccedere ; una luce superflua abbaglia qualche volta e fa smarire la via quanto la mancanza di essa. Mi pare che l' autore avrebbe potuto rendere il suo discorso più utile estendosi maggiormente nelle conseguenze di suoi principij che egli lascia al quanto nudi.

Mi ha piacciuto [sic] assai quella maniera *derisoria* di rispondere all' objezione che una buona rappresentazione distruggerebbe il Re e la Camera dei Lord. Dopo di aver provato che i tre principij sono incombinabili l'eccellente costituzione Inglese diventa molto meno eccellente.

L' articolo *upon the Elective body* è il più sviluppato a mio parere e sì [?] avrei anche le mie osservazioni da fare ma siccome troppo lunghe gliene farò gratia per ora.

Nel saggio sopra la Giurisprudenza si trova un articolo diretto contro i parolai metafisici che dobbiamo mostrare al nostro Sta Rosa.

Quel libretto mi ha occupato la mente ed in simil caso mi è forza talvolta il discorrere delle mie Idee. Per questo gliele indirizzo gentilissima Signora trovando con ciò una occasione di forzarla a non dimenticarmi.

Quando avrò la sorte di rivederla *talkeremo* di queste cose intanto mi creda

Suo Dev° ed aff°

S.M°.

[See p. 116, footnote 1]

[Unpublished letters from San Marzano to Mrs. Austin, lent to the Author by the late Mrs. Janet Ross.]

APPENDIX III.A

I

Note on address page : Mr. Panizzi about Mr. Pistrucci as Assistant, Liverpool—24 Feby. 1828)

9 Gt. George St.—Liverpool
Feb. 24th, 1828.

Dear Sir

I beg to apologize for not having sooner written to you, as it was certainly my duty to have done, in order to thank you for the very kind manner with which you have been pleased to treat me during my stay in town. I can assure you that I never shall forget it, and I hope that a longer acquaintance will make you think me not unworthy of your friendship, which I shall be proud to deserve. I have been however so much engaged that I could not absolutely find time to write a letter, and I flatter myself you will forgive me for the delay.

Before leaving London this day week I spoke to our mutual friend Ct. dal Pozzo, about the person whom I thought the most fit as teacher of Italian in the L. University. As I have to answer for him, I must find a reasonable man, who will allow himself to be directed, and who is not a sturdy pedant, or a conceited coxcomb. He must likewise be a man of good character, and of agreeable and gentlemanly manners. Now it appeared both to Ct. dal Pozzo and myself that a gentleman of the name of Pistrucci has all the requisite qualities, and so I called upon him, and spoke to him in general terms of a situation which I thought was likely to suit him. He appeared to me a man such as we want. He has, besides, a quality which the Council will like in him. He is a Roman. I am of opinion that the idea of a Roman speaking better than the other Italians is quite a chimera, yet if the University can have a man as teacher, who may satisfy even the prejudices of certain people, so much the better, particularly at the commencement. I should like you to have the goodness to tell me, whether there is any objection on the part of the Council to my making any specific proposal to that gentleman, who, as far as I can learn is a very honorable man. This must be done as soon as convenient, partly to give him time to learn very well your language, which I think he knows but indifferently, and partly to have time to look for someone else, should he not suit the Council, or should he not find it convenient to accept the office.

I should think that a teacher attending the pupils every other day

266

would be quite sufficient. To learn a language is matter of memory, and the student must have time to learn ; and moreover the pupil who studies Italian is likely to have three or four more professors to attend to. I pledge myself to the Council that in a scholastic year, young men of fair abilities and diligence will be able to translate any Italian author, taking lessons thrice a week. . .

As I begged Ct. dal Pozzo to take some more informations about Pistrucci, I shall feel obliged to you if you will be kind enough to present him my compliments, and consult him about the contents of this letter regarding that gentleman.

> Believe me, dear Sir,
> Most truly yours,[1]

Address : Leonard Horner, Esq., 29 Percy St., Bedford Sq.

2

Dated : Gt. George St., L'pool ; April 19th, 1828.

[*Returning proofs and newspaper with mention of the last report of the University*]

The gentleman I alluded to in my letter before last as the one whom I could entirely rely upon as my assistant is Mr. Tealdi now living in Manchester where he has resided for several years. He is very well known there and the highest references can be given to the Council both as to his capability and respectability. I can fully answer for him both for the one and the other. As however the Council have acted with so much kindness towards me, I think I owe to the University to do not only my duty, strictly speaking, to the best of my abilities, but also whatever they may think I can do with advantage to the establishment. If it should therefore be thought more desirable that for this first year I should myself both lecture and teach the Language, I will submit to do it.

> I remain, my dear Sir,
> Yours very truly,

3

MY DEAR SIR

I have to thank you for the trouble you have taken in communicating to the Council my letter of the 19th inst., as well as them for their kind opinion on the subject of an assistant, in which I see a new proof of their benevolent attentions to me. I must however take the liberty to observe that the number of pupils is not at all a matter of consideration to me on this head, since it is not the *quantity* of work but the *quality* which I object to. As I think I had the honor to tell you formerly my repugnance to be obliged to teach beginners altogether is so strong that neither loss nor gain can balance it. I shall not however take any step about an assistant till I have further directions from you, and there is sufficient time for it. I have only to add now that so anxious am I that the choice of such an assistant may prove a real assistance not only to me, but to the students, as well as an acquisition to the University, that having heard of another gentleman, perhaps better qualified than the one I proposed, I am making enquiries about him, and should he appear to be preferable, I should suggest

[1] The letters in Appendix III.A are all signed *A. Panizzi.*

him, although he is not such a personal friend of mine as the one already mentioned.   But of course I neither did nor shall ever pledge myself to any one until I have the full approbation of the Council.

[Then follow enquiries *re* soundness of Mr. Taylor, the University bookseller, for whom the book of extracts was being printed.]

I am almost ashamed of giving you so many troubles, which I hope you will pardon and remain

Very sincerely Yours

9 Gt. George St., L'pool.   *April 29th.* 1828.

4

MY DEAR SIR

. . Respecting the *Assistant* I beg to remind you of a few circumstances.   I think you will remember that when I had the honor to speak to you for the first time I told you that the only thing which could induce me to leave Liverpool was *not* to be obliged to teach beginners, and that therefore I should engage at the University (a situation which I consider the most honorable I could wish for) only with the view of not being obliged to do it.   This I had the honor to repeat to the board of Council, and then it was said that I should be allowed to have an Assistant for that purpose, I only being obliged to lecture according to the sketch left in your hands and then read by Mr. Brougham.   Mr. Warburton then observed that I was to answer for this Assistant in every respect, that I ought to see he did his duty, and that the Council in fact looked upon me as responsible for the whole department.   And this I thought right, and agreed to . . .

[Discusses the book to be used instead of *Leo X.*, which is unobtainable in a cheap edition ; objects to *Charles V.* on account of size ; shows concern for his students in considering weight of books ; suggests one work for all translation into Modern Languages.] . . . of a small size, conveying useful information, avoiding to discuss *ex professo* any peculiar tenet either religious or political, and of an interest so general, as to be in some parts connected with the literature and history of those countries whose Language is taught.   [Suggests, on advice of a friend, Hallam's *Middle Ages*.]

9 Gt. George St., Liverpool.   *June 7th* 1828.

Address : L. Horner, Esq., Warden, London University.

5

DEAR SIR

I am ready to deliver a course of ten lectures on any of the following subjects which the Council may be pleased to prefer.

1st.   On the Heroic and mock Heroic Poetry of the Italians.
2nd.   On the Italian Opera, Comedy and Tragedy.
3rd.   On some of the best Italian Prose-writers.
4th.   On Dante and some of his imitators.
5th.   On the Lyric Poetry of the Italians.

Few persons would understand the 4th and 5th course.   The 3rd would be unquestionably more profitable to the student ; but not relished by persons who attend such lectures for their amusement.   I should suppose the 1st and 2nd more popular.   I rather incline to the first, because Tasso (whose *Gerusalemme* would occupy a prominent part in the course) is more known than any other Italian poet. I am moreover of opinion that the subject would give occasion to new and interesting critical inquiries.

Believe me, dear Sir,
Yours most truly,

2 Gower St. North.   *Tuesday, March 31st* [1829].

6

Dated : 25 April, 1829.

MY LORDS AND GENTLEMEN
I have been requested by several friends to deliver a course of Lectures on Italian Life, rather out of the University of London, and in a place where Ladies might attend. I hope that considering the smallness of my class in this establishment you will not object to my complying with the wishes of my friends, and I have the honor to be

My Lords and Gent^n
Your most obed^t Servt

University of London.   *April 25th* 1829.
To the Council of the Univ^y of London.

7

DEAR SIR
I did not answer your note sooner, waiting for notice of a meeting of the Senate to whom you might communicate my answer. I have this moment received such notice.

The scheme of delivering lectures on Italian Literature in hopes of attracting persons not belonging to the University, who might be conversant with the Ital. language has been repeatedly tried and failed. In 1829 a course was announced soon after Easter : I had *two pupils*, now members of the Council, Mr. Booth and Mr. Romilly, who would not have attended, if they had not been my private friends. On the following year a course was advertised and no person entered. I then, at the suggestion of the present Lord Chancellor, advertised a course of lectures to which Ladies should be admitted. Thanks to the strong exertions of influential friends I mustered an audience of about 50 persons, *every one of them my personal friend.* The lectures were delivered at Willis' Rooms.

Do not these facts prove that it would be mere loss of time to prepare lectures, and of money to advertise them ?

Believe me,
Very truly yours,

B.M.   *May 1st.*
Address : Thomas Coates, Esq., University of London.

8

MY LORDS & GENTLEMEN
Several publications having lately appeared in some Sunday Papers, which I conceive highly injurious to this establishment, I consider it due to the Council & to myself to say

1st That I am not connected either directly or indirectly with any such publications

2ndly That the attacks aimed at Mr. Horner appear to be only the

effect of personal malice against that gentleman. I think him entitled
to the Proprietors' & Professors' gratitude for his useful exertions in
support of this establishment, and I think it not only just to him, but
necessary to the prosperity of the University that he should not be so
unfairly & ungenerously abused :

3rdly   That it is the humble opinion that if an effectual end be not
put to these unworthy proceedings, the success of the University is
utterly impossible.

I have the honor to be
My Lords & Gentlemen
Your most obd. humble Ser.

To the Council of the University of London.

University.   *March* 13*th* 1830.

(*No address*)

9

BRITISH MUSEUM.   *December* 6*th* 1837.

MY LORDS & GENTLEMEN

The Keepership of the Printed Books in the British Museum to
which I have been lately promoted being incompatible with any other
situation, I am obliged to resign the professorship which I have had
the honor to hold in the University College since its foundation.
Nothing but the obedience which I owe to the rules of this House
could have induced me to resign a chair which I was always proud to
hold in an Institution in the success of which, now put beyond doubt,
I always took and shall always continue to take the most lively interest.
Allow me, My Lords & Gentlemen, to offer you my grateful thanks
for the many acts of kindness which I have received from you in your
official as well as private capacities, and to subscribe myself with the
greatest respect

My Lords & Gentlemen
Your very Obed[t] H[le] Ser[t]

To the Council of University College.

(*No address*)

[From the original letters in the possession of University College
London]

APPENDIX III.B

I

1 OLD PALACE YARD. *16th Dec*^r 1831.

MY LORD,

I have the honor of laying before your Lordship a memorial on behalf of Professor Panizzi praying your Lordship to grant him the usual certificate with a view to his naturalization—to which I hope your Lordship will give a favourable answer.

I have the honor to be
My Lord
With the greatest respect
Your very humble servant
GEO. WEBSTER.

The Viscount Melbourne, Home Office.

Petition
To the Right Honorable
Viscount Melbourne, His
Majesty's Secretary of State for
the Home Department,
The Memorial of
Antonio Panizzi, one of
the Assistant Librarians at
the British Museum,—

Humbly Sheweth,

that the Memorialist is a native of the Dukedom of Modena, having been born at Brescello on the 16th September 1797—

that in the year 1823, the Memorialist came to this country, and has resided therein ever since without any intermission, occupying himself with literary pursuits—

that in the year 1828, the Memorialist was appointed Professor of Italian Literature in the London University, which situation he now holds in conjunction with the office of an Assistant Librarian at the British Museum conferred upon him by the principal Trustees of that Establishment in April last.

that the Memorialist has now resolved to adopt this Country for his permanent residence, and as he holds the offices above referred to, he hopes that he may be thought to be a fit person on whom to confer the privileges of naturalization, and that your Lordship will be pleased

271

to certify, in the usual manner, Your approbation of a Bill for that purpose, which the Memorialist intends to apply for during this Session of Parliament.

(Sgd.) ANTONIO PANIZZI.

Middlesex

Antonio Panizzi one of the Assistant Librarians at the British Museum, Gentleman, maketh oath and saith that the facts set forth in the preceding Memorial (which is signed by this Deponent) are true as the Deponent shall answer to God.

(Sgd.) ANTONIO PANIZZI.

Sworn at Bow Street this 13th day of December 1831 before me (Sgd.) G. R. MINSHULL.

2

GROSVENOR ST., *Dec.* 21 1831.

DEAR SIR

In case my testimony either to a long acquaintance with you or in favor of your character should be required for the purpose of forwarding the bill for your naturalization I shall be most happy to give it in any manner that may be most convenient.

Very faithfully yours
AUCKLAND.

A. Panizzi, Esq.

BRIGHTON. *Dec*ʳ 30 1831.

MY DEAR SIR

There is an Italian Gentleman of the name of Panizzi, who is now seeking the approbation of the Home Office to a Bill of Naturalization for himself. I called one day with the hope of seeing you on the subject, & removing any difficulties that might arise from his want of landed property ; a want, which he supplies by having the engagement of Assistant-Librarian to the British Museum. I then saw Mr. Noble, the Clerk through whose hands such matters pass, & thought that I had satisfied his scruples. I have however since learned, that there must be two sponsors, & am therefore anxious to add my name to that of Lord Auckland in that capacity. I have known him myself for four or five years, & know others who have done so more intimately for much longer. He was originally a Refugee from the North of Italy, & is an accomplished & well-conducted man. I shall be very glad, if this word of recommendation can serve him.

Believe me, my dear Sir,
Yours very truly,
SANDON.

J. Phillips, Esq.

[Home Office Records, 1, 15. 1835. Naturalization Bills.]

APPENDIX III.C

I

DEAR MR. PANIZZI

It is the sonnet to Death that I think I never shewed you, and it is the last line in which Mr. Smith objects to the word " charms "—so I must alter it, I suppose, but I like it rather best as it stands.—Pray come to us to-morrow evening (Friday the 5th)—

We go to Mr. Smith's Saturday when I will see what I can do to *vindicate my " charms "* and I should be glad to have something to say from you in corroboration of his dislike or my partiality for them.—

We must come to a decision when I return whether I am to print or burn my attempts. Pray come to-morrow evening.—We shall have some pretty singing & pretty people.

Yrs. truly

Thursday Even. the 4th.

Address : A. Panizzi, Esq. [*Evidently delivered by hand*].

[Panizzi Correspondence, B.M., Add. MSS. 36714, Vol. I., fol. 410.]

2

[1835]

DEAR MR. PANIZZI

I have been looking at the 3 *Sisters* and cannot think them by any means adapted to english [*sic*].—We are a matter of fact plodding people & we insist on a little common sense. Now here are 19 stanzas of 15 lines each, 285 lines, all about Laura's Eyes.—There is a sameness—indeed there is—pervading the whole.—The stanza is unfavorable—the rhymes are often so far apart that they would be lost on an english ear.—The short lines do not always rhyme with the preceding one, which does not please in english.—There are many repetitions.—the thoughts are spun out.—*The eyes* are addressed as persons—In short I cannot for the soul of me take to these Canzoni con amore. Their merits are essentially Italian.—The graces of diction are unattainable, & they have not the pith and substance we require—" Nella stagion che' 1 ciel rapido inchina ", which I translated 30 years ago, contains in each stanza a picture equally beautiful in any language.—" Di pensier in pensier " the same.—The dream relates a succession of emotions, & is dramatic—" Italia mia " is full of strong argument—but these *Sisters* are merely love-sick. There is something *decousu* [*sic*],—a want of connection that worries me.—It is one thing to read & admire, and another to translate.—A translator must ask his author a thousand questions a reader would never think of. For example, pray tell me, as Petrarch is not here to do so, *precisely* what he means by—" E per lungo costume Dentro là dove sol Con amor seggio ? "—Where does he sit ? And what does " dentro là " *exactly* mean ? If I attempt any, it must be the second sister.—I think it possible I might make something of her but I decidedly would take some little liberty with the stanzas or rather with the rhymes.—I have had no time as yet.—We have been full of worry & anxiety about Elections.—It is at length resolved our nephew does not stand for the County. Lord Dacre has been excessively annoyed & engaged, which has not done him any good, but I hope he will now be quiet & recover from the mischief done.

I wrote thus far several days ago and was interrupted.—It looks as if I set up my opinion in opposition to that of all the great Italian critics for 500 years. Far from it.—I do not doubt the beauty of the 3 sisters. I only contend that they are not willing to change their Italian costume for an english dress, & that my plodding old Muse (if I have such a menial in my establishment) as their *tire-woman* declares, (with my Abigail in the little piece acted at Hatfield) that they would look " no how at all "—when so attired.—I can put them into English and very literally too, but if when done they are ugly things to english eyes, then I give no idea of things that are renowned for their beauty. Tell me however what that passage in the first stanza of the 2nd Canzone means, & I will try a bit of *that*, to show you I am not obstinate, & I will do my *very best* upon *honor.*—

Lord Dacre is better than when I began this scrawl.—I hope you have quite recover'd your strength & your sleep & above all your spirits.—

> Believe me
> Dear Mr. Panizzi
> Yrs. truly

The Hoo. *Sunday.*

(*No address.*)

[*Ibid.*, fols. 412–13.]

3

[Castle Martyr, Ireland.   1836]

DEAR MR. PANIZZI

The title page appears to me perfect. I hope you will find Italics to please your fastidious taste in these matters.—I put my fame as to authorship entirely into your hands, and if I have not a fine *recolte* of Laurels I shall lay all the blame on you. You will be glad to hear that Lord Dacre is remarkably well for him & enjoys his trip. The Sullivans are a boy & girl about the age of their own Brand & Barbarina, and I am wonderfully better. We leave this delightful place next Monday & go to Dublin and then work our way home by Liverpool & thro' Wales, and shall be at the Hoo by the 15th of next month—My daughter will then begin collecting from the four quarters of the globe the integral parts of the *Vie* now scatter'd abroad over the face of the earth.—A propos of *faces* we hear that darling Franky's face is much

improved by the Sea.—Your pupil Barbarina writes us most pleasant
letters.—

In great haste
Yrs truly obliged

Castle Martyr.   *Friday*.
My daughter bids me say how much she is obliged to you for going
to see her children.

(*No address*.)

[*Ibid*., fol. 456.]

4

[1836]

Thanks, dear Mr. Panizzi—it looks so much better thus, that I am
quite pleased.   I begin to think I look very handsome in black & white.—
They *read* much better than they did in MS. & my dormant vanity is
beginning to stretch itself & yawn & throw off its sluggishness.—Once
thoroughly awaken'd it will lead me into some folly unworthy of my
sober age.   I am afraid I have done mischief by trying to introduce a
comma . . . I feel almost ashamed of the trouble you take, but it is your
own fault—Why will you be so obliging ?   I mean to cut down my
little odious preface to very few words—Indeed I believe I had best
say nothing.   Let the *things* speak for themselves.   I am in good humour
with them this morning & think they *may* plead their own cause pretty
tidily.

Yrs truly

Wedy. Morn.

I had called you *Signor* to do you honor, but I see you are determined
to be a John Bull to all intents & purposes, so good bye *Mr*. Panizzi
for to-day.

Address : A. Panizzi, Esqr.

[*Ibid*., fol. 458.]

5

[*Undated*]

DEAR SIR

The Archbishop of Canterbury assures me that it is quite a mistake
that the Bishop of Lincoln is appoined tutor to the Princess Victoria,
that the Duchess of Kent herself employs whom she pleases to instruct
her, and that he could not with the slightest prospect of success interfere
in the business.—I am very sorry to have been thus unsuccessful in my
negociation.—I mention'd your book to him in the hope he might be
induced to read it, for in his youth he was fond of belles lettres, & a
good italian [*sic*] scholar, tho' I fear his present situation allows him
little time to indulge in such pursuits now.   We shall return to Town
early next week, and I hope shall have the pleasure of seeing you ere
long.

Believe me,
Dear Sir, Yrs truly

The Hoo, Friday.

(*No address*.)

[*Ibid*., Vol. XIII., fols. 49–50.]

6

DEAR MR. PANIZZI

Lord Dacre bids me enclose this to you, & desires you to read it before you take it to Lord Willoughby. He says you will then know what to do.—I myself could of course do nothing in the business.—

He hopes you will succeed, especially as the young Lady is so handsome.

Yrs. truly

The Hoo. *Wedy.*

The chamberlain's office is in Abingdon St. just beyond the House of Lords.

Address : A. Panizzi, Esqr., British Museum, London, *and stamped with a* 1^d. *stamp,* 30 *May* 1845.

[*Ibid.*, Add. MSS. 36715, Vol. II., fol. 22.]

7

CASTLE MARTYR,
September thirteen 1836.

DEAR MR. PANIZZI

Mr. Coke's letter follows us to this place, & reaches us this morning. Lord Dacre bids me enclose it to you, & advise you to write to Mr. Coke to announce yourself immediately—Lord Dacre says you will find there some of the most interesting MSS. in the world.—So make haste, for Mr. Coke is going from home soon, you see. The place too is magnificent, & the immense tract of country that he has brought into the finest state of cultivation in Europe, makes him rank high as a benefactor to the human race.—The excursion will be delightful to you as a scholar, & as a " good man ", as Franky [1] esteems you.—

We all arrived safely here last night, thro' perils & difficulties which served but to enhance our amusement—such as storms of rain—restive or completely knocked up horses—Steam packet in a gale of wind to such *land-lubbers* as most of us, etc. etc. but here we are, all the better for our journey & our voyage. Lord Dacre remarkably well for him, & my lameness incalculably better.—Mr. & Mrs. Sullivan in high glee, & Mr. Brand in his usual state of perfect equanimity.

Mr. Coke's direction is simply

T. Coke, Esqr,
Holkham
Norfolk

ours

Castle Martyr
Ireland.

Yrs truly

Castle Martyr. *Tuesday Morn.* 13*th.*

Address : as before.

[*Ibid.*, Add. MSS. 36714, Vol. I., fol. 442.]

[1] Lady Dacre's grandson.

APPENDIX III.D

LETTER FROM THE RT. HON. THOMAS GRENVILLE TO ANTONIO PANIZZI

CLEVELAND SQUARE, 21 *May* 1835.

DEAR SIR,

I have this moment received, with the two editions of the Boiardo, the beautiful and valuable copy of the Sonetti which accompanied them. For that estimable addition to my Collection, & for the kindly expressions of the dedication, I must not delay to offer to you my best acknowledgments, as well as the assurances of the pleasure which I look for in the improvements which this edition of the Sonetti will have received from the talents of its commentator. It reconciles me much to the very costly terms on which my books have been collected, when any of them can, as in the present instance, be found to promote or assist the literary labours of those who are best qualified to profit by them.

Receive therefore my best thanks & believe me always

Dear Sir,

Very truly & faithfully Yours

(*No address.*)

[Panizzi Correspondence, B.M., Add. MSS. 36714, Vol. I, fol. 353.]

APPENDIX III.E

Antonio Panizzi to Andrew Rutherfurd, Lord Advocate of Scotland.

1

DUNKELD, *Saturday evening.*

MY DEAR LORD

Eccomi, dopo aver seguito appuntino l'itinerario da lei cortesemente tracciatomi, ed aver fatto anche di più, nel più bel luogo, o per dirle alla Rediana [?], nel *arcibellissimo* dei luoghi, dopo una bellissima giornata di ottimo viaggio. Non è piovuto che tre volte quest'oggi. Gli altri giorni piovve almen venti volte al giorno, ed Erle [?] aveva lasciato la sua reggia costì per recarsi meco a visitare Loch Katrine ed Invernesnaid [*sic*] Hill sul Lomond. Credo sia ora ritornato in città.

Non poteva—tuttochè assai stanco—lasciar di farle sapere quanto io le debbo per avermi così ben diretto. Domani credo andrò ad Inverness senza veder Perth non avendo tempo di far tutto.

Accetti, mio caro Signore ed amico, i miei ringraziamenti e per questi e per tanti favori compartitimi costì, & faccia la grazia di farli accettare co' miei ossequii alla sua Signora. Se il Se. Fox Maule [1] è costì lo saluti e gli dica che ho veduto, ammirato, e invidiato la sua graziosa e deliziosa casa.

Mille volte e di cuore
Suo vero Serv^e. ed Amo.

2

BRIT. MUSEUM. *Wednesday* [1851 ?]

MY VERY DEAR RUTHERFURD

I got here yesterday after the pleasantest tour I have ever made not excepting that from Glenquoich to Mrs. Mikie's (is that right ?). I got yours at Milan. Answer this to say that you as well as Mrs. Rutherfurd, and also Amos & John—besides Duke & Prince—are very well & you cannot write any thing that will give me greater pleasure. Lauriston I suppose beautiful & cold without, as well as beautiful & warm within. I shall answer a letter of Mr. Maitland in two or three days. I cannot now : & please tell him so if you see him. Where is the Lord of Glenquoich ? I mean Edward I. [2] I wish to write to him—Nothing new here : I have seen nobody. Lord Spencer is very dangerously ill.

Ever *Ever*
Yours truly

[1] Later 11th Earl of Dalhousie.   [2] Edward Ellice, senior.

APPENDIX III.E 279

3.[1] *To the Editor of the " North British Review "*

BRITISH MUSEUM. *Saturday* [1844]

MY DEAR SIR

I direct to Edinburgh as I suppose you either are or will soon be back there. I am glad we agree about the Jesuits. The post office article will be longer than I thought : there is a great deal important unsaid that we must say. The Jesuits shall follow : Both by the middle of Septr. shall be ready.

I got the *two* numbers of the Review only yesterday—or rather the day before & I thank you for them. I think it good as far as I have seen it yet ; but as you ask me I have some observations to make as to what is *not* in it. There is no article on any subject of immediate, striking, and *now* exciting interest. For inst. the Post Office is one of them, Algiers & French Ambition is another, the Jesuits is a third & that is why I chose them. Any article on Ireland, or Sugar & free trade, or the Slave trade, or the Oregon question, or Puseyism, &c. &c. &c. would be would be [*sic*] welcome to the general readers. Puseyism I know you have touched upon, but with the Dublin Review on the one hand, & Newman's publications on the other you might pay off these two inveterate enemies of yours most capitally. Then, altho' I know *your* difficulties about it as it is a *serious* review, you want light amusing articles ; anecdotes of shooting, fishing &c. of old highlanders & robbers (or gentlemen who took what they wanted), travels &c. I put down at random what I think may illustrate what I mean. The number is in fact *too good* for this age of light reading : we are impatient if we don't get on in reading as we do travelling—by steam. *Rutherfurd ought to give you a paper on Scotch education.*

Ever yours truly

Antonio Panizzi to Andrew Rutherfurd

4

UPLEATHAM [MARSKE BY THE SEA, YORKSHIRE.] *Wednesday mng.* [1852]

MY DEAR RUTHERFURD

I went to Richmond[2] the day before yesterday & saw the head master of the school there and his wife. I was so much pleased with him & with her and with every thing I saw & heard that I determined upon sending Louison[3] there. Yesterday Mr. Tate, who is the headmaster, came here and carried back to Richmond with him Louison who went off in better spirits than I expected. I confess I am weak enough to feel parting with him.

Nothing could be kinder than these excellent people here. They were pleased at my sending him to Richmond and if he behaves well they will be his friends for life, & he their pet.

They wish me to say all that is kind to you & how sorry they are about Mrs. Rutherfurd's health. They will be in Scotland about the 20th of Sept. & Lord Z [etland] wishes me to say that they hope to see you there as well as here whenever it is convenient to you. I start in

[1] Quoted by Fagan, I., p. 319, with some inaccuracies and incompletely. He addresses it in error to the Editor of the *Edinburgh Review.*
[2] Yorkshire.   [3] Raffaele Settembrini.

a couple of hours for London where I hope to be at half past nine this evening.

With kind remembrances to Mrs. Rutherfurd believe me
My dear friend
Ever thine

5

BRITISH MUSEUM. *Dec. 21st* [1852]

MY VERY DEAR RUTHERFURD

I dined at Ellice's last evening & he showed me a letter of yours which has determined me on writing to you. I have long thought of doing so, but as I had something very unpleasant to write I put it off. The fact is that young Louison has behaved so ill at Richmond—and I found on my return from Scotland that he had behaved as ill here—that nothing remained for me to do but to send him to Italy—not to Naples however—to see what can be done for him there. I will tell you more about it when we meet. I will also explain to Wm. Murray when I see him that the money is to be applied for Louison in Italy, but should he behave so ill as to be unworthy of farther care, I shall return the balance to each contributor in proportion. I have sent him to Genoa ; friends of mine & of his father will take the care of him which I took here. I have suggested that he should be placed in a military or naval school. I shall let you know what has been done when I know more myself. . . .

[Rutherfurd Papers in the keeping of the Faculty of Advocates, Edinburgh, See p. 147, footnote 3.]

APPENDIX IV.A

SIR,

I receive with the greatest pleasure the news, you communicate, of my having been chosen Professor of the Italian Language & Literature at King's College.

I must request you will do me the favour to express my gratitude to the Electors, to whom I am indebted for having thought me worthy of an honour, the duties dependant on which I shall always endeavour most zealously to fulfil.

> I remain, Sir,
> Your most obed. serv.
> (Signed) GABRIEL ROSSETTI.

38, Charlotte Street, Portland Place. 9 *June* 1831.

H. Smith, Secy.

KING'S COLLEGE LONDON. 7, *April* 1843.

GABRIEL ROSSETTI ESQRE.

Having submitted your application that the Council will dispense with your attendance at the College during the ensuing term, I am directed to acquaint you that the Council accede to your request, and desire at the same time to express their very sincere regret at the cause which has compelled you to make the application. With this feeling permit me to conjoin my own cordial sympathy and believe me to be &c. . . .

To the

Revd. Jelf.

REVD. SIR,

God has seen fitting to afflict me with a terrible calamity and I resign myself to His supreme will. After repeated vain attempts under the first oculists to procure a restoration of my nearly lost sight, I am compelled to acquiesce in the conviction that I have no longer the power to be of active service as Professor of Italian Literature in King's College. I must therefore request the Council to accept my resignation in order that the College may not suffer detriment from the want of an effective Italian Professor. Having had the honour of being chosen as Professor at King's College at the time of its foundation, I trust that I have given satisfaction by my conduct and zealous endeavours to promote the advancement of my pupils in the knowledge of my native tongue. I

281

have ever considered it a high honour to be connected with so noble an institution, and shall with pride entitle myself to the day of my death late Professor of King's College.

With a sincere desire that my successor, if not more zealous, may be still more adequate to the advancement of his pupils, and requesting you to have the goodness to lay before the Council this communication, with my thanks for a long period of courteous consideration, and for the kind indulgence of the last four years ; with most sincere wishes for the continued prosperity of King's College, I remain

Revd. Sir,
Your obedient Servant,
(Signed) GABRIEL ROSSETTI.

April 28th, 1847
50, Charlotte Street, Portland Place.

P.S.—If the Council of King's College would wish to hear my conscientious opinion concerning an Italian worthy to succeed me in this Institution, I will give it, and am sure that my wishes for the well being of the College will guide me to a right decision.

(Signed) GABRIEL ROSSETTI.

KING'S COLLEGE, STRAND. *May* 15th, 1847.

G. Rossetti Esq.,
    Charlotte Street,
    Portland Place.
DEAR SIR,

I have laid before the Council your letter of the 28th ult. resigning your appointment as Professor of Italian Literature within this College.

I am desired to communicate to you the satisfaction which your services in the College have afforded to the Council, and their regret at the necessary discontinuance of those services. This regret is aggravated by their knowledge of the calamity which has fallen upon you.

I remain, Dear Sir,
Yours very truly,
(Signed) J. W. CUNNINGHAM,
Secretary.

[From the original letters in the possession of King's College, London.]

APPENDIX IV.B

LETTER FROM GABRIELE ROSSETTI TO F. LEIGH

[*Dated by recipient :* 13 July 1835. Signor Rossetti, London.]
MON CHER MONSIEUR
Je suis bien charmé d'entendre que j'aurai le plaisir de vous revoir.
Je serai chez moi demain (Mardi, 14 de Juillet) pour vous recevoir à
dix heure [*sic*] et *demi* [*sic*] (half past ten) ; et je passerai une heure et
un quart avec vous.   Son sicuro che da che non si siamo veduti avete
fatto un tal progresso grammaticale da lasciarvi indietro le spine per
procedere tra i fiori della letteratura, nella quale vi sarò fedel guida.
E salutandovi me ripeto
Divotiss. servo
38 Charlotte Str., Portland Place.
il 13 *di Luglio del* 1835.
Address : F. Leigh, Esqre., T. P. Platt's Esqre., Child's Hill, Hampstead.
[Correspondence of the Family of Leigh, 1651–1837. B.M., Add.
MSS. 36663.]

APPENDIX IV.C

The Honble, the Council of King's College.

MY LORDS & GENTLEMEN,
   I humbly take the liberty of proposing myself as a Candidate for the now vacant Professorship of Italian Language and Literature at King's College. I am encouraged to make this application from the great experience which I have had, during the last ten years, in teaching my native language, and by the knowledge I flatter myself to have acquired of the English tongue.
   Should I be honoured by your election, I would unremittingly devote my energies to merit your approbation.
   In support of my application I beg most respectfully to forward the annexed testimonials.

I have the honour to be
My Lords and Gentlemen
Your most Obednt, humble servnt.
(Signed) VALERIO PISTRUCCI.

1. Jeffreys Street, Kentish Town. *May 29th*, 1847.

1, JEFFREYS STREET, KENTISH TOWN.

SIR,
   In reply to your polite request I beg to state that my birth-place being Rome, I was in my earlier years brought up as a member of the roman Catholic religion, but that at a later period, when able to reflect on such important matters, I have adhered to the creed of the reformed Church as more consonant with reason and just. The consequence I unhessitatingly declare that I belong *de facto* to the Church of England.
   To make more manifest the truth of my assertion, I take the liberty to inform you that my wife is english and that my children were cristened, and are brought up as members of the Church of England.

I remain, Sir,
Your obednt. servnt.
(Signed) V. PISTRUCCI.

June 12th, 1847.

J. W. Cunningham Esqre.

APPENDIX IV.D

LETTER FROM COUNT CARLO PEPOLI TO JANE WELSH CARLYLE

CARA SIGNORA JANE, e Scuolara *Modello*—
Permettetemi di mandarvi il primo Articolo inglese che (*dopo molte correzioni magistrali*) ho stampato.
Malgrado ch' io non sto bene interamente, cerco tutto *il dì* e *la notte* di avere occupazioni *che mi mancano assolutamente*. In mezzo dunque de' miei studj, mi sono rinfrescata la memoria delle cose studiate nel tempo passato sulle Belle Arti tutte ; ed ora mi troverei abile ad avere preparati alcuni materiali per simili Articoli. Si voi poteste procurarmi (*anche a soggetto obbligato*) il modo di farmi scrivere alcun' articolo in qualche *Periodical*—io vi sarei ben Molto, Molto, riconoscente, perchè ho BISOGNO di *utilizzare* assai il mio tempo !—
Ho per esempio, tutti li materiali in ordine per fare un quadro sullo stato attuale della *Pittura* in *Italia* ; *sullo Stato attuale della Musica*, etc : etc :
So che il primo articolo che vi mando è piccola cosa ; ma la mia Scuolara antica, ma la buona Mrs. Carlyle, lo guarderà con occhi benevoli.
Fui a Windsor ; domani vi anderò ancora ma Lunedì tornerò in Città, ed avrò presto il piacere di visitarvi.
Credo che il Sig. Tommaso sarà tornato—Presentate gli i miei complimenti ; e ricevete quelli del grato vostro amico
Sabato. 65 Quadrant.

[Leigh Hunt Correspondence, Vol. II., 1825-41. B.M., Add. MSS 38109, fol. 149.]

KING'S COLLEGE, STRAND.   *June 30th,* 1847.

Sig. Pistrucci, 1, Jeffreys Street, Camden Town.

DEAR SIR,

I have much pleasure in informing you that at a Meeting of the Council held this day, you were elected to the office of Professor of Italian Literature at this College.

I remain, Dear Sir,
Yours very faithfully,
(Signed) J. W. CUNNINGHAM
Secretary.

1. JEFFREYS STREET, KENTISH TOWN, *July 2nd,* 1847.

DEAR SIR,

I beg to acknowledge the receipt of your kind communication, informing me that the Honble. Council have elected me to the office of Professor of Italian Literature at King's College. With feelings of sincere gratitude I accept the honour thus conferred upon me, and trust I shall fulfil my duties to their satisfaction.

I remain, Dear Sir,
Yours very faithfully,
(Signed) V. PISTRUCCI.

J. W. Cunningham Esq.

[From the original letters in the possession of King's College, London.]

APPENDIX IV.E

To the Secretary of the University College London.
(Received my testimonials Co. Pepoli.)

28 *March* 1838.

SIR

May I request you to present the inclosed testimonials to the Council of the University College London, and announce me as a Candidate for the vacant Professorship of Italien [*sic*] Literature. Will you farther allow me to state that as my chief friends lie in other countries, and as the enterprise of starting for this honour was but very lately suggested to me, my claims to it cannot yet for some time be fully laid before the Council. I have written to Mr. Sismondi in Geneva ; to the University of Bologna, to Dr. Oridi my late collegue [*sic*] there now Professor in Corfu ; and to several other friends. Their answers with various new documents I hope to have the honour of presenting in a more legible shape before the day of election.

Such of my writings as happen to be in my possession, and certain printed pieces by others in which mention is made of me, are sent herewith.

I have the honour to be

Sir

Your most obed^t

Cte CARLO PEPOLI Ph.D^r.

London, 1th [*sic*] *February* ; 1838.

(65 Quadrant.)

late) Dottore Collegiato (*Member of the Senate*) nella facoltà filologica della Università di Bologna : Vice-Presidente dell' Accademia Letteraria Felsinea in Bologna.

actual) Membro effettivo dell' Accademia di Belle Arti in Bologna.

Socio delle Accademie Latina, e Tiberina in Roma, delle Accademie di Pisa, Livorno &c &c &c.

(*No address.*)

(*Postmark :* M^r 22. 1838)

(7 *April* 1838. Announced to Council)

In answer to your communication of the 19th Instant, I beg you to lay before the Council my grateful acknowledgments for the distinction they have conferred upon me, together with my earnest wishes of doing every thing in my power for the attainment of their object.

I regret that in consequence of a short absence from town, I have not been able to come to the college to learn the duties of my office, but I will do so immediately

I am, Sir,

Your very obe^t Servt

CARLO PEPOLI.

65 Quadrant, 21 *March.* 1838.

Address : Chas. C. Atkinson, Esq. &c &c &c

University College Gower St., London.

INDIA HOUSE. 13*th Feby.* 1838

MY DEAR SIR

I do not know whether the appointment to the professorships of languages at the University College is referred by the Council to the consideration of the Professors, but if it is I hope you will excuse my saying a word to you in favour of a candidate for the Italian Professorship, Count Pepoli, a member of the Provisional Government of Bologna. I know nothing of him personally, but I can vouch for his high literary reputation & acquirements on the authority of one of the most competent witnesses living, though not a very producible one perhaps, Mazzini, the celebrated President of La Jeune Italie who appears to me one of the most accomplished & every way superior men among all the foreigners I have known, & profoundly versed in his country's literature. As you probably have not Mazzini's testimony before you, I have thought it but right to tell you what I have learned from him. I should consider his testimony sufficient by itself to warrant any such appointment.

Ever yours truly

J. S. MILL.

(No address.)

[From the original letters in the possession of University College, London.]

APPENDIX IV.F

VIA SARAGOZZA 149. PALAZZO PEPOLI.

GENTILISSIMO CAV^e

Vi ringrazio ben mólto per la vostra lettera che mi reca sì buone novelle pubbliche, ed al tempo medesimo mi assicura ch' Elisabetta va ricuperando la sanità. Ve ne ripeto li più ringraziamenti!—Qui si diverte la gente in questi giorni carnevaleschi in modo straordinario tra la neve altissima caduta e crescente sotto un cielo cupo, mentre a stento sui carri vengono a centinaia li cannoni, li mortari, le palle e le bombe e le munizioni di ogni guisa per fortificare la città seguendo li piani del generale Menabrea, del g^{le} Cavalli e di Fanti nostro.

Il momento delle elezioni è grave di per sè stesso : ma lo rendono gravissimo poi tutte le voci che ad arte si fanno spargere dal partito clericale, e dai pochi ma noiosi repubblicani. Nondimanco le cose camminano con calma operosa, nè l' ansietà dell' incertezza impedisce, *ripeto*, alle genti di godere le divertimenti vedendosi *anche di notte*, molte maschere correre le vie cantando, o seguendo la banda Musicale, o andando agli affollati teatri, od alle Feste di ballo. Ma poi con molta energica guisa corre parimente la gente alle diverse elezioni, sia nella Città, come ne' castelli, e nelle campagne.

Ieri l' altro volli andare io medesimo alle Elezioni Comunali e Provinciali a Crevalsore—Provincia di Ferrara.

Io credeva che que' campagnoli sarebbero stati *o indifferenti* o forse avversi, perchè intimoriti dal clero . . . Ma che ?—

Partito io alle 5 del mattino, giunsi alle 9 e trovai il paese come a festa, come ad una fiera . . . tutto in moto. Appena giunto sulla piazza fui circondato dalla folla che di tutte, ma tutte le cose mi chiese : la folla m' accompagnò su alla sala del Palazzo Comunale dove trovai altra folla, e sempre delle nuove politiche bramosissima. La votazione fu numerosa, savia, e senza la minima cosa non conveniente. Io rimasi a fare la mia votazione ed a vedere compiuta quella di tutti : noi attorniati sempre da tanti *antichi* amici delle campagne dove nei tempi floridi io avea molti beni rurali, fui condotto ad un Palezzetto che già fu mio, e dove il presente Padrone volle ospitarmi con somma ospitalità cordialissimamente, acciò ch' io ricevetti le visite innumerevoli de' paesani, che volevano discutere sulle contingenze politiche nostre, e *tutti tutti tutti* aspettando bramosamente l' *annessione* delle Provincie a formare un Regno Italico forte. V' erano giovani, vecchi d' ogni classe, ed alcuni ricchi molto.

Poi rammentai il nome e la faccia di un vecchio, il quale discuteva di cose politiche prima e dopo della sua votazione. . . . E chi era? Il SACRISTANO che da 45 anni ha questo ufficio. E bene ; quando veggonsi li villani, e li chierici e li sacristani discutere *con senno* e fare le votazioni venendo da 10 miglia lontani a tal fine nel cuore d' un severo inverno, bisogna dire veramente che la rivoluzione intellettuale *è un fatto compiuto* : e così essendo, non si ponno più aver dubbi sulle conseguenze ! Io lavora = *totis viribus* = e forse " *ultra vires* " : il Senatore ed il Municipio ed il Comune e l' Università mi danno incombenze ch' io cerco di compiere alla meglio che so per corrispondere alla fiducia in me posta e per giungere a vedere il paese ov' ebbi cura in quello stato d' Indipendenza ; cosa che fu il sospiro della mia gioventù nelle prospere e nelle avverse fortune, e lo sarà sino allo estremo della mia vita. Se vedrò tal beatitudine io vecchio, ma lieto, canterò col vecchio Simeone " *Nunc dimitte, Domine, servum tuum* " e morrò felice.

Li giovani hanno forza . . . noi vecchi abbiamo costanza. Gli amici ad uno ad uno vi salutano caramente. E voi fate il simile favore per me col nostro Panizzi " muss regular ", con " el Señor Settembrini, e De Viniensi ed Avesani . . . in somma con " *todos los amigos* ". Il Cardinale Viale = *per la prma volta* = si trovò ad una funzione sacra [per la restituzione di una Madonna già rubata] col Senatore d il Mu icipio in formalità. Ed il Cardinale fu cortese molto. Ciò piacque moltissimo al popolo che vide " *los excomunicados* " trattati con rispetto . . . da un Viale !—Addio. Scrivete.

L'Amico

[Layard Papers. B.M., Add. MSS. 39068, fol. 76.]

APPENDIX IV.G

To Antonio Panizzi from Antonio Gallenga

TURIN *November* 8 1856.

MY DEAR PANIZZI

I find myself all at once under a cloud in this country, and I expect the same cloud will cast its shade as far as England.

Mazzini has published a letter charging me with the *intention* of killing Charles Albert in 1833. The newspapers have rather clumsily taken up the matter and so represented it as if I had actually *killed* the present King, or at least Charles Albert in 1848. The uproar against the *regicide* has been so very high that I have thrown up my seat in the Chamber and my cross of St. Maurice. I have found no friend or defender here.

I hear now that Count Carlo Arrivabene, who is at the bottom of all the intrigue, is trying to stir up the Senate and Council of University College to oust me as a *Regicide*. Masson, Newman & other *friends of Italy*, are strongly in favour of some measure highly injurious to my character : Arrivabene has received very great and signal favours from me, therefore is implacable.

I wish you would see Mr. Atkinson. Tell him if the College wish to appoint a New Professor, I shall gladly resign : but they must neither expel nor pointedly ask me to resign : for in that case I should fight my battle with them *à outrance*.

Last August I received an intimation from the Secretary, asking me whether I intended to resume my duties at the College. I saw Atkinson, and told him I *would* provided there were a class of four according to the rules and regulations of the college ; but that if the class was less than four, *I would not attend*, and only allow my substitute Arrivabene to take my place as usual. Atkinson answered *the matter might be left as it was for this season.* Understand I care not a straw for the Professorship, but I would not wish to give it up in a manner reflecting disgrace upon Me, and I should be sorry to see it fall into the hands of Arrivabene who is another Angeli in learning, and has proved a viper to me in character.

Write to A. Gallenga, *Castellamonte*, and believe me,

My dear Panizzi

Yours truly

[Panizzi Correspondence, Vol. V. B.M., Add. MSS. 36718, fol. 468.]

THE ATHENAEUM PALL MALL, 1. W. 11 *Aprile*, 1857.

CARO PANIZZI

Vi sovverrà che al tempo di tutto quel gran fracasso nato dalle rivelazioni delle cose del 1833, io vi scrissi da Torino pregandovi di difendermi ad *University College* contro le insidie di Arrivabene.

Vi sovverrà anche che non solamente voi mi rispondeste che la cattedra non correva pericolo, ma che di più non credevate che Arrivabene avesse mai fatto mala opera contro di me.

Autore di quel sospetto, anzi di quell' accusa, contro Arrivabene era il Sig^r Weir, Redattore del *Daily News*, il quale ora riconosce di essere stato tratto in errore, e desidera discolpare ottimamente Arrivabene.

Certo che a voi farà piacere di riconoscere il torto che c' era fatto ad uno dei nostri ; io mi affretto di comunicarvi l' avvenuto e vi prego di credermi sempre

Vostro di cuore

[Panizzi Correspondence, Vol. V. B.M., Add. MSS. 36718, fol. 67.]

APPENDIX IV.H

Monday noon.

My dear Sir

Indisposition prevents me to have the pleasure of coming to you on Saturday last and perhaps lost the chance of meeting Lord Rosse.

Would it be agreable to you to give me few lines for him simply stating that I have been much interested on the same subject of reflecting telescopes and having great admiration for his talents—I wish very much to know him—Should it not be agreable to you to give me a note will you have the kindness to send me his address ?—

I have been for the last three weeks in the hope of receiving a visit from you but knowing that your time is too valuable I do not expect such pleasure—

I have a speciment [*sic*] of casting which I wish to show to Lord Rosse.

Your obt.

Serv.

10 Pelham Crescent Brompton.

[Correspondence of Charles Babbage, Vol. XIX. B.M., Add. MSS. 37200, fol. 253.]

APPENDIX V

Statement of aims of the 'Associazione Nazionale' signed by the 'Depositari del Fondo'—Gius. Mazzini, G. Giglioli, 5 Albion Gn., Hyde Park. A. Gallenga, 21 Thurloe Square, Brompton. W. J. Linton [85 Hatton Gardens].

[Announcement of the state of affairs between Italy and Austria, of the necessity for the whole of Italy to unite in driving out Austria and of the need for funds.]

" 1° E istituto in Londra un Fondo Nazionale Italiano, destinato esclusivamente a soccorrere con tutti i mezzi materiali possibili all'impresa Nazionale Italiana, ogni qualvolta venga efficacemente iniziata sia dall' assalto straniero, sia dal sorgere spontaneo della Nazione, e inalienabile prima di quell' unico caso.

2° Il Fondo Nazionale Italiano si comporrà delle offerte pecuniarie degli Italiani, e degli stranieri bramosi di promovere la causa Nazionale Italiana.

L' ammontare delle offerte verrà di mano in mano messo in deposito presso uno o più banchieri noti e sicuri, il nome del quale o dei quali sarà comunicato ad ogni offerente.

3° Le offerte si ricevono in Londra dai sottoscritti e dal Segretario della Lega Internazionale dei Popoli (People's International League) W. J. Linton, 85 Hatton Garden : altrove, dai Collettori autorizzati. I collettori saranno muniti d' autorizzazione scritta di proprio pugno dal primo fra i tre sottoscritti [Mazzini] e firmata da tutti. Rilasceranno ricevuta immediata a ciascun' offerente ; e più dopo giunte le offerte in Londra, ricevuta legale dai tre sottoscritti. . . .

5° L' intera lista degli offerenti verrà pubblicata quando col trionfo della causa Nazionale ogni pericolo sarà svanito per essi.

Possano gl' Italiani intendere la chiamata dei loro fratelli e provare a tutti amici e nemici com' essi amino la loro patria a fatti e non soltanto a parole ! Noi ci accostiamo rapidamente a un momento supremo, decisivo, europeo : a un momento, in cui potremo, vincendo, risorgere a un tratto giganti, o dovremo, cadendo, subir la condanna di forse un'altro mezzo secolo di schiavitù e d' impotenza. E quel momento, noi non lo afferreremo pascendoci improvvidamente di cieche speranze, ma procedendo logicamente, severamente, ne' preparativi com' uomini che hanno misurata anzi tempo tutta quanta la via da percorrersi e ne accettano deliberatamente le necessità. Un partito Nazionale non può dirsi costituito, non esiste attivo, vigoroso, potente, se non rappresentato da

una cifra positiva d' elementi materiali che ne esprima a un tempo la
forza e l' animo deliberato, capace di sagrificio. . . . Noi dobbiamo
conquistarci vita, patria, nome, bandiera, unità, libertà, prosperità,
potenza ed onore ; e saremmo da meno ? "
    Londra.   1º *Agosto*, 1847.

[Panizzi Correspondence, Vol. II., 1837–48.   B.M., Add. MSS. 36715.]

APPENDIX VI

THE MOTHER OF FLORIANA FOSCOLO

THE question of the identity of Floriana's mother is a perplexing one. Chiarini concludes after a careful examination of two drafts of letters, one to ' Fanny ' and the other to ' Sofia ', Foscolo's loves during the period of his service in northern France, that the former was the English girl and the latter the French.[1] Montazio, without quoting any authority, calls her ' Sofia Emerytt '.[2] The Editors of the *Epistolario* suppose ' Emerytt ' to be the mother's family name from Floriana's, and even Foscolo's use of it after the sale of the Totteridge house.[3] Pickering and George Robinson in letters to Foscolo, refer to ' Miss Hamilton '.[4] The latter are the earliest references that we possess, and the name ' Hamilton ' suggested a line of investigation which has at least the merit of throwing light on certain interesting personalities of the time. Towards the end of the eighteenth century there lived in Lille a family of the name of Hamilton, whose history has not been difficult to trace. Lady Mary Leslie, daughter of the 6th Earl of Leven and Melville, married in 1762 Dr. James Walker of Inverdovat.[5] They had at least five children, three sons [6] and two daughters. The *Scots Peerage* by Paul, Volume 6, 1909, page 115, only mentions one daughter, but in the Archives Communales de Lille there is recorded under the date May 29th, 1793, the marriage of Joseph Jouy to Isabelle Henriette Walker " 22 ans, native de Londres, à Lille depuis huit ans, demeurant chez son beau-père rue Nationale, fille de feu James, natif de Iverdivil [*sic*], province Fife en Ecosse, décédé en Amérique et de Marie Leslie, native d' Edimbourg en Ecosse, 51 ans, mariée en 2es noces à Georges Robinson Hamilton, 39 ans, natif de Success, province de St. James, île Jamaïque " [7] and the birth of a son on the 4 *ventose an v* [Feb. 22nd. 1797] to Paul Thiébault and Betty Mackercher Walcker [*sic*]. The Walkers must thus have taken up residence in Lille about 1785. In the Records Office in London there is the last will and testament of George Robinson Hamilton, dated ' the twentieth day of November in the year of our Lord one thousand seven hundred and eighty-six ', of which we have a photostat. The said George Robinson Hamilton ' of

[1] Chiarini, *Gli Amori*, II., p. 132. [2] *ibid.*, p. 132.
[3] *Epist.*, III., p. 270. [4] See above, p. 41.
[5] Register of Proclamations and Marriages for the Parish of Edinburgh, New Register House, Edinburgh.
[6] Fraser, *The Melvilles*, I., p. 336.
[7] Excerpts from the registers of the Archives Communales de Lille for which we are indebted to the Archiviste du Nord.

the parish of Saint James in the County of Cornwall and Island of Jamaica, now residing at the village of Los near the City of Lisle in French Flanders ' provides for the payment of all just debts and funeral expenses first and thereafter, to quote the terms of the will, ' do hereby Give Devise and Bequeath all my Estate Real and Personal whatsoever and wheresoever unto the Right Honourable Mary Walker, commonly called Lady Mary Walker at present residing at the above named village of Los, to hold the same and every part thereof to her own sole and seperate [sic] use during her natural life with full Liberty to bequeath at her death ten thousand pounds Sterling Money of Great Britain to any person or persons she shall think proper. But it is my express will and desire and it is the true meaning of this my last Will and Testament that the Estates so bequeathed by me to Lady Mary Walker should remain, continue and be in the hands of and in trust to the Right Honourable James the Earl of Hopetown of Hopetown House near Edinburgh, the Right Honourable Alexander Leslie commonly called Lord Balgonie (her nephews) and the Honourable General Alexander Leslie of Edingburgh (her Bro^r.) . . . for the sole benefit use and behoof of the said Lady Mary Walker and without any claim or demand by James Walker her husband to any part or parcel thereof '. Lady Mary Walker was appointed executrix of the will, but ' in the case of any interference, molestation or interruption from the said James Walker ' the abovenamed trustees were to be the executors. The date of the will is significant—less than one year from the arrival of the Walkers in Lille. The family would appear still to be resident in Edinburgh in 1783 from a reference in a letter dated ' Edinburgh, 17th. May 1783 ', from David, Earl of Leven and Melville, to his son.[1] In a letter to her nephew, Alexander, Earl of Leven and Melville, dated ' London 14th. September, 1818 ',[2] Lady Mary Walker (or Hamilton) says, after speaking of her literary works, ' Having been unhappy in marriage, instead of dissipation I had recourse to literature for my consolation, but I never presumed on the idea of becoming an author ! Notoriety to women is destructive, at least collectively, and generally speaking ; but with a family of young children left on my hands, abandoned by their father, I was necessitated to hazard the effronterie of publication to cloath [sic], feed and educate them ! ' One of the young children, the eldest, James, Lieutenant in H.M. Navy, seems, when he was not yet eighteen years of age, to have taken unto himself a wife who divorced him eleven years later. It transpired in the course of the process that the wife was in receipt of an annuity of £40 a year from James Walker's mother, Lady Mary Walker. Except in legal documents Lady Mary signed her name Hamilton after her liaison with George Robinson Hamilton and she was known as his wife, although there seems no evidence of their marriage. The record of Hamilton's death is in the Archives de Lille in the following words : ' 8 brumaire an VI [Oct. 29th, 1797]—Décès de George Robinson Hamilton, natif de la Jamaïque, 44 ans, rentier, veuf de Henriette [illeg.], native de Londres et y décédée, époux de Marie Lesley Waker [sic], native d' Ecosse, 56 ans.' The will was proved on November 21st, 1797, ' by the Oath of the Right Honble Ladye Mary Walker (wife of James Walker) the sole Exrix.' [3] In the

---

[1] Fraser, *The Melvilles*, II., p. 282.　　　　[2] *ibid.*, p. 328.
[3] Principal Registry of the Probate Divorce and Admiralty Division of the High Court of Justice.

notice de l'éditeur which introduced Lady Hamilton's *Famille de Popoli*,
Charles Nodier who had translated and in fact re-written the novel in
part, gave some biographical details of the authoress among which he
said ' elle a marié deux de ses filles avec des Français '.[1] ' Deux de ses
filles ' suggests that there was at least a third.

The identity of this third daughter is interesting. In her letter to
her nephew, quoted above, Lady Mary Walker or Hamilton speaks of
' my daughter, Mrs. Alderson (now a widow, who resides with me) '.
The *Gentleman's Magazine* of 1821 [2] announces the death at Exeter on
February 28th of the Right Hon. Lady Mary Hamilton, great-aunt to
the Earl of Leven and Melville, at the age of eighty-two. Careful
search in the Records produced her last will and testament, and we
quote it in full from the photostat in our possession. " This is the
Last Will and Testament of me The Right Honourable Lady Mary
Walker late of Woburn place in the parish of Saint Pancrass but now
of Brompton in the County of Middlesex, Widow commonly called
Lady Mary Hamilton, whereas I am possessed of a bond from George
Robinson Hamilton, Esquire, deceased, bearing date on or about the
first day of May in the year of our Lord one thousand seven hundred
and eighty-five by which he became bound to me in the penal sum of
twelve thousand pounds conditioned for payment by him, his Executors
or Administrators unto me my Executors, Administrators or assigns of
the sum of six thousand pounds with lawful interest for the same in
twelve calendar months after the same should be demanded and whereas
the said George Robinson Hamilton by his last Will and Testament in
writing bearing date on or about the twentieth day of November one
thousand seven hundred and eighty six and thereby after subjecting his
Estate real and personal unto the payment of his debts gave and devised
the same unto me for my own separate use during my natural life with
full power to bequeath at my death the sum of ten thousand pounds
sterling to any person or persons I should think proper and that during
my life the interest rents issues and profits of the said bequest from and
after his decease should be regularly paid to me for my private use by
the Trustees therein named named [*sic*] and be declared that it was his
Will and desire that after my death his estates real and personal except
the said sum of ten thousand pounds should descend to his heirs at law
and their heirs for ever and he thereby nominated me Executrix of his
said Will and other persons therein named Executors thereof now I do
hereby in pursuance and in execution of the power and authority given
to me in and by the said last Will and Testament of the said George
Robinson Hamilton and of all other powers and authorities, me hereunto enabling do bequeath the said sum of ten thousand pounds and
do give and bequeath all other my estate and effects both real and personal to the persons and in the manner following that is to say in the
first place I direct that all my just debts and funeral expenses be in the
first place paid and in the next place I give and bequeath out of the
said sum of ten thousand pounds and my other Estate and effects unto
my daughter Sophia Saint John Hamilton Alderson the widow of
Doctor Alderson the sum of five thousand pounds sterling and after
the payment thereof I give and bequeath unto my Son Lieutenant

[1] P. L. Jacob, *Charles Nodier chez Lady Hamilton*, Bibliophile Français,
1869, p. 277.

[2] p. 283.

Colonel Leslie Walker the sum of three thousand pounds sterling but the payment thereof is to be postponed until the said sum of five thousand pounds is fully satisfied and I give devise and bequeath all the residue and remainder of my estate and effects both real and personal unto my said daughter Sophia Saint John Hamilton Alderson her heirs Executors Administrators and assigns to and for her own use and benefit and I appoint my said daughter Executrix and William Peatt Litt of Berkeley Square in the county of Middlesex Esquire Executor of this my Will and I revoke all former Wills by me at any time heretofore made. In witness whereof I have hereunto set my hand the nineteenth day of April in the year of our Lord one thousand eight hundred and nineteen *M. Walker Hamilton.* Signed and published by the said Lady Mary Walker otherwise Hamilton in the presence of us who in her presence have hereunto subscribed our names as Witnesses. *Henry Rivington Fenchurch Buildings London. Ann Duval Servant to Lady Mary Hamilton.*" [1] Two facts emerge clearly from this will. Lady Mary Walker who was not the wife of George Robinson Hamilton, as is clear from the proving of his will by ' Ladye Mary Walker (wife of James Walker) ', although she had assumed his name, had a daughter Sophia Saint John Hamilton, possibly his child, and she had the right which she endeavoured to exercise, to bequeath ten thousand pounds of the fortune left by him ' to any person or persons she shall think proper ' as he stated in his will. It would seem that Hamilton about the year 1786 felt the necessity of making some provision for Lady Mary Walker and through her for someone else. For whom else but a child of whom he was the father ? It is true that Lady Mary Walker was then at least forty-five years of age, some twelve years older than he, but the supposition is not impossible. Unfortunately Hamilton's fortune seems to have been much less than he anticipated, for the modest sum of £2,000 is noted in the Principal Registry of the Probate Division of the High Court of Justice against the record of the proving of the will. From her own letters we know that Lady Mary at the age of seventy-five undertook a journey to Jamaica to look into her affairs, as the annual income paid to her by her trustees was only four hundred pounds instead of the three thousand that the estate had produced.[2]

Some time certainly elapsed between the date of Lady Mary's death and the proving of her will ; perhaps there were difficulties connected with her estate. Whatever the cause of the delay we hear none of it. At the end of her will appear merely the words, " Proved at London 5th July 1822 before the Worshipful Samuel Rush Meyriot Doctor of Laws and Surrogate by the Oaths of Sophia Saint John Hamilton Alderson one of the Executors to whom Admon. was granted having been first sworn duly to Admr. power reserved to William Peatt Litt Esquire the other Executor." The report of this in the Principal Registry of the Probate Division of the High Court of Justice notes that the estate was under £6,000.

If Sophia Hamilton was born about the year 1785-6, she would be about nineteen or twenty years of age during Foscolo's sojourn in Valenciennes. We have no evidence of the Hamiltons' living in Valenciennes but also none to the contrary. Hamilton was dead, Lady Mary's residence in Amiens is first mentioned with reference to the year 1809,

---

[1] From the photostat made from the original document.
[2] *The Melvilles*, II., p. 310.

and Valenciennes is at no great distance from Lille. If Sophia Hamilton was the mother of Floriana, there is every possibility that Foscolo after his arrival in England had some contact with her or her mother who in 1815 was living at No. 11 Lower Kennington Green, Staines,[1] and arranged to assume responsibility for his daughter who should be provided for, if indirectly, in her grandmother's will. What one finds difficult to understand is that the mother, if she was alive in 1827, left the poor child to the chance if kindly help of strangers.

Lady Mary's will was proved in the year 1822 before the Worshipful Samuel Rush Meyriot. The name is unusual. In 1825 when Foscolo took up residence in Totteridge he assumed the name of *Marriatt* which passed through at least the form *Merriatt* before it became Emerytt, a name which was taken without further investigation by some writers to be the name of Floriana's mother. " Mi pare d'aver dimostrato che, se il Foscolo non ebbe in Francia altri amori che quello della signorina inglese a Valanciennes e quello della signorina francese a Calais," says Chiarini, " la prima probabilmente è Fanny, e la seconda è Sofia. Ma il terreno degli amori foscoliani è così lubrico, che anche caminandovi su con le maggiori precauzioni, si può, quando uno se lo aspetta meno, sdrucciolare e trovarsi per terra. Io non giurerei quindi che non potesse un giorno o l'altro venir fuori qualche nuovo documento il quale buttasse in aria la mia dimostrazione." [2] We cannot claim to have found the document which would ' buttare in aria ' the theory of so eminent a Foscolo scholar as Chiarini, but there was a Sophia Hamilton in northern France about the end of the eighteenth century and possibly a few years later, whose home was hospitable, not to say romantic, as witness the benevolent reception accorded Sir Herbert Croft and later Charles Nodier and his young wife,[3] where literary interests predominated, and where, to judge from the husbands of the two eldest daughters, there reigned a certain freedom of manners and customs. This Sophia Hamilton, then a widow, inherited in the year 1822 from her mother who had died on February 28th of the previous year, the sum of £5,000 or possibly less. There seems therefore some justification for the theory that she, and not some unknown Fanny Emerytt, was the mother of Foscolo's child.

[1] *The Melvilles*, II., pp. 312 *et seq.*
[2] Chiarini, *Gli Amori*, II., p. 136.
[3] *D.N.B., Sir Herbert Croft* ; Michaud, *Nouvelle Biographie Générale*, with many inaccuracies ; P. L. Jacob, *Charles Nodier chez Lady Hamilton.*

DOCUMENTARY SOURCES AND WORKS CONSULTED

MANUSCRIPTS

ALIEN OFFICE RECORDS. Records Office. H.O.1. H.O.3. H.O.5.
BABBAGE, C. Correspondence. Vol. X., Oct. 1838–Dec. 1841. Vol.
XIX., Undated. British Museum. Add. MSS. 37191, 37200.
BROUGHTON CORRESPONDENCE. Vols. II., IV., XI. British Museum.
Add. MSS.
COPIALETTERE dal dì 24 ag. 1821. N. 14. 83 letters of F. Dal Pozzo.
MS. in MS. Room in Biblioteca Nazionale, Florence. (See *Dieci
Mesi di Carteggio di Ferdinando dal Pozzo*.)
HUNT, LEIGH. Correspondence. Vol. II, 1825–41, 1845–59. Vol. IV,
1851–9. British Museum. Add. MSS. 38109, 38111, 38524.
LAYARD PAPERS. Vol. CXXXVIII. Letter from Carlo Pepoli. British
Museum. Add. MSS. 39068.
LETTERE DA INGLESI AD UGO FOSCOLO, non tutte pubblicate. In the
Biblioteca Labronica, Leghorn.
LETTERS FROM GABRIELE ROSSETTI TO F. LEIGH, 1835–7. Correspondence
of the Family of Leigh, 1651–1837. British Museum. Add. MSS.
36663.
LETTERS FROM SANTORRE DI SANTA ROSA and other Refugees to Mrs.
Sarah Austin. (Including letters to Signor Prandi.)
Unpublished. From the MSS. in possession of the late Mrs.
Janet Ross, Florence. A few extracts published by Professor Guido
Ferrando in an article on " Un'amica inglese di Santorre di Santa
Rosa ", in the *Vita Britannica*, Florence, of Nov.–Dec. 1919,
Anno II, N. 6, and by Guido Biagi in " Una Dinastia di scrittrici
inglesi " in *La Lettura* of July 1, 1924, Anno XXIV, N. 7.
LETTERS FROM SANTORRE DI SANTA ROSA to the Enfield Family.
Unpublished. In the possession of H. H. Enfield, Esq., of
Bramcote, Nottingham.
LETTERS TO FRANCIS PLACE. Vol. I, 1813–52. British Museum. Add.
MSS. 37949.
MANOSCRITTI FOSCOLIANI, già proprietà Martelli, della Reale Biblioteca
Nazionale di Firenze.
PANIZZI, ANTONIO. Correspondence in the British Museum. Vols. I.,
II., III., IV., XII., XIII., XIV.
PANIZZI, ANTONIO. Correspondence in the possession of University
College, London. 932–43, 1177, 1179 (19), 1530–1, 2138, 2444,
2489, 2725, 2767, 2985, 3167, 3173, 3379, 4193. Also Box XXXI.

PEPOLI, CARLO.   Correspondence in the possession of University College, London.   4218, 4219, 4238, 4250, 4485, 4846.
PISTRUCCI, VALERIO.   Correspondence in the possession of King's College, London.
ROSSETTI, GABRIELE.   Correspondence in the possession of King's College, London.
RUTHERFURD CORRESPONDENCE, 90 Letters from Antonio Panizzi.   (In the care of the Faculty of Advocates, Scottish National Library.)

PUBLISHED WORKS

GENERAL

Centenary History of King's College, London, 1828–1928.   By F. J. C. Hearnshaw, London, 1929.
Early Life and Letters of Cavour, 1810–1848.   By A. J. White.   Oxford, 1925.
Garibaldi and the Thousand.   By G. M. Trevelyan.   London, 1909.
" Gli Italiani morti per la Grecia."   (Extract from *Il Nuovo Giornale.*) By Carlo Paladini.   Pub. Florence, Dec. (year not on extract).
History of Italian Unity.   2 vols.   By Bolton King.   London, 1912.
Life of Peter Stuart, the " Ditton Doctor ".   By Mr. L. Finigan for Mazzini Stuart, Esq.   1920 (for private circulation).
Making of Modern Italy, The.   By Arrigo Solmi, with an Introduction by Arundell del Re.   London, 1925.
Rebellen and *Guerra.*   Novels dealing with the revolutions in Tuscany, by Alfred Neumann.   Stuttgart, 1928–9.
Scenes from Italy's War, 1915–18.   By G. M. Trevelyan.   London, 1919.
Statutes of the United Kingdom.
Acts for the Registration of Aliens, and Naturalisation & Denization
  56 Geo. III. c. 86.
  1 Geo. IV. c. 18, c. 105.
  3 Geo. IV. c. 15, c. 97.
  5 Geo. IV. c. 37.
  7 Geo. IV. c. 54.
  6 & 7 Guliel. IV. c. 11.
  7 & 8 Vict. c. 66.
Theory and History of Historiography.   By Benedetto Croce ; trans. by Douglas Ainslie.   London.
Times, The.   1815–48.
University College, London, 1826–1926.   By H. Hale Bellot.   London, 1929.

UGO FOSCOLO

Adolphe.   By Benjamin Constant.
Baronage of Scotland, Vol. I.   Edinburgh, 1798.
Book of Memories of Great Men and Women of the Age, Wiffen, Lady Sydney Morgan, John Banim, Thomas Campbell, Samuel Rogers, Ugo Foscolo.   By S. C. Hall.   London, 1871.
Catalogo dei Manoscritti foscoliani, già proprietà Martelli, della Reale Biblioteca Nazionale di Firenze.   By Giuseppe Chiarini.   Rome, 1885.
Da Ponte, Memorie, a cura di G. Gambarin e F. Nicolini.   2 vols.   Bari, 1918.

Due Lettere inedite a Carolina Russell. Ed. by Giuseppe Chiarini. Bologna, 1888.

Epistolario. In 3 vols. *Opere edite e postume di Ugo Foscolo.* Ed. by F. S. Orlandini and E. Mayer (1852). Florence. New ed. 1923.

Fifty Years' Recollections, Literary and Personal. (3 vols.) Vol. II. By Cyrus Redding. London, 1858.

Giornale Storico della Letteratura Italiana.
1883. Vol. I.
1885. Vol. V.
1902. Vol. XXXIX. " Lettres inédites de Ugo Foscolo à Hudson Gurney "—p. 56. (R. Tobler.)

Gli amori di Ugo Foscolo nelle sue lettere : ricerche e studî. By Giuseppe Chiarini. Bologna, 1892. 2 vols.

Gurney, Hudson, in *Dictionary of National Biography.*

Life and Letters of William Bewick. (2 vols.) Vol. I., Chapter V., " Wordsworth and Foscolo." Ed. by Thomas Landseer, A.R.A. London, 1871.

Manuale della Letteratura Italiana. Vol. V. Articles on Foscolo, Perticari, Sanvitale, Rossetti, Berchet, Mamiani, Mazzini and Amari. By Alessandro d'Ancona and Orazio Bacci. Florence.

Melvilles, Earls of Melville and the Leslies, Earls of Leven. 3 vols. By Sir William Fraser, K.C.B. Edinburgh, 1890.

Mirror of Literature, Amusement, and Instruction, The. No. 276. Oct. 6, 1827. " Anecdotes of Ugo Foscolo, the Italian Poet," p. 229.

New Monthly Magazine and Literary Journal. Vol. V., 1822. Articles by Foscolo on " Guido Cavalcanti ", and G. on " A Sabbath in London ".

" On the Antiquarians and Critics of Italian History ", article by Ugo Foscolo. In *The Retrospective Review*, Vol. XIV., 1826, p. 136.

Publisher and His Friends, A. Memoir and Correspondence of the late John Murray. 2 vols. By Samuel Smiles. London, 1891.

Recollections of a Long Life. By Lord Broughton. 2 vols. London, 1909.

Recollections of Past Life. By Sir Henry Holland, Bart. London, 1872.

Roscoe, W., in *Dictionary of National Biography.*

Roscoe, William. *The Life of Lorenzo de' Medici*—(With a Memoir of the author from the biography by his son, Henry Roscoe.) 8th ed. revised by Thos. Roscoe. London, 1846.

Scots Peerage, ed. by Sir James Balfour Paul. Edinburgh, 1909.

Studî su Ugo Foscolo. Editi a cura della R. Università di Pavia nel primo centenario della morte del poeta. Turin, 1927.

Ugo Foscolo. 4 vols. By Camillo Antona-Traversi and Angelo Ottolini. Milan, 1928.

Ugo Foscolo in Inghilterra. By Francesco Viglione. Catania, 1910.

Vita di Ugo Foscolo. By Giuseppe Chiarini. Florence, 1910.

Westminster Review, Vol. VII., 1826-7. Article on " La Commedia di Dante Alighieri : Illustrata da Ugo Foscolo. Tom. I. Londra. Pickering. 1825." Page 153.

HOLLAND HOUSE

Creevy Papers. 2 vols. Ed. by Rt. Hon. Sir Herbert Maxwell. London, 1903.

DOCUMENTARY SOURCES AND WORKS CONSULTED

Holland House. 2 vols. By Princess Marie Liechtenstein. London, 1874.

Holland House Circle. By Lloyd Sanders. London, 1908.

Holland, Lord and Lady, in *Dictionary of National Biography.*

Journal of Elizabeth, Lady Holland. Ed. by the Earl of Ilchester. London, 1908.

Memoir of the Reverend Sydney Smith, by his daughter, Lady Holland. With a Selection from his Letters, edited by Mrs. Austin. 2 vols. London, 1855.

Relazioni letterarie fra Italia e Inghilterra. Lady Holland e i suoi ospiti italiani, pp. 317–420. By Carlo Segrè. Florence, 1911.

The Exiles of 1820–1

Anecdotes of the Spanish and Portuguese Revolutions. By Count Pecchio. Introduction by Edward Blaquiere. London, 1823.

Correspondence of Henry Crabb Robinson with the Wordsworth Circle (1808–1866). 2 vols. By Edith J. Morley. Oxford, 1927.

Dante Gabriel Rossetti, His Family Letters, with a Memoir. Vol. I. By William Michael Rossetti. London, 1895.

" Dante Gabriel Rossetti and his Godfather, Charles Lyell of Kinnordy." In *University of Edinburgh Journal,* Vol. IV., No. 2, 1931.

De la Révolution Piémontaise. [By S. di Santa Rosa.] Paris, 1822.

Delle Speranze degli Italiani. By Santorre di Santa Rosa. *Opera edita per la prima volta con prefazione e documenti inediti da Adolfo Colombo.* Milan, 1920.

Diario dell' Assedio di Navarino. Memorie di Giacinto Collegno precedute da un Ricordo Biografico dell' Autore scritta da Massimo D' Azeglio. Turin, 1857.

Dieci mesi di carteggio di Ferdinando dal Pozzo (24 agosto 1831—2 giugno 1832). Pub. (with omissions), by L. C. Bollea, Pavia, 1916. [Biblioteca della Società Storica Sub-alpina, diretta da Ferdinando Gabotto. XIX., ii., Testi, I.]

Gabriele Rossetti. A Versified Autobiography. Trans. and supplemented by William Michael Rossetti. London, 1901.

L'Anno Mille ottocento ventisei dell' Inghilterra colle osservazioni di Giuseppe Pecchio. Lugano, 1827.

La Révolution du Piémont. By M. de Beauchamp. Paris, 1821.

La Rivoluzione Piemontese del 1821. Studi e Documenti raccolti di Teofilo Rossi, e da Carlo Pio Demagiotris. Vol. I. Turin, 1927.

Le Mie Prigioni. By Silvio Pellico. Florence.

Memoirs of Count John Arrivabene, with Documents, Notes, and Six Original Letters of Silvio Pellico. Translated from the original with notes by C. Arrivabene. London, 1862.

Memoirs of General Pépé, written by himself. 3 vols. London, 1846.

Memorie e Lettere Inedite di Santorre Santa Rosa, con Appendice di Lettere di Gian Carlo Sismondi. Ed. by Nicomede Bianchi. Turin, 1877.

Memories of Lenton. By M.C.M. Letchworth, 1910 (for private circulation).

Nel Primo Centenario della Morte di Santorre di Santarosa. By Adolfo Colombo. Casale, 1925.

Osservazioni Semi-serie di un Esule sull' Inghilterra. By Giuseppe Pecchio. Lugano, 1831.

English Translation—*Semi-serious observations of an Italian Exile during his residence in England.* By Count Pecchio. London, 1833.
Relazione degli Avvenimenti della Grecia nella primavera del 1825. Prima edizione italiana tratta dal manoscritto originale. By Giuseppe Pecchio. Lugano, 1826.
First pub. in England under title, *A Picture of Greece in 1825 as exhibited in the narratives of James Emmerson, Esq., Count Pecchio and V. H. Humphreys, Esq.* London. 2 vols.
Rossetti Family, The. 1824–1854. By R. D. Waller. Manchester, 1932.
" Santa-Rosa." By Victor Cousin. *Revue des Deux Mondes.* Tome XXI., 4me Série, pp. 640 *et seq.* Paris, 1840.
Santorre di Santarosa verso l' esilio. By Adolfo Colombo. Lucca, 1920.
Three Generations of English Women. New, revised and enlarged edition. By Janet Ross. London, 1893.
" Una Dinastia di scrittrici inglesi." By Guido Biagi. *La Lettura.* 1 Luglio, 1924, Anno XXIV., N.7.
" Un' amica inglese di Santorre di Santa Rosa." By Guido Ferrando. *Vita Britannica* (review pub. by the British Institute), Florence. Anno II., N. 6. Nov.-Dec., 1919.

ANTONIO PANIZZI

Annual Register. 1827. Law Cases, &c. " The King *v.* Edward Gibbon Wakefield, William Wakefield, Edward Thevenot, and Frances Wakefield." London, 1828.
Antonio Panizzi, Scholar and Patriot. By Constance Brooks. Manchester, 1931.
Biographical Sketch of Sir Anthony Panizzi, K.C.B. By Robert Cowtan. London, 1873.
Catalogue of the Library of the Reform Club, with revised historical introduction. (Printed for the Members.) London, 1894. (2nd edition.)
Catalogue of Panizzi Pamphlets in the Reform Club, issued by the Library Committee. London, 1920.
Foreign Quarterly Review, Vol. XV. Article on Panizzi's *Bojardo, Ariosto,* etc., p. 48.
Lettere ad Antonio Panizzi di uomini illustri ed amici italiani. Ed. by Luigi Fagan. Florence, 1880.
Letters of Prosper Merimée to Panizzi. 2 vols. Ed. by Louis Fagan. London, 1881.
Life of Sir Anthony Panizzi, K.C.B., 2 vols. By Louis Fagan. London, 1880.
Life of William Ewart Gladstone, 3 vols. By John Morley. London, 1903.
Panizzi, Sir Anthony, in *Dictionary of National Biography.*
" Sir Anthony Panizzi." *Quarterly Review.* Vol. 151. 1881.

1831 AND AFTER

Autobiography of Mrs. Fletcher. Edinburgh, 1875.
Birth of Modern Italy. Posthumous Papers of Jessie White Mario, edited, with introduction, notes and epilogue by the Duke Litta-Visconti-Arese. London, 1909.

x

Castellamonte. An autobiographical sketch, illustrative of Italian life during the insurrection of 1831. 2 vols. Preface signed " Castellamonte " (A. Gallenga), 1852. London, 1854.

Cracovia, Carmi di Gabriele Rossetti, Nardini, Pepoli, Ricciardi, ecc. Lausanne, 1847.

Episodes of my Second Life. By A. Gallenga (L. Mariotti). 2 vols. London, 1884.

Epistolario di Giuseppe Mazzini. Per cura della Commissione Editrice degli Scritti di Giuseppe Mazzini. 2 vols. Florence, 1904.

Epistolario. Edizione Nazionale degli Scritti editi e inediti di Giuseppe Mazzini. Vol. VI. Ed. by Pro. Mario Menghini. Imola.

Giovine Italia, La. Anno I–II. Pistoia, 1892. (In 4°.)

Italian Characters in the Epoch of Unification. By the Countess E. Martinengo Cesaresco. London.

Jane Welsh Carlyle ; Letters to her Family, 1839–1863. Ed. by L. Huxley. London, 1924.

Land of Manfred. By Janet Ross. London, 1889.

" La Signora Carlyle e Mazzini." By P. R. [Piero Rèbora.] *I Libri del Giorno,* Luglio, 1924.

Lettere ad Aurelio Saffi e alla famiglia Crauford, 1850–72. By G. Mazzini. Pub. in the *Biblioteca Storica del Risorgimento Italiano,* Ser. IV., No. 7. Rome, Milan, 1905.

Letters and Memorials of Jane Welsh Carlyle. 3 vols. Prepared for publication by Thomas Carlyle. Edited by James Antony Froude. London, 1883.

Letters and Recollections of Mazzini. By Mrs. Hamilton King. London, 1912.

Life of Mazzini. By Bolton King. Everyman's Library. 1912.

Life of Robert Browning. By W. Hall Griffin and H. C. Minchin. London. (Undated.)

" Mazzini and his Scottish Friends." *The Merchant Maiden.* Vol. XV., No. 2. Edinburgh, 1923.

Mazzini's Letters to an English Family. 3 vols. Edited with an introduction by E. F. Richards. London, 1920.

Mazzini, the Story of a Great Italian. By Edith Hinkley. London, 1924.

Memories of Two Cities. " An Edinburgh Brotherhood." By David Masson. Edinburgh, 1911.

Memories of London in the Forties. By David Masson. Edinburgh, 1908.

New Letters and Memorials of Jane Welsh Carlyle, annotated by Thomas Carlyle and edited by Alexander Carlyle, with an introduction by Sir James Crichton-Browne. London, 1903.

North British Review. Vol. II. 1844. Article viii., on " Post Office Espionage " [by A. Panizzi].

Studî e ritratti letterarî. Tommaso e Giovanna Carlyle. 1889. By Giuseppe Chiarini. Leghorn, 1900.

Westminster Review. Sept.-Dec. 1844. Vol. XLII. Article on " Mazzini and the Ethics of Politicians ", dealing with the reports from the Secret Committee of the House of Lords upon the Detaining and Opening of Letters at the General Post Office, and from the Committee of Secrecy of the House of Commons on the same subject.

INDEX OF NAMES

Scalvini, Giovita. 75, 79, 80, 82, 103, 127, 215.
Scandiano, Count of (*see* Bojardo).
Schiller. 112, 183.
Schorno, Andrea. 50, 51, 109.
Schulze & Dean. 12.
Scott, John, Lord Eldon. 248.
Scott, Sir Walter. 24, 262.
Segrè, Carlo. 7, 62, 84.
Senior, Mr. 215.
Sette-Comuni, Count Vela dei. 77.
Settembrini, Luigi. 156, 290.
Settembrini, Raffaele. 156, 279, 280.
Seymour, Lord. 152.
Shaen, William. 194.
Shakespeare. 106, 121, 183, 236, 238, 243.
Shaw, Benjamin. 139.
Shelley, Percy Bysshe. 183.
Shepherd, Dr. William. 126, 128.
Sicard, Mr. 1, 199.
Sicard, Mrs. 199.
Sidoli, Giuditta. 185, 186, 189.
Sismondi. 74, 93, 94, 99, 184, 219, 287.
Smith, " Bobus ". 137, 273.
Smith, H. 281.
Smith, John. 114, 139.
Smith, Miss. 94, 102, 226, 227, 231, 235.
Smith, Rev. Sydney. 8, 84, 208.
Smith, T. 262.
Smith, William. 94.
Smith Carpenter, Mr. 258.
Sofia. 296, 300.
Solmi. 161.
Sorreno, Colonel. 121.
Southern, Henry. 220, 246.
Spathis, Diamantina (Signora Foscolo). 15.
Spencer, Lavinia. 13.
Spencer, Lord. 278.
Spenser, Edmund. 169.
Spina, Cardinal. 239.
Sta.....d, Isabella. 46.
Stanley, Lord. 151.
Stansfeld, Caroline. 196.
Stansfeld, James. 196.
Stati, Giuseppe. 212.
Stephen, Sir James. 94.
Stuart, Lady Dudley. 164.
Subula, Colonel. 91.
Sullivan, children. 274.
Sullivan, Mrs. 138, 274, 276.
Sullivan, Rev. Frederick. 274, 276.
Sussex, Duke of. 69, 134, 236.
Sutherland, Duke of. 176.

Tancione, family. 192, 193.

Taruzzi, J. 212.
Tasso. 51, 126, 268.
Tate, Mr. 279.
Taylor (London University Bookseller). 268.
Taylor, Edgar. 58, 62, 63, 65.
Taylor, Edward. 220.
Taylor, John. 243, 245, 256.
Taylor, John (junior). 220, 221.
Taylor, Mrs. 93, 94, 99, 103.
Taylor, Richard. 220, 221.
Taylor, Sarah (*see* Austin, Sarah).
Tealdi. 267.
Tedaldo. 113.
Teleki, Countess (*see* Bickersteth, Jane Frances).
Thevenot, Edward. 129.
Thiébault, Paul. 296, 300.
Thiers. 159.
Thomson, James. 255.
Tiraboschi. 59.
Tito, A. 219.
Tooke, Eyton. 220.
Tooke, William. 139.
Toynbee, Dr. Joseph. 193, 194.
Trechi, Sigismondi. 2, 38.
Turner, Ellen. 129.
Turner, Mr. 258.
Turner, Mrs. 258.
Turner, Rev. William. 176.

Ugoni, Baron Camillo. 2, 80, 82, 84.
Ugoni, Count Filippo. 74, **80–81**, 86, 88, 89, 96, 103, 127, 142, 189, 224, 226.
Usiglio, Angelo. 187, 188, 197.

Valencia, Archbishop of. 228.
Vanelli. 80.
Vardon. 145.
Vasto, Marchese del. 163.
Vaudoncourt, General. 242.
Vecelli. 96.
Venturi, Carlo. 196.
Viale, Cardinal. 290.
Viarigi, Baron. 216, 217, 218, 219.
Viarigi, family. 88, 216.
Viarigi, Gaetano. 88, 216, 218, 219.
Viarigi, Madame. 216, 217.
Viarigi, Sophie. 88, 217.
Viaris (*see* Viarigi).
Victor Emmanuel I., King of Sardinia. 74, 155.
Victoria, Queen. 137, 155, 275.
Viglione, Professor Francesco. 10, 11, 20, 21, 22, 23, 27, 32, 33, 34, 35, 36, 37, 38, 42, 43, 45, 46, 47, 50, 51, 52, 53, 54, 55, 57, 62, 78, 80, 104.